CONNECTIONS IN *Swing*

A Collection of Articles about the
Musical Greats of the Big Band Era from Jazz
Connection Magazine

Volume One: The Bandleaders

CONNECTIONS IN *Swing*

A Collection of Articles about the
Musical Greats of the Big Band Era from
Jazz Connection Magazine

Volume One: The Bandleaders

By Stephen Fratallone

Connections in Swing: Volume One: The Bandleaders
© 2018. Stephen Fratallone All rights reserved.

All illustrations are copyright of their respective owners, and are also reproduced here in the spirit of publicity. Whilst we have made every effort to acknowledge specific credits whenever possible, we apologize for any omissions, and will undertake every effort to make any appropriate changes in future editions of this book if necessary.

No part of this book may be reproduced in any form or by any means, electronic, mechanical, digital, photocopying or recording, except for the inclusion in a review, without permission in writing from the publisher.

Published in the USA by:
BearManor Media
P O Box 71426
Albany, Georgia 31708
www.bearmanormedia.com

Printed in the United States of America
ISBN: 978-1-62933-263-5 (paperback)

Book & cover design and layout by Darlene Swanson • www.van-garde.com

Contents

Volume One: The Bandleaders

Dedication vii
Introduction ix
Foreword xv

Van Alexander 1
Ray Anthony 23
Louis Bellson 41
Tex Beneke 63
Les Brown 73
Bobby Byrne 89
Benny Carter 109
Ray Conniff 117
Del Courtney 133
Bob Crosby 155
Larry Elgart 165
Frank Foster 177
Lionel Hampton 193
Woody Herman 207
Elliot Lawrence 225

Ted Lewis 245
Billy May 259
Buddy Moreno 277
Buddy Morrow 293
Alvino Rey 307
Artie Shaw 323
Orrin Tucker 343

The "Ghost Bands"

Michael Berkowitz and the New Gene Krupa Orchestra 357
Les Brown Jr. and the Les Brown Band of Renown 375
Chris Calloway and the Cab Calloway Orchestra 385
Dick Johnson and the Artie Shaw Orchestra 401
Larry O'Brien and the Glenn Miller Orchestra 423
Don Pentleton and the Hal McIntyre Orchestra 441
Bill Tole and the Jimmy Dorsey Orchestra 459

Author Photos with the Bandleaders 473

Dedication

To the wonderful and inspirational men of music who led their Big Bands to help create some of the best music this side of heaven and in so doing, provided a rich foundation for American popular music, I dedicate this humble offering with gratitude and thanks.

To my parents, Stephen and Ursula Fratallone, who encouraged me with the gift of music through their love and sacrifice, my loving thanks.

To my junior high school music teacher, Mr. Thomas Cate, and my high school music teacher, the late Mr. Hugh Wallace, both men bandleaders in their own right, who encouraged me in my journey with music, my sincere appreciation and thanks with the opportunities you afforded me.

To the late Don Raffell, an alumnus of the Big Bands, stellar studio musician, and my private instructor on the saxophone, for your patience with me and for lessons learned.

And last but certainly not least, to my two beautiful children, Stephen and Rachel, who have taken interest in playing music. May doing so bring you a lifetime of pleasure. You are my love.

Introduction

"You can have the men who make the laws, but give me the music makers."
~ William Shakespeare (1564 – 1616)

Biting brass. Smooth saxophone lines. Pulsating rhythm. It was music that showcased exciting and creative instrumental soloists. It made stars out of number of band singers. It was compelling music with catchy arrangements to dance and dream to at ballrooms all across America. The music was both hot and sweet. It was melodic, romantic and sometimes had silly vocals. It was music that a person could hum a tune to with lyrics that wouldn't embarrass one's grandmother. It was a time when people were looking to divert themselves from the painful realities of the Great Depression and a world at war. Swing was the thing and for the most part, it helped to define the music of the Big Bands.

My love for the music of the Big Bands of the 1930s and 1940s came quite by accident. I was ten years old and living with my folks in Garfield, New Jersey, a small town in Bergen County, with a population of approximately 29,000, situated in the northeast section of the state, about a fifteen-minute drive from the George Washington Bridge. One Saturday morning on an early October day I volunteered at the local American Legion Hall helping members of that organization collect recyclables from residents around the neighborhood. The "pay off" for our altruistic efforts was a homemade, hot chilly lunch served at the Legion hall. I thought that was a pretty good deal. But then, I'm easy.

I boarded a pick-up truck with two Legionnaires who drove to an elderly widow's home to collect her stacks of newspapers and other recyclables that she had stored in her garage. While the two men were talking with her, I noticed a pile of 78 RPM records in their album books. Out of curiosity, I took the liberty of looking through them. I didn't recognize any of the titles of songs or their recording artists in the first batch of records, but leafing through the second album of records I recognized one song title: "Flight of the Bumblebee" recorded in 1941, on Columbia Records by Harry James and his Orchestra.

This was 1966 and my favorite television show at that time was *The Green Hornet* starring Van Williams and Bruce Lee. Of course, I recognized "Flight of the Bumblebee" as the Green Hornet's theme song. I thought that was cool. I asked the lady if I could have the record and she graciously said yes, as the records were to be part of the items we came to collect.

When I returned home with my "treasure," I enthusiastically showed my mother who immediately said, "Oh, yes, I remember this recording. Harry James was one of my favorite bands that I listened to as a kid."

Fortunately, our stereo console was equipped to play 78 RPM records. Once I heard James's record, I was hooked. I loved the recording and the technical prowess of James on the trumpet. I played that record a lot in the months ahead.

When my family and I moved to Glendale, California the following May, that fragile 78 record unfortunately got broken in transit. Was I disappointed!

Sometime later I was surfing the dial on my radio one evening and I abruptly stopped because I heard a familiar sound. It was "Flight of the Bumblebee," of all things - that same Harry James recording I once had. I continued listening as the radio host said his name was Chuck Cecil and that I was listening to his *Swingin' Years* radio program, a show dedicated to playing music of the Big Bands.

I was captivated, not being able to break myself away from the radio as if I was under the spell of the Sirens of Greek mythology. A seemingly endless array of magical recordings from other power-house bands broke through the air waves: music created by Benny Goodman, Artie Shaw, Count Basie, Gene Krupa, Woody Herman, Kay Kyser, Duke Ellington, Glenn Miller, and Charlie Barnet. There were even some hilarious moments thanks to the creative genius of Spike Jones, who was credited as "The Man Who Murdered Music." Overall, the music I heard on *The Swingin' Years* was pulsating, enticing, and alive with electricity!

I made it a point to tune in to *The Swingin' Years* program every week. As a result, I became a "Big Band junkie," quickly becoming familiar with the music and its creators. While my teen peers were digging the rock sounds of The Beatles, The Rolling Stones, Black Sabbath, and The Grateful Dead, I was entrenched in the music of the 1930s and 1940s. Musically, I indeed walked to the beat of a "different drummer," but without any qualms or regrets.

Then one early Saturday evening I was turning the dial on the television when I came across *The Lawrence Welk Show*. It just so happen that Welk's program that evening was a salute to the Big Bands.

The theme songs of all my favorite bands were showcased on that program and Welk's magnificent musicians, many of whom were Big Band alums, performed them with delectable authenticity.

Notable standout soloists from the Welk aggregation included clarinetist Peanuts Hucko who handled the Benny Goodman, Artie Shaw and Woody Herman tasks with perfection; trombonist Bob Havens who nailed down the Tommy Dorsey and Glenn Miller covers in swinging style; trumpeter Johnny Zell, mastering the varied musical styles of Harry James, Clyde McCoy, and Henry Busse; and tenor saxophonist Russ Klein, who brought genuineness to works by Charlie Barnet, Tex Beneke, and Freddy Martin. Because of Welk's talented instrumentalists, I became a regular viewer of Maestro Welk's television show just to hear these men play.

Over time, thanks to the presenting efforts of men like Cecil and Welk, my interest in the music of the Big Bands grew. I was then able to see a number of bandleaders at Disneyland during the summer months when the Magic Kingdom hosted various Big Bands each week throughout the 1970s and 1980s.

The very first bandleader I saw ironically, was Harry James. Other bandleaders I was fortunate enough to see lead their aggregations at Disneyland were Woody Herman, Count Basie, Duke Ellington, Lionel Hampton, Bob Crosby, Charlie Barnet, Cab Calloway, Benny Carter, and Orrin Tucker. I was also blessed see to Les Brown, Alvino Rey, Tex Beneke, Freddy Martin, Buddy Morrow, Louis Bellson, Larry Elgart, and Stan Kenton at other venues.

Over time, I collected the music these wonderful bandleaders made and I would go see them perform at various venues whenever I could. When I started *Jazz Connection*, my Internet magazine about jazz and Big Band music, I made it a point to interview as many of the stalwarts from this wonderful era of music as I could, especially the bandleaders, as their ranks were quickly thinning due to death. Other series of articles include sideman who played in these bands and the vocalists who sang in them.

It is these articles, based on in-person and telephone interviews I conducted with these bandleaders, that comprise the first volume of this trilogy of musical greats from the Big Band Era. It is my hope that reading about these particular bandleaders will bring back a fond memory or two for those that do remember that magical era and its music, and for those readers who weren't able to remember, may this serve as a proper introduction - a *connection*, if you will - to these mighty men of music who were the architects of that golden era in American popular music.

I echo the sentiments of that great English bard, William Shakespeare, when he wrote, "You can have the men who make the laws, but give me the music makers." Thanks for reading!

Musically,
Stephen Fratallone
Chico, CA
2016

Foreword

The Big Band Era was a unique period in American popular music. Although it can be argued that it lasted only a decade (1935-1945) the big band sound continued for years to follow. Each band had a unique sound and personality. That sound and personality was certainly brought about by the instrumentalists and singers, and by the arrangers who wrote the scores, but at the heart of each of the bands was its bandleader. It was the incomparable sound of Tommy Dorsey's trombone playing that became the central focus of his band. The same can be said of the particular clarinet styles of Benny Goodman, Artie Shaw, and Woody Herman. For an arranger like Glenn Miller, the sound of his band was built upon the unique reed sound he crafted. For other bandleader-arrangers like Duke Ellington, Van Alexander, and Billy May, the life of the band was rooted in the arrangements that they wrote.

My introduction to the big bands and their great leaders came at an early age when I heard some old, live recordings of Glenn Miller's orchestra. I was eleven years old and already had a developing love for music. It was Miller's sound that set me on a new musical course. I soon learned of other bands of the period and would think of each band in terms of its leader. Each leader inspired me in a different way and although this was the music of my grandparents' era, I was gaining a sense that being a professional musician and performing this style of music was what I wanted to do as a career.

By the time I was twenty-five years old, I had spent several years on the road as the male vocalist with the Glenn Miller Orchestra under the direction of Larry O'Brien. It was also during this period that I recorded my first solo album with the GMO. Soon after this, I made a wonderful connection with author Stephen Fratallone who interviewed me for *Jazz Connection Magazine*. Stephen and I have maintained that relationship over the years as both of us have continued in our particular pursuits in this wonderful genre of music.

Stephen's love for the big bands came at a young age as well. Perhaps when something so powerful comes along at such an early stage, one can't help but go in that direction. It is his love for the music and those who made that music that is so compelling. Stephen has devoted many years to connecting with and developing relationships with so many of the great musicians of that era. In turn, he has done a great service by allowing us to make that connection with those musicians as well. It was Stephen who personally introduced me to Garry Stevens, "The Boy Singer," when I myself was a young boy singer with the Glenn Miller Orchestra. Garry was very complimentary of me during those early days in my career and that was extremely encouraging.

It is these types of relationships that Stephen has cultivated which demonstrate the importance of his work. He has developed relationships with sidemen, singers, and bandleaders throughout his career, and shared the lives of these great musicians with us. In this compilation of the bandleaders interviewed for *Jazz Connection Magazine*, Stephen gives an enjoyable and informative look into the lives of some of the musical greats that helped create and develop one of the greatest genres in American music. From bandleaders like Louis Bellson and Buddy Morrow (who I had the wonderful privilege of working with) to Tex Beneke, Les Brown, and Billy May (bandleaders I've known about for years and would love to have met) and others like Van Alexander and Benny Carter (bandleaders for whom I have gained an even greater appreciation), this is a wonderful and enlightening collection. I also appreciate the inclusion of Stephen's interviews of the bandleaders from various "ghost bands," many of whom are still bringing this music to audiences all over the world.

My hope is this music will continue for many more generations and that the lives and careers of those who created and developed it would be recognized for their important contributions to American music. *Connections in Swing* is a valuable resource to this end.

Nick Hilscher
Music Director, The Glenn Miller Orchestra
August 2016

Still Truckin' On Down The Avenue

Van Alexander's Life Set To Music While In Semi-Retirement

The following article on Van Alexander was originally published in the November 2000 issue of Jazz Connection Magazine.

Van Alexander may very well be the only arranger and co-composer in the annals of American popular music to take a simple nursery rhyme and turn it into a mega-hit in its day. That song was "A-Tisket, A-Tasket," recorded by drummer Chick Web and His Orchestra on May 2, 1938, and sung by the incomparable Ella Fitzgerald. The song has secured for Alexander, who wrote the tune under his birth name of Al Feldman, a bit of musical immortality.

"I think "A-Tisket, A-Tasket" will go down through the generations," said Alexander, 85, via telephone from his high-rise condominium on Wilshire Boulevard in the Westwood section of Los Angeles. "Ella added her own special ideas to the lyrics. It was her idea to put the piece down in writing in the first place. It's a public domain nursery rhyme so that's why we were able to claim authorship of it."

"A-Tisket, A-Tasket" hit the charts at the No. 10 position on June 18 of that year and skyrocketed to No. 1 two weeks later. It stayed on the *Hit Parade* at the No. 1 position for a total of nineteen incredible weeks. It eventually became a million seller in 1950, its sales helped after it was revived in the 1944 movie, *Two Girls and a Sailor*, starring June Allyson, Gloria DeHaven and Van Johnson. The song was first sung in films by Fitzgerald in the 1942 Abbott & Costello musical-comedy, *Ride 'Em Cowboy*.

"I had no idea at the time that it would be such a great hit," Alexander admitted.

Because of the enormous success of "A-Tisket, A-Tasket," both Fitzgerald and Alexander were inducted in to the Grammy Hall of Fame in 1986, as part of a pantheon of music to honor recordings of "lasting qualitative or historical significance that are at least 25 years old."

"That was a big honor," Alexander humbly said. "Unfortunately, Chick passed away (on June 16, 1939) right at the height of the song's popularity. He never really got to reap the benefits of it."

Besides arranging for Webb, Alexander also led his own full-time swinging outfit for two years. He also arranged material for the bands of Benny Goodman, Larry Clinton, Abe Lyman, Tommy Tucker, Bob Crosby, Kay Kyser, and earlier this year, for Les Brown on his newly recorded CD.

Alexander continued his long and fruitful musical career in Hollywood beginning in the mid-1940s as an arranger-composer for radio, recordings, film, and television. He was arranger-conductor for singers Gordon MacRae and Guy Mitchell and worked as an arranger and assistant conductor for *The Dean Martin Show* on television. He's scored twenty-three movies and was nominated three times for Emmy Awards for his work on various television specials.

Born Alexander Van Vliet Feldman, on May 2, 1915, in the Harlem section of New York City. He was the youngest of two sons of Jacob Feldman and Mildred Van Vliet. The future arranger-composer-bandleader was named after his maternal grandfather who was born in in Rotterdam, Holland, and who worked as a head prison guard at Welfare Penitentiary on Welfare Island (now Roosevelt Island) situated on the East River separating the New York boroughs of Manhattan and Queens.

"My grandfather would jokingly say, 'If you ain't Dutch, you ain't much!'" Alexander said with a laugh.

Alexander's father was pharmacist who owned a Rexall drugstore on 131st Street at Amsterdam Avenue while his mother was a concert pianist for WEAF in New York during the early days of radio. She taught her son to play the piano at age six.

While growing up Alexander became more and more absorbed with music. He became fascinated with the mechanics of how a song was orchestrated. It wasn't until he attended George Washington High School in Manhattan that he first started experimenting with arranging, he said.

"I was always in awe of listening to bands on radio in those days," Alexander said. "I loved the Mills Brothers and how they imitated instruments with their voices. I never dreamed that someday I'd be writing arrangements for them. I put together and led a small eight-piece ensemble at the time and when I heard my first arrangement played, I was hooked and I knew this is what I wanted to do."

Also attending George Washington High at the time was Henry "Butch" Stone with whom Alexander struck up an endearing and long-last friendship. Stone later played in Alexander's big band and went on to greater notoriety in 1941, after joining Les Brown and His Band of Renown. At age 88, Stone still performs with Brown together as a featured vocalist.

"Butch and I still talk on the phone to each other almost daily," Alexander said of his 70-plus years of friendship with Stone.

After graduating high school in 1933, Alexander entered Columbia University to study music, concentrating on arranging and orchestration. It was during this time that Alexander regularly frequented the Savoy Ballroom in Harlem to hear the great black bands of the day such as Don Redman, Erskine Hawkins, Lucky Millinder, and of course, Chick Webb, who was the house band at the famed dance spot.

After going to the Savoy for as long as he did, Alexander developed what he called a nodding acquaintance with Webb which led to his first break in 1936.

"One night I got up the nerve to approach Chick and told him I had a couple of arrangements at home that I thought might fit his band,"

Alexander said. "He told me to bring them to his rehearsal the following Friday night. I was bluffing. I didn't have any arrangements. I went home and started to write out two charts: Fats Waller's 'Keepin' Out of Mischief,' and the Dixieland classic, 'That's a Plenty.'"

Alexander brought the arrangements to the Webb rehearsal which started at 2 a.m. *after* the band played the Savoy gig, he said.

During the rehearsal, the charts by Edgar Sampson, Webb's saxophonist and stellar arranger, were played first, Alexander recalled. It was Sampson who collaborated with Benny Goodman and Webb on the famed swing piece, "Stompin' at the Savoy," so named in honor of the famous ballroom. He also had a hand in writing and arranging other swing classics such as "Don't Be That Way," "Blue Lou," and "Clap Hands! Here Comes Charley!"

"Chick finally got to my arrangements about 4 a.m.," Alexander said. "By then, the guys in the band were a little tired. Since I hadn't come home at my usual time, my mother was in a panic and called the police."

Webb liked Alexander's work and the drummer took a $20 advance on his salary from Charlie Buchanan, the Savoy manager, to pay the young arranger for both pieces.

"It was my first sale and I went home on Cloud Nine!" Alexander said.

Alexander soon was hired as a full time arranger for Webb's band. His main area of concentration was to do arrangements for the band's up-and-coming and popular female vocalist, Ella Fitzgerald, who had joined the band less than a year earlier.

"I did all her early Decca recordings," Alexander said. "They were successful."

Some of those successful Alexander-Fitzgerald recordings include "Sing Me a Swing Song" and "Love, You're Just a Laugh" (both recorded on June 2, 1936); "I've Got the Swing Fever Blues" and "Vote For Mr. Rhythm" (October 29, 1936); "I Got a Guy" (October 27, 1937); "If Dreams Come True" (December 17, 1937); "I'm Just a Jitterbug" (May 2, 1938); and "Everybody Step" (June 9, 1938).

Alexander also contributed some outstanding swing instrumental arrangements for the Webb band including 'Liza' (the "B" side to "A-Tisket, A-Tasket"), which featured the drum-playing leader.

"A number of publications at the time mistakenly gave credit for that arrangement of 'Liza' to Benny Carter," Alexander said. "Even Benny himself will tell you that it was my arrangement."

The date of May 2, 1938, proved to be a double blessing for Alexander. Not only was he celebrating his 23rd birthday and working as a successful arranger with one of the top swing bands in the nation, but he would gain greater recognition for a recording waxed that day on an arrangement he did on a nursery rhyme that dated back to 1879. The arrangement was "A-Tisket, A-Tasket."

Webb's band was playing at Levaggi's Restaurant in Boston and was broadcasting over the radio coast-to-coast four times a week. Alexander was writing three arrangements a week for the band and he would make the weekly trek from his home in Manhattan to Boston to drop off the new music to Webb.

"One time Ella pulled me to the side and told me she had a great idea for a song," Alexander recalled. "She suggested that I put something together on the old nursery rhyme, 'A-Tisket, A-Tasket.' I thought it was a great idea and told her to let me think about out. I didn't get around to it because I was busy doing other arrangements and that I didn't have the time. When I'd come up to Boston every week, Ella would ask me about it and I kept putting her off. Finally, one week she got a little huffy and told me if I can't do it or didn't want to do it, she'd ask Edgar Sampson to work on it.

"I asked her not to do that and to give me one more week to make good on my intentions. I went home and sat up all night to write it. I put the piece in a 32-bar frame and wrote all the novelty lyrics including the dialog between Ella and the band where they sang 'Was it blue? No! No! No! No!', etc. Ella loved my arrangement but wanted to change some of the lyrics. I had originally written in the middle part of the song, 'She was walkin' on down the avenue without a single thing to do.' Ella suggested we don't use 'walkin' on down the avenue,' but rather, *'truckin'* on down the avenue' to make it sound more 'hip.' The rest, as they say, is history."

Alexander and Fitzgerald worked well together from the start and became life-long friends.

"There will never be anyone like Ella," Alexander said. "Her intonation and her projection were impeccable. She never lost her innocence from the day I met her until she passed away (on June 15, 1996). I guess she never realized just how great she was."

Some of the other jazz stalwarts who made Webb's band such a powerhouse outfit at the time included trumpeter Taft Jordan and saxophonists Louis Jordan and Teddy McRae.

Although the intermingling of black and white musicians on the same stage was not widely accepted in a number of areas in America during this period, however, Alexander's association arranging for a black band was not problematic at all, he said.

"The guys in the band were wonderful to me," Alexander said. "I even traveled with them on the bus on occasion and I really got an education. Chick was magnanimous and gracious of his praises for me. He even introduced me to Benny Goodman and others who played at the Savoy. It was a blessing for me."

As a result of Webb's introduction, Alexander was able to do some arrangements for "The King of Swing."

"I did some things he never recorded," Alexander said. "I did an arrangement of 'Mean to Me' and some selections in early 1937 when Francis Hunt was Benny's vocalist at the time."

Alexander was even in attendance at the Savoy Ballroom the night of May 11, 1937, during the famous "Battle of Swing," pitting Goodman's outfit against the formidable Webb band. The event proved to be legendary in the history of swing music.

"The consensus was that Chick won that night," Alexander recalled.

"As far as individual musicianship I thought Benny had the better band. But Chick's band had a spirit that night that was unbeatable. Even Gene Krupa said publicly that he was cut by a better man. There were thousands of people crammed in front of both bands and thousands more lined the streets outside. It was a night to remember and something I'll never forget."

As a result of the tremendous commercial success of "A-Tisket, A-Tasket," Alexander was approached by Eli Oberstein, head of RCA-Victor Records, to form his own band. Oberstein wanted to add Alexander to his stable of songwriting bandleaders which included Larry Clinton and Les Brown, offering the fledgling bandleader a good deal to record on the RCA Bluebird label for $100 a week against all royalties.

"It sounded to be a very good deal at the time, so I jumped into the band leading business," Alexander said. "That's when I changed my name to Van Alexander. Eli said to me that Al Feldman and his Orchestra wouldn't sound that exciting on a marquise. He asked me to take my middle name of Van, and make it my first name, and to take my first name, Alexander, and make it my last name. That's how I became Van Alexander."

The initial roster of Alexander's band included Bob Person, Milt Davidson, and Hy Small on trumpets; Jerry Rosa and Bill Schallenberger (later know as Bill Schallen), trombones; Sol Kane and Butch Stone, alto saxes; Jack Greenberg and Harry Steinfeld, tenor saxes; Ray Barr, piano; Joel Livingston, guitar; George Hanrahan, bass; and Roger Segan, drums. Shirley Brown was the band's vocalist.

The first tune the new Van Alexander and His Orchestra recorded for Bluebird was Alexander's own composition of "Alexander's Swinging" (November 3, 1938). It would be the bandleader's theme song, based on a variation of Irving Berlin's ever-popular, "Alexander's Ragtime Band."

Originally, Alexander used Berlin's piece as his theme song, but soon received a cease-and-desist telegram from the renowned composer's publishing company stating that Berlin didn't want anyone associated with that song except himself. So, Alexander had to write another theme.

Soon after, the band's first radio broadcast was on the popular *Fitch Bandwagon Show*. They played mostly at New York City's Roseland Ballroom, the Paramount Theater and Loew's State Theater. Band promoter Cy Scribman, the loyal benefactor of Glenn Miller, booked the band at all the fine spots in Boston and the New England states. The band also frequented Atlantic City and traveled to play venues as far west as Chicago.

"It was a good swing band," Alexander said. "I tried to emulate the good brass sound or that 'fat' sound of the brass section that Isham Jones had in his band. I could never tolerate 'under-nourished' brass. We always had a good rhythm section with solid drummers."

Some of the more drummers of note to filter through the Alexander ranks were Irv Cottler, who later became Frank Sinatra's regular drummer for years, and a very young 16-year-old Shelly Manne.

"I gave Shelly his first start," Alexander said proudly.

Other well-known Alexander alumni include trombonist Si Zentner, who had a hit recording with his orchestra in 1961 of his catchy version of "Up a Lazy River" (which also won a Grammy Award for "Best Pop Instrumental Performance"); pianist Ray Barr who later carved out for himself a long career as singer Frankie Laine's accompanist; saxophonist Frank Socolow; trumpeter Neil Hefti, who went on to be a contributing architect to the compositional success of Woody Herman's First Herd and Count Basie's band during the 1950s. He composed such jazz standards as "Li'l Darlin'," "Cute," and "Coral Reef." A multi-Grammy Award winner, Hefti also wrote the theme music for the *Batman* and *The Odd Couple* television shows; and saxophonist Butch Stone who also sang novelty tunes.

"Butch was a big asset for my band," Alexander said proudly. "When he was with me, he did my arrangement of 'A Good Man Is Hard to Find.' Every time he did it, he broke up the place. When he left my band he took the arrangement with him and he continued to break up the place while with Jack Teagarden and then with Larry Clinton. When Butch went with Les Brown, Les had the foresight to record it (on July 20, 1942). It sold something like a half-million copies. To this day I still haven't gotten paid for my arrangement!" (laughing)

Some of the more prominent novelty tunes that Stone recorded while with Alexander include "Got a Pebble in My Shoe" (recorded November 3, 1938), Alexander collaborated with lyricist Charlie Tobias, who also wrote popular songs as "Don't Sit Under the Apple Tree" and "Trade Winds"; "The Girl Friend of the Whirling Dervish" (December 27, 1938); "Hooray for Spinach" (February 16, 1939); "The Jumpin' Jive" (June 21, 1939); "Hot Dog Joe" (August 1939, another Alexander composition); "The Yodelin' Jive" (October 10, 1939); "On Behalf of the Visiting Firemen" and "Jungle Jive" (both recorded on May 10, 1940).

Between November 3, 1938, and June 21, 1939, Alexander recorded 52 sides for the Bluebird label.

From August 1939 to May 10, 1940, Alexander waxed 30 sides on Oberstein's new and now-defunct Varsity label. Other Varsity label mates included bandleaders Harry James and Johnny Messner.

Alexander's body of recorded work during this period focused more on an ensemble sound than it did showcasing individual soloists.

"We featured soloists, to be sure," Alexander said. "But to do that consistently, you had to have outstanding jazz players. If a fellow tries to plays jazz and doesn't make it, it's embarrassing. We also had some fine singers like Shirley Brown, Jane Dover (an alumna from the Bunny Berigan band), and Phyllis Kenny."

During his tenure as bandleader, Alexander could only recall one performance that he considered a disaster. In reality, it turned out to be the band's "Waterloo." It was at New York City's Paramount Theater in 1940.

"The most important element of a stage band show was the accompanying picture," Alexander said.

"We had the unfortunate luck of playing with the picture, *Geronimo* (starring Preston Foster, Ellen Drew, Andy Devine and Chief Thundercloud). It was a terrible movie! We ended up only getting one week's engagement when we were looking for three or four. I could have gotten healthier financially if we could have stayed there longer."

Shortly after the Paramount Theater engagement, Alexander disbanded.

In the aftermath, Alexander found outside arranging work for the bands of Larry Clinton, Les Brown, and Kay Kyser.

"Kay was the most commercial of all the bands," Alexander said. "He was a great personality. You have to have that in order to be a successful bandleader."

By late 1942, Alexander led a band for special weekend engagements in the New York area and for wartime bond rallies but concentrated on writing and teaching orchestration to supplement his income. His first student was 13-year-old Johnny Mandel, who later became an Academy Award-winning and Grammy Award-winning composer and arranger.

During this period Alexander began writing a how-to book on arranging, entitled *First Arrangement*. Initially published in 1946 by Criterion Music Corporation, the book was geared for novice arrangers by outlining the fundamentals of orchestration along with information about each instrument with its ranges and capabilities. It was designed to help them write their 'first arrangement,'" he said.

"The book sold very well and to this day I have well-known people coming up to me saying that they've used my book," Alexander said. "It's gratifying to hear. Along with my teaching, writing this book was a natural progression."

Musical luminaries who have used *First Arrangement* include Quincy Jones, Elmer Bernstein, and Jonathan Tunick.

Alexander's book was updated in the 1960s and was re-titled *First Chart*, to give it a more contemporary title. The book is still in print and is published by Criterion Music Corporation in Los Angeles, according to Alexander. Amazon.com sells the book on its website at www.amazon.com.

In 1943, Alexander was ready to heed Uncle Sam's call to military service but was rerouted instead to do defense work at home. Classified as

1-A by the draft board, his orders for military service were rescinded two days prior to his induction into the Army because he was married with two small children, he said.

"No fathers were being drafted so I worked for the Russian War Relief," Alexander said. "The Russians were our allies during World War II and we were supplying them with meat. I was working at a wholesale meat factory in New York City. I worked the job for six months doing the 4 a.m. to 10 a.m. shift."

In his off hours Alexander still privately taught arranging and leading outfits for various local war time events.

The following year Alexander arranged for the Abe Lyman and Tommy Tucker bands.

"Tommy wanted to have his band swing a little more so he called me to do some arrangements for him," Alexander recalled.

The "new" sound to Tucker's outfit was short-lived as fans identified him with "Mickey-Mouse-music" and they didn't go along with the switch. Fans clamored for the old "Tommy Tucker Time" persona with which he was associated. Tucker eventually reverted to his "rodent" brand of music.

By World War II's end in 1945, Alexander teamed up with bandleader and singer Bob Crosby, an association which opened up a whole new chapter in the arranger's life.

"Bob had just been discharged from the Navy and he and I put on a four-week show together at the Capitol Theater in Manhattan," Alexander recalled. "He didn't have a band at the time so will billed it as 'Bob Crosby with the Van Alexander Orchestra.' We developed a good rapport with each other and after the show ended he invited me to go out to California with him to put together a band for him and to do his arranging. It sounded like a great opportunity. My wife and I talked it over and decided to make the move."

Unfortunately, the honeymoon between Crosby and Alexander was short lived. After three months, Alexander was fired due to a major disagreement he had with Crosby.

"It was a blessing in disguise," Alexander said. "I probably wouldn't have gotten out here to California if it weren't for dear ol' Bob. We made up since that disagreement."

Alexander's blessing came by way of *The Jack Benny Show*. He heard that Benny's popular Irish tenor, Dennis Day, was searching for a new arranger and conductor. Alexander was hired and spent a full season working with Day on Benny's radio show.

"Working with Dennis helped to get me established in Hollywood," Alexander said.

During the late 1940s throughout the 1950s, Alexander also worked for Capitol Records, orchestrating for many of Capitol's recording artists, including comedian/impersonator Mel Blanc (a fixture on the both the Jack Benny radio and television shows and the voice of all the Warner Bros. cartoon characters) who waxed some children's novelty sides; singing cowboy Tex Ritter; Dakota Staton; George Chakiris; and Keely Smith, among others. He also worked on some transcription recordings for Doris Day.

In 1954, Alexander also landed a spot arranging for Mickey Rooney's *Hey, Mulligan!* television show which led to scoring Rooney's next five films, including the last of Rooney's Andy Hardy films.

When Rooney's television show came to a close in 1955, Alexander was hired by singer Guy Mitchell to be his musical director for *The Guy Mitchell Show*, which aired for thirteen weeks.

One of the more endearing personal and professional associations Alexander had was with baritone crooner Gordon MacRae. As musical director for the singer, they performed together at many of the top venues around the world and recorded thirteen albums together on Capitol Records, the first being *The Best Things in Life Are Free* (1956). Others that followed were *Cowboy's Lament* (1957); *Motion Picture Soundstage* (1957); *Gordon MacRae in Concert* (1958); *Seasons of Love* (1959); *Songs for an Evening at Home* (1959); *Hallowed Be Thy Name* (1960); *Our Love Story* (1960); *The Desert Song* (1963); *New Moon* (1963); *The Student Prince* (1963); *Kismet* (1964); and *If She Walked into My Life* (1966).

Despite MacRae's issues with alcoholism and excessive gambling, MacRae was great to work for, and both his family and Alexander's family would often go on vacations together, Alexander said.

"He had such a magnificent voice," he said.

Alexander also arranged and conducted for singer Kay Starr on four of her consecutive albums she recorded for Capitol after her three-year hiatus at RCA-Victor: *Movin'!* (1959); and a trilogy of LPs from the follow year with *Losers, Weepers; Movin' on Broadway;* and *Jazz Singer.*

While at Capitol Records, Alexander was also given the opportunity to produce three of his own albums: *Home of Happy Feet* (1958, which was later re-issued as *Savoy Stomp*); *Let's Dance the Last Dance* (1960); and *Swing! Staged For Sound* (1961).

Alexander said that his favorite of the three albums is *Savoy Stomp*, a dedication of songs of twelve different black bands that frequently played at the Savoy Ballroom. Joining the recording session were some of the best studio musicians in Los Angeles including Abe Most, Plas Johnson, Chuck Gentry, Ronnie Lang and Butch Stone on saxophones; Uan Rasey, Conrad Gozzo, Manny Klein and Shorty Sherock, trumpets; Tommy Pederson, Milt Bernhart, Ken Kusby and Joe Howard, trombones; Ray Sherman and Paul Smith, piano; Joe Mondragon, bass; Barney Kessel, guitar; and Irv Cottler and Shelly Manne on drums.

Throughout the mid-1950s and early 1960s, Alexander was a respected musical name in the television industry working for Screen Gems doing arrangements and orchestration for such shows as *Bewitched, Dennis the Menace, Donna Reed, Hazel, The Farmer's Daughter,* and *I Dream of Jeannie.*

He also scored several movies including two Joan Crawford films: *Straight Jacket* and *I Saw What You Did.* Other movie scores include *Baby Face Nelson, The Atomic Kid,* and *Safe At Home,* starring the late New York Yankees sluggers Mickey Mantle and Roger Maris.

In 1965, Alexander embarked on an eight-year run as the arranger and assistant conductor for *The Dean Martin Show.* Les Brown was the show's musical director.

"Les originally asked me to help him out by working on some arrangements for the show which led to the assistant musical director slot," Alexander said. "Les still had his band and with the Vietnam War still going on, he would frequently travel overseas a lot with Bob Hope to entertain the troops. Every time Les would go out of town, I would conduct for the show."

Alexander's association with Martin proved to be a wonderful experience, he said.

"Dino was a pussy cat," he said.

As a result of working on Martin's show, Alexander got to meet many big stars that he was able to conduct for which eventually led to future television work on *The Dom DeLuise Show* (the 1968 summer replacement for Jackie Gleason), *The 1969 Emmy Awards*, and several NBC specials including *Gene Kelly's Wonderful World of Girls* (1970); *The Gold Diggers Chevy Show* (1971-1972); and *The Wacky World of Jonathan Winters* (1972-1973). Alexander was nominated three times for Emmy Awards between 1970 and 1973 for his work on the latter three specials.

"Receiving such recognition was quite an honor for me," Alexander said about his three Emmy Award nominations.

When *The Dean Martin Show* ended in 1974, Alexander went into semi-retirement to spend more time with family and to improve his golf game. Today, he remains active doing occasional freelance work if the project appeals to him, he said.

Earlier this year, Alexander did some arrangements for Les Brown's latest CD, *Session 55: The New Les Brown CD* (Jake/Doc Hollywood Records). Released this past August, the 21-track disc features updated and fresh versions of standards from Brown's musical library as well as Brown signature tunes of "Leap Frog" and "Bizet Has His Day." Singer Lou Rawls guests on the project singing "I Only Have Eyes for You" and "They Can't Take That Away From Me."

"Les is a dear friend and when he asked me to do some arrangements for his new CD, I gladly did it," Alexander said.

Alexander is a member and past-president of the American Society of Music Arrangers and Composers (ASMAC), and serves as vice-president of the Big Band Academy of America. In 1997, the BBAA presented him with its coveted Golden Bandstand Award. He was also honored for a Lifetime Achievement in Jazz Award by the Los Angeles Jazz Society, and in 1996, he received the Pacific Pioneer Broadcasters' prestigious Diamond Circle Award. Both Alexander and trumpeter/arranger/bandleader Billy May were inducted into the American Society of Composers, Authors and Musicians (ASCAP) Hall of Fame.

With over sixty-five years invested in the music business, Alexander admitted that arranging has been more personally fulfilling for him than leading a band.

"Arranging went into composing and the life of those things that I've done goes on and on," Alexander said. "Some of the things I've done for television are still being shown around the world."

Despite all the different musical entities that he has arranged for, writing for a particular style of music has always come pretty easy for him, Alexander said.

"I prided myself even to this day as being able to write for whatever anyone wanted," he said.

And Alexander knows better than anyone else that a good arrangement is crucial to a song's success and that arrangers are often under-recognized for their contributions.

"A good arrangement can make a song or let it die," he said. "It's really the most important element, I think. It's important first of all to the songwriter to have his song arranged properly, and of course, to the record company for its sales. Arrangers are still not given their dues for a song. Frank Sinatra did a lot for arrangers. He never performed any place or recorded anything without giving the arranger credit."

Even in semi-retirement Alexander keeps his ear close to today's music scene and admitted that he likes some of the contemporary sounds.

"I don't like distortion of any kind," he said. "Some of the contemporary things I can dig except rappers and heavy metal."

This past September, Alexander and his wife, Beth, celebrated 62 years of marriage. They wed on September 22, 1938, in New York City.

"As Henny Youngman used to say, 'I've been in love with the same woman for 62 years and if my wife ever finds out, she'll kill me'" Alexander quipped.

The Alexander's have two daughters, Lynn Tobias and Joyce Harris, and four grandchildren, and three great-grandchildren, all living close by in the Los Angeles area.

With his vast successes in the music industry, Alexander remains somewhat modest about the legacy that he has given to American popular music.

"Outside of 'A-Tisket, A-Tasket,' some of my recordings I made with people like Gordon MacRae and some of the jazz things I did may endure," he said. "I have a well-rounded musical background and the variety of music that I've done will count a little bit, I think."

** Coda - Here is an update on Van Alexander since this article was published:

Alexander was a frequent attendee and speaker at the annual Society to Preserve and Encourage Radio, Drama, Variety and Comedy (SPERDVAC) luncheons in Los Angeles.

On May 2, 2004, Alexander had his arrangement of a medley of songs from the Big Band Era performed at Carnegie Hall as the opening piece for a concert given by Michael Feinstein.

On Sunday, September 21, 2008, Van and Beth Alexander celebrated 70 years of marriage together. Their daughter, Joyce Harris, opened her lovely home in Bel Air to host about 100 guests which included family and friends from the music business: Butch and Shirley Stone, Kay Starr, Bea Wain, Lee Hale (former associate producer of *The Dean Martin Show*) Ray Charles (fondly known as the *other* Ray Charles, the leader of choral groups on recordings and television shows), John and Tenieka Clayton, Vic Mizzy (composer/arranger who wrote the theme songs for *The Addams Family* and *Green Acres* television shows), among others.

In June 2009, Alexander's autobiography, *From Harlem to Hollywood: My Life in Music*, was published by BearManor Media. The book was co-written with Stephen Fratallone.

The following year Alexander and Fratallone were awarded the Certificate of Merit for "Best Research in Recorded Jazz Music" from the Association of Recorded Sound Collections based in Eugene, Oregon. The recognition was part of the 2010 ARSC Awards for Excellence in Historical Recorded Sound research.

In 2010, Alexander was videotaped to share his memories of his association with the Chick Webb Orchestra as part of the oral history project through the auspices of the Smithsonian Institute in Washington, D.C. Alexander was the last surviving member of that great orchestra.

On February 13, 2011, Beth Alexander passed away from complication after suffering a broken hip from a fall the previous year. Van and Beth Alexander were married 72 years.

In January 2012, Alexander launched his new website, www.vanalexandermusic.com.

Later that same year, Alexander collaborated with Lee Hale to compose, "(It Comes Around) The Same Time Each Year," a Christmas holiday song. It was recorded in May 2013, as a single and for iTunes by Grammy-nominated singer Michael Feinstein.

In October 2013, Alexander joined fellow arrangers Johnny Mandel, Pat Williams, Bill Holman, Jorge Callendrelli, Ralph Carmichael, and Tim Somonic to be interviewed and videotaped about arranging for a documentary called *Vintage Masters of Swing* for PBS.

Early in 2015, Alexander and other Los Angeles-based arrangers were honored by having their music played by a Big Band compromised of the best Los Angeles musicians at the Catalina Bar and Grill Jazz Club on Sunset Blvd. in Hollywood, CA.

On March 17, 2015, Alexander was interviewed via telephone along with Stephen Fratallone by radio hosts Walden Hughes and Larry Gassman of Orange County, CA, about his career in music in honor of his upcoming 100th birthday. The interview was taped and later aired over Internet radio on Friday, May 1, 2015.

On May 2, 2015, Alexander celebrated his 100th birthday with a party at the Catalina Bar and Grill in Hollywood. Of the 200 people who attended were family, friends, and members of the music, television and film community including Bea Wain, Johnny Mandel, Peter Marshall, Lee Hale, Ginny Mancini, Florence Henderson, Terry Gibbs, and Sammy Nestico.

On Sunday, July 19, 2015, Van Alexander passed away quietly of heart failure after spending the preceding five days in the hospital. He is survived by his two daughters, Lynn Tobias and Joyce Harris, four grandchildren and fourteen great-grandchildren. He is interred alongside Beth, his wife, at Hillside Memorial Park Cemetery in Los Angeles, CA.

A handsome and debonair Van Alexander as a fledgling bandleader in 1938.

Drummer Chick Webb was Van Alexander's first boss.

Van Alexander presenting Ella Fitzgerald with her seventh Grammy Award in Las Vegas in 1962.

Van Alexander celebrating his 100th birthday with his daughter, Joyce Harris, on May 2, 2015, at the Catalina Bar and Grill Jazz Club in Hollywood. - *Photo by Stephen Fratallone*

The cover of Van Alexander's autobiography, *From Harlem to Hollywood: My Life in Music*, written with Stephen Fratallone and published by BearManor Media in 2009.

The Man With The Horn

Bandleader Ray Anthony Champions Big Band Music For Over Six Decades With Consistency

The following article on Ray Anthony was originally published in the February 2002 issue of Jazz Connection Magazine

Bandleader Ray Anthony took his exceptional trumpet chops, Cary Grant-like looks, and a relentless energy for self-promotion and turned them into a long and prosperous series of music business enterprises.

"I can't remember a time when music wasn't part of my life," said Anthony, 80, via telephone from his home in Beverly Hills, CA. "Music puts wings on the human soul. Nothing can touch people the way music can. And every day is a new opportunity to create, change, stretch and reach for new heights doing something that I absolutely love - entertaining people through great music."

For over sixty years Anthony has been entertaining people through great music from the bell of his golden trumpet first as a sideman with the Al Donahue, Glenn Miller and Jimmy Dorsey orchestras and then as a bandleader in his own right with a Navy aggregation during World War II and then leading one of the most popular and successful bands during the post-World War II period.

Throughout the 1950s and 1960s Anthony was one of Capitol Records' biggest recording artists cranking out such hits as "The Bunny

Hop," "Dragnet," "The Peter Gunn Theme," "Thunderbird," and "Mr. Anthony's Boogie," among others.

Anthony is slated to be honored for his contribution to Big Band music with the presentation of the coveted Golden Bandstand Award by the Big Band Academy of America at its annual reunion at the Sportsmen's Lodge in Studio City, CA, on Sunday, March 3. The theme for this year's BBAA gala is the celebration of the 60th anniversary of Capitol Records.

"Ray was a Capitol Records star," said BBAA president Milt Bernhart. "Our program will concentrate on bands that recorded for Capitol during its 60-year history and Ray shouldn't be left out."

Anthony put the accent on excitement in Big Band music with his lush, rich tone that projected from his trumpet coupled with his band's bright, spanking arrangements.

"I'd like to think that I play with a lot of feeling," he said.

Anthony was born Raymond Antonini on January 20, 1922, in Bentleyville, Pennsylvania. His father taught him music and he began his musical career at age five playing cornet in the "Antonini Family Orchestra" comprised of his sister, two brothers, and father.

"I was heavily influenced by Louis Armstrong, Roy Eldridge and Harry James," Anthony said.

The Antonini Family eventually settled in Cleveland, Ohio. While in high school, Anthony played in various high school bands as well as in local professional outfits like those led by Vince Patti and Jack Crawford.

"I learned a lot from Vince and the first time I went on the road I was with Jack's band," Anthony said. "I always kept coming back to Cleveland which was my home town."

By the time he was a junior in high school, the young trumpeter made the decision to change his name, he said.

"We thought that Antonini would be hard for people to remember," Anthony said. "I started to go by the last name of Anthony and I changed it legally a few years later."

The teen trumpeter was soon making a name for himself in the Cleveland area. In the fall of 1940, Anthony auditioned and was hired by violinist Al Donahue to play lead trumpet in his "Low Down Rhythm in a Top Hat" band, named after his theme song by the same name. Donahue began his career as a society band leader but by 1940 he was leading a swing band. The band featured two young singers, Phil Brito and Dee Keating. For two years Paula Kelly had been the featured vocalist but left a few months before Anthony joined the outfit. The two would eventually work together as members of trombonist Glenn Miller's band.

"This was the first nationally known band that I had played with and I enjoyed my time with Al very much," Anthony said.

Anthony's first recordings with the Donahue band were waxed on September 11, 1940, for Okeh Records with "Burning the Midnight Oil" and "The Blue Jump," both instrumentals; and "My Disposition," with Phil Brito on the vocal, and "Too Much Love," featuring Dee Keating on the vocal. In the over four months he was with Donahue, Anthony recorded a dozen sides.

In early December 1940, Anthony had a chance to listen to Miller's band in person while in Boston and it impressed the young trumpet player.

"Their showmanship, what they did with their hats and trumpets and movements, was unreal!" Anthony recalled.

Anthony admitted that his real reason for seeing the Miller band in Boston was in hopes of securing a job from the renowned trombone-playing bandleader.

"I had heard that Glenn was looking for a trumpet player and I thought that being the ripe old age of 18, that I could fit the bill," Anthony said. "Glenn also heard about this young kid, me, playing pretty good trumpet. I almost lost out, though. When I told Glenn I was under contract to Al Donahue and that I'd have to get out of it, he hired Billy May, not believing I could do it. When I came back to Glenn and told him that I did get out of my contract, he said, 'Well, I already hired somebody.' I told him that I was now out of a job. He fired another guy and hired me right on the spot."

Donahue, knowing that the young trumpeter could go farther in Miller's band than with his, released Anthony from his contract. Anthony's first recording with the Miller band was "Anvil Chorus, Parts I & II" (December 13-27, 1940) for RCA's Bluebird label. Arranged by Jerry Gray, the Giuseppe Verdi piece was recorded on two sides of a 78 RPM platter and was often used as a rousing finale for Miller's *Chesterfield* radio broadcasts.

Other Miller personnel on this recording session included Dale "Mickey" McMickle, Johnny Best and Billy May, trumpets; Jim Priddy, Paul Tanner and Frank D'Annolfo, trombones; Hal McIntyre, Tex Beneke, Willie Schwartz, Ernie Caceres and Al Klink, saxophones; Chummy MacGregor, piano; Trigger Alpert, bass; Jack Lathrop, guitar; and Maurice Purtill, drums.

While Best and May would split the jazz solos, McMickle and Anthony split the lead book, Anthony said.

"Strangely enough, at a young age, I was a good lead trumpet player," Anthony said. "Where I got the conception of being able to lead a big band like that, I don't even know myself."

From the perspective of an 18-year-old, Anthony felt as if he was on top of the world being in Miller's band, he said.

"I was playing in the most popular band in the country at that time," Anthony said. "We played all kinds of music, swing tunes as well as sweet tunes. Every place we went to perform was sold out before we arrived. Miller was like the Elvis Presley of his day."

During his year-and-a-half stay with Miller, Anthony's relationship with the noted bandleader was often times stormy. Some musicians from the band tried to describe the personalities of the two men as Anthony to oil and Miller to water; the two never mixed well together.

"Glenn fired me twice," Anthony said. "And I often say to this day, if I had a punk like me in the band, I'd fire him, too! I didn't know how cocky I was, but I must have been. Now, Glenn was an ordinary-looking man and he'd play just ordinary. He wasn't a great musician. There was no reason I couldn't be doing the same thing he was doing."

During his tenure with Miller, Anthony helped to record numerous hits that have become associated with the Miller orchestra such as "Song of the Volga Boatmen" (January 17, 1941); "Adios" (June 25, 1941); "Perfidia" (1941); "Elmer's Tune" (1941); and "A String of Pearls" (November 3, 1941).

During that year the Miller orchestra went out to Hollywood to film its first appearance in a movie, *Sun Valley Serenade,* starring John Payne, Sonja Henie and Milton Berle. One of the songs that Miller performed in that film, "Chattanooga Choo-Choo," turned out to be a tremendous hit for him. The song, both in the film and on record (May 7, 1941), featured Tex Beneke, Paula Kelly and The Modernaires on the vocal.

"Chattanooga Choo-Choo" was such a big hit that RCA Victor presented Miller the first actual golden disc of that recording for selling a million copies, on February 10, 1942, according to *The Guinness Book of World Records.*

After America entered World War II, Anthony left the Miller band in early 1942 to enlist in the Navy. It would be a few months before he would have to report for active duty, so Jimmy Dorsey hired him during that interim period.

"Jimmy was a sweet man," Anthony said. "He was very much a musician and led a really popular band."

While Miller and Dorsey had good commercial bands, both played different styles, Anthony said.

"Jimmy's big hits came from vocalists Bob Eberly and Helen O'Connell which were slower, romantic pieces," he said. "Miller's band recorded every week. We recorded four sides once a week. His big hits, even though he was also known for his ballad style, were mostly swing numbers like "In the Mood."

After his first year in the Navy, Anthony was placed in charge of a service show band which toured island bases in the Pacific, where his aggregation won an award as the top service band.

"It amazed me that at some of the more obscure islands that we played at, we were able to cross other Navy bands led by Artie Shaw, Bob Crosby, Dick Jurgens and Claude Thornhill," Anthony said.

The date of December 15, 1944, is a sad day for Glenn Miller aficionados. It was on that foggy day that Major Glenn Miller and two other officers boarded a Norseman UC-64A aircraft from England to Paris which never reached their destination. Anthony was on Midway Island during that time when he heard the news of his former boss's disappearance over the English Channel.

"It was like hearing about the death of the President of the United States," Anthony said. "It was that powerful."

Upon his discharge from the Navy in 1946, Anthony formed his own dance orchestra which opened at the Chase Hotel in St. Louis for a five-week engagement beginning on February 15, 1946. Joining the band at this time was Anthony's brother, Leo Anthony, who played alto and baritone saxophones. He would be a mainstay in his brother's band for several decades.

While in Chicago in November 1946, the newly-formed Anthony band recorded their first sides on Sonora Records. Those songs were "I'll Close My Eyes" (vocal by Bill Johnson), "Margie" (vocal by the ensemble), "Please Be Kind" (vocal by Dee Keating who was with Al Donahue's band during the same time as Anthony was), "Isn't This Better Than Walkin' in the Rain?" (vocal by Bill Johnson), "We Knew It All the Time" (Dee Keating and Bill Johnson, vocals), "Meet Me at No Special Place" (Dee Keating, vocal), "Would You Believe Me?" (Bill Johnson, vocal) and "That's My Desire" (vocal by Dee Keating), a cover version of singer Frankie Laine's first million-selling hit.

In February 1947, Anthony and his band trekked out to Hollywood for a three-week stint at the Hollywood Palladium and to Columbia

Pictures to make their first film short. The songs they recorded for the film's sound track included "I'll Close My Eyes" (vocal by Bill Johnson), "Let's Go Back and Kiss the Boys Again" and "Funiculi, Funicula."

The Anthony band would go on to make two other film shorts, one for Will Cowan Films in July 1950, and the other in October 1952. Both are currently distributed on the MCA Video Cassette series, *Swing: The Best of the Big Bands, Vol. 1 - 4*. The selections that Anthony plays on these video cassettes include "Skip to My Lou," "All Anthony and No Cleopatra," and "Mr. Anthony's Boogie."

Anthony's band was just starting to build momentum when the second musicians' union strike of the decade was set to take place throughout 1948. The trumpet-playing leader and his band went into the studios on December 30, 1947, to record eight sides on Signature Records: "Bye, Bye Blues," "Gloria," "London Bridge is Falling Down," "Passing Fancy," "Peace of Mind" (all featuring Ronnie Deauville on the vocal), and three instrumentals: "Oh! Moon," "Trumpet Time" and "The Man with the Horn," which Anthony would use as his theme song.

During this time Anthony was developing his band's sound and eventually combined elements of the top bands of his day into his, he said.

"We were searching for our own identity as a band and until we got one, we took the best of the best," Anthony explained. "We took the sax sound from the Glenn Miller band, we took the trombone sound from Tommy Dorsey. I, being a trumpet player, was naturally compared to Harry James at the time and so we felt the combination of sounds might be one of our own."

In 1949, Anthony signed a five-year contract with Capitol Records but ended up staying with the Los Angeles-based recording company for much longer.

"Signing with Capitol was a lucky break for us," Anthony said. "We wound up staying with Capitol for nineteen years."

By signing with Capitol, Anthony joined a pantheon of top-name recording artists that would help to make the seven-year-old company a formidable force to be reckoned with in the recording industry: Margaret Whiting, Kay Starr, Jo Stafford, Tennessee Ernie Ford, Peggy Lee, Nat "King" Cole, Ella Mae Morse, Les Paul and Mary Ford, Gordon MacRae, Mel Blanc, Skitch Henderson, Buddy Cole, Jan Garber, Tex Ritter, Billy May, Woody Herman, June Christy, Dean Martin, and a few years later, Frank Sinatra, along with Nelson Riddle, among others.

Anthony recorded his first sides for Capitol on March 23 of that year with "House Party," "Veloa" (vocals by Pat Baldwin, Ken Trimble and The Skyliners), "A New Shade of Blues" (vocal by Dick Noel), and two days later with "The Wreck on the Highway" (vocal by Ken Trimble), "Darktown Strutters' Ball" and "Yesterdays." Veteran arrangers Dean Kincaide, Charles Shirley and George Williams were also hired to arrange for the band.

Staying that long in partnership with a major record label such as Capitol was a feat in itself. Maintaining a big band during this period of time was nothing short of a miracle as many top-name bands of the day were folding at the end World War II. Despite some early disappointments, Anthony remained focused.

"It was difficult for us in the beginning because we weren't popular enough," Anthony recalled. "Once we became popular, we ranked as the Number One Band in the country in all trade magazine polls from 1950-1955. It was after the important 'Big Band time,' but we did quite well."

Doing quite well is an understatement for Anthony. During this period he seemed to have had the "Midas touch." His band toured exclusively and played all the top spots across the country. He has probably played more college prom dates than anyone else in recent history. He was also the most played instrumental recording artist on radio.

During his stay at Capitol Records, he released over 100 albums and 500 singles. His biggest album of all time is *Dream Dancing* (recorded January 11-20, 1956). With arrangements provided by George Williams, personnel on the album included a stellar line up Big Band era and studio stalwarts in Johnny Best, trumpet; Murray McEachern, trombone; Abe Most and Willie Schwartz, alto saxophones and clarinet; Georgie Auld, tenor sax; Al Hendrickson, guitar; and Larry Bunker, drums.

Other hit albums include *Worried Mind, Ray Anthony Plays Steve Allen* (June 1958), *Dancing Over the Waves* (1958), and *Dream Dancing Memories.*

Anthony's first hit single was his interpretation of the standard, "Tenderly" (February 21, 1950), followed by "Stardust" (February 22, 1950) and a remake of his theme song, "The Man with the Horn" (May 6, 1950), which showcased his rich, lush tone. Other hit singles include "Slaughter on Tenth Avenue" (April 16, 1952); and compositions Anthony wrote in collaboration with arranger George Williams: "Mr. Anthony's Blues" (August 20, 1950), "Mr. Anthony's Boogie" (December 17, 1950), with its brassy sound and infectious shuffle, and "Thunderbird" (December 12, 1952); and "Oh! Mein Papa" (November 17, 1953, with vocal by the Anthony Choir).

Anthony's first million-seller, a piece co-written with Leonard Auletti, was a dance tune that sparked a craze even shorter-lived than the Macarena. That song was "The Bunny Hop" (recorded March 7, 1953).

His biggest hit came in 1954, when, after bugging Jack Webb for months to get him to release the recording rights, Anthony recorded a cover of the theme to Webb's cop television show, *Dragnet.* The song was recorded on July 25, 1953, with drummer Mel Lewis playing a prominent role on the tune.

Anthony's third million-selling single was his rockin' cover of Henry Mancini's theme song from the television detective drama, *Peter Gunn.* Recorded on August 4, 1958, it's the best-selling single recording of that tune.

"We did a lot of singles in those days and we did about four albums a year," Anthony said. "That's a lot of recordings. I always remember the big hits like 'Dragnet,' 'Bunny Hop' and 'Peter Gunn.' They stand out and they were great recordings for me."

In 1955, at the height of his popularity, Anthony gave up touring with his big band to stay in Los Angeles to study voice and acting with Sanford Meisner and Estelle Harmon.

"The band business was getting even less effective for big bands and I was tired of the constant traveling," Anthony said. "The band went out occasionally like for a ten-week tour."

By 1960, Anthony, seeing the coming trend away from big bands, developed a small group for nightclub variety performances called "Ray Anthony and the Bookends." Anthony's instrumental group included his own trumpet, Bob Fitzpatrick, trombone; Joe Maini, tenor sax; Leo Anthony, Ray's brother, baritone sax; Arnold Ross, piano; Don Simpson, bass; and Jerry McKenzie, drums. Featured vocalists included Anthony and two female "Bookends" - Diane Hall and Annita Ray. The ensemble lasted for twenty years and was a big draw at the Sahara Hotel in Las Vegas for many years.

"We traveled all over the world performing with that group," Anthony said.

Anthony appeared as an actor and bandleader in fifteen motion pictures. The Anthony band's first appearance in a feature film occurred in 1955 in Twentieth Century Fox's *Daddy Long Legs* starring Fred Astaire and Leslie Caron. The band was used in a college dance scene.

Other films in which Anthony's band appeared include *The Girl Can't Help It* (1956) starring Jayne Mansfield, Tom Ewell and Edmund O'Brien; and *This Could Be the Night* (1957) starring Jean Simmons, Paul Douglas and Tony Franciosa.

As an actor, Anthony had speaking roles in *High School Confidential* (1958) starring Russ Tamblyn, Jackie Coogan and Mamie Van Doren; *Girls Town* (1959) starring Mamie Van Doren; *The Beat Generation* (1959) starring Steve Cochran and Mamie Van Doren; *Night of the Quarter Moon* (1959) starring Julie London; *Five Fingers* (1959) starring David Hedison and Oscar Homolka; *The Big Operator* (1959) starring Mickey

Rooney, Steve Cochran, and Mamie Van Doren; *Birds Do It* (1968) starring Soupy Sales; and his most prominent acting role in *The Five Pennies* (1959) starring Danny Kaye, Barbara Bel Geddes, Tuesday Weld, and Louis Armstrong. Loosely based on the life of jazz cornetist Red Nichols, Anthony portrayed his former boss, Jimmy Dorsey, in the film.

Anthony took the new medium of television and made it work for him hosting five of his own television shows, two of which were syndicated. Anthony's first television program, *The Ray Anthony Show*, sponsored by Chesterfield cigarettes, aired over the CBS network in 1953 as the summer replacement for Perry Como. Anthony did three 15-minute Big Band variety shows per week for thirteen weeks that featured singers Helen O'Connell and Bob Eberly. The show was such a hit that it was aired again the following summer.

During the 1956 - 1957 season, Plymouth sponsored *The Ray Anthony Show* for thirty weeks over the ABC network. The weekly one-hour Big Band variety show featured its own family of entertainers as well as occasional guests.

In 1963, *The Ray Anthony Show* went into syndication as *Club Anthony*. The 30-minute TV show, shot in a night club setting, lasted for twenty-six weeks and featured Anthony's small band and "The Bookends," one of whom was Vikki Carr, as well as outside guests.

During 1969 - 1970, Anthony's new show, *Swinging Scene*, also went into syndication. Broadcast in color, the one-hour weekly variety show featured Big Bands, "The Bookends," plus numerous outside guests.

Anthony has also appeared as a guest on *The Merv Griffin Show*, *The Steve Allen Show*, *The Mike Douglas Show*, *The Tonight Show*, *The Chevrolet Comedy Hour with George Goebel*, and *The Jerry Lewis Telethon*, among others. He served as musical director and co-host for the *Stop Arthritis Telethon*.

In August 1980, Anthony and his band performed for two hours live on KCET, the Public Broadcasting Station's affiliate in Los Angeles, for their pledge festival.

Anthony also won a place in the hearts of exotica lovers by marrying buxom B-movie queen Mamie Van Doren, but the marriage ended in divorce.

Anthony received a star on the Hollywood Walk of Fame. His star is appropriately situated across from the place he helped to build, the Capitol Records Towers Building.

In 1968, with the trend toward big band music waning, Capitol Records decided not to renew its contract with Anthony. That year, he entered into an agreement with Ranwood Records and stayed with them for nine years releasing ten albums and thirty singles.

In 1976, Anthony formed his own record label, Aero Space Records, producing over 40 albums to date since its inception.

"There are still records coming from other companies, so that has upped our total to about 40 CDs out on the market right now," Anthony said.

Anthony's latest CD, *Dream Dancing III: The Romantic Mood*, has just been released, he said.

In 1980, he formed an organization of bandleaders called "Big Bands '80s" to perpetuate the revived interest in Big Band music. As president, he started out with a group of Los Angeles-based leaders who, together with Anthony, compiled a comprehensive mailing list of Big Band fans and radio stations. Anthony then produced an LP featuring himself and five other big bands playing two tracks each and shipped it to 500 radio stations. At that time there were less than a dozen stations playing Big Band music. Today, through Anthony's efforts, there are close to 1000, he said

In 1981, Anthony formed the Big Band Record Library, a mail order business for Big Band CDs.

"People were looking for this kind of music and they couldn't find it, so we created a place for people to order these records," Anthony said. "It's gotten bigger."

To order any CDs, audio cassettes or videos from Aero Space Records or the Big Band Record Library, log on to Anthony's web site at www.bigbandrecordlibrary.com

Other entrepreneurial ventures that Anthony was affiliated with include running a music publishing house, contracting bands (he bought out Billy May's short-lived Big Band when it folded), and a nightclub in Hollywood.

During the early 1980s, Anthony reorganized his Big Band to play dates in an around the Los Angeles area such as Disneyland and the Hollywood Palladium. In January 1985, Anthony and his Big Band were invited to play for the 50th Presidential Inaugural Ball for President Ronald Reagan, and were also asked to perform at The White House for the opening festivities of the week-long event.

These days the Anthony aggregation plays quite often for the public at the Cocoanut Club at the Beverly Hilton Hotel in Beverly Hills.

"We do more special engagements these days staying pretty close to Los Angeles," Anthony said. "Occasionally we'll do Palm Springs or Las Vegas. We go out on Big Band cruises about twice a year. We also do a lot of private parties."

While Anthony's love for Big Band music is widely known, his impressions of today's music is less than complimentary.

"It's all bad," he said. "You don't have music anymore. There are a few songs out there with melodies, but not many."

For the past six decades Anthony has been a champion of Big Band music and one of its leading standard bearers. His contribution to that musical genre can best be summed up in one word: consistency, he said.

"We became the Number One band for five years following in the footsteps of Glenn Miller and bands like that," Anthony said. "For a good period of time we consistently put out records, and had some hit records along the way. We kept Big Band music going when there wasn't any."

** Coda - Here is an update on Ray Anthony since this article was published:

Anthony is semi-retired and plays only a few special dates a year.

He maintains an official Ray Anthony website at: www.rayanthonyband.com and has Facebook and Twitter pages.

Ray Anthony on the album cover of his *Dragnet* album on Capitol Records from 1954.

Ray Anthony doing "The Bunny Hop" with Tony Curtis and Janet Leigh.

Ray Anthony and wife, Mamie Van Doren.

Ray Anthony and his horn in the mid-1990s.

Ray Anthony at age 93 in December 2015.

Hail, King Louie

Drumming Great Louis Bellson To Be Honored With Golden Bandstand Award

The following article on Louis Bellson was originally published in the March 2005 issue of Jazz Connection Magazine

Louis Bellson was referred to by the late jazz critic Leonard Feather as "one of the most phenomenal drummers in history." And Bellson has lived up to that high praise throughout his illustrious 65-year career in music.

The four-time Grammy Award-nominee has been considered by many to be one of the three top jazz/swing drummers - along with Gene Krupa and Buddy Rich - to come out of the Big Band Era. All three giants of the traps consistently exhibited charismatic appeal to both peers and public alike. All three have raised the bar by giving distinction and respectability to the drums as a legitimate musical instrument. All three have generated high-powered excitement with their often times spectacular and torrid drum solos.

"For me to be in that class it's wonderful," said a humbled Bellson, 80, via telephone from his home in San Jose, California. "But I have to give just dues to two guys who really got me off on the drums - Big Sid Catlett and Jo Jones. They were my influences. All three of us realized what Jo Jones did and it influenced a lot of us. We all three looked to Jo as the 'Papa' who really did it. Gene helped bring the drums to the foreground as a solo instrument. Buddy was a great natural player. But we also have to look back at Chick Webb's contributions, too."

While two members of this elite triumvirate were noted as percussive stylistic innovators, Bellson took his own innovation a step further by developing the double-bass drum set up, which is used by many drummers today, and by his creative and stimulating compositions and arrangements, many of which have become jazz classics.

As Feather once again enthused, "Musicians and public alike respect him as a drummer without peer in technique, taste and originality; and as a composer whose works are a consistently effective fusion of melodic, rhythmic and harmonic ideas."

As a musician, Bellson is a "total drummer," meaning he knows how to play dynamic and tasteful solos but he also knows how to drive and support a band during a performance.

"Having been brought up during the Swing Era, I've always felt that a great drummer needed to learn how to play solos, but the most important thing is knowing how to back up soloists and play for the band," Bellson said. "The best comment I would get from the guys in the band would be, 'You really swung the band tonight, Louie,' rather than, 'That was a great solo.' Solos are fine but a drummer may play one or two solos a night. What about the rest of the evening? It's how you play the ballads, it's how you play the bossa novas, it's how you fit in with the rest of the rhythm section, it's how you support the band - that's what makes a great drummer."

As one of the greatest drummers of our time, Bellson will be honored by the Big Band Academy Of America at its annual reunion on Sunday, March 6, 2005, at the Sportsmen's Lodge in Studio City, CA. He will receive the fine arts organization's esteemed Golden Bandstand Award. Other honorees joining Bellson on that day include trumpeters Eugene "Snooky" Young, a veteran of the Jimmie Lunceford orchestra and a mainstay in the Los Angeles jazz and studio arenas, and Clora Bryant, a jazz pioneer for women and one of the last living musicians of the Be-Bop jazz era.

Louis Bellson was born Luigi Paulino Alfredo Francesco Antonio Balassoni on July 26, 1924, in Rock Falls, Illinois, near Chicago. His parents were Italian immigrants. His father hailed from Naples, his mother came from Milan.

"People were either misspelling or mispronouncing my father's last name, so he changed it to Bellson," Bellson said. "In those days, many immigrants shortened their names to Americanize it."

Bellson's father played numerous instruments and he eventually opened his own music store in Moline, IL, across the Mississippi River from Davenport, Iowa.

The young Bellson's love affair with the drums began at age 3 when his father took him to see a parade and he heard the wonderful sounds of the drums thundering down the street.

"I told my dad that I wanted to play that (the drums)," Bellson said. "My dad said I was so definite about it that he started me on the drums. That was the beginning."

Because his father was gifted musically, Bellson, along with his three other brothers and four sisters, received a very thorough training in music, he said.

"By the time I was 12, I was teaching drums at my father's music store," Bellson said. "He taught my brothers and sisters and me all the instruments. I also had brass, woodwind and string students. We even played a lot of tarantellas at home!" (laughing)

By age 13, Bellson also studied conducting from his father and was well-versed with most of the arias from the major operas, he said.

"I'm called a jazz drummer and I chuckle a little bit because most people don't realize that I had all that 'legit' training," Bellson mused. "I was into all the classics."

Wanting to learn more about playing the drums, the then-15-year-old Bellson started studying privately with Roy Knapp in Chicago. Knapp previously had given lessons to Gene Krupa, who by this time had become the icon of the traps after having reached stardom with Benny Goodman's band and who was now a bandleader in his own right.

"Roy was not only a great all-around percussion teacher, but also a great musician," Bellson said.

The young teen also showed a great aptitude for art. As a result for his fondness for drawing, Bellson is credited with pioneering the double-bass-drum set-up, which would be his trademark. His detailed sketch of his new "invention" earned him an 'A' in his high school art class.

"My art teacher saw me draw two round circles and he asked me what I was drawing," Bellson said.

"I told him I was developing a new drum set: a two-bass drum set up. He thought it was an interesting concept and passed me on that drawing. It was my art project for the year."

The purpose of the double-bass drum is to give the drummer added support, Bellson said.

"I've been of the opinion that all a drummer really needs is one bass drum, a snare drum, some tom-toms, a ride cymbal, a crash cymbal, sticks and brushes," Bellson said. "If you can't do it with that, you better go back to the drawing board. The extra bass drum is frosting on the cake. It doesn't mean that every drummer needs to play two bass drums. For me, it works."

Eventually Gretsch Drum Company picked up on the young drummer's vision and made the first double-bass drum kit, Bellson said.

Bellson was a musically hungry student and he grew quickly at his craft. At 17, two important events occurred in Bellson's young life: he gained national attention by winning the Gene Krupa-Slingerland Drum Contest, triumphing over 40,000 drummers who entered the contest, and he got his first professional job with a name band.

"A representative from Slingerland Drum Company came to my dad's music store and encouraged my dad to have me enter the contest," Bellson said. "I didn't care much for contests in those days. My dad persuaded to enter."

However, once entering the contest, Bellson played to win, thus prevailing at each level of competition through the local, regional, semi-finals and eventually, the finals.

"I felt that some of the stiffest competition was from around the Chicago area," Bellson said. "There were about 750 drummers from the Midwest that were really hot."

As one of the five finalists, Bellson was sent to New York to play for Krupa at the Paramount Theatre. Krupa judged the finalists himself.

"When I won, it was a feather in my cap," Bellson said. "The contest was covered in *Down Beat* and *Metronome* magazines. I realized at that moment the value of the contest itself even if I didn't win. The value that was important to me was just being there and learning something and being with other drummers and learning from them and being with Gene."

After the contest, Bellson got to meet his idol.

"Gene was a wonderful man," he said. "He said to me, 'Kid, you have lots of talent. Keep on going. Lots of love.'"

From that moment on, a life-long friendship developed between the two drummers until Krupa's death from leukemia and heart failure in October 1973. He was 64.

"Gene was so humble," Bellson recalled. "Buddy Rich and I went to see him a few times. He said to Buddy and me, "I can't play well like you guys can. I just struggle along.' We said, 'Yeah, like you struggle along.'"

In addition to perfecting his own drumming style, Bellson spent time listening to other drummers. As a teen, he went to hear all the major bands that came to Moline or Davenport, he said.

One of the bands that came through the area was led by pianist Ted Fio Rito. Fio Rito led a sweet band and was also a prolific songwriter with such hits to his credit as "Laugh, Clown, Laugh," "I Never Knew," and "Toot, Toot, Tootsie, Goodbye." In the early 1930s, Benny Goodman was a sideman in Fio Rito's orchestra and Betty Grable, who became the G.I.'s favorite Pin Up Girl during World War II, was his girl singer.

Word got back to Fio Rito about the talented 17-year-old drummer from Moline and the veteran bandleader offered Bellson a job with his band right on the spot.

"This was in March or April of my senior year in high school and I told Ted I wanted to graduate high school first," Bellson recalled. "Ted told me to call him after I graduated. I did. He kept his word. He sent for me to come to Hollywood to play with the band at the Florentine Gardens. The Number One act on that bill was The Mills Brothers. They taught me so many things. They were great."

While performing with Fio Rito at the Florentine Gardens in September 1942, bassist Harry Goodman, Benny's brother, happened to come in to catch the show. Goodman was impressed with Bellson's playing and asked the young drummer if he would like to audition for the "King of Swing's" band.

Goodman and his orchestra were in Hollywood at the time filming *The Powers Girl*, starring George Murphy, Anne Shirley, Carol Landis, Dennis Day and Alan Mowbray. Goodman was trying out drummers to replace his current drummer, Hud Davies, who would be leaving the band at the conclusion of filming.

"When Harry asked me if I would like to audition for Benny's band, I just started stuttering!" Bellson said with a laugh. "I was just floored."

The next day, Harry Goodman brought Bellson to Paramount Studios to play a few numbers for his brother. The audition turned out to be more like a screen test for a part in a motion picture.

"I was dressed in a tuxedo and make up was put on my face and they started filming me while I played," Bellson said. "That was my audition!"

Bellson made an impression because Goodman told him that he was hired. Feeling both elated and stunned at the same, Bellson found himself in a quandary, he said.

"Before I had a chance to tell Benny that I was tied up with Ted Fio Rito, Benny said that the band would leave for New York in a few days," Bellson said. "I went back and told the guy's in Ted's band what happened and asked them what I should do. They said to me that I should go because it's not everyday one gets a chance to join Benny Goodman's band and that they would explain things to Ted."

Fio Rito initially got mad at his young drummer for "jumping ship," but his anger was short lived.

"Ted sent me a nice letter and called to wish me lots of luck," Bellson said.

Bellson would do two major stints with Goodman. His first stint lasted eight months and was filled with a number of highlights. The drummer's first gig with the "King of Swing" was on October 9 when the band opened at the Hotel New Yorker. Band personnel at the time included trumpeters Jimmy Maxwell, Lawrence Stearns, and Tony Faso; trombonists Lou McGarity and Charlie Castaldo; alto saxophonists Hymie Schertzer and Clint Neagley; tenor saxophonists Jon Walton and Al Klink; baritone saxophonist Bob Poland; pianist Jimmy Rowles; guitarist Dave Barbour; bassist Cliff Hill; and the band's vocalist, Peggy Lee.

During the Goodman band's three-month stay at the Hotel New Yorker, Hollywood beckoned the clarinet genius to appear in his fourth motion picture, *Stage Door Canteen,* starring Lon McAllister, William Terry, and Cheryl Walker, with cameo appearances by many of Hollywood's most popular stars. The film also included the orchestras of Count Basie, Kay Kyser, Guy Lombardo, Freddy Martin, and Xavier Cugat.

Because of wartime travel restrictions and Goodman's commitment to the New Yorker, his segment of *Stage Door Canteen* was filmed in New York. With more wartime personnel changes, Conrad Gozzo, Carl Poole and Lee Castaldo (Castle) became the new replacements in the trumpet section, and pianist Jess Stacy rejoined the band. In the film, Bellson can be seen periodically over Goodman's right shoulder as the band plays "Bugle Call Rag" and "Why Don't You Do Right?", a vocal by Peggy Lee. The latter tune was originally recorded five days prior to the recording ban in July 1942, and by the time the movie was being filmed, it was a hit for Goodman. *Stage Door Canteen* was released in July 1943.

Another memorable gig for Bellson while with his new boss began on December 30, 1942. The Goodman band was part of a stage show at New York's Paramount Theatre backing up crooner Frank Sinatra. Sinatra had left Tommy Dorsey to forge a solo career for himself (Goodman's Dick Haymes had taken Sinatra's spot with Dorsey), and this was his first major booking.

On February 23, 1943, Goodman and his orchestra opened at the Hollywood Palladium and the following month performed in the Twentieth Century-Fox film, *The Gang's All Here,* starring Alice Faye, Carmen Miranda, Edward Everett Horton, Charlotte Greenwood, and Phil Baker.

In the film, the band was featured on a couple of obscure tunes: "Minnie's in the Money" (with vocal by Goodman) and "Paducah" (vocal by Goodman and Miranda). In fact, Bellson shares Miranda's spotlight along with Goodman in the "Paducah" scene toward the end of the movie.

After *The Gang's All Here* was completed, Goodman remained in California as his wife, Alice, gave birth to their first daughter, Rachel, on May 2 in Los Angeles. Bellson, in turn, found his next gig to be with Uncle Sam as he was drafted into the Army.

"I was supposed to go with Ziggy Elman's band at March Air Field in Riverside, CA, but instead the Army took me the other way to Washington, D.C., to play in concert and dance bands," Bellson said.

In 1946, Bellson was discharged from the Army, and in May of that year, he rejoined Goodman. Band personnel at the time included trumpeters Bernie Privin, Johnny Best, Nate Kazebier (an alumnus of Goodman's 1935 outfit) and Jimmy Blake; trombonists Lou McGarity and Cutty Cutshall; French hornist Addison Collins (an alumnus of Glenn Miller's AAF Band); alto saxophonists Bill Shine and John Prager; tenor saxophonists Gish Gilbertson and Cliff Strickland; baritone saxophonist Danny Bank; pianist Mel Powell (a standout from Goodman's 1941-42 band and Glenn Miller's AAF Band); guitarist Mike Bryan; bassist Barney Spieler; vibraphonist/vocalist Johnny White; and Art Lund, who also rejoined Goodman as the band's vocalist. A few months later Hymie Shertzer returned once again as lead alto saxophonist, and Joe Bushkin as the band's pianist.

On May 14, Bellson waxed his first four sides (in actuality, his first commercial cuts) with Goodman on the swinging Powell arrangement of "Oh, Baby!" (vocal by Goodman), "Blue Skies" (vocal by Art Lund), and

"I Ain't Mad at Nobody" (vocal by White). The swinging "Oh, Baby!" was recorded in two parts on 12-inch platters. The first side of the tune begins with a small group. The flip side, which is slightly faster, features the rest of the band with solos by Gilbertson, Best and McGarity. Bellson gets part of the action with some characteristically clean and accurate drumming.

Bellson stayed with Goodman through the end of 1946, doing *The Benny Goodman Radio Show*, *The Victor Borge Show Starring Benny Goodman*, as well as other radio remote broadcasts with the band, and recording commercial 20 sides. Some of those commercial cuts include "Fly-By-Night" (July 18), "A Kiss in the Night" (vocal by Art Lund), "For You, For Me, For Evermore" (vocal by Eve Young) and "Put That Kiss Back Where You Found It" (vocal by Goodman - all three on August 7), "Hora Staccato" (October 15), "Man Here Plays Fine Piano" (vocal by Eve Young, featuring Joe Bushkin on piano - October 22), and a pair of sextet tracks: "I'll Always Be in Love with You" and "Honeysuckle Rose" (October 22 with Johnny White, vibes; Joe Bushkin, piano; Barney Kessel, guitar; and Harry Babasin, bass).

"Benny was a genius," Bellson said of his boss. "I learned so much from Benny as to how to rehearse a band. I got to know Benny very well. If you get to know a person and get into knowing what they're all about, then you know how valuable they are."

But the good will between Bellson and Goodman wasn't always there. In fact, three months into his first stint with Goodman, Bellson was fired. Bellson explains:

"I had heard many stories about the Benny Goodman 'Ray.' When I first joined the band, Hymie Shertzer was playing lead alto and he was like a second father to me on the road. He said, 'Look, Kid, you probably heard of Benny's Ray. Don't let it bother you. Do what Lionel Hampton used to do - just dig into your instrument and play. Don't even look at him.'

"Everything went well for about the first three months. We were playing at the Hotel New Yorker and we were playing a terrific show. We were doing "Sing, Sing, Sing" and suddenly the focus was on me. Soon after,

Benny gave me my notice. Hymie went to Benny and said, 'Benny, are you crazy? This kid is breaking it up.' Hymie told me he detected a tone of jealousy in Benny because I was getting more applause on 'Sing, Sing, Sing' then he got. Whatever it was, I never found out.

"I went back to Chicago and hung out with Louis Jordan for the night. By the time I got home, my dad was at the train station to meet me. I was surprised to see him because I didn't notify him that I was coming home. He told me Benny kept him up all night on the telephone. He told my dad to tell me to get my butt on that train back to New York. I returned to New York on the next train and rejoined the band. Benny never bothered me again."

Bellson reunited with Goodman in 1948 for the Howard Hawks' film, *A Song is Born*, starring Danny Kaye and Virginia Mayo. Also in the film were Louis Armstrong, Lionel Hampton, Charlie Barnet and Tommy Dorsey.

In 1947, Bellson joined Tommy Dorsey's band, staying until 1949.

"Tommy was a genius, too," Bellson said. "My time with Tommy's band was a marvelous experience."

In "The Sentimental Gentleman of Swing's" band at the time were trumpeters Charlie Shavers and Doc Severinson, tenor saxophonist Boomy Richmond, and pianist Paul Smith, who would later go on to be Ella Fitzgerald's accompanist.

"Charlie (Shavers) and I roomed together for three years," Bellson said. "Charlie was a marvelous trumpet player and a great musician. In fact, Tommy had a lot of fine musicians in his band."

Bellson may have propelled the Dorsey band into a swinging unit, but what the charismatic drummer really wanted to do was to write music. He wanted to study with the best, and he found the best in Norman "Buddy" Baker, who wrote numerous scores for Walt Disney and helped to create one of the finest film scoring schools in the United States: The Thornton School of Music at the University of Southern California (USC). Baker died in 2002.

"I wanted to really get into music so I had heard about Buddy Baker," Bellson said. "I listened to the wonderful string writings he did with Herb Jeffries and I knew I had to meet him and study with him."

Bellson left Dorsey to briefly co-led a sextet in 1950 with Shavers that featured clarinetist Buddy DeFranco and vibraphonist Terry Gibbs.

Bellson then join trumpeter Harry James, whose band wasn't working steady at the time.

"Harry was working one or two days a week, which gave me a chance to study with Buddy," Bellson said. The move to James' band proved to be good for Bellson as he immersed himself in his musical studies.

Bellson stayed with James for a year before Duke Ellington wooed him, and fellow band members Juan Tizol (valve trombone) and Willie Smith (alto saxophone), over to his side.

"Duke had a lot of things in store for us and we went to Harry and told him about it," Bellson said. "Harry looked at the three of us and said, 'Take me with you!'"

Bellson's two-year association with Ellington was artistically productive. He was able to put into practice many of the things he studied while with Baker as well as the things he picked up from Ellington himself and composer/arranger Billy Strayhorn.

"The techniques of learning music from Duke and Billy really impressed me," Bellson said. Ellington was also impressed with his drummer's ear for composition and arranging. He was the first bandleader who asked Bellson to bring arrangements to him, Bellson said.

"I said to Duke, 'No way! Not with you and Billy around,'" Bellson said.

Through Tizol's prodding, however, Bellson reluctantly showed his boss and mentor two pieces that he composed - one back in 1946 called "Skin Deep," and a more recent effort, "The Hawk Talks."

"I wrote 'The Hawk Talks' for Harry James," Bellson said. "Harry was known by musicians as 'The Hawk,' as was (tenor saxophone giant) Coleman Hawkins. To my utter surprise and joy, Duke said he wanted to record the songs. That catapulted me into the arranging class. To have Duke rehearse just one of my songs would have been good enough. Here he wanted to record them."

Some critics felt that Bellson helped to re-vitalize Ellington's orchestra with his great, swinging arrangements. In fact, Bellson's material such as "Skin Deep," "The Hawk Talks" and "Ting-A-Ling," has stood the test of time as Ellington features.

"Duke's band was unbelievable," Bellson said. "He and Billy were true geniuses in every sense of the word. Being with Duke was a marvelous experience. That was probably one of the highlights of my life. Duke spent as much time with the newspaper boy on the corner as he would with the President. He always had a kind word for everybody. He was just a marvelous man."

In 1952, Bellson left Ellington to marry singer/actress Pearl Bailey, with whom he worked as her musical director over the next few years, and leading his own band which included Taft Jordan on trumpet, Eddie "Lockjaw" Davis on tenor sax; and George Duvivier on bass.

"Pearl and I met when she did a few shows with Duke which were fantastic," Bellson said.

Pearl Mae Bailey, the youngest of four children born to a preacher and who was Bellson's senior by eight years, was featured both as a singer and dancer with jazz bands led by Noble Sissle, Cootie Williams, and Edgar Hayes. She began performing as a solo act in 1944, and wooed nightclub audiences with her relaxed stage presence and humorous asides. After briefly replacing Sister Rosetta Tharpe in Cab Calloway's Orchestra during the mid-1940s, she debuted on Broadway during 1946 in the musical, *St. Louis Woman*. Bailey earned an award for Most Promising Newcomer, and made her first film, *Variety Girl*, in 1947.

Though it wasn't a hit, her version of "Tired" (from *Variety Girl*) increased her standing in the jazz community. She recorded for several different labels, including Columbia, during the 1940s and finally found a hit in 1952 after signing to Coral. Her version of "It Takes Two to Tango", backed by Don Redman's Orchestra, hit the Top Ten. In that same year she married Bellson, her fifth husband.

"After I became Pearl's musical director, Don Redman helped front the band," Bellson said. "He was a fantastic musician who never got his just dues. Between Don and Benny Carter, they did most of Pearl's arrangements."

As theirs was an interracial marriage, Bellson and Bailey encountered only few incidents of racial prejudice during their thirty-eight years together, Bellson said.

"Because Pearl was the kind of lady she was, there were many people who by-passed that," Bellson said. "She was one of those people everyone loved. We had a few incidents over the years, but not many. I received a letter when we first got married that was very derogatory, very racial. We didn't think anything of it, but rather, we felt sorry for the person who wrote the letter."

With her career continuing to move forward, Bailey recorded several albums for Coral during the early 1950s, and starred as a fortune-teller in the 1954 film, *Carmen Jones*. More starring roles followed: in the W.C. Handy biopic, *St. Louis Blues*, as well as the first filmed version of Gershwin's classic operetta, *Porgy and Bess*.

In 1959, a new recording contract with Roulette Records resulted in a change of direction. After her double-entendre LP, *For Adults Only*, was banned from radio play, it became a big seller and occasioned a string of similar albums during the early 1960s. She continued to perform on Broadway, and won a Tony award in 1970 for her title role in *Hello, Dolly!* She briefly hosted her own television variety show in 1971.

"We are still trying to uncover those fifteen shows that Pearl did on *The Hollywood Palace*," Bellson said. "She had three heavy-weights on every week. Louis Armstrong, Bing Crosby and Andy Williams were on her first show. We had a 40-piece orchestra with strings. (Guitarist) Joe Pass and (bassist) Ray Brown were in the orchestra."

Bailey also provided voices for animations such as *Tubby the Tuba* (1976) and Disney's *The Fox and the Hound* (1981). She wrote humorous and inspirational books, including *Hurry Up, America, and Spit*. In

1989, she published an autobiography, *Between You and Me*. Bailey was named to the American delegation to the United Nations in 1976, and was awarded the Medal of Freedom in 1988.

The Bellson's adopted two children: a son, Tony, who died in 2004, and a daughter, Dee Dee. Bailey died on August 17, 1990, at age 72.

In May 1952, Bellson led an all-star group in Los Angeles to record eight sides for Capitol Records as part of Gene Norman's Just Jazz series. All-star members included Clark Terry, trumpet; Juan Tizol, valve trombone/arranger; John Grass, French horn; Willie Smith, alto saxophone; Wardell Gray, tenor saxophone; Harry Carney, baritone saxophone; Billy Strayhorn, piano/arranger; Wendell Marshall, bass; and Shorty Rogers and Buddy Baker, arrangers.

In 1955, Bellson received a call from jazz promoter Norman Granz inviting him to be a member of the Jazz at the Philharmonic aggregate. He would do return stints with the JATP in 1967 and 1972.

"I have Norman Granz to thank for that," Bellson said. "Buddy Rich and I were the two drummers to go out on that 1955 tour. We had Dizzy Gillespie, Ella Fitzgerald, Lester Young, Roy Eldridge, Clark Terry, Flip Phillips, Oscar Peterson, Zoot Sims, Herb Ellis and Ray Brown with us, too."

Under Granz's supervision, Bellson recorded a number of sides on Granz's Norgran Records label leading his own quintet. The ensemble included Charlie Shavers, trumpet; Zoot Sims, tenor sax; Don Abney, piano; and George Duvivier, bass.

"Through Norman, I got a chance to record with Art Tatum before he died and with Louie (Armstrong) and Ella (Fitzgerald)," Bellson said.

The album with Armstrong and Fitzgerald that Bellson is referring to is *Ella and Louis Again*, recorded on Granz's Verve Records in August 1957. In addition to Bellson and Armstrong's trumpet and vocals, other musicians for that session were Oscar Peterson, piano; Herb Ellis, guitar; and Ray Brown, bass.

Armstrong and Fitzgerald give swinging renditions on "Don't Be

That Way," "They All Laughed," "Autumn in New York," "Stompin' At The Savoy," "I Won't Dance," "Gee, Baby, Ain't I Good to You?", "Let's Call the Whole Thing Off," "I've Got My Love to Keep Me Warm," "I'm Putting All My Eggs in One Basket," "A Fine Romance," "Love Is Here to Stay," and "Learning the Blues."

"I owe a lot to Norman for giving me the opportunity to play with all those great players," Bellson said.

From 1955 to 1956, Bellson was featured with the Dorsey Brothers band. Two years earlier, Jimmy and Tommy Dorsey patched up their differences and reunited to lead an orchestra they started together eighteen years earlier. The partnership lasted until Tommy's untimely death in November 1956. Brother Jimmy died of lung cancer seven months later.

Throughout the 1950s, Bellson continued touring with his wife while free-lancing as a drummer, composer and arranger.

Over the years, Bellson took several bandleaders' holidays to play under the direction of other leaders or to lead someone else's band. During the 1960s, he rejoined Ellington for his Emancipation Proclamation Centennial stage production, *My People*, the motion picture soundtrack of *Assault on a Queen*, and for what Ellington called "the most important thing I have ever done" - his Concert of Sacred Music.

In 1966, Bellson toured briefly with both Basie and ex-boss Harry James. A few years later, Buddy Rich paid Bellson the supreme drummer-to-drummer/bandleader compliment. Rich asked Bellson to lead his (Buddy's) band on tour while he was temporarily disabled by a back injury. Bellson proudly accepted.

Bellson has led his own orchestra almost steadily for more than forty-five years. He maintains four separate bands located in Los Angeles, New York, Chicago, and at Stanford University. His sidemen have included Blue Mitchell, Don Menza, Larry Novak, John Heard, Clark Terry, Pete and Conte Candoli, Snooky Young, and Dave Stone, among others.

His most current aggregation, "Big Band Explosion," displays zest, humor, fervor and exultation. Everybody is having a good time, as well they should, inspired by their drummer-leader. One of his former employers understands. The distinguished Mr. Ellington has been quoted as saying, "Louis Bellson has all the requirements for perfection in his craft. He is the world's greatest drummer."

As a leader, Bellson has recorded over 100 albums on various labels including *150 MPH* (1974), *Explosion* (1975), *Prime Time* (1977), *Raincheck* (1978), *Dynamite* (1979), *Don't Stop Now* (1984), *Stephane Grapelli With Phil Woods and Louie Bellson* (1987), *Airmail Special: A Salute To The Big Band Masters* (1990), *Louie Bellson and His Big Band: Live From New York* (1994), *Explosion Band* (1995), *Louie in London* (which "The London Suite," a track from that album, was performed at the Hollywood Pilgrimage Bowl before a record-breaking audience. The three-part work includes a choral section in which a 12-voice choir sings exquisitely sensitive lyrics by Bellson. "Part One" is the band's rousing "Carnaby Street," a collaboration with Jack Hayes).

In 1987, at the Percussive Arts Society convention in Washington, D.C., Bellson and Harold Farberman performed a major orchestral work titled, "Concerto For Jazz Drummer and Full Orchestra," the first piece ever written specifically for jazz drummer and full symphony orchestra. This work was recorded by the Bournemouth Symphony Orchestra in England, and was released by the Swedish label, B. I. S.

As a prolific creator of music, both written and improvised, Bellson's compositions (more than 300 to date) and arrangements embrace jazz, jazz/rock/fusion, romantic orchestral suites, symphonic works and a ballet. Little known to many of his listeners, the versatile Bellson is also a poet and a lyricist.

In June 1993, he performed "Tomus I, II, III" with the Washington Civic Symphony in historic Constitution Hall. A combination of full symphony orchestra, big-band ensemble and 80-voice choir, "Tomus," had been a collaboration of music by Bellson and lyrics by his late wife, Pearl Bailey.

Continuing the tradition of keeping performances as a "family affair," Bellson's daughter, Dee Dee, occasionally performs with her father's groups.

"Dee Dee is an excellent singer," said the proud father. "When people come to hear our band and she sings, they want to know if she has any records out. I'm trying to get her recorded."

Wherever Bellson performs, his second wife, Francine, with whom he married in 1992, accompanies him for P.R. support and to help sell her husband's CDs.

Even in his twilight years, Bellson is always creating, delving into new projects. In March 2000, the drumming great finished what he called "a very important project at USC." It was a scared concert/jazz ballet done in the spirit of Ellington's Sacred Concerts.

"After Duke did his first Sacred Concert, and I was with him when he did that at Grace Cathedral in San Francisco in 1956, and he told me that I should do one of these concerts in the future," Bellson said. "We did one. We had a full string section, choir and big band."

The first half of the concert featured twelve original pieces of scared music composed by Bellson with the second half an original jazz ballet, Bellson said.

"Bobby Shew did the jazz ballet playing a trumpet that Dizzy Gillespie performed on in 1962," Bellson said. "We recorded it and it came out great. We are still looking for a recording company to pick it up."

With the exception of the late comedian, Bob Hope, who has made the most White House appearances, Bellson holds, along with his late wife, Pearl Bailey, the second highest number of White House appearances.

As an author, Bellson has published more than a dozen books on drums and percussion. He is currently at work with his biographer on a book chronicling his remarkable career and bearing the same name as one of his compositions - *Skin Deep*.

Bellson's numerous accolades are legion. He has been voted into the halls of fame for both *Modern Drummer* magazine and the Percussive Arts

Society. Yale University named him a Duke Ellington Fellow in 1977. He received an honorary Doctorate from Northern Illinois University in 1985. He received the prestigious American Jazz Masters Award from the National Endowment for the Arts in 1994.

Now, as he has throughout his career, Bellson devotes as much time as possible to drum and band clinics at high schools, colleges and music stores. Aimed at student musicians of all ages, there are frequently as many professional musicians in attendance as there are youngsters, all eager and fascinated by the magic of the Bellson touch.

Bellson has attributed longevity to his craft from taking care of himself in the early years, he said.

"If you take care of yourself early on, then when you get into your 70s and 80s, you can still have some chops," Bellson asserted. "I never neglected pasta. I eat pasta almost every day. I've never been a drinker. I never smoked or got into heavy drugs. That's an important factor I impress on youngsters when I do my clinics. You have to be physically and mentally in shape to be a good player."

While "Old Man Time" cheats no one, Bellson also realizes that there will come a time when his playing days will come to an end.

"One thing that gets all of us is age, when your muscles go out," he said. "When that time comes, I'll just bow out because I've had a good career. I do know eventually that time creeps up and I'm not going to fool myself or my public and have them say, 'What is that old man doing up there?'"

But that time will have to wait, as Bellson still has some more serious drumming to do.

"I can still swing," he said. "My solos are still clear."

Whether fronting a big band or small, whether at colleges, clubs or concert halls, Bellson still maintains a respectable schedule of clinics and performances each year. He also continues to create new drum technology for Remo, Inc., of which he is vice president.

Through it all, Bellson has given to the jazz arena and for all who love the thrilling sounds of drums done wild, a high-level of artistry graced with humility, gentleness, creative brilliance, and above all, a sense of tradition.

"I'd like to know that I've created something artistic to the percussion world, both as a player and as a composer/arranger," Bellson said. "I'd like to think of myself as being creative and having created something that will last. I feel that I have to give credit to guys like Big Sid Catlett, Jo Jones and Chick Webb for my being the player I am today. Gene (Krupa) and Buddy (Rich) were big influences on me, too. Music is a very vital force in everyone's lives. What these teachers have given me, I feel it's important for me to continue that wonderful legacy. It makes me feel good that I've done something for our young people that they can pass on. That's better if someone gave me a million dollars to record some corny thing. I can't do that."

** Coda - Here is an update on Louis Bellson since this article was published:

Bellson died on February 14, 2009, in Los Angeles, from complications of a broken hip in December 2008 and Parkinson's disease. He was 84. He is buried next to his father in Riverside Cemetery in Moline, Illinois.

Dee Dee Bellson died on July 4, 2009 at age 49.

Francine Bellson maintains an official website on her husband called "The Bellson Beat!" designed to promote her late husband's music and to keep his legacy alive at www.louiebellson.info/

Louis Bellson at his double-bass drum set as his Big Band Explosion played for listeners at Warner Park in Canoga Park, CA, on June 23, 1985, during a free summer concert series. The bassist behind Bellson is bassist Dave Stone. - *Photo by Stephen Fratallone*

The ever-energetic Louis Bellson diving his Big Band Explosion at an outdoor concert on June 23, 1985, at Warner Park in Canoga Park, CA. - *Photo by Stephen Fratallone*

Louis Bellson sitting in command of his signature double-bass-drum setup.

Louis Bellson in 2003.

He Was Texas To A "T"

Iconic Saxophonist/Bandleader/Singer Tex Beneke Dead At Age 86

The following article on Tex Beneke was originally published in the June 2000 issue of Jazz Connection Magazine

Tenor saxophonist, singer, and bandleader Gordon "Tex" Beneke, who helped to make hits of such songs as "Chattanooga Choo Choo" and "(I Got a Gal in) Kalamazoo" for the Glenn Miller Orchestra in the early 1940s, died on Tuesday, May 30, 2000, at a convalescent home in Costa Mesa, California. He was 86.

Born in Fort Worth, Texas, on February 12, 1914, Beneke shot to fame with the Glenn Miller Orchestra in 1938. As a featured saxophone soloist and vocalist, he helped turn "Chattanooga Choo Choo," originally recorded on May 7, 1941, into the first certified gold record for the trombone-playing bandleader while also helping to make other hits for Miller, turning them into signature tunes such as "In the Mood" (August 1, 1939); "Little Brown Jug" (April 10, 1939); "Sunrise Serenade" (April 10, 1939); "Tuxedo Junction" (February 5, 1940); "Pennsylvania 6-5000" (April 28, 1940); "A String of Pearls" (November 3, 1941); "Don't Sit Under the Apple Tree" (February 18, 1942); "American Patrol" (April 2, 1942); and "Juke Box Saturday Night" (July 15, 1942).

Beneke was hired by Miller in March 1938 and became the most important and featured sideman in Miller's band.

In George T. Simon's book, *Glenn Miller and His Orchestra*, Beneke recalled how he teamed up with Miller: "I was playing in Ben Young's band in Detroit when Glenn called me to come join his outfit in New York. I drove for twenty-four hours through the snow to make that first rehearsal. When I got there, I was going to ask Glenn to let me get some sleep, but he said, 'No, get out your sax.' So I went downstairs to my 1936 Plymouth and got my horn and started playing. I remember I was playing Jerry Jerome's book, and everything was fine until we got to the vocal part of the arrangement. Jerry had been singing some part of it – I think it the tune was 'Doin' the Jive' – and Glenn would sing, 'Hi there, Buck, what'cha say?' But when it came to me, he sang, 'Hi there, Tex, what'cha say?' That's when the whole business of calling me Tex began." Beneke and his new boss initially haggled over how much he would be paid per week. Miller wanted to pay his new saxophonist $50 while Beneke held out for and won $52.50.

Miller reportedly said, "I'll give it to you, but you are going to have to prove you are worth the extra $2.50." From 1939 to 1942, Glenn Miller had the hottest band in the land, chalking up hit tunes after hit tunes and consistently taking Number One honors in music polls conducted by the trade magazines of the day. In September 1942, Miller dissolved his civilian band to join the Army Air Corps where he organized and led the Army Air Force Band for the G.I.s in Europe.

Miller's plane disappeared over the English Channel during a flight from London to Paris on December 15, 1944, shocking the music world.

Beneke formed his own band after the war in 1946, following in his ex-boss's footsteps utilizing his name and style.

"I feel very badly about Tex's passing," said singer Garry Stevens, 83, of Benicia, California, who sang with Beneke's band from 1946 to 1948. "I got along very well with Tex. We were good friends. He was a warm, amiable kind of guy. He never fluffed anybody off. He was easy to work with and we had a lot of fun together. I had a good time with the band."

I had the privilege of seeing Tex Beneke perform twice while I was living in the Los Angeles area. The first I saw him was as a guest soloist with the Ralph LaPolla Big Band during the free summer outdoor concert series on June 15, 1986, at Warner Park in Canoga Park, California.

The final encounter was in on March 7 the following year when Beneke was leading a big band for a dance at the Glendale Civic Auditorium in my old home town of Glendale, California.

Both meetings I had with Beneke were delightful. He was warm, friendly, gracious, and very accommodating to talk about Glenn Miller and his music. And at age 73, he was still blowing the heck out of his sax!

I had written an article in 1987 for *Artbeats,* a (now defunct) magazine about the fine arts scene in Ventura County, California, based on a brief interview I had conducted with Beneke in between sets at the Glendale Civic Auditorium engagement. In honor of this iconic figure of the Big Band era and the great music and memories he helped to create, it is reprinted here.

Tex Beneke Still Providing Great Expectations For His Listeners

Gordon "Tex" Beneke is a musician who doesn't mind playing the kind of music his audience "expects" of him.

He's unlike his musical contemporaries, Woody Herman and Artie Shaw. Herman usually doesn't like to yield to nostalgia but rather likes to forge ahead with new sounds and ideas. In 1940, Shaw walked off the bandstand during an engagement and headed off to Mexico for a one year hiatus because he had difficulty handling his public's artistic "expectations" of him.

Beneke, on the other hand, enjoys assuming that role.

"This is what everyone expects me to do," said the 73-year-old Beneke. "I like the Big Band sound and I enjoy playing the Glenn Miller sound." Beneke and his fourteen-piece orchestra were playing for a March 7, 1987, dance at the Glendale Civic Auditorium in Glendale, California. The sold-out crowd was appreciative of dancing once again to the magic of Glenn Miller's music, á la Beneke.

Beneke's West Coast band rosters some of the best sideman from the Big Band era. The saxophone section boasted the talents of Mahlon Clark, a Will Bradley and Lawrence Welk alumnus who is also an outstanding clarinetist; Chuck Gentry, a fellow Miller graduate with Beneke who did stints with Benny Goodman and Harry James; and Don Lodice, a standout with Tommy Dorsey in the early 1940s. Providing most of the solo spots on trombone was Bill Tole, a contemporary swing bandleader in his own right. Lead trumpet duties were handled by Art DePew, who currently leads the Harry James Orchestra. Plucking on the bass strings was former Miller classmate Rolly Bundock. Vocals were performed by Carole Dulaine. Beneke confided that he maintains four separate bands that are geographically situated throughout the country. It is easier and economically more feasible for him to travel alone to a specific area to perform and having local veteran musicians there to be part of the Beneke aggregation than for him to maintain a full-time road band.

Keeping in tune with his assumed role, Beneke played many of the Miller favorites at the Glendale gig of which he helped to create, including "Moonlight Serenade," the band's theme song, "Little Brown Jug," "In the Mood," "Pennsylvania 6-5000," "A String of Pearls," "Don't Sit Under the Apple Tree," "(I Got a Gal in) Kalamazoo," and the first-ever certified million seller, "Chattanooga Choo Choo."

Although Beneke is not considered by music critics to be a jazz saxophonist (as Beneke himself agrees), yet he remains a much under-rated soloist. Saxophone "purists" would never consider Beneke in the same league as Bud Freeman, Eddie Miller, Lester Young, Coleman Hawkins or Ben Webster.

The fact is, Beneke is an outstanding saxophonist and a creative and exciting soloist. It wasn't by accident that he was one of the top tenor saxophonists named in *Metronome's* All-Star Musicians' polls during the 1930s and 1940s.

"I've played with guys such as Coleman Hawkins, Bud Freeman and Eddie Miller before," Beneke said. "They are great musicians and I tried to learn something from each of them in developing my own style."

Despite being a celebrated sideman in the Miller band and as a bandleader himself for over forty years, Beneke is quite modest about any impact he has left on American popular music.

"I don't know if I've made any impact," Beneke said. "I've just tried to carry on the Miller band as Glenn would to have done. Before he died, he was in the process of forming a new band after the war with a new sound. I'm only trying to do what he would have wanted."

Beneke went on to say that he enjoys playing for dances and has noticed more and more young people attending these dances who are "digging" this kind of music.

"Today, whenever we play a 'far out' piece, these young people still want to hear 'In the Mood' or 'Kalamazoo' or something like that," he said. "People expect me to play a 'stereo-type' of the Miller style."

By playing the Miller book, Beneke insists that he isn't trying to convey any special message about the music he plays.

"I'm just happy playing the Miller style (a clarinet lead over the doubled tenor saxophone parts accompanied by the "wah-wah" derbies of the brass)," Beneke said.

In addition to fronting his own orchestra, Beneke says he enjoys from time-to-time performing as a soloist with various groups. On June 15, 1986, he joined Ralph LaPolla's Big Band in Canoga Park, CA, as part of a free summer concert series held at Warner Park sponsored by the Musicians' Union, Local 47, and more recently with the San Fernando Valley's Poor Angel Jazz Society playing in a Dixieland ensemble.

"I enjoy playing Dixieland jazz on occasion," Beneke said. "It's a lot more work having to solo, but it's also a lot of fun." Beneke stated that he is in planning stages of making an album that will contain material completely foreign to the Miller book.

"We want to bring in and try some new things," he said. "We want Billy May to do the arranging." Beneke's music – new or old – with or without the Miller sound – will undoubtedly be appreciated by Big Band enthusiasts everywhere. As one of the last few Big Band leaders remaining that are working full time, Beneke's music can probably be rightly called a "Moonlight Serenade" of listener expectations.

Tex Beneke, 73, on March 7, 1987, at the Glendale Civic Auditorium in Glendale, CA.
– *Photo by Stephen Fratallone*

Tex Beneke blowing his tenor sax on March 7, 1987 at the Glendale Civic Auditorium in Glendale, CA.
– *Photo by Stephen Fratallone*

Tex Beneke (third from left) leads his orchestra for a dance at the Glendale Civic Auditorium in Glendale, CA, on March 7, 1987. Band personnel pictured are Mahlon Clark (third from right); Chuck Gentry (second from right); Don Lodice (far right). Vocalist Carole Dulaine is seated at Beneke's right. – *Photo by Stephen Fratallone*

Tex Beneke and the band's girl singer, Marion Hutton, go over an arrangement with their boss, Glenn Miller, prior to waxing a recording in 1940.

Tex Beneke, 72, blows a hot solo as a guest artist with the Ralph LaPolla Big Band at Warner Park in Canoga Park, CA, on June 15, 1986, as part of the free outdoor summer concert series sponsored by the Musicians' Union, Local 47. - *Photo Stephen Fratallone*

Tex Beneke, 72, leading the crowd in the refrain to "Pennsylvania 6-5000" at Warner Park in CanogaPark, CA, on June 15, 1986.
- *Photo by Stephen Fratallone*

Still Young At Heart (And Loving It!)

Les Brown And His Band Of Renown Keeps Toes Tapping And Feet Dancing

The following article on Les Brown was originally published in the January 2000 issue of Jazz Connection Magazine

Les Brown and His Band of Renown may hold the distinction of being the oldest existing band in America, but they sure don't sound like it.

They are still giving fans what they expect – those familiar Big Band arrangements that start toes tapping and feet shuffling on the dance floor.

Now at age 88, Brown hasn't skipped a beat since organizing his first band in 1936 and is only one of a small handful of original Big Band-era leaders still active.

"We're still going after 63 years," Brown said during an interview prior to his December 2, 1999, performance at the Jackson Rancheria Casino and Hotel in Jackson, California. "We're the only organized band left. Nobody comes close to us. Some have gotten to 50 years, some 45. I guess I can owe it to my health." In April 1996, the *Guinness Book of World Records* awarded Brown the distinction of being the leader of the longest lasting musical organization in the history of American popular music.

"I don't know if I made a big contribution to the history of American popular music, but I made a long one," Brown said with a laugh.

Brown's longevity in the music business has produced such popular tunes as "Leap Frog" (the band's theme song), "Bizet Has His Day," "Mexican Hat Dance," My Dreams Are Getting Better All the Time," and "Joltin' Joe DiMaggio," his first big hit honoring the Yankee Clipper's 56-game hitting streak in 1941. The piece was written by Ben Homer with lyrics by disc jockey Alan Courtney. DiMaggio died on March 8, 1999, in Florida after having surgery for lung cancer. He was 84.

"I don't know why we haven't gotten requests to play that song ("Joltin' Joe Di Maggio") since Joe's passing," Brown said.

Brown's two top hits, both million-sellers, were the 1944 standard, "Sentimental Journey," which Brown had co-written with Ben Homer and Bud Green, and Irving Berlin's "I've Got My Love to Keep Me Warm," recorded on September 19, 1946.

However, if the band hadn't played "I've Got My Love to Keep Me Warm" one night in 1948 while doing one of the Bob Hope radio shows, chances are the song wouldn't have been a hit, Brown said.

"An executive from Columbia Records was listening to the show and he loved the song," Brown recalled. "I received a wire telling us to record the number. I wired back saying we recorded that tune two years earlier and it was never released and for him to look for it in the Columbia vaults. Our recording was found and then released. It became a big hit for us."

Born Lester Raymond Brown on March 14, 1912, in Reinerton, Pennsylvania, he was the eldest of three sons. Brown's father, R.W. Brown, was a baker and musician. The senior Brown played soprano saxophone and led the hometown concert and parade bands. He made sure that his three sons – Les, Warren, and Clyde, nicknamed "Stumpy" because of his physical stature – all played instruments.

"Our dad *made* us to be musicians," said Stumpy Brown, 74, the Band of Renown's bass trombonist, specialty singer, and band manager. "If you didn't play your horn, you almost had to move out of the house!"

Middle brother Warren also took up the trombone while Les concentrated on the clarinet and alto saxophone.

A music scholarship took Brown to the Ithaca Conservatory of Music in Ithaca, New York, where he received a degree in music. He later attended the New York Military Academy and graduated in 1932 as class valedictorian. He then enrolled at Duke University in Durham, North Carolina, where he became the leader of the "Duke University Blue Devils" dance band.

Band personnel at that time included Bob Thorne, William Irvin, and Jack Atkins, trumpets; Joe Pilato, Dan Mairs, trombones; Herb Muse and Joe Candreau on alto saxes; Dutch McMillan and Gus Brannon, tenor saxes; Coon Plyler, piano; Stacey McKee, guitar; Ken Dutton, string bass; and Don Kramer, drums. Brown played alto sax, clarinet and shared the vocal duties with Muse.

The band's first appearance on platters came on April 11, 1936, in New York, when it waxed five transcription recordings of twenty medley of tunes, arranged by Brown himself: "You Never Looked So Beautiful," "Tormented," "You," and "Us on a Bus" (Thesauras 243); "It's Got to Be Love," "Would You?" "At the Codfish Ball," and "Hawaiian Paradise" (Thesauras 243); "Welcome Stranger," "Swing Me a Lullaby," "I'll Stand By," and "It Ain't No Fun" (Thesauras 242); "Cabin in the Sky," "A Waltz Was Born in Vienna," "I've Got A Heavenly Date," and "The Glory of Love" (Thesauras 249); "All My Life," "There's a Small Hotel," "You're Toots to Me," and "Count Your Kisses" (Thesauras 242).

After graduating from Duke in 1936, Brown and the "Duke Blue Devils" spent that summer performing at Budd Lake, New Jersey, then toured the East Coast for well over a year before breaking up.

On October 15, 1936, Brown and the Duke University Blue Devils recorded five songs for Decca Records in New York, four of them were rejected. The lone song that was a "keeper" was "Papa Tree Top Tall," with vocal by Herb Muse.

The following month the band made five more transcription recordings of twenty-one tunes.

On March 18 the following year, the band cut ten commercial sides for

Decca Records before waxing their final appearance on record on September 13, with another five transcription recordings of twenty-one songs.

A few changes to band personnel occurred on the final batch of transcription recordings: Corky Cornelius and Earl Kirk replaced William Irvin and Jack Atkins in the trumpet section; John Goodman replaced Plyler on piano; Howard Smith replaced Don Kramer on drums; and Jack Wilmot was showcased on the vocals.

After the breakup of the Duke Blue Devils Band, Brown went to New York City and supported himself by doing freelance arranging for Rudy Newman, Isham Jones, Jimmy Dorsey, Larry Clinton, and Red Nichols.

In 1938, Brown formed a new band after being signed to RCA-Victor Records by its executive, Eli Oberstein. Brown would record on the RCA Bluebird label, the company's less expensively-priced record. In that same year, Brown married Georgia Claire DeWolfe. A few years later, the Brown's became parents of two children, Les Jr., and Denise.

Brown waxed his inaugural recordings on Bluebird as "Les Brown and his Orchestra" on September 2, 1938, with "Stop Beatin' Around the Mulberry Bush," "With You on My Mind," "Peelin' the Peach," and "Why Doesn't Somebody Tell Me These Things?" The vocal duties were performed by the band's girl singer, Wendy Bishop on "With You on My Mind," and on the remaining pieces by Blue Devils alum, Herb Muse, who joined the band for a short time as its boy singer.

Personnel in Brown's new aggregation included Max Herman, who went on to be Bob Crosby's lead trumpeter and in later years became the long-standing president of the Musicians' Union, Local 47 in Los Angeles, Jimmy Blake, and Les Kriz, trumpets; Fred Ohms, trombone; Stuart McKay and Steve Madrick, alto saxes; John Pepper and Wolffe Tayne, tenor saxes; Abe Osser, piano; Allan Reuss, a veteran guitarist with later played Benny Goodman and with other bands; Bassie Deter, string bass; and Lew Koppleman, drums.

Brown and his orchestra were gaining momentum in popularity.

During the summer of 1939, Warren Brown joined his older brother's trombone section. Vocalist Miriam Shaw sang with the band beginning in early 1939 and left in the spring the following year. Brown was in the market for a female singer and found one just what he was looking for.

In August 1940, a very attractive seventeen-year-old former dancer from Cincinnati, Ohio, named Doris Day joined the band as its girl singer. Day would be Brown's girl singer on two separate occasions.

"I went to the Edison Hotel in New York City to hear Doris sing with the Bob Crosby band," Brown said. "I had heard that she was dissatisfied and was ready to leave. I listened to her for five minutes and immediately went backstage and signed her for my band. She was every bandleader's dream: a vocalist who had natural talent, who had a keen regard for lyrics, and an attractive appearance."

Three months after joining Brown, Day cut her first recordings on the Okeh label, a subsidiary of Columbia Records, on November 29, with "Let's Be Buddies," "Three at a Table for Two," "While the Music Plays On," and "Dig It."

Her next recording date with the band occurred on January 7, 1941, waxing three sides. Between that date and April 1941, Day recorded eleven sides for Brown all on the Okeh label.

Day stayed with the Brown band until mid-1941, before leaving to marry Al Jordan, a trombonist with the Jimmy Dorsey Orchestra.

Betty Bonney was soon hired to replace Day as the band's new girl singer and she helped to cut such notable Brown sides as "Joltin' Joe DiMaggio" (August 8, 1941) and "He's 1-A in the Army and He's A-1 in My Heart" (November 15, 1941).

Also hired during this period was a brilliant clarinetist named Abe Most, who today, is a much-in- demand studio musician, and who also went on to play the majority of the clarinet solos for the Time-Life Records series, *The Swing Era*. Produced in early the 1970s, the series contained Big Band recreation recordings done in in stereo.

"Les hired me to play most of the clarinet solos," Most said. "I'm the one who played the quirky clarinet solo on 'Mexican Hat Dance.' Everyone thinks it was Les, but it wasn't."

Another hit tune for Brown and the band came on September 17, 1941, when they recorded "Bizet Has His Day" on the Okeh label, an opus arranged by Ben Homer. It has stomping rhythm, hand-clapping, the united "Hey!" of the sidemen, and some exciting solo work by band members.

The band was spending most of the summer of 1941 playing at the Log Cabin Farms in Armonk, New York. Bands were playing a lot of public domain songs and swinging the classics such as "Marche Slave," the "Anvil Chorus," and "Song of the Volga Boatmen," in response to the ASCAP boycott.

"I don't remember whether I thought of the idea for this piece or whether my arranger, Ben Homer, did," Brown recalled. "Anyway, he arranged the farandole from Georges Bizet's *L'Arlésienne* music and called it 'Bizet Had His Day.' We thought the title sounded too negative so we changed the word 'had' to 'has.' We still get requests for that 'Bizerte thing' or 'the Biz-ett piece.' We always know what they mean."

Band personnel during this period included Bob Thorne, Eddie Baily, and Don Jacoby, trumpets; Si Zentner, Warren Brown, and Ronnie Chase, trombones; Les Brown, Steve Madrick, Abe Most, Wolffe Tayne, and Eddie Scheer, saxophones; Billy Rowland, piano; John Knepper, bass; Joe Petroni, guitar; and Nat Polen, drums.

The band's novelty tunes took on an exciting new dimension when baritone saxist Butch Stone was hired. A veteran musician who played in the Van Alexander, Jack Teagarden, and Larry Clinton outfits, Stone was playing in Clinton's band at Lowe's State Theater in New York City in the fall of 1941 when Brown saw the show. Clinton was to be inducted into military service soon and would be disbanding his aggregation. Brown asked Stone to join his band at his band's upcoming engagement at the Blackhawk Restaurant in Chicago. Stone has been with Brown ever since.

"Les likes good music and the band plays good music," said Stone,

87. "For me, he's great. He's perfectionist. He wants everything just right from the way the boys look to the way they play."

Stone's first big hit he recorded with the Brown band was "A Good Man Is Hard to Find" (recorded July 20, 1942), which sold a half-million copies. The piece has since become his signature tune. Other songs graced with Stone's humorous vocals that sold well commercially include "Everybody's Making Money but Tchaikovsky" (with Betty Bonney on December 23, 1941), "Everybody Wants to Go to Heaven But Nobody Wants to Die," "Triskaidekaphobia," "Robin Hood" (1945), "Green Apples," and "Baby, I Need You."

Now legally blind, Stone has "retired" from playing his sax with the band but continues to wow audiences as he belts out such numbers as "Bad, Bad Leroy Brown," "Mack the Knife," and "I've Got the Shiniest Mouth in Town."

Brown's band has always been a "family affair." Middle brother and trombonist Warren Brown joined his brother's band in 1939, staying until he went into the service in 1942. After his return from World War II, he rejoined the band in 1946 staying only for a few months. He went on to become vice-president of music publication for Universal Studios. Now retired at age 84, he resides in Carlsbad, California.

Brown's kid brother, Stumpy, rounded out the trombone section and also sings some of the band's jump tunes.

Les Brown's son, Les Jr., currently sings with the band and occasionally plays drums.

"When my brothers needed a job, they got one," Brown said. "Stumpy came out of military school in 1943 and he's been with me ever since."

"I joined up with Les during the recording ban and it wasn't until November 20, 1944, that I recorded my first tune with the band," Stumpy Brown said. "That tune was 'Sentimental Journey.'"

By this time the band was known as "Les Brown and the Band of Renown," a moniker christened on the spot by a radio announcer when the band was performing live one night on the radio from the Hollywood Palladium.

It was during this period that Doris Day rejoined the band. Day's marriage to Jordan produced a son but the union was extremely abusive, and the couple soon divorced. Day returned to her home town of Cincinnati and became a staff singer for WLW. Brown heard her on radio and persuaded her to return to the band in 1943.

Day remained with the Band of Renown until September 1946, afterwards branching out on a solo career in films and recordings. During her second stint with Brown, she recorded twenty-four commercial sides on the Columbia red label, mostly romantic "returning-home-from-the-war"-type songs such as "He's Home For a Little While" and "My Dream Are Getting Better All the Time" (both on February 1, 1945); "He'll Have to Cross the Atlantic" (May 17, 1945); "Aren't You Glad You're You" (September 15, 1945, from the movie, *The Bells of St. Mary's*); "You Won't Be Satisfied" and "We'll Be Together Again" (both on November 5, 1945); "I Got the Sun in the Morning" (February 25, 1946); and Mel Torme's holiday classic, "The Christmas Song" (August 29, 1946).

But Day's biggest hit recording with Brown that will always be associated with her was "Sentimental Journey" (November 22, 1944), the first tune the band was able to wax since Columbia Records' defiance of the musicians' union strike begun over two years earlier.

"Shortly after Doris joined the band, my arranger, Ben Homer, came to me with an original song that he had been trying to peddle," Brown recalled as quoted in Doris Day's book, *Doris Day: Her Own Story* by A. E. Hotchner. "He had a good eight bars but that's all. I added the bridge, smoothed out what he had, and got Bud Green to write a lyric for it. The song was 'Sentimental Journey,' and Doris introduced it during our stand at the Pennsylvania Hotel. Most often you don't know what a new song will do, but the minute Doris sang that song I knew that it was going to be a big love affair between her and the public."

"Sentimental Journey" became the perfect theme song for all the young men returning home from World War II. It remained the Number One sing in the country for sixteen weeks.

Brown and the Band of Renown's star would shine brighter worldwide as a result of one man: Bob Hope.

Hope was looking for a replacement for Francis Langford who had been the long-time vocalist on his radio show. Someone brought Hope a copy of Day singing "Sentimental Journey," with the idea that Day would get hired by the popular comedian. Hope listened to the recording but decided that he wanted the band and not the singer. When Stan Kenton, Hope's musical director, had quit, Brown got the job.

With popularity of the Big Bands waning in the late 1940s, the decision to hook up with Hope proved to be a wise one for Brown.

"Besides his hit recordings, being with Bob Hope was the greatest thing that ever happened Les. Les himself will tell you that," Stumpy Brown said.

"My association with Bob has been wonderful for us," Brown confirmed.

Brown and the Band of Renown have provided musical accompaniment for eighteen of Hope's Christmas tours for members of the U.S. armed forces stationed overseas and three of his around-the- world junkets.

Long-time veterans of the band recall that entertaining the troops overseas was their most memorable highlight with the Brown organization.

"The outstanding years were from 1950 to 1972 when we went to see the troops," Stone said. "It's hard to describe how wonderful it was and to see how much the guys appreciated people entertaining them from home. Parents are still thanking me for having called them to tell them about their sons."

"It was so rewarding," Stumpy Brown said. "I was 4-F during World War II, and doing the tours I felt I was really doing something in my duty. I think I saw more places of war than some of my friends who were in the service at the time."

Brown and the Band of Renown have recorded with a pantheon of singers over the years including Bing Crosby, Johnny Mercer, Nancy Wilson, Dick Haymes, Herb Jeffries, the Ames Brothers, and Julie London.

Adding to Brown's popularity were regular appearances on weekly network television shows, starting in 1959, when the band was the featured house band on *The Steve Allen Show*.

The orchestra's longest run on television was from 1965 to 1974 on *The Dean Martin Show*.

The Band of Renown has played for Grammy Award telecasts, New Year's Eve shows in Las Vegas, celebrity golf tournaments, staged concerts, and commercial business functions.

The band is also popular on VIP calendars, having played for the inauguration balls for presidents Richard Nixon (1973) and Ronald Reagan (1981 and 1985), and for California governors George Deukmejian (1983) and Pete Wilson (1991 and 1995). The band also entertained at a gala for Queen Elizabeth II in Beverly Hills in 1983, arranged by Frank Sinatra.

Brown and his orchestra appeared in two movies: *Seven Days' Leave* (1942), starring Lucille Ball and Victor Mature; and *The Nutty Professor* (1963), starring Jerry Lewis.

Brown and his orchestra participated on a royal recording at the behest of the King of Thailand, His Majesty King Bhumiphol. The King, a staunch jazz aficionado and saxophonist, wrote twelve songs that the band recorded in honor of His Majesty's 50th Anniversary as King of Thailand. The record was released only in Thailand.

The Band of Renown also plays occasionally for cruises to the Caribbean as they did for one week last April.

Brown and company are slated to return to Northern California on July 13, 2000, to play for another dinner/dance at the Jackson Rancheria Hotel and Casino.

"The response we had for Les and his band when he was here in December was so overwhelming that we just had to bring them back," said John Taylor, Events Center Manager at Jackson Rancheria.

In this day and age when Big Bands are not economically feasible, Brown still likes to maintain a regular band.

"A lot of bandleaders pick up musicians to form a band, but I don't," Brown said. "I don't care how good the musicians are, unless they work together a lot, they'll never jell."

Nevertheless, Brown and the Band of Renown – a nucleus of seventeen, but sometimes as many as thirty-five for large concerts – are not overworked.

"We do alright although we command a pretty good price," Brown said. "We work about three or four days a month and band members book around that. They can play all kinds of gigs with other groups around Los Angeles or Las Vegas, but when the time comes then they come to work for me."

"Big Bands aren't hired like they used to be," Stumpy Brown said. "Thank God for places like this! (Jackson Rancheria)"

Despite playing for a variety of social engagements, the Band of Renown is still recognized primarily as a dance band that is synonymous with good music.

"We are basically a dance band," Brown said. "We enjoy playing for dances more than anything else. In the old days we'd get all kinds of awards for being the best dance band in the country – not necessarily the best band, but the best *dance* band. I myself like to dance and I like to play danceable tempos and play anything from a ballad to a waltz to a Latin number."

Brown's leadership has provided musicians with a certain amount of stability over the years. Musicians come and go, but many of the Band of Renown's tenured veterans have been together almost since the band's genesis, and many others date from the 1950s.

"When you are happy, you might as well stay happy," Stone said of his fifty-eight-year association with Brown.

"I hate to say this because Les is my brother, but he's very easy to work for," Stumpy Brown said of his fifty-six years with his brother's organization. "He's a very fair person. Besides that, he's not a typical leader. He's a musician. He knows what he wants out of a musician and he loves to conduct. Whenever we get a new arrangement of a tune, Les would be the one to run through it, not the arranger."

"If a band member joined us in the last three years, he's considered a rookie," Brown quipped.

With more young people taking part in the retro-swing craze during the past few years, Brown said he has seen a notable increase in younger fans at his performances.

"It (the retro-swing craze) has brought a new audience to us," Brown said. "Most of our work now is done at private parties so we don't get to see young people much. But when we do play for the public, we see more young people than we have seen in a long time."

As the Band of Renown swings into the new millennium, Brown hasn't any plans of retiring, he said.

"It's still enjoyable," he said. "This is what I enjoy doing."

Brown and the Band of Renown maintain a website at: www.bandsofrenown.com

** Coda - Here is an update on Les Brown since this article was published:

Dancers can still "cut a rug" to Brown's music in their own homes as the Band of Renown has recorded a new CD of classic Les Brown songs called, *Session 55: The New Les Brown CD* (Doc Hollywood Records). Recorded in March 2000, this twenty-one-track disc features updated and freshly recorded versions of standards from the band's library as well as Brown signature tunes of "Leap Frog" and "Bizet Has His Day." Singer Lou Rawls joins in on "I Only Have Eyes for You" and "They Can't Take that Away From Me." The CD was released on August 19, 2000.

Shortly after the CD was recorded, Brown's health began to rapidly deteriorate. He would front his band of a few occasions throughout the year 2000. Les Jr. assumed more of that responsibility of fronting the band.

According to close friends, Brown was in a wheelchair but was alert and maintained his sense of humor right up to the end.

"When I visited Les a few days ago, he jokingly said to me, 'Wanna buy a band, Van?'" said Van Alexander via telephone from his home in Los Angeles. "Les had a great sense of humor. I was No. 4 on his automatic telephone dialing system. He would often call me and say, 'No. 4? This is No. 1...." He maintained his dignity both professionally and personally throughout his life."

On Thursday, January 4, 2001, Brown died of lung cancer at his home in Pacific Palisades, California. He was 88. He is interred in a wall niche in the Garden of Serenity sector at the Westwood Village Memorial Park Cemetery in the Westwood section of Los Angeles. His marker reads, "Les Brown, A Man of Renown, 1912-2001."

He was survived by his wife of three years, Evelyn Joyce Wells Brown, and his two children, Les Brown Jr., and Denise Brown Marsh, and several grandchildren.

In 2009, Evelyn Brown died and is interred in an adjoining niche next to her husband. She was 83.

In 2004, Les Brown's Band of Renown, now under the direction of Les Brown Jr., moved from their home base in Los Angeles to Branson, Missouri. The band is the only Big Band in the area and entertains audiences about twenty days out of the month. For updated information about the band log on to www.bandofrenown.com

Bandleader Les Brown, 87, ready to front his Band of Renown on December 2, 1999, at the Jackson Rancheria Hotel and Casino in Jackson, California. –
– *Photo by Stephen Fratallone*

Budding bandleader Les Brown fronting the Duke University Blue Devils, circa 1935.

Butch Stone shows no timidity in letting everyone know at the Jackson Rancheria Hotel and Casino in Jackson, CA, on December 2, 1999, that "A Good Man Is Hard to Find." His boss, Les Brown, looks on with pure delight.- *Photo by Stephen Fratallone*

Les Brown, 87, strikes an inviting pose for dancers as he fronts his Band of Renown at the Jackson Rancheria Hotel and Casino in Jackson, CA, on December 2, 1999.
– *Photo by Stephen Fratallone*

Sliding Into Position

Trombonist Bobby Byrne Talks Of Leading Bands, Working In Studios, And As A Record Exec

The following article on Bobby Byrne was originally published in the May 2001 issue of Jazz Connection Magazine

If Bobby Byrne hadn't been talked in to leading his own band in 1939, he might well have been content to remain the trombonist in Jimmy Dorsey's orchestra. The handsome twenty-one-year-old sensation who has been described as an "excellent trombonist whose cool jazz solos were ahead of their time," went on to lead a very popular and successful band.

"Jimmy's agent talked me into it," said Byrne, 82, in a telephone conversation from his home in Irvine, California. "He decided it would be good for me at that point. I didn't know whether it would be good for me or not. I had no true aspirations along those lines. I got a group of people together to do just that for the next several years."

In addition to his band leading notoriety, Byrne also became a much-in-demand freelance and studio musician after World War II, and later as the A&R (Artists and Repertoire) for Command Records.

When Byrne started out on his adventure, he was more fortunate than most aspiring bandleaders. Besides possessing exceptional mastery of his instrument and having band experience, he had a booking agency that was behind him one hundred percent and a recording contract with Decca Records.

Byrne and his orchestra waxed fifty-four sides for Decca from October 18, 1939, to March 13, 1942, most of which were swinging original novelty-type dance tunes.

"In many cases, the companies that I was working for at the time, would help me with the material," Byrne said. "They were much more interested in making a saleable product, obviously. I was young in those days and not as bright as I thought I was. Some of those recordings are very dated, now that I look at them. How in the world could I have done something like that?"

Some of those "dated" tunes in the Byrne canon include "Speaking of Heaven" and "Make With the Kisses" (both recorded Oct. 18, 1939, with vocals by Jimmy Palmer); "If It Wasn't For the Moon" (vocal by Jimmy Palmer); "Two Little Doodle Bugs" (vocal by Dorothy Claire); "One Cigarette For Two" (vocal by Jimmy Palmer); and "Barnyard Cakewalk" (all recorded Dec. 14, 1939); "Way Back in 1939 A. D." (vocal by Jimmy Palmer) and "Busy As a Bee" (vocal by Dorothy Claire - both on Feb. 14, 1940); "If I Could Be the Dummy on Your Knee" (vocal by Dorothy Claire - April 2, 1940); "I Found a Million-Dollar Baby (In a Five-And-Ten Cent Store)" (vocal by Dorothy Claire and Stuart Wade - April 29, 1941); and "Down, Down, Down (What a Song)" (vocal by Dorothy Claire - June 18, 1941).

During this period Byrne wrote, "My Colleen," a hit song for the band which was never recorded commercially. He was also noted for the arrangement of the band's signature tune, "Danny Boy" (recorded September 4, 1940).

One of the biggest human interest stories from the Big Band era involved the young and up-and- coming bandleader when he was stricken with acute appendicitis during an engagement in October 1940, at New York's Paramount Theater. The twenty-two-year-old Byrne received heavy media coverage not so much because of his malady, but rather, from the response he received from members of the musical community. During his hospitalization, a host of top name leaders filled in for him during their days off to front the band in Byrne's absence so that he would not lose his position at the Paramount.

"Even though the band business was competitive, there's a sense of fraternity among leaders to help each other out when they can," Byrne explained. "It was publicity for all of us. Let's put it this way, it was a major theater and it was exposure. I don't think any of them (bandleaders) got paid for it, but after all, the publicity never hurts."

Bandleaders such as Benny Goodman, Charlie Barnet, Jan Savitt, and even Guy Lombardo, to name a few, pitched in to help. According to music critic George T. Simon, the Byrne orchestra's favorite substitute during this period was veteran sweet bandleader Abe Lyman.

"I never heard that," Byrne said about Simon's comment. "If that happened, I'd be surprised."

Robert "Bobby" Byrne was born on May 13, 1918, on his grandfather's farm twelve miles south of Columbus, Ohio. He great up in Detroit, where his father, an accomplished music professor, taught in the Detroit school system and also taught during the summers at New York University in New York.

Music was such the life-blood of the Byrne family that Bobby and his younger brother, Don, who later played tenor saxophone and did some of the arranging duties in his brother's band, started taking music lessons at five years of age.

"There was nothing else," Byrne said. "Music in our family was every day, including weekends. We went through various instruments over the years: piccolo, piano, harp, you name it." After going through a myriad of musical instruments, Byrne finally settle on the trombone.

"I was just handed a trombone by my father and I was required to learn how to handle it," Byrne said. "My embouchure seem suitable for a brass instrument so my father decided that the trombone would be the instrument for me. It was my duty to play it day in and day out."

Being classically trained, Byrne soon developed a reputation of being a child prodigy, a term he dismisses.

"I don't even think of that in those terms," he said. "It was a duty that I truly felt that would be helpful to me in a career. I was oriented in that area."

Byrne honed his trombone-playing skills without benefit of listening to any jazz-oriented trombonists of the day, he said.

"I was involved in what I laughingly called the 'legitimate area,'" he said.

As a sixteen-year-old student at Cass Technical High School in Detroit, Byrne led a small dance band. Through contacts made by his father, Byrne was first introduced to alto saxophonist/clarinetist Jimmy and trombonist Tommy Dorsey when they visited his school during the spring of 1935.

"Jimmy and Tommy were in Detroit with their band playing at one of the major theaters and my dad invited them to visit the music students at school," Byrne recalled. "I had never heard of them before and my dad was quite insistent that I go listen to them. The brothers were having students sit in with the band during their presentation at school. I was required to play a little with the group. I did. After it was over, I walked away thinking nothing more about it."

But that wasn't the end of it. As a result of Byrne's exceptional playing, Tommy Dorsey invited the teenage brassman to sit in with the band during its Detroit theater engagement. Byrne accepted the invitation. Other musicians in the Dorsey Brothers band at the time were George Thow, trumpet; Joe Yukl and Don Mattison, trombones; Jack Stacy, alto saxophone; Arthur "Skeets" Herfurt, tenor saxophone/vocals; Bobby Van Eps, piano; Roc Hillman, guitar/vocals; Del Kaplan, bass; Ray McKinley, drums; and band vocalists Kay Weber and Bob Crosby. Glenn Miller was arranging for the band. (*Note of interest:* As of this writing, Roc Hillman, now age 90, who resides in Woodland Hills, California, and Kay Weber Sillaway, age 91, a resident of Dallas, Texas, are the two surviving members of the original Dorsey Brothers band.)

"My parents drove me to the theater and I played a few sets," Byrne said. "I went back home thinking that was the end of it."

About a month later, Byrne received a letter from Corcoran O'Keefe, the Dorsey Brothers' booking agent, asking him to join the band, he said.

Tommy Dorsey had abruptly walked off the bandstand at the beginning of the band's summer engagement at the Glen Island Casino in New

Rochelle, New York, in May 1935, as a result of heated misunderstanding that had been building up between he and his brother, Jimmy. (When Tommy started to count off the tempo to "I'll Never Say 'Never Again' Again," Jimmy said it seemed a little too fast. Jimmy's remark, innocuous in itself, was the last straw in a partnership that had been simmering with resentment for a long time. Tommy glared at his brother, then packed his trombone and walked off. An attempt at reconciliation failed and soon both men were leading their own outfits). Byrne joined the band at Glen Island Casino, which, by default, was led by Jimmy.

"I sat in and I thoroughly enjoyed myself," Byrne said. "I played Tommy's book."

According to future bandleader Larry Clinton, who was arranging for the band then, Tommy's book was tough to master and Byrne handled it flawlessly.

It has been said that many trombonists of that period looked to Tommy Dorsey as a leader in developing "new" trombone styles. Byrne is somewhat hesitant to confirm or deny such an assessment.

"My own feeling in this area is a little bit different," he said. "Tommy was a marvelous player. I thought of him as a fine player and a good friend. Without question, he made the trombone recognized for its artistic quality."

After a month playing with the band led by Jimmy Dorsey, Byrne had heard that Tommy was technically under contract to properly finish his involvement with the Dorsey Brothers band and that he would be rejoining the group soon.

"I figured that would be the end for me, so I was ready to head back for Detroit," Byrne said. "As it turned out, Tommy only played for a week and he insisted that I stay on. When he left for good, I was in the band from that point on."

Byrne stayed with Jimmy Dorsey from 1935 to 1939. During those years he played with such outstanding musicians as Ray McKinley, drums; Roc Hillman, guitar; Skeets Herfurt, alto saxophone; Tutti Camarata, Shorty Sherock, and Ralph Muzillo, trumpets; Don Mattison, trombone; Bobby Van Eps, piano, and later Freddy Slack; Fud Livingston and Herbie

Haymer, tenor saxophones; and vocalists Kay Weber, Bob Eberly, June Richmond, and Helen O'Connell, who joined Dorsey during Byrne's last few months with the band.

Herfurt, Hillman and Mattison, forming a vocal trio, usually sang the novelty rhythm numbers, with McKinley joining in on occasion, while Eberly and Weber sang the ballads, and O'Connell doing the rhythm tunes.

"It was a fine orchestra," Byrne said. "It was basically the Dorsey Brothers orchestra without Tommy."

Jimmy Dorsey officially took over the band under his own name in September 1935, after the completion of the summer season at Glen Island Casino.

In 1936, the Jimmy Dorsey aggregation landed a great job as the house band on the Bing Crosby *Kraft Music Hall* radio series that originated from Hollywood. The job lasted for almost two years. However, due to a freeze on personal appearances and touring stipulated in the band's contract, J. D.'s band lacked the commercial successes that initially came Tommy's way.

J. D.'s band was under recording contract with Decca Records and waxed a number of outstanding sides with top name artists, including crooner Bing Crosby on "I Can't Escape You," "The House That Jack Built For You," and "I'm an Old Cowhand (all on July 17, 1936); songstress Frances Langford on "Easy to Love" and "Rap Tap on Wood," "I've Got You Under My Skin," and "Swingin' the Jinx Away" (all from early August 1936); trumpeter and jazz icon Louis Armstrong, who fronted the band on "Skeleton in the Closet," "When Ruben Swings the Cuban," "Hurdy-Gurdy Man," "Dipper Mouth Blues" and "Swing That Music" (all recorded August 7, 1936); and the Andrews Sisters (Patty, Maxene and LaVerne) on "Tu-Li-Tulip Time" and "Sha-Sah" (both on July 27, 1938), and "Billy Boy" and "Hold Tight," one of the female vocal trio's biggest hits (both on November 21, 1938).

The J.D. band also waxed some early hits of their own including the two-beat instrumental, "Parade of the Milk Bottle Caps" (July 7, 1936); a pair of swinging instrumentals, "John Silver" and "Dusk in Upper Sandusky" (both on April 29, 1938); and some Bob Eberly ballads on "They Can't Take Away From Me" (March 17, 1937), "Love Is Here to Stay" (January 25, 1938), "Deep Purple" (February 10, 1939, which climbed to Number Two on the chart), and "Stairway to the Stars" (June 16, 1939).

"We did our share of recordings and it was great training ground," Byrne said.

In spite of his relaxed manner when it came to leading a band, Byrne considers Jimmy Dorsey, known as "The World's Greatest Saxophonist," an outstanding instrumentalist, he said.

"In this area, I'd say Jimmy was equally musically proficient as Tommy," he said. "They both had the same background. Their father taught both of them."

Many musicians have come to the conclusion that as a result of the original band's split, J. D. would hire exceptional trombonists in his band as a way of "getting back" at his brother, while T. D. would showcase superb clarinetist in retaliation. Byrne disagrees.

"I don't think it even happened that way," he said.

Byrne's own outfit showcased not only his fabulous trombone tone, but some good ensemble sounds; some great arrangements by veteran Don Redman; a fine bassist in Abe Siegel; an exciting clarinetist in Jerry Yelverton; a trio of fine vocalists: Jimmy Palmer, Dorothy Claire, and later, Stuart Wade; and a kid drummer who later became a big name in the jazz world - Shelly Manne.

It has been said that Byrne was a musical perfectionist who drove his men exceptionally hard, and a result, the band as a whole was unusually tense. Byrne described his band leading style in this way: "I was trying music that would 'fit' the capabilities that I had, limited though they may be on my instrument. I found a few singers that could handle a lyric. They weren't great, but they were good singers. I tried to make the music I was dealing with and make it acceptable as I possibly could and to it with respect. I worked diligently at trying to make it sound well. People did their best for me."

When the band waxed its first three recordings on October 18, 1939, its vocalist was a young man by the name of Jimmy de Palma. De Palma's given surname was printed on the record labels as providing the vocal refrains on "Speaking of Heaven," "Make With the Kisses" and "Can't We Be Friends." After these recordings, he became known as Jimmy Palmer.

"For some reason our management decided that they didn't want to emphasize Jimmy's surname So they came up with a new surname for him," Byrne said.

Palmer stayed with Byrne until the end of 1940 and then returned briefly in early 1942, replacing Stuart Wade. Palmer made nineteen commercial cuts with Byrne. He later led a popular territory band in the Midwest.

At the next recording session on December 14, 1939, singer Dorothy Claire had joined the band cutting her first sides with "Two Little Doodle Bugs" and "How Many Times?" She quickly became a popular attraction with the Byrne aggregation. She was also the source of some heated controversy between Byrne and rival bandleader Glenn Miller.

In early 1941, Marion Hutton left Miller, and Miller wooed Claire over to his camp, resulting in some ill feelings between the two bandleaders. Claire stayed with Miller less than three months before returning to Byrne. During her absence, Kay Little, another fine vocalist, took over the girl singer chores for Byrne. While with Byrne, Claire recorded seventeen commercial sides.

"Dorothy was a real prominent fixture in our band at the time," Byrne said.

Upon Claire's return, Byrne also hired new boy singer Stuart Wade, a handsome baritone with a fine sense of phrasing who later became a standout with Freddy Martin's band. From April through July 1941, Wade recorded ten songs with the Byrne orchestra.

"I didn't discover Stuart Wade," Byrne said about the misconceived notion that he somehow discovered the singer. "I took advantage of his talents!"

The Byrne Orchestra traveled the usual band circuit, did their share of one-nighters in various parts of the country, and played at Frank Daily's Meadowbrook, the landmark night spot in Cedar Grove, New Jersey. Another big break that came Byrne's way was when his band was hired to play at Glen Island Casino in New Rochelle, New York, the country's top dance spot and also nicknamed "The Cradle of Name Bands." Byrne also captured the Raleigh Cigarette-sponsored radio show which added greater exposure for his band.

Just as things were going well, some setbacks occurred. In addition to his appendicitis attack, one of Byrne's most important engagements at the Hotel New Yorker was canceled at the last moment due to an electricians' strike.

There was also an embarrassing moment on stage when Byrne wanted to showcase his harp-playing abilities for the audience at New York's Strand Theater. Byrne was also a fine harpist, and he played the stringed instrument by identifying the notes using colored strings.

"The harp strings are set up by a color scheme," Byrne explained. "The C-naturals are green and F's, blue. All the rest of the strings are the same color. That's the way you find the respective notes."

Just as Byrne was about to play, the lighting man in the theater thought he would lend mood to the performance by bathing the bandleader in a purple spotlight. Chaos ensued.

"When the stage guy hit me with the purple light, all the strings looked white!" Byrne said. "I couldn't tell one string from the other. That was the end of my performance right there."

By the end of 1942, Byrne was very popular and he and the band went to Hollywood to appear in the "B" film, *Follies Girl,* directed by William Rowland and starring Wendy Barrie, Doris Nolan and Gordon Oliver. A young, attractive up-and-coming starlet named Virginia Mayo also appeared in the film as an uncredited extra.

Byrne disbanded his outfit in early 1943 to heed Uncle Sam's call to arms when he was offered a commission in the Army Air Corps due to his interest and ability to fly airplanes. He was trained as a P-47 pilot.

"I went where they told me to go," Byrne said. "I graduated in Class 44-A, that's how classes were differentiated when finished," Byrne said. "I started in the Army Air Corps and transferred to Air Service to complete pilot training school."

After World War II ended, Byrne organized another band that briefly featured alto saxophonist Larry Elgart and arrangements by Charlie Albertine, who later helped to create the Elgart band style. Stuart Foster often appeared as guest male crooner in Byrne's new band, while Karen Rich provided the "feminine touch" to the vocal duties. She helped to create a minor hit for Byrne with the bouncy tune, "Hey, Bobby!" (recorded May 20, 1946). Trumpeter Dick Luther was also on board to sing the novelty rhythm tunes. In 1946, Byrne and crew were also the subject of the two-reel musical short, *Bobby Byrne and his Orchestra.*

Indicative of most big bands that regrouped after the war, Byrne's was also short lived. He gave up leading a full-time outfit at the end of 1947.

"The first few years after the war the band business was pretty good but then it went all to pieces," Byrne said. "I decided that life is too short and I didn't want to live this way any longer. We did an honest job and tried to play good music as best we could, but I was also dog-tired of one-nighters!"

Byrne then became a "hired gun," so to speak, working as a freelance artist in jazz clubs in the New York City area with cornet legend Bobby Hackett. He also went into the studios working as a solo trombonist for radio, recordings, and television.

"I worked with everybody," Byrne said. "Whatever the music was, I played it. I picked up my check and went to another date. Sometimes I'd do three or four recording sessions in a day. It was a good way to be comfortable in music and to play all kinds of music. I enjoyed the remuneration."

Byrne's television work included being a cast member on the series, *Club Seven* (1948-1949 season); musical director from 1952-1954 for *Tonight!* hosted by Steve Allen and sponsored by Knickerbocker Beer. The show originated as a local New York City late night program, thus giving late night television its start; weekly appearances for three years as a musician on *The Lucky Strike Hit Parade*; a three-year stint on *The Milton Berle Show*; an eleven-year run on *The Perry Como Show*; and numerous Patti Page specials.

In February 1953, Byrne was part of an all-star orchestra led by Benny Goodman to record a memorial album for the late arranger Fletcher Henderson, who played an important role in Goodman's early success. Appearing in the band with Byrne on "Wolverine Blues," "You're a Heavenly Thing," "What a Little Moonlight Can Do," and "I'll Never Say 'Never Again' Again" were trumpeters Billy Butterfield, Chris Griffin and Jimmy Maxwell; trombonists Lou McGarity and Cutty Cutshall; alto saxophonists Milt Yaner and Hymie Shertzer; tenor saxophonists Boomie Richmond and Al Klink; pianist Bernie Leighton; guitarist Barry Galbraith; with Eddie Safranski on bass; and Don Lamond on drums; and former Goodman vocalist Helen Ward.

From the late 1950s throughout the 1960s, Byrne worked as a musician, orchestra leader, producer and promoter for Grand Award Recording Company, a division of ABC Records, and spent the next seven-plus years rising to the position of Director of Artists and Repertoire for Enoch Light's Command Records.

"Enoch hired me," Byrne said. "I did everything that had to do with practicing music. We had many great artists and with my classical background, it helped."

Albums that Byrne recorded during this period as a musician and orchestra leader include *The Great Themes of America's Greatest Bands Played by the All-Star Orchestra Conducted by Bobby Byrne* (Grand Award Records); *Dixieland* (Grand Award Records); *Greatest Hit Songs of Glenn Miller* (Grand Award Records 1958); *Greatest Hit Songs of Dorsey* (Grand Award Records 1958); *Jazzbone's Connected* (Grand Award 1960); *1966 Magnificent Movie Themes Played by Bobby Byrne and His Orchestra* (Command Records); *The Roaring '20s: The Charleston City All-Stars Conducted by Enoch Light* (series recordings Grand Award Records); and *A Shade of Brass* (Command Records).

As the A&R man for Command Records, one of Byrne's functions was to seek out artists to record. Prominent artists who signed on with the label included trumpet sensation Doc Severinsen, noted for his flashy suits and who went on to direct Johnny Carson's *Tonight Show* band; and the Pittsburgh Symphony Orchestra, who did the bulk of the company's symphonic works.

"My classical background came in handy in this area because I was familiar with the music we were recording," Byrne said. "I was qualified to make certain judgments on pieces."

While Byrne was busy seeking musicians out, younger trombonists never sought him out for technical and artistic tips on the instrument, he said.

"That didn't bother me in the least," he said.

Byrne also led an all-star group on the project, *Dixieland Jazz,* for Waldorf Music Hall Records featuring clarinet great Peanuts Hucko. Rounding out the group for the session were Pee Wee Erwin, trumpet; Lou Stein, piano; Jack Lesberg, bass; and Cliff Leeman, drums.

"Peanuts is a good friend and we enjoyed those sessions together," Byrne said. "We had a good time playing that type of music."

In March and April 1958, Byrne was part of an all-star aggregation recording session led by trumpeter and Duke Ellington stalwart, Cootie Williams, for RCA Records called *Cootie Williams in Hi-Fi.* The trumpet-less band (save for Williams himself) also included in various groupings, Billy Byers, Lou McGarity, Chauncey Welch and Dick Hixson, trombones; Phil Bodner, Elwyn Fraser, Nick Caiazza, Romeo Penque and Boomie Richmond, saxophones; Lou Stein, Hank Jones and Henry Rowland, piano; George Barnes, Tony Mottola and Barry Galbraith, guitar; Eddie Safranski, bass; Don Lamond and Osie Johnson, drums; and Bill Stegmeyer, arranger.

On the topic of today's music, Byrne chooses to pose the rhetorical question of "Who can argue with taste?" as his guide.

"Everyone has their own tastes in music," he said. "They are all entitled to it. Their thoughts are as good as mine. I'm not going to criticize it. I know what I like. If others differ, that doesn't bother me at all."

In the early 1970s Byrne completely left the music industry for the business world, though he occasionally continued to perform. He retired permanently in the late 1980s.

"I served my apprenticeship," he said. "I have no interest in it anymore. I can't stand to see the pain in people's eyes when they hear me. I don't go backwards. I had my shot at it and I enjoyed it. I got great pleasure out of doing what I was doing."

Byrne also retired with the rank of major in the Air Force Reserve and retained his pilot's license until a few years ago. He also enjoys going skeet shooting.

Byrne looks and sounds like an energetic man in his fifties and he wants to keep things that way, he said.

"When you consider what the alternative is, it's not that great," he said with a laugh. "I feel well and my wife, Marilyn, takes good care of me."

Byrne has been married three times. He has a daughter from his first marriage, Shellye Hayden of Alvarado, Texas; and three daughters from his second marriage: Barbara Fuhrman of Poway, California, Kathleen Kennedy of Paramus, New Jersey, and Eileen Mail of Encinitas, California. Byrne has twelve grandchildren; and two great-grandchildren. He is married to his current wife, Marilyn, a former elementary school teacher. They wed on January 1, 1977.

Byrne is somewhat reluctant when it comes to sharing his thoughts as to what his contribution may have been to Big Band music.

"I truly couldn't even comment on that," Byrne said. "I have never thought of it in those terms. It would be fatuous in my thinking to think of myself in that area. If I gave pleasure to people who listened to my music, that's great. If I didn't, then turn the dial. I enjoyed working as a musician and playing all kinds of music with many people over the years. I tried not to embarrass myself by playing poorly."

** Coda - Here is an update on Bobby Byrne since this article was published:

Bobby Byrne was in the advanced stages of Alzheimer's disease the last year of his life and was cared for at the Green Hills Care Home in Irvine, California. He died in his sleep after suffering from a stroke on Saturday, November 25, 2006. He was 88.

A memorial service celebrating his life was held on Saturday, December 9, 2006, at Light of Christ Lutheran Church in Irvine, California.

 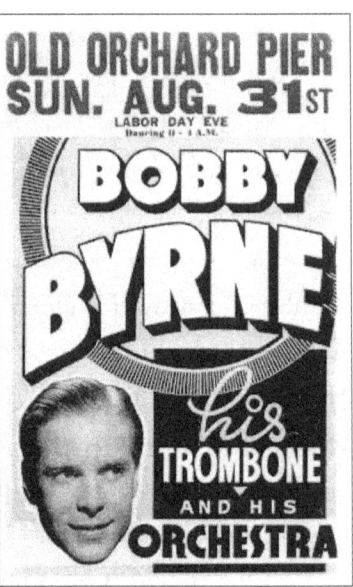

A publicity photo of Bobby Byrne, circa 1940, and a poster from 1941 advertising Bobby Byrne, His Trombone and His Orchestra, appearing at the Old Orchard Pier in Maine.

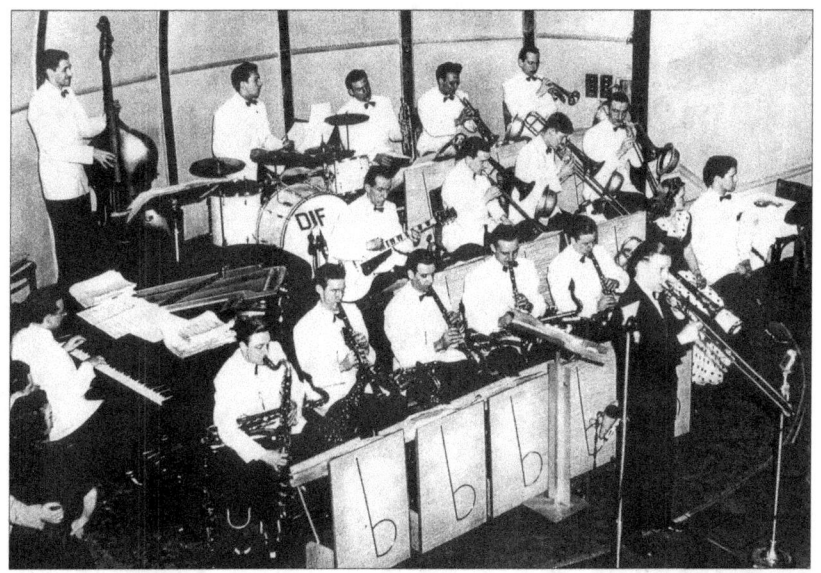

At Frank Daily's Meadowbrook in Cedar Grove, New Jersey, circa 1941.

Bobby Byrne and His Orchestra, 1946.

Jimmy Dorsey and His Orchestra, 1936. Four future bandleaders apprenticed in this band: trombonist Bobby Byrne, seated front left; trumpeter Tutti Camarata, over Byrne's right shoulder; pianist Freddy Slack, standing far left with arms crossed; and drummer Ray McKinley, standing third from right.

Bobby Byrne and His Orchestra, 1941. Standing next to Byrne is Dorothy Claire, the band's girl singer.

Lt. Bobby Byrne sits in with Tommy Dorsey and His Orchestra in 1944 at the University of Texas. Dorsey is at far left. Playing drums is Gene Krupa.

In this March 2003 photo, 83-year-old Bobby Byrne plays his harp at his home in Irvine, California.
– *Photo by Stephen Fratallone*

Above - Bobby Byrne with his trombone and together with his wife, Marilyn, in March 2003.
— *Photo by Stephen Fratallone*

Remembering Benny Carter

Jazz Icon Benny Carter Dead At Age 95

The following article on Benny Carter was originally published in the August 2003 issue of Jazz Connection Magazine

Benny Carter, the saxophone dynamo who became a jazz icon for eight decades as a musician and bandleader, and was one of the first black composers/arrangers to find success in Hollywood, died on Saturday, July 12, 2003, at a hospital in Los Angeles. He was 95.

Carter had checked into Cedars-Sinai Medical Center two weeks ago with bronchitis and had been ailing for some time.

Carter, who made hundreds of recordings from 1927 to 1998, did not simply endure as a musician. He remained a fresh and vital force in music for decades and is often mentioned as one of the four jazz giants of the alto saxophone, along with Johnny Hodges, Willie Smith, and Charlie Parker.

He gave early sophistication to jazz arranging that evolved into the big-band sound, was a distinguished multi-instrumentalist and helped end restrictions on black membership in a musicians union after settling in California in the 1940s. He was among the first blacks to receive credit for scoring movies and television shows, paving the way for contemporary black arrangers/composers such as Quincy Jones and Isaac Hayes.

Carter, a largely self-taught musician, was performing professionally in Harlem by age 15. Within a few years, he solidified his reputation as one of the foremost talents of his day as a player and arranger for such bandleaders as Fletcher Henderson, Chick Webb, Lionel Hampton and Duke Ellington.

He wrote such songs as "When Lights Are Low," "Once Upon a Time," "Cow-Cow Boogie," "Key Largo" and "Blues in My Heart." He also wrote the all-black musical, *Stormy Weather*. He performed and recorded with all the jazz greats of the day including Coleman Hawkins, Ben Webster, Benny Goodman, Nat "King" Cole, Django Reinhardt, Dizzy Gillespie, Oscar Peterson, Fats Waller, Chu Berry, Teddy Wilson, Sarah Vaughn, Ella Fitzgerald and Louis Armstrong, among others. He hired for his early 1940s bands such progressive players as trumpeter Miles Davis, trombonist J.J. Johnson and drummer Max Roach.

Bennett Lester Carter was born on August 8, 1907, in New York City. By the age of ten, he was studying piano. He quickly mastered brass instruments. At age fifteen, he had already ditched school for jam sessions in Harlem clubs. Carter tried the trumpet, but when he could not master it in a weekend decided to trade it for a C-melody saxophone, which he had been told was easier to play. He said Frankie Trumbauer, the gentle C-melody saxophone player of the 1920s, was his greatest reed influence.

He began playing at Harlem clubs, where pianist Willie "The Lion" Smith persuaded him to switch to alto sax. By the late 1920s, he was showing enormous promise as an arranger, replacing Don Redman with the Fletcher Henderson band. He followed the Henderson-Redman tradition of crafting an early Big Band sound that years later was borrowed by Benny Goodman and others who popularized the style. With Redman, Carter pioneered the full, block-chord sound that emphasized the richness of the saxophones on melody. His style lent depth and distinction to two of his early 1930s compositions: "Lonesome Nights" and "Symphony in Riffs."

In 1932, Carter formed his own band with stars like saxophonist Chu Berry and pianist Teddy Wilson, but the group failed commercially during those Depression years. Carter, in Europe for an engagement, soon settled in England at the behest of Leonard Feather, the influential musician and jazz writer. He became arranger for the British Broadcasting Corp.'s dance orchestra and went on tour with other European bands. In Holland, he led an interracial, international band. When he returned to the United States in 1938, the sound he had innovated years earlier had become a sensation. He led several groups and played and arranged for others, such as Lionel Hampton. He also was a featured performer and arranger in all-star groups featuring such greats as saxophonist Coleman Hawkins, clarinetist Benny Goodman and trumpeter Harry James.

After returning from Europe in the late 1930s, Carter made his way to California, where he became one of the first African-American composers to work in Tinseltown, arranging music for numerous films (including *An American in Paris* and *The Guns of Navarone*) and TV shows (*M Squad, Ironside, The Name of the Game* and *It Takes a Thief*).

On May 21, 1942, his song, "Cow-Cow Boogie" (co-written with Don Raye and Gene DePaul) was recorded and quickly became a juke-box favorite. The infectious, Western-themed boogie-woogie number was a hit for Ella Mae Morse and Freddie Slack and His Orchestra and helped launch Capitol Records. Between arranging duties, he played with the Jazz at the Philharmonic touring concert series and conducted seminars at Princeton University.

He arranged Ray Charles's 1963 Grammy Award-winning rhythm and blues recording of "Busted." Carter's most recent recordings included *All That Jazz* (1990), with trumpeter Clark Terry and singer Ella Fitzgerald. Even in his nineties, his music was considered as meticulous and mesmerizing as in his youth.

Carter received a lifetime achievement Grammy Award in 1987, a Grammy for "Best Instrumental Composition" in 1992 for his work *Harlem Renaissance Suite* and a Grammy for "Best Jazz Instrumental Solo" in 1994 for his recording of Ellington's "Prelude to a Kiss." He also was nominated for the coveted award seven times.

In 2000, President Bill Clinton presented Carter with the National

Medal of Arts, an award of the National Endowment for the Arts.

For all the tributes, Carter remained a soft-spoken, slightly bashful personality. An elegant man, he had a penchant for precise wording and a surefire memory for dates. He continued to be regarded in later years as the exemplar of elegance, on recordings as well as in person.

I had the opportunity to hear Carter lead his seventeen-piece Big Band on October 25, 1986, when he was making a one-night appearance at Disneyland. I was thrilled at the prospect of seeing this jazz great not fully aware of just how pervasive his influence in American music really was. I basically recognized him as bandleader and one of three major jazz innovators on the alto sax.

From the moment the band played the explosive opening number of "Strike Up the Band" (a Carter arrangement, of course!), the whole evening was a textbook example of classy, swinging, pulsating jazz in a Big Band format. And at 79 years of age, Carter was blowing his alto sax with grace and fluidity of a musician half his age. His ideas were fresh, vibrant and filled with verve. Also performing with Carter that evening was special guest jazz singer Ruth Olay, a musical protégé of his.

And yet I had to wonder as I listened to this superb music and this outstanding band, why such a remarkable talent such as Carter was not better appreciated by mainstream Big Band aficionados? Perhaps Carter's music was just a little ahead of its time for most people to grasp. Perhaps it was just a bit too elegant, a bit too precise, a bit too "other dimensional." Who knows?

During the dance, I took some wonderful close up photos of Carter while he was playing his sax. I got to meet Carter briefly after the performance. He was friendly and soft-spoken, eloquent and gracious. He was nice enough to provide me with an autograph while allowing me to have a photo taken with him. I have that photo framed and hanging on a wall in my office.

The next and final time I saw Carter in person was at the Big

Band Academy of America's annual reunion on March 3, 2002, at the Sportsmen's Lodge in Studio City, California. He attended with his wife, Hilma. I snapped a few quick photos of him as he was mingling with other "royalty" of the Big Band Kingdom.

While Carter's overall musical impact ranks second to that of the revered Duke Ellington, time may be the key in which greater appreciation for "The King's" music will occur. Very few artists are hailed as National Treasures while they are still alive. Carter was fortunate that he was recognized by many inside the music world as such. While Ellington held a much broader appeal with the general public, Carter, for the most part, was pretty much a musical insider. Individuals inside the music arena were more savvy to his work. Hopefully soon, the key to unlocking Carter's treasures will be found so that the riches that this great icon of jazz and American music had bestowed upon us can be greater appreciated.

Carter's first wife, whom he married in 1925, died of pneumonia three years later. Three other marriages ended in divorce. In 1979, he married Hilma Ollila Arons, who survives him, along with a daughter, a granddaughter and a grandson.

Benny Carter, 94, at the Big Band Academy of America's annual reunion on March 3, 2002.
–Photo by Stephen Fratallone

Benny Carter, 79, claps his hands to the beat (left photo) and blows a hot solo on his alto sax (right photo) as he fronts his band on October 25, 1986 for dancers at Disneyland. - *Photos by Stephen Fratallone*

Benny Carter, 79, solos on his alto sax as he fronts his band at Disneyland on October 25, 1986.
– *Photo by Stephen Fratallone*

'S Wonderful

Happiness Is Music For Bandleader/Arranger/Conductor Ray Conniff

The following article on Ray Conniff was originally published in the June 2000 issue of Jazz Connection Magazine

If you ask bandleader/trombonist/arranger Ray Conniff to sum up his career in music, he'll probably say it's been "'S Wonderful." The arranger king of easy listening music who blended voices with Big Band instrumentation and whose record sales are at 78 million, made a conscious choice to stick with a formula that guaranteed commercial success beginning with his first LP for Columbia in 1956, *'S Wonderful*.

"Music has been wonderful to me," said Conniff, 83, during a recent telephone interview from his home in Los Angeles, California. "I'm very fortunate. I don't think too many guys have something in life that they like doing and are able to do that pays them well and gives them a wonderful living."

In his over sixty years as a musician/arranger/conductor, Conniff has played with and scored for many of the top bands of the Big Band era like Bunny Berigan, Bob Crosby, Artie Shaw and Harry James. As chief arranger for Columbia Records during the 1950s, he worked with such artists as Don Cherry, Johnnie Ray, Frankie Laine, Guy Mitchell, Tony Bennett and Johnny Mathis. As a recording leader, he recorded 103 albums earning him ten national gold records and twenty foreign gold records, a Grammy

Award, two Grammy Award nominations, a spot on Billboard's All-Time Top 10 albums list, and a fanatical international following.

"I think timing had a lot to do with it," Conniff said about his commercial successes. "If I came out now with those kind of songs, I don't think it would be successful. For the time when those songs came out, it was a Big Band sound with voices."

Born on November 6, 1916, in Attleboro, Massachusetts, Conniff was exposed to music at an early age by his father, the leader/trombonist of the local Jewelry City Band, and by his mother, who played piano.

Conniff took up the trombone at age nine because his father played the instrument, Conniff said.

During his junior year in high school, some kids up the street heard Conniff practicing his trombone one day and they talked him into joining their band.

"I told them I wasn't good enough, but they still wanted me," Conniff said. "At rehearsal, I was the best one in the band and I couldn't play very good, so you can imagine what the band sounded like."

As a teen, Conniff and friends would go see the name bands of the day that would come through their area like the Cosa Loma Orchestra, Mal Hallet, and Tommy Dorsey.

"I would stand at the front of the stage to hear Tommy play," he said.

Always fascinated as to how songs were played in bands, Conniff noticed a *Billboard* magazine on his father's desk opened to a page with an ad for a "lightning arranger" that read, "learn to arrange quickly." It was a musical slide rule, costing one dollar. Using this simple transposing device, Conniff wrote his first arrangement, "Sweet Georgia Brown," and the guys in the band loved it.

Out of high school, Conniff got his first professional job with Dan Murphy's Musical Skippers, out of Boston. Staying with Murphy for six months, Conniff then started working for society bands in Boston. He was encouraged by fellow musicians to leave Boston and go to New York where his musical talents would be better appreciated.

"I would bring my arrangements to bands just to hear them rehearsed," Conniff recalled. "I didn't care if I got paid. I just wanted to hear how the arrangement sounded."

One day in early May 1938, Conniff ran into Joe Dixon, an old friend from Boston who was at the time playing clarinet with trumpeter Bunny Berigan's band. He invited Conniff to try out for the band and to sit in at a rehearsal that evening.

"When I tried out, this was the first time I ever played in a band where the musicians were better than me," he said. "What a thrill it was!" Suddenly, I thought, 'Wow! This is the way it's supposed to be!'" Conniff said.

During the try out, while Ruth Gaylor, the girl vocalist, was singing her refrain to "It's Wonderful," Berigan asked Conniff to solo during the next chorus.

"Most bandleaders, especially Bunny, had someone in the band whom they respected," Conniff said. "While I was playing my solo, I could see Bunny out of the corner of my eye looking at Georgie Auld who was nodding in approval. Then Bunny looked over to Joe Bushkin and he also nodded, so I knew I was in. It was one of the highlights of my whole life."

On May 26, 1938, Conniff cut his first recordings with the Berigan band for RCA-Victor Records with "Somewhere with Somebody Else" (vocal by guitarist Dick Wharton); "It's the Little Things That Count" and "Wacky Dust" (pair of vocals by Ruth Gaylor): and an instrumental, "Wearin' of the Green."

Conniff waxed thirty-four commercial recordings with Berigan and nine transcription recordings totaling thirty-eight songs.

He was also a featured member of Berigan's small nine-piece jazz ensemble, "Bunny Berigan and His Men," which recorded a half-dozen tunes: "In a Mist," "Flashes," "Davenport Blues" and "Candlelights" (all four on November 30, 1938); and "In the Dark" and "Walkin' the Dog" (both on December 1, 1938).

Rounding out this group were Irving Goodman (Benny's older brother) on trumpet; Georgie Auld, tenor sax; Murray Williams and Gus

Bivona, clarinet and alto saxes; Joe Lippman, piano; Hank Wayland, bass; and Buddy Rich, drums.

Other notable musicians who filtered through the Berigan ranks during Conniff's tenure were tenor sax man Don Lodice who went on to star in Tommy Dorsey's orchestra; guitarist Allen Ruess, a stalwart in Benny Goodman's rhythm section; and trumpeter Steve Lipkins, later played in both Dorsey bands as well as the bands of Artie Shaw, Glenn Miller, and Will Bradley.

After a fifteen-month stint with Berigan, Conniff joined Bob Crosby in July 1939.

"Bunny had a great band but there were always problems like finances and Bunny's alcoholism, so when the opportunity came, I went with Bob Crosby," Conniff said. "It was a better job for me."

Conniff played with Crosby's band for eighteen months even though it was a different style than what he was used to playing.

"Bunny's style of music was patterned after the black bands like those of Count Basie, Duke Ellington and Jimmy Lunceford," Conniff said. "Crosby was more Dixieland-oriented. Although Crosby's style of music wasn't the type I liked as in Bunny's band, it was a really great band."

Crosby's band became very popular on the basis of the leader's outgoing personality (he sang a little even though he was unable to read a note of music or play an instrument) and the powerhouse of talented sidemen he fronted. From the outfit's inception in 1935 until it disbanded in 1942, the band possessed a team spirit that could not be rivaled with few key sidemen departing for other endeavors.

When Conniff joined the band Crosby's personnel read like an all-star baseball lineup, each person was a multi-talented musical force to be reckoned with in their own right: Zeke Zarchy, Billy Butterfield and Shorty Sherock in the trumpet section; Warren Smith, trombone; Irving Fazola, clarinet; Joe Kearns and Bill Stegmeyer on alto saxes; Eddie Miller and Gil Rodin, tenor saxes; Joe Sullivan, piano; Nappy Lamare, guitar and vocals; Bob Haggart, bass; and Ray Bauduc, drums.

A unique and thrilling feature in the Crosby outfit was the presentation of the "Bob Cats" – a band within a band - an eight-piece group that played the most energetic and swinging Dixieland sounds ever heard north of New Orleans.

Members of the Bob Cats during the Conniff period were Billy Butterfield, trumpet; Warren Smith, trombone; Irving Fazola, clarinet; Eddie Miller, tenor sax; Joe Sullivan, piano; Nappy Lamare, guitar; Bob Haggart, bass; and Ray Bauduc, drums. Cornetist Muggsy Spanier, clarinetist Hank D'Amico, trombonist Floyd O'Brien, and pianist Jess Stacy, who came over from Benny Goodman's band, also saw action as a Bobcat.

Other "heavy hitters" associated with the Crosby orchestra during this period include lead trumpeter Max Herman, who in later years became the long-standing president of the Musicians' Union, Local 47 in Los Angeles; Arthur "Doc" Rando, alto sax; former Benny Goodman vocalist Helen Ward who recorded "Day In, Day Out" on July 24, 1939, and was a guest vocalist for a brief period with the Crosby band on the *Camel Caravan* radio show; and Doris Day, who stayed three months as the band's girl singer, but wasn't recorded.

Conniff helped to record seventy-three sides for Crosby including such classics as "Boogie Woogie Maxie" (August 29, 1939, featuring Joe Sullivan on piano); "High Society" (October 2, 1939); "Run, Rabbit, Run" (February 19, 1940); and "Dry Bones" (September 6, 1940).

With Conniff's reputation growing as an arranger and soloist, he joined clarinetist Artie Shaw's band in December 1940.

"Actually, I was with three different Artie Shaw bands," Conniff said. "The first band had a string section. Jerry Jerome and Les Robinson on tenor saxes were in it as was Billy Butterfield on trumpet; Johnny Guarnieri, piano/harpsichord; Nick Fatool, drums; Al Hendrickson, guitar; and Jack Jenny, trombone. I sat beside Jack in the band. Then I played in the 1943 and 1945 Shaw bands."

During his first stint with Shaw, Conniff helped to record a number of hits for the clarinet great including "Concerto For Clarinet, Parts 1 and 2" (December 17, 1940); "Dancing in the Dark" and "Moonglow" (both on January 23, 1941); "Beyond the Blue Horizon" (September 3, 1941); and "St. James Infirmary, Parts 1 and 2" (November 12, 1941, vocal by "Hot Lips" Page).

During the summer of 1941, the Shaw aggregation saw the addition of Orin "Hot Lips" Page, Lee Castle, and Steve Lipkins in the trumpet section; Les Robinson switched from tenor sax to playing lead alto sax; Georgie Auld and Mickey Folus occupied the tenor sax chairs; Mike Bryan on guitar; and Davey Tough, drums.

Conniff was also on hand on January 20, 1942, when Shaw waxed three tunes with vocals by Fredda Gibson on "Somebody Nobody Loves," "Not Mine," and Absent-Minded Moon." During the next decade Gibson became pop hit maker "Her Nibs, Miss Georgia Gibbs."

Conniff was also present in the Shaw band working on the weekly (George) *Burns and* (Gracie) *Allen Show* on radio heard on Monday evenings from 7:30 to 8 over the NBC network. Shaw and his twenty-two piece orchestra became the house band on the show replacing Ray Noble. Shaw's stint began on the season opener on July 1, 1940, lasting until the season closer on March 24, 1941. Other regulars on the show included the singing trio, The Three Smoothies (Rosalind "Babs" Stuart, and brothers Charlie and Little Ryan), and announcer Bud Hiestand, and Jimmy Wallington, for the last eight weeks of the show when it moved production from Hollywood to New York.

While Shaw lead great bands, the leader was very difficult to know, Conniff said.

"Artie didn't socialize with the guys in the band - at least he didn't with me," he said. "He'd have a cool hello every night. He was an excellent musician and a very learned man. He invited me up to his room one time to play chess. He beat the heck out of me, two games in a row! That was the only time I really ever got to talk with him."

It was with his final stint with Shaw that Conniff inked his big hit arrangement of the George and Ira Gershwin tune, "'S Wonderful." Recorded for RCA Victor on January 9, 1945, the tune turned out to be one of the best of a batch of sides the "new" Shaw band recorded; eighteen sessions in six months, or an average of three a month.

"I got paid for the arrangement but Artie got the success off the record," Conniff said. "As far as I was concerned, the arrangement was a great success. I'm a perfectionist. It was one of the few arrangements I wrote that I really liked that turned out great. I said to myself, 'If I ever have a band of my own, I'm going to record this same arrangement for myself.' I did so eleven years later. It was the title song of my first album for Columbia. It was practically the same arrangement."

Personnel in Shaw's band include Roy Eldridge and Ray Linn, trumpets; Herbie Steward and Jon Walton, tenor saxes; Chuck Gentry, baritone sax; Dodo Marmarosa, piano; Barney Kessel, guitar; and Lou Fromm, drums. "'S Wonderful" was full of surprises and with inspired solos by Shaw, Herbie Steward and Dodo Marmarosa.

Other swinging tunes Conniff helped Shaw to wax during this period include "Lady Day" and "Jumpin' on the Merry-Go-Round" (both on November 23. 1944); and "Bedford Drive" (January 9, 1945).

On April 5, 1945, Shaw and the orchestra recorded four sides for RCA Victor. One of those sides was Maxwell Anderson and Kurt Weill's "September Song," a brand new song at the time that was featured in the Hollywood musical *Knickerbocker Holiday*. Conniff made the arrangement of the piece.

Conniff finally received his draft notice and left Shaw in the early spring of 1945 to serve in the Army during the concluding months of World War II, arranging for the Armed Forces Radio Services in Hollywood. After his discharge in 1946, Conniff began arranging for trumpeter Harry James.

"Harry was even more distant than Artie was as an employer," Conniff said. "However, I think he liked my work." Conniff arranged another version of "September Song" that James was nuts about, recording the piece on November 6, 1947. James played the song every night without fail, Conniff said.

"Harry was an arranger himself," Conniff said. "I think he sensed that 'September Song' was a great arrangement. For me to say that it was a great arrangement is very unusual. I don't think many of the things I did could described as great. As I look back, I don't know how I ever thought that one up."

Living in Hollywood while the James band was on the road, Conniff would get calls from James telling him to go to Columbia Records to pick up tunes that the band would be recording when they returned.

"Harry would leave it up to me to put my ideas into these arrangements," Conniff said.

When "be-bop" hit the musical scene in the late 1940s, Conniff's musical tastes did not connect with the new music, so he stopped arranging for a while, he said.

"Harry also wanted me to write some things in the bop style, but I couldn't," Conniff said. "I didn't like it and I didn't 'feel' it, so I got out."

Conniff found himself digging tract-housing ditches for two years while reinventing his music, studying the elements of hit songs and teaching himself how to conduct.

Conniff bumped around the studios for a few years until Mitch Miller hired him in 1951 as a house arranger with Columbia Records.

For five years, Conniff wrote back-up arrangements for vocalists, and took the assignments other Columbia arrangers were too busy to write.

In 1955, Miller asked Conniff to arrange a single, "Band of Gold," for crooner Don Cherry (no relation to the late jazz trumpeter who worked with Ornette Coleman). Recorded on October 17, Conniff used a tightly harmonized chorus in place of a string section, and the sound was an instant hook, taking the single to No. 5 on the Top 40 and giving Cherry his biggest hit.

This led to a series of Conniff-arranged Columbia recording sessions, which resulted in many hit records such as Johnnie Ray's "Just Walking in the Rain" (1956), Frankie Laine's "Moonlight Gambler" (1956), Guy Mitchell's "Singing the Blues" (1956), Marty Robbins' "A White Sport Coat," and Johnny Mathis' "Chances Are," "Wonderful, Wonderful" and "It's Not For Me to Say." While Miller was difficult to get along with at times, a mutual admiration developed for each other, Conniff said.

"I got along great with Mitch even though we fought a lot," Conniff said. "The differences we had with each other were well taken and one of us would catch something the other would have missed." Conniff recalls the time on June 25, 1956, when Johnnie Ray recorded "Just Walking in the Rain." Listening to the playback, Conniff told Miller that the recorded take needed reverb and echo. Miller yielded to Conniff's suggestions. The result produced a million seller for Ray.

While working on the *'S Wonderful* album, Miller wanted to have voice doubling on the song "Sometimes I'm Happy." During the scheduled three-hour recording session, Conniff spent the first two hours and 15 minutes rewriting the arrangement to include voice doubling, he said.

"I was thoroughly disgusted, but Mitch was right!" Conniff said. "The singles I previously did under my own name ("Begin the Beguine" and "Stardust") were getting fantastic airplay and he wanted the same sound."

Conniff's success in arranging for other recording artists prompted Columbia to let him record an album under his own name.

He was the first to use voices and vocal arranging as part of the instrumentation. His formula was to use female voices to double with trumpets, high saxes and clarinets and male voices with trombones or saxes in the lower register.

'S Wonderful was in the Top 20 for nine months, ultimately selling about fifteen million copies. *Cash Box* voted Conniff "the most promising up-and-coming band leader of 1957." In 1959, disk jockeys voted the Ray Conniff Orchestra and Singers "the most programmed studio orchestra."

Conniff recorded with two groups: his "Orchestra and Chorus" and his "Singers." The former was a typical big band line-up of saxophones, trumpets, trombones, and rhythm section and a chorus of four men and four women. The latter was a chorus of twenty-five singers - twelve women and thirteen men - with minimal instrumental backing.

Conniff produced twenty-five straight Top 40 LPs for Columbia during the 1950s and 1960s. Although the first albums were strictly compilations of standards, be began introducing current pop hit songs in the late 1950s and within a few years had made these the mainstay of his repertoire.

"I picked songs that people had fallen in love with," Conniff said about his formula of success. "All the songs in those early days were songs that were in the Top 10 at one time or another. I thought that if I did songs in the Top 10, I'd strike people's heart strings when they first fell in love."

In addition to the choice of material and the particular use of voices and instrumentation, Conniff's final ingredient to his successful formula included the use of simple rhythmic sounds.

"Everything in life is rhythm from the seasons of the year to our heart beats," he said. "The rhythm sound was predominate in my recordings as is the use of reoccurring patterns."

In 1966, Conniff won a Grammy Award in the category of "Best Performance by a Chorus" for "Somewhere My Love," an adaptation of Maurice Jarre's "Laura's Theme" from the movie, *Doctor Zhivago*. He earned two other Grammy nominations – in 1968 for "Honey" and in 1969 for his version of the Rod McKuen song "Jean."

During the 1960s, Conniff brought to the public his "Concert in Stereo," the first live stereo concert ever to take place in the world. It became an instant hit with listeners.

During the 1970s, Conniff performed throughout South America, Japan and England. He also performed at the White House. In 1974, Conniff was the first pop artist from the West to record in Russia, where he used a local chorus to make *Ray Conniff in Moscow*.

Conniff has developed a major following over the years in Brazil and tours there quite often. He is scheduled to tour that country during September and October of this year.

"I'm still doing an album or two a year but that's with Abril Music, a Brazilian record company," Conniff said. "You don't hear much about my records here in the States."

Fans of Ray Conniff make sure that the general public is kept aware of news concerning their musical idol. The Ray Conniff Fan Club operates an official web site at: http://members.aol.com/dmitchell9/index.htm

The president of the fan club, Manfred Thoenicke of Germany, also hosts a Ray Conniff web site at: http://members.aol.com/thoenicke/index.htm

In 1997, after forty years with Columbia Records/CBS Records/Sony Music, Conniff signed on with Polygram Records and recorded three albums for them: *Ray Conniff Live in Rio, I Love Movies,* and *My Way,* a tribute to the late Frank Sinatra.

Conniff's two most recent albums, both recorded in July of last year on Abril Records, are *Ray Conniff 'S Country,* featuring Brazilian Country music; and *Ray Conniff 'S Christmas,* his fourth Christmas album.

"Abril Records wanted me to do the Brazilian songs to sell down there," Conniff said. "They don't have a lot of value up here."

When not recording or touring, Conniff and his Swiss-born wife of thirty-two years, Vera, and their two dogs and two cats, spend time traveling in their motor home, logging almost 20,000 miles a year.

"My life has settled into a routine," Conniff said.

During their RV travels, the Conniff's often hook up with their children, son Jimmy, who drives an 18-wheel semi, and daughters Patti and Tamara.

Conniff is rather modest about the contributions he has made to the history of American popular music.

"I don't think my peers think of me as having made a great contribution," he said. "My wife gets sore that my peers don't give me some kind of recognition. I don't think I have a legacy. I do know that I came up with a sound that was a little different. Maybe that's the legacy."

** Coda - Here is an update on Ray Conniff since this article was published: In 2001, Ray Conniff and his Orchestra and Chorus toured Brazil for a series of concerts.

Conniff's last public appearance was in March 2002, in which he conducted a choir singing "Somewhere My Love" at the wedding of Liza

Minnelli and David Gest.

Later that month, Conniff suffered a stroke. He died on Saturday, October 12, 2002 at Palomar Medical Center in Escondido, California, after falling down and hitting his head in the bathtub. He was 85.

He is interred at Westwood Village Memorial Park Cemetery in Los Angeles. His grave marker bears a musical score with the first four notes of "Somewhere My Love."

Conniff was survived by Vera, his wife of thirty-four years; a son, Jimmy Conniff; a daughter, Tamara Conniff; and three grandchildren and four great-grandchildren. Jimmy Conniff died in 2015.

Family and fans of Ray Conniff maintain a web page devoted to Conniff's life and music at www.rayconniff.info/

Ray Conniff in the 1970s.

Ray Conniff in 1955.

Ray Conniff conducts his orchestra at the Columbia's 30th Street studios in New York City.

Ray Conniff in the 1980s.

Ray Conniff in the 1990s.

Striking Up The Band

"The Old Smoothie," Del Courtney, Leaves Musical Legacy Spanning Over Seven Decades

The following article on Del Courtney was originally published in the January 2001 issue of Jazz Connection Magazine.

If Del Courtney had listened to his father who wanted his son to become a music teacher, the music business would have lost out on a very successful and innovative bandleader. For over seven decades, Courtney has led one of the most popular orchestras of the Big Band era.

"My dad wanted me to be a teacher because he thought it was an honorable profession and that I would be looked up to in the community," said Courtney, 90, via telephone from his high-rise apartment in Honolulu, Hawaii. "I got my teacher's degree and taught at a high school for six months. It wasn't to my liking. I went back to my father and said, 'Dad, I did it your way, now I'm going to go out and do it my way.'"

And Courtney did indeed go out and do things his own way. Nicknamed "The Old Smoothie" because his band played a very smooth and danceable-type of music, Courtney and his orchestra played every major hotel in the nation as well as for four U.S. presidents. During his long career, he appeared in movies and television and was surrounded frequently by some of the biggest names in show business. He was a popular radio host and a prominent fixture in early television in the San Francisco area. He formed the original Oakland Raiders band and was one of the first to bring Big Band music to Hawaii.

"I consider myself blessed by the 'Man upstairs' and very fortunate to have enjoyed a successful career in the music and entertainment world," Courtney said. "I was lucky to have had a number of 'firsts' in my profession as well as enjoying a good part of my life in sports both as a player and in my relationship with the Oakland Raiders football organization."

The desire to play professional sports almost kept Courtney out of the musical line-up. While pursuing a degree in music and leading a dance band at the University of California, Berkeley, he played semi-pro baseball in the Maxwell League in the San Francisco Bay area, earning $10 per game playing centerfield, and $15 if he pitched, he said. He turned down a professional contract with the Pacific League San Francisco Seals.

"I wanted to play professional baseball but I also wanted to lead a band," Courtney said. "I had a decision to make. I figured I could last longer in music than I could in baseball. If I got a couple of broken fingers playing baseball I would never be able to play the piano."

Born on September 24, 1910, in Oakland, California, Courtney's interest in music began at age nine when his parents, George and Mary, started him on piano lessons from a lady who lived in the neighborhood. She charged the then-exorbitant price of twenty-five cents per thirty-minute lesson.

"Being able to play the piano so fascinated me that I wanted to increase the time of each piano lesson," Courtney recalled. "That's pretty unusual for a nine-year-old kid! I knew that I wanted to continue to study music."

At age sixteen, Courtney first became acquainted with jazz through a chance contact with Waterman's Jazz Piano School, a small piano school located in Oakland. After taking a number of jazz piano lessons with the owner, Mr. Waterman, Courtney was encouraged to try out for the piano spot with a small jazz band from nearby Alameda.

"I thought I wasn't good enough to play jazz with this band but I auditioned anyway," Courtney said. "I was so nervous that I think I played more on the wooden part of the piano than on the keys! I was hired and that was the beginning of my interest and activity in the jazz field."

As a student at St. Mary's High School in Oakland, Courtney led his first dance band playing in the area with quite a bit of success.

Upon graduation from high school, Courtney attended St. Mary's College in Moraga, California, but left after two years because of the school's lack of music courses.

"By this time I had definitely decided I wanted to be in music," he said.

With a heartfelt desire to study music, Courtney transferred to the College of the Pacific in Stockton, California (now known as the University of the Pacific). UOP, an expensive private college, had the reputation of being the best music school west of the Mississippi River.

Courtney joined the Rho Lamda Phi fraternity and was a roommate with Henry "Dutch" Brubeck, the older brother of famous jazz pianist, Dave Brubeck.

"Dutch's mother was a piano teacher and she allowed us to use her big studio in her home in Concord for band rehearsals," Courtney said. "Her younger son, Dave, sat on the floor and watched us rehearse. This, he had said many times publicly, inspired him to a life of playing jazz music."

Between the high tuition rates and the costs incurred of being in a fraternity, Courtney left UOP after his junior year to transfer to the University of California, Berkeley.

Liking the sound of jazz and the sound of a big band, Courtney soon formed a jazz band on the campus of Berkeley. His first engagement as an orchestra leader paid $20.

"The money aspect of it almost discouraged me and whetted my appetite to return to professional sports," Courtney said. "However, I stuck it out."

Courtney graduated with a degree in classical piano and spent an additional year at Berkeley to earn his master's and teaching degree.

"I always had it in my mind that having a teaching degree in my back pocket would be a safety net for me if my professional dance band career didn't prove successful," he said.

In 1933, Courtney signed a booking contract with Music Corporation of America (MCA) and took his newly-formed sixteen-piece band to Seattle, Washington, for its first job: a four-week engagement at the Trianon Ballroom.

Arriving in Seattle a day early, Courtney met with the ballroom's owner/manager, John Savage, who was also part owner of a Seattle baseball team in the Pacific Coast League and part owner of the Rainier Beer Company.

Savage told Courtney, "Kid, you are not opening up in this ballroom tomorrow night. We have a local band the people like."

Courtney felt like crying, he said, but reminded Savage about the contract he signed with MCA to which Savage replied, "I signed that contract when I was in a bad mood one day. You're still not opening here."

After some pleading by the fledgling bandleader, Savage offered a compromise. He told Courtney, "Kid, this is what I'll let you do. You can open here tomorrow night. If the people like you, you can stay for the weekend."

Elated, Courtney returned to the hotel and told the members of his band the news.

"I told my band that if we were to keep this first engagement, we had to play with both hands and with both lips," Courtney said.

The people attending the Trianon Ballroom that Friday evening liked the Courtney band and true to his word, Savage let the band play out the weekend.

The people liked the band so much that before the weekend was over, Savage extended the band's stay to one week - then to four weeks.

"He kept extending the contract and we ended up playing there for eight months!" Courtney said.

During that time, Vic Meyers, a former bandleader turned nightclub owner, invited Courtney and his band to play at his swanky downtown Seattle nightspot, The Club Victor, which broadcasted nightly over NBC.

When Courtney gave Savage his two weeks' notice, the Trianon Ballroom manger responded, "Kid, not leaving here!"

"The only way that I got out of the Trianon was to go to the musicians' union in Seattle and they helped me so I could go to The Club Victor," Courtney said. "That was a big step up for me being only twenty-four years old."

After a twelve-week stay at The Club Victor, Courtney's booking agency booked the new band in Hawaii, which ironically, led to greater public exposure.

In 1935, MCA booked Courtney at the Alexander Young Hotel Roof Garden in Honolulu, a move the young bandleader stoutly resisted.

"I was against going to Hawaii," Courtney said. "The band was just getting known and I didn't want to be stuck playing on some rock in the middle of the ocean! I figured no one was ever going to hear about us."

He grudgingly took the job, and as luck would have it, the whole world ended up hearing about Del Courtney and his Orchestra. He was picked by the Hawaii tourist bureau to play the very first broadcast of the long-running radio series, *Hawaii Calls*.

"At that time, Harry Owens and his Royal Hawaiians were the big name in the Islands and I told the show's producer that I thought Harry should be the first to play on the show," Courtney recalled. "I got the nod to be the first so the rest of the world would know that Hawaii had big name bands playing here, too. Harry was pretty angry about it. He didn't speak to me for weeks."

The Courtney and Owens bands alternated broadcasts weekly for twenty-six weeks, each airing the show from their respective locations: Courtney from the Alexander Young Roof Gardens and Owens (who wrote "Sweet Leilani") from the Royal Hawaiian Hotel.

It was while in "Paradise" that Courtney first met Alex Anderson, Hawaii's most prolific songwriter, who wrote such tunes as "Lovely Hula Hands," "Keep Your Eyes on the Hands" and "The Kakaied Mayor of Kaiankakai," among others. He even wrote a song for Courtney based on the bandleader's physical discomfort he experienced shortly after arriving to Hawaii.

"I got so sunburned the first week I was in Hawaii that I could hardly walk," Courtney said. "Alex asked me what the matter was. I told him I felt like I was on fire, especially my stomach. He said, 'Oh, you mean your *opu*.' The next week he came to me and said, 'I wrote a song about your sunburn. It's called 'My Little Red Opu.' That song is still played today."

Courtney and his band were one of the first to play the song, "Hawaiian War Chant."

"We worked with a number of Hawaiian troupes," Courtney said. "There was one little Hawaiian girl who did a number called 'Tahawahawai.' I asked her to write down the words, and my arranger took down the notes as she sang the melody. We recorded it back on the mainland as 'Hawaiian War Chant' (December 27, 1939). Fortunately, the record sold pretty well. Tommy Dorsey also recorded it earlier (July 1938), as did Guy Lombardo."

The *Hawaii Calls* broadcasts captured a lot of interest on the mainland for Courtney's band. He was soon booked into every major hotel, ballroom and theater in the country, including such famed sites as the Coconut Grove in Los Angeles, the Aragon-Trianon ballrooms in Chicago, New York's Paramount Theatre, the Glen Island Casino in New Rochelle, New York, the Mark Hopkins Hotel in San Francisco and Chicago's Blackhawk Restaurant, where the band was booked for nine straight months in 1946, its longest engagement.

"We didn't have trouble getting jobs after that," Courtney said. "We never played in Hawaii again, until I moved here in 1978. I always knew that this was where I wanted to end up."

Engagements in these major hotels led to recording contracts over the years on such labels as Vocalion, Okeh (a Columbia affiliate), Bluebird (an RCA-Victor affiliate), Mercury and Capitol.

The band's most notable recordings include "An Apple for the Teacher" (July 7, 1939); "Monstro the Whale" (August 28, 1939); "The Singing Hills" and "Hawaiian War Chant" (both on December 27, 1939). Many of Courtney's early recordings featured vocals by guitarist Joe Martin and tenor saxophonists Sherman Hayes and Dick Dildine.

In 1946, Courtney missed out on what could have been biggest hit of his career. The song was "To Each His Own," subsequently made famous by Eddy Howard on Majestic Records.

Courtney was sent a copy of the Jay Livingston and Ray Evans tune and recorded it for Mercury Records in Chicago. By the time he recorded the piece, there was an internal shake up within the record company and as a result, Courtney's recording of the song never got released, he said.

"Every time I hear that song, I cry," Courtney said. "Eddy made a pile of money off it."

Although music critic George T. Simon in his book, *The Big Bands*, labels Courtney's band as "part Mickey Mouse and part society," Courtney said he disagrees with that assessment.

"We fell into the category of playing 'smooth music,'" he said. "We were never a Mickey Mouse band. We leaned more toward the touch of jazz than strictly being a society band. We played a pretty solid brand of music. We were a solid band leaning more on the smooth side of music than the high- powered jazz/swing bands. We did play some jazz but the mainstay was 'smooth' danceable music."

And that earned Courtney his nickname of "The Old Smoothie."

"A writer from *Down Beat* magazine reviewed the band and said it was a very smooth danceable- type of a band," Courtney said. "I guess I had personality, too. It was suggested in the article that I be called 'The Old Smoothie.' The moniker stuck."

Even with his love for jazz, Courtney peddled his brand of music for commercial reasons, he said.

"The first big band I had, we played jazz, but it was loud and we didn't get too many jobs," he said. "Making it more danceable gave us our niche."

Courtney patterned his band after the sweet band of saxophonist Orville Knapp. In 1936, after Knapp was killed piloting the plane he crashed, Courtney used as his theme song, "Three Shades of Blue," a song from the late popular bandleader's library.

Courtney used that piece as his theme until 1941 when problems arising with the American Society of Composers and Publishers (ASCAP) surfaced, which prohibited playing or recording any song of a publisher associated with ASCAP.

"I came to work at the Stevens Hotel in Chicago," Courtney recalled. "About an hour before we were to broadcast, we were told that we couldn't use 'Three Shades of Blue' as our theme. I went over to the piano and with the help of my piano player, the two of us wrote a song we could play as our theme. We called it 'Good Evening,' because that's what we first say when we come on the air. We kept it as our theme song until the day I retired."

Not all of the venues the band played for during the early days held fond memories. Once while the band was playing a one-nighter at a ballroom in Lexington, Kentucky, a dancer pointed a gun at Courtney. Courtney explains: "This guy danced by the bandstand and asked us to play 'Sweet Sue.' We always tried to honor requests so we played the song for him. About twenty minutes later the same man danced by and again wanted us to play 'Sweet Sue.' I told him that we had already played it and we don't like to repeat numbers, but that we would play it again. About thirty minutes later the same man came up to me and the band to play 'Sweet Sue' again. This time I told him no since we played it for him two times. At that moment the man pulled a revolver out of his pocket, aimed it at me and said, 'I said, play 'Sweet Sue.' My knees were knocking. I shouted to the boys in the band, 'Hey, guys, stop whatever you're playing and play 'Sweet Sue.'"

There were also times of struggle as to when the next booking would come from so that the band could eat.

"We finished an engagement in Gallup, New Mexico, and we didn't have another booking lined up. We were starving," Courtney said. "We had six guys in a room eating beans, and five more guys in another room sharing a hamburger. I went to Chicago see a band booker named Bob Weems, the brother of bandleader Ted Weems. He said, 'I've canvassed every place in the Midwest and nobody wants your band. My advice to you, kid, is to go home. You'll never make it as a bandleader.'

"I went to my room that night and cried. Then I borrowed money to get some gasoline in my car, drove up to Minneapolis, thinking I'd find us a job myself. I was walking down the street when I bumped into Horace Heidt. He and his band were playing the Orpheum Theater. He knew the Radisson Hotel was opening a room and didn't have a band yet. He took me to see the manager, and right under the band booker's nose, I got a four-week job. The worst thing was I had to pay him commission for the job even though I got it myself, because we were under contract. Then we switched agencies and the first job we were booked into was the Ambassador Hotel on Park Avenue in New York. The hotel sent out embossed invitations that said, 'The Ambassador Hotel is proud to present the music of Del Courtney and his Orchestra.' I got a hold of one those invitations and sent it to Bob Weems in Chicago with a note: 'Dear Bob, I'm sorry I didn't take your advice. If you're ever in New York, I'll buy you a drink.' That was the sweetest revenge in my life, to open in a swank room in New York when he told me I'd never make it in the band business."

As the Big Bands began to fade out in the late 1940's, Courtney reluctantly decided that it was time for him to disband as well. Courtney's father by this time had opened a television retail store on Franklin Street in Oakland and wanted his son to come home and help him run the business.

"The first television station had not yet been built in San Francisco and we had no 'real' television sets to sell," Courtney said. "Dad's store was set up in anticipation of the first TV station being built. We put a TV cabinet in the store window with a movie camera behind it so that people passing the store could see what they thought was a television set. People became interested and wanted to buy one. Since no TV stations were built yet in the area that was selling televisions the hard way! A few months later when the local television station was completed, we sold TV's by the truckloads."

This led Courtney to a new phase of his career as a pioneer in early television in San Francisco on KPIX Channel 5. He re-formed his band and hosted a musical variety/talk show which lasted almost five years.

"Because of the name that I had built up in the band business, the management of the TV station asked me to do a three-hour daily television show," Courtney said. "I turned down their first few offers until they told me that I could mention my family television stores on the show as many times as I wanted. Realizing this would save us thousands of dollars in advertising, I accepted the job."

Working out of a small room from the Mark Hopkins Hotel, doing a television show at that time was a great challenge, Courtney said. The news, for example, was flown in from Los Angeles. Some days after doing three hours on the air, the station manager would stick his head in the door and ask Courtney to stay on the air since the news hadn't arrived from L.A. yet.

"I thought to myself, 'What could I do for three hours a day that I hadn't done yesterday or last week or last month?'" Courtney said. "We did everything on this show from having animals to interviewing people outside the studio to comedy skits to broadcasting weddings. Our receptionist at KPIX was getting married and we did the wedding live on television. This was the very first wedding done on television anywhere."

Since Courtney made so many contacts in show business as a bandleader, it wasn't much of a problem to have these celebrities appear on his television show, he said.

"We were fortunate to have had people from Hollywood come up to San Francisco who wanted to plug their latest motion picture, recording, book or whatever," Courtney said. "Whoever they were, we interviewed them. We had such greats as Ella Fitzgerald on six times. Sammy Davis Jr., was such a hit and he loved being on the show that whenever he came to play the Fairmont Hotel, he'd always call me and ask for an appearance."

Besides featuring established stars on his show, Courtney also introduced then-unknown performers such as comedian Phyllis Diller, singer Johnny Mathis, and the vocal group, The Kingston Trio, he said.

With all the Hollywood greats with whom he has been associated, Courtney counts conducting for crooner Frank Sinatra as a career highlight, he said.

"KPIX just opened its studios on Van Ness Avenue so were able to have a live audience," Courtney said. "The station manager asked me if I knew Frank Sinatra. I told him I did. He wanted me to get Frank to appear on the opening night of the new studios. Frank was still recording with Columbia Records at the time and since the station was a Columbia Broadcasting affiliate, he was hoping there wouldn't be a problem. If Frank liked you, he'd do you a favor. If he didn't like you, he'd be apt to put a contract out on you. Frank was appearing in Los Angeles at the time and he agreed to show up at the studios. Half way through the show, I looked in the wings and there was Frank, impeccably dressed in a tuxedo. I introduced him and he asked me if the band knew "Somebody Loves Me" in B-flat. I said, 'They sure do.' Frank responded with, 'Well, let's do it.' He was off singing. I also conducted another number for him."

While working for KPIX, Courtney would put a band together for special performances at various posh hotels in San Francisco including the Mark Hopkins, the St. Francis, the Palace, the Fairmont and the Claremont in nearby Berkeley.

In addition to being a television personality, Courtney also hosted his own daily three-hour radio show in the early afternoons on KSFO in San Francisco for twelve years. The radio show was broadcasted from the Tonga Room at the Fairmont Hotel. Courtney interviewed many top performers including Louis Armstrong, Duke Ellington, Tommy and Jimmy Dorsey, Buddy Rich, Mel Torme, Nat "King" Cole and Abbott and Costello, who did what seemed to be a never-ending and funny take-off on their famous "Who's On First?" comedy routine Courtney said.

As a self-confessed workaholic, Courtney always seemed to have three or four jobs going at the same time. The pace got really hectic when for years beginning in 1958, he was simultaneously working on television, radio and driving 400 miles a day to lead the house band at Harrah's at Lake Tahoe, Nevada, he said.

"After I'd get off the air at KSFO, I'd jump in my car and drive 200 miles to Sacramento," Courtney said. "That was before they had the by-pass. You had to stop at every light. I'd get to Tahoe just in time to give the downbeat for the 8:15 dinner show. I'd do the dinner show, do the midnight show, get through with work about 2 a.m., get in my car, drive all the way back from Lake Tahoe to San Francisco, get three hours of sleep, four if I was lucky, get up and do it all over again."

The routine got to be too strenuous for Courtney and he decided not to do anything more with the band but to just concentrate on his radio and television career, he said.

Courtney also gave Hollywood a try, appearing in the 1955 sci-fi film, *It Came From Beneath the Sea*. He also appeared in other flicks such as *The Hideous Sun Demon*, *Chicago at Night* and *John Loves Mary*, and on the television shows *Dragnet*, *San Francisco Beat* and *Harbor Command*.

In 1964, Courtney began working on *The King Family Show* television series which lasted about five seasons and was named the show's General Manager. The idea behind the show came from Yvonne King, one of the four King Sisters, a female quartet who rose to notoriety as the featured act with guitarist Alvino Rey and his band. Courtney was married to Yvonne King at the time, his second marriage.

"I got taken off the air at KSFO and Yvonne, my wife, said to me that she was going to make me the best-known MC in the United States," Courtney said. "The fact that I was married to the brainchild of the show made it easy for me to be named General Manager. The show consisted of forty-one family members and I couldn't fire any one of them!"

The cast rehearsed six days a week and the show was performed live on the seventh day over ABC. Managing such a "menagerie" was a real challenge at times, Courtney said.

"Some family members would come late to rehearsals, which was very frustrating, he said. "When we took the show on the road during the summer months, one teenager may not want to room with another teenager because they had a falling out the day before. Or, one mother would want to know why her daughter was being paid a certain amount of money while her cousin was being paid a different wage. It just went on and on."

One of the bright spots of being affiliated with *The King Family* show was working with his brother-in-law and co-host of the program, Alvino Rey, who was married to Luise King, Courtney said.

"They just don't come any better than Alvino Rey," he said. "He's a great musician and probably the best guitarist ever."

Courtney also helped to infuse show biz into the world of sports in 1960 when he formed the band for the then newly-formed football franchise, the Oakland Raiders. He was also instrumental in establishing pro football's first corps of cheerleaders, the Raiderettes.

At first Courtney turned down offers made to him by the owners of the Raiders to lead the "Silver and Black" band, citing that he had a "full plate" of interests going already. He did agree, however, to put the initial forty-piece band together and to produce home game half-time shows for the first season, he said.

"The owners kept after me to come aboard and pretty soon they made the offer better and better and so I went to work for the Oakland Raiders," Courtney said. "I started out as entertainment director, conducting the band at half-time and getting the national anthem singer. When Al Davis came to Oakland, I was soon elevated to the role of the team's director of administration, overseeing virtually all Raider operations except those directly involving the players. I represented Al in contracts for television and radio rights and a myriad of other things."

Courtney utilized his vast array of contacts in show business by inviting celebrities to sing the National Anthem or to participate in Raider half-time extravaganzas, he said.

During his nineteen years with the Raiders organization, the team made four Super Bowl appearances, winning three: Oakland Raiders - Super Bowl II, January 14, 1968, lost; Super Bowl XI, January 9, 1977, won; Super Bowl XV, January 25, 1981, won; Los Angeles Raiders – Super Bowl XVII, January 22, 1984, won.

In 1971, Courtney was stricken with the rare Guillam-Barre syndrome, which attacks the nervous system. The condition left Courtney completely paralyzed and in a coma for nearly five weeks.

"I could hear what was going on, but I couldn't move or speak at all during that time," Courtney said. "Eight doctors said I had about an hour to live." But Courtney proved the doctors wrong and in six months, three of which were spent in the intensive-care unit, he walked out of the hospital with the aid of canes and returned to his job with the Raiders.

"A lot of people may not like Al Davis, but he used to visit me when I was in the hospital and he continued to pay me my salary and the Raiders took care of the hospital bills, which were astronomical," Courtney said. "He did right by me."

By 1978, Courtney decided the time was right to relocate to Hawaii and planned to completely retire from show biz, but his plan was short lived. Less than a month after arriving in Honolulu, Courtney was recruited by the Royal Hawaiian Hotel's manager, Joe Hiebert, to put together a band to play for Sunday afternoon tea dances in the hotel's Monarch Room.

"A couple years earlier, Joe came to the Hyatt Regency Hotel in San Francisco where my band was playing every Friday and he gave me a standing invitation to run such dances if I ever came to Honolulu," Courtney said. "A week after I got to Honolulu, I went to see Joe and asked when I could start. Two weeks later I had a band together working for a twelve-week contract."

So successful were those Sunday afternoon tea dances that like the Trianon Ballroom engagement in Seattle forty-five years earlier, Courtney's contract kept getting extended until it turned into an unprecedented fifteen-year stint that finally ended in 1993.

"I finally said to Joe that I was retiring," Courtney said. "You have to know when it's time to let go."

Little did Courtney realize that his association with the Raiders football team did not end when he retired from the organization and moved away. In 1983, when the Raiders moved to Los Angeles, Al Davis telephoned the semi-retired bandleader and wanted him to come to Los Angeles to work once again for six months.

"I didn't want to but before I knew it, I was on a plane going to Los Angeles," Courtney said. "Al Davis is a very persuasive man."

Courtney helped put together a new Raider band and produced all the half-time shows. He was also looking for someone to permanently take over the band when friend and former bandleader Horace Heidt contacted him.

"Horace asked me if his son, Horace Heidt Jr., who was starting out in the band business, could get the job of leading the Los Angeles Raiders Band," Courtney said. "I was happy to give him the job. It was something I could do for Horace because he helped me when I was down."

In 1986, Courtney released a tape cassette, *Del Courtney Swings in Hawaii*, and in August of that year appeared with the Honolulu Symphony in a tribute to the Big Bands at the Waikiki Shell in Honolulu.

Since his retirement, Courtney has undergone major back surgery and has had two knee operations, which limit his activities. He spends a good deal of time in his condo reading or listening to music, he said. He occasionally leads a band for special engagements as he did for his 90th birthday party last September 24. Hosted by the Royal Hawaiian Hotel, many celebrities came out to celebrate including singer Herb Jeffries (who celebrated his 89th birthday on the same day and who has worked with Courtney on many occasions in the past), singer Jimmy Borges, alto saxophonist Gabe Baltazar, John Norris, Kanoe Miller, Sonny Kamahele, and trombonist Ira Neptus.

The Musicians' Association of Hawaii Local 677 AFM, even awarded

Courtney with its first-ever Distinguished Life Member Gold Card and through resolution declared that *"...September 24 of each and every year henceforth be declared 'Del Courtney Day' in Hawaii... and that the Local (musicians' union) sponsor a Big Band concert, featuring the music that Del made famous around the world, in honor of Del and his contributions to the life of music and musicians in Hawaii."*

Courtney is also in the process of writing a book about his life in the music business, an idea encouraged to him by friend Herb Jeffries.

"Herb kept reminding me that music has treated me very well and that I have to give something back," Courtney said. "He's right."

Courtney has been married and divorced four times. His wives include Nalani Courtney, Yvonne King (m. 1957-1966) and singer Connie Haines (m. 1966-1972). Courtney has no children.

Although he favors good jazz music, Courtney likes all kinds of music except rock, which he abhors, he said.

"There really isn't any live music here in Hawaii right now," Courtney said. "My music has deteriorated to the point where there isn't any."

The high-water mark of Courtney's career was playing for four different U.S. presidents, he said.

"I don't know of any other band who ever played for four presidents," Courtney said. "I consider this a great honor. I was lucky enough to have bands play for presidents Truman, Eisenhower, Nixon and Reagan. We played for President Truman in Kansas City for the 35th reunion of his Army Division. Every big star in the country attended the reunion which was hosted by Jack Benny. We played for one of President Eisenhower's Inaugural Balls in Washington, D.C. Then we played for President Nixon for one of his functions in California. We were a hit with President Reagan at one his Inaugural Balls held at the Space Museum in Washington, D.C., when we played "Nancy with the Laughing Face." He always liked our band. I knew him when he was governor of California. He told me that he ordered Del Courtney tapes to be played on Air Force One. I thought that was quite an honor."

With such an illustrious career in music, Courtney feels that his contribution to the history of American popular music is directly connected with his association with the Aloha State, Hawaii, he said.

"I think I've done some things for Hawaii by bringing good Big Band music here which it never had before," he said.

Would Courtney do all over again?

"You bet I would!" he said. "With my love of music and the successes I enjoyed, I would do the whole thing all over again. I enjoyed every minute of it."

** Coda - Here is an update on Del Courtney since this article was published:

During the past five years, it has been reported that Del Courtney had been suffering from ill health and was confined the majority of the time to his bed. Courtney put health concerns aside and felt well enough to lead a Big Band that played for his 94th birthday party in 2004, according to Donna Johnson, Courtney's caregiver.

In January 2005, Del Courtney self-published his autobiography, *Hey! The Band's Too Loud* (AuthorHouse Publishing), written with Stephen Fratallone.

Courtney died on Saturday, February 11, 2006, at Queen's Medical Center in Honolulu after suffering a weeklong bout with pneumonia. He was 95.

Courtney is interred at Holy Sepulcher Cemetery in Hayward, California.

Del Courtney and His Orchestra from 1943.

Del Courtney, circa late 1950s

Del Courtney, Honolulu's newest nonagenarian on September 24, 2000.

Del Courtney, far left, leading his band at his 90th birthday bash on September 24, 2000 in the Monarch Room of the Royal Hawaiian Hotel in Honolulu. At far right is alto saxophonist Gabe Baltazar.

Del Courtney in the 1940s.

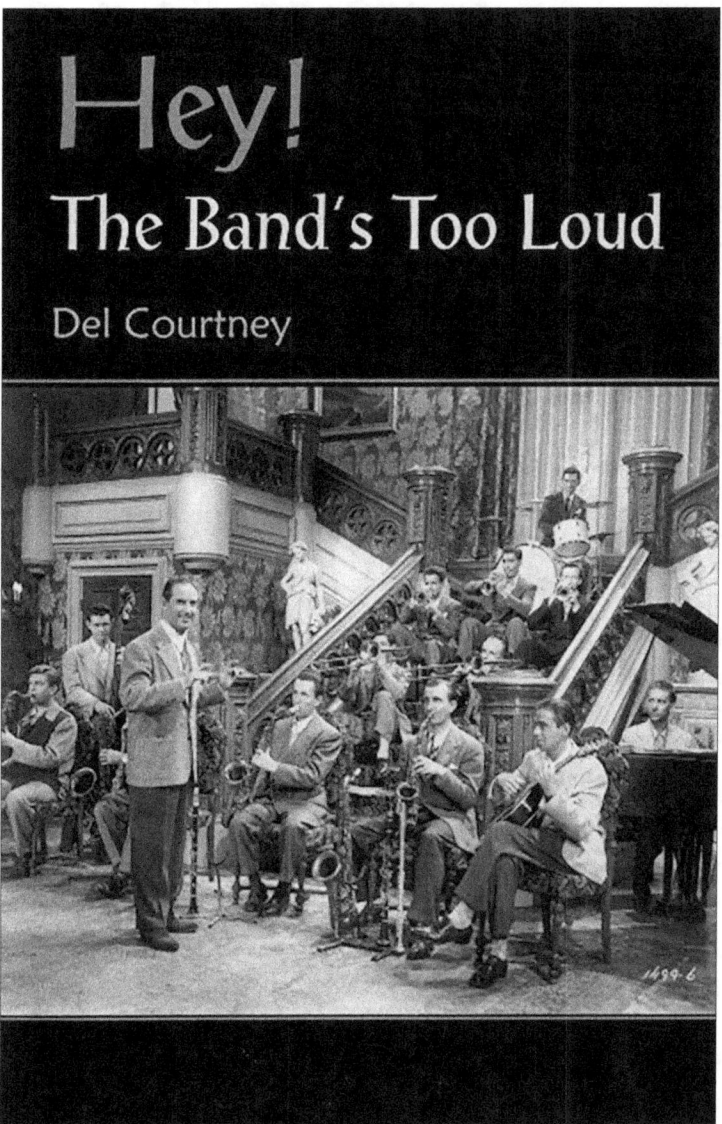

Del Courtney's autobiography, *Hey! The Band's Too Loud*, written with Stephen Fratallone, was published in January 2005 by AuthorHouse Publishing.

- Photo by Stephen Fratallone

Big Noise From Ojai

Bob Crosby and the Bob Cats Roar Big at Ojai Jazz Festival

This article about Bob Crosby originally appeared in the October 9, 1986, edition of The Fillmore (CA) Herald and was later reprinted in Jazz Connection Magazine.

The 1986 Jazz at Ojai (CA) matinee Saturday, September 27 was a Dixieland class reunion for some familiar musical faces and a famous first-time visitor to the rustic Ojai Festivals Bowl.

The newcomer was Bob Crosby, who provided personable commentary, a few jokes and a couple of vocals, while fronting an octet billed as his Bob Cats – a Dixie combo within his big band. Crosby was joined by two members of the original Bob Cats – tenorman Eddie Miller and bassist Bob Haggart. Rounding out the Bob Cats were recognizable "A-List" musicians and all veteran sidemen from the Big Band era who are no strangers at Ojai: Abe Most, clarinet; Johnny Best and Dick Cathcart, trumpets; Bob Havens, trombone; Ray Sherman, piano; and Nick Fatool, drums.

The seventy-three-year-old Crosby, who is celebrating his 50th anniversary as a band leader, took the audience on a "musical tour" of jazz. Beginning at New Orleans, the Bob Cats started the set off with a toe-tapping rendition of "Way Down Yonder in New Orleans."

Crosby had each sideman spotlighted as the tour of jazz made its way up the Mississippi River. Two of the Crosby band's biggest hits were featured during the trek. The first, "South Rampart Street Parade" (originally recorded on November 16, 1937), garnered enthusiastic audience approval.

Going "Up a Lazy River," the tour went past "Memphis," up to "St. Louis Blues," to Davenport, Iowa, to take the train for some "Honky Tonk Train Blues," enroute to "Chicago." There's a suburb of Chicago called Winnetka and no Bob Cat performance would be complete without doing "Big Noise From Winnetka" (originally recorded on October 14, 1938, with Bob Haggart, string bass and whistling, and Ray Bauduc, drums), the Crosby band's second biggest hit for the Ojai performance. Haggart reprised the trademark whistle-through-the-teeth and Fatool's drumsticks-on-the-bass's "G-string" routine during "Big Noise" had the Ojai crowd creating a "big noise" itself by shouting their approval.

The final destination of the jazz tour ended in California as the Bob Cats played "California, Here I Come." Not wanting the tour to end, patrons clamored for more.

As an encore, Bob Havens brought down the house with "Tiger Rag," displaying his inimitable combination of musicianship and showmanship by sliding his trombone with the use of his feet.

Reflecting upon his 50 years as a bandleader, Crosby, age 73, never thought when he started in the music business that he would have made such an impact upon American music one half century later.

"When you're young nothing really seems to mean anything," Crosby said during the break between sets. "No, I never thought we'd ever amount to anything because we never stayed in one spot long enough for people to get to know us."

Crosby, who described himself as "the only guy in the band business who made it without talent," was an above-average singer who didn't play an instrument, but his expansive stage presence made the most of the band's talented musicians, and soon the band's Big Band-Dixieland sound was getting top billing on radio shows and at hotels, theaters and ballrooms.

A critic once described Crosby's tentative baritone as having "a tremolo wide enough to drive a Mack truck through." But what he lacked in vocal confidence, he made up for in personality, bridging the gap between the audience and the bandstand with a mellow charm that made him one of the more popular bandleaders of the Swing era.

Such jazz names as trumpeters Yank Lawson and Billy Butterfield, cornetist Muggsy Spanier, clarinetists Matty Matlock and Irving Fazola, guitarist Nappy Lamar, trombonists Ward Silloway and Warren Smith, drummer Ray Bauduc, pianists Joe Sullivan, Bob Zurke, and Jess Stacy, and vocalists Kay Weber, Doris Day, Kay Starr, and Liz Tilton worked with the band at various intervals. The band's arranger was Deane Kincaid, with contributions by Matty Matlock and Eddie Miller.

Born George Robert Crosby in Spokane, Washington, on August 25, 1913, Crosby was the youngest of seven children. By the time he graduated from Gonzaga University intent upon a show business career, his older brother, Bing, was already a well-known entertainer. Bob went directly from college to the Anson Weeks orchestra in 1933 as band vocalist, and within a year booking agent Tommy Rockwell got him a spot as a singer in a new band being organized by Jimmy and Tommy Dorsey (1934-35).

After the Dorsey Brothers Orchestra split up, Crosby looked to branch out on his own in the entertainment world while desperately wanting to get out of the pervasive shadow of his brother, Bing. Crosby led his first band in 1935, as a cooperative corporation when the former members of Ben Pollack's band elected him their titular leader.

The new band initially struggled to gain recognition as all new bands were prone to do, but Crosby was able to see light-at-the-end-of-the-tunnel through the intervention of one man.

"Fortunately, we had a chance to play in a hotel chain that was owned by Ralph Hitz," Crosby said, continuing with his remarks during the Ojai interview. "He took us to New York and put us in the Lexington Hotel. That was the first acknowledgement that I ever made to myself that we ever had a chance of making the big time. We were very successful in New York.

That's when I started thinking that this wasn't going to be a one or two-week engagement, but this was going to be a future. It proved to be so."

By March 1938, the Crosby band's popularity soared through a series of coast-to-coast radio shows during its long-standing booking at Chicago's famed Blackhawk Restaurant. This led to being tapped in 1939, as the summer replacement for the popular *Camel Caravan* radio shows.

The Crosby band was also beckoned to Hollywood to appear in a handful of "B" films including *Sis Hopkins* (1941), *Let's Make Music* (1941), *Reveille with Beverly* (1943), and *Presenting Lily Mars* (1943). The band helped to supply some of the music while band members had cameo appearances in *Holiday Inn* (1942), starring Bing Crosby and Fred Astaire When America entered World War II and the draft began taking sidemen, the band decided to break up rather than continue with less talented substitutes.

Crosby joined the Marines in 1944, as a second lieutenant leading a service band in the Pacific.

After his discharge, Crosby hosted *Club Fifteen*, a musical variety radio show which ran from 1947- 1953. A half-hour CBS daytime television series, *The Bob Crosby Show*, followed from 1953 to 1957. In 1952, Crosby replaced Phil Harris as the bandleader on *The Jack Benny Program*, remaining until Benny retired the radio show in 1955 after twenty-three years. He was one of two featured singers (himself and Dennis Day) in mid-1950s episodes of *The Jack Benny Program* on television. Crosby married socialite June Kuhn on September 22, 1938. They had five children, three boys (Christopher, George, and Stephen) and two girls (Cathleen and Junie).

During the 1960s, Crosby fronted various reincarnations of the Bob Cats before settling in La Jolla, California.

Crosby went on to say that he was very fortunate to have had wonderful musicians in the band.

"I've got to give them more credit than I can give myself," he confessed at Ojai.

Crosby believes that the impact he has made on American popular music is in the compositions that were written by the musicians themselves.

"We had a very close-knit band," he said. "Everyone contributed in some way on all those wonderful songs. We took Dixieland, which was pretty much of a bar-type music, and we enhanced it by making the harmonies a little more intricate and adding more changes in the songs we wrote. We took the music of New Orleans and brought it to New York City and to all the big cities, playing in all the best spots."

With the help of the Ojai Rotary Club, jazz and Big Band radio host Fred Hall, and jazz entrepreneur Lyn Stewart, produced and hosted this eleventh annual festival.

** Coda - Here is an update on Bob Crosby since this article was published.

Bob Crosby continued to lead various manifestations of a dance band along with the Bob Cats throughout the 1980s and early 1990s.

I first saw Crosby at Disneyland on July 1, 1985, leading a dance band under his name comprised of various Big Band era veterans and Los Angeles-based studio musicians. In that band were clarinetist Peanuts Hucko, alto saxist Skeets Herfurt, tenor saxist Dick Hafer, trombonist Bob Havens, trumpeter Johnny Best, pianist Frank Scott (who was our jazz band leader for a semester in 1979, when I was a budding student sax player in that band at California Lutheran College in Thousand Oaks), and bassist David Stone. Special guest for that Disneyland engagement was diva Kay Starr, who briefly sang with her former boss in the early 1940s.

I took slide photos of Crosby during his Disneyland engagement and had a few enlargements printed to mail to him to autograph for me which he graciously did. Accompanying the returned autographed 8 x 10s was a letter from Crosby liking the photos I had taken while telling me that I can be his photographer "any time." He also wrote requesting if I would send him the negatives so he could use the photos for publicity purposes. I responded by saying I would be honored, but since the photos were taken on slides, I did not wish to depart with them, but I would be willing to have duplicate slide copies made for him at the cost at that time of one dollar per slide. I never heard back from him.

Crosby died on Tuesday, March 9, 1993, of cancer at a nursing home in Torrey Pines, California, just north of La Jolla. He was 79. He was the last of the seven Crosby siblings to die.

Bob Crosby and the Bob Cats performing at the Ojai (CA) Jazz Festival on September 27, 1986. Bob Cat members include (l-r) Ray Sherman, piano (hidden); Abe Most, clarinet; Eddie Miller, tenor sax; Bob Haggart, bass; Johnny Best and Dick Cathcart, trumpets; Bob Havens, trombone; Nick Fatool, drums; and leader Bob Crosby.
– Photo by Stephen Fratallone

Bob Crosby with Eddie Miller and Bob Haggart, two original Bob Cats, at the Ojai Jazz Festival on September 27, 1986.
— *Photo by Stephen Fratallone*

Bob Crosby and Judy Garland starring in the movie, *Presenting Lily Mars,* from 1943.

Bob Crosby, 72, fronting his Big Band at Disneyland on July 1, 1985.
– *Photos by Stephen Fratallone*

Kay Starr with her ex-boss Bob Crosby at Disneyland.
– *Photo by Stephen Fratallone*

Bob Crosby, (72) fronting his band at Disneyland on July 1, 1985. Musicians pictured are Frank Scott, piano, far left; Dave Stone, bass; tenor saxist Dick Hafer; and alto saxist/clarinetist Peanuts Hucko.
— *Photo by Stephen Fratallone*

Ambassador Of Swing

Larry Elgart Continues To Revitalize Swing In To New Millennium

The following article on Larry Elgart was originally published in the February 2000 issue of Jazz Connection Magazine.

Larry Elgart has probably done more to revitalize swing music than any other musician around. Long before the neo-swing craze took hold, Elgart, known as "The Ambassador of Swing," has been providing listeners with an assortment of swing tunes accented with a contemporary dance beat. His 1982, *Hooked on Swing* album, which helped to keep swing music popular, has sold five million copies worldwide to date, making it the largest selling swing/big band record in history.

"Swing is my style of music, my musical identity," said Elgart, 77, during a telephone interview from his home in Longboat Key, Florida, prior to his January 13, 2000, dinner/dance engagement at the Jackson Rancheria Hotel and Casino in Jackson, California. "I've always been hooked on swing. It is a valid musical form and as such endures, always taking on new shapes and colors, whereby new generations can relate to it. It is the kind of music people react to – actively and posively. It's a happy form of music. The music of the Swing Era was fun *then*, and still is *now*!"

Elgart has been a professional musician for sixty years. In 1952, his music first reached a broad spectrum of listeners following issuance of his first

Columbia album titled, *Sophisticated Swing*. He shared leader credit on that album with his brother, trumpeter Les, and for years the name of "Les and Larry Elgart" described the style of music first heard on that initial album.

That style of music, the "Elgart Touch," as it has become known, features a certain graceful lilt to the saxophone sections phrasing led by Elgart himself playing lead alto saxophone. The reeds are accompanied by a piano-less rhythm section, an unmuted rich brass unit emphasized by the bass trombone, and the use of a percussionist augmenting the drums.

"Our rhythm style is a close sound to that of the Count Basie band, with emphasis on the guitar and bass," Elgart said about having a piano-less rhythm section. "Basie didn't play rhythm at all. He did it through accents. He played simple solos and 'punched in' things."

Elgart went on to say that during the early days of his band there were practical reasons for not electing to have a piano player.

"We played at ballrooms that didn't have air conditioning," he said. "It raised havoc with the piano, so we never knew where to go to tune."

The collaboration as co-leader with his brother, Les, who died in 1995, lasted about four years before the brothers parted ways to front their own respective bands, Elgart said.

Forming a Big Band after the end of World War II was a bold venture. Many existing bands folded and it looked as if the Big Band sound was dying out.

"It worked two ways," Elgart aid. "It was much easier because there was less competition."

The Larry Elgart band proved to be a success. It toured universities and ballrooms around the country and soon became known as America's Number One College Prom Favorite.

Jazz critic Barry Ulanov summed up the appeal of the Elgart orchestra when he wrote, "It seem so easy, you think, as you listen to these performances by the Larry Elgart orchestra. Just make sure it's always danceable and listenable. Isn't that what the Big Band era was all about?"

Ulanov went on to describe the sax section: "They sound as a section the way (Elgart) does on as an alto saxophonist: sweet to the ear, always under control, always with a suggestion of a hidden reserve of power, always with a delicate kind of humor, the humor of understatement."

Larry Elgart was born on March 20, 1922, in New London, Connecticut, four years younger than his brother, Les. Their mother was a concert pianist; their father played piano as well, though not professionally and encouraged both sons to pursue music as a career.

Les took up the trumpet, while Larry started playing the clarinet at age eight and then took up the alto saxophone at thirteen. By age seventeen, the younger Elgart was playing professionally on radio shows and in musical productions in New York City.

He later worked with clarinetist Joe Marsala and did stints in the Bobby Byrne, Charlie Spivak, Jerry Wald, Tommy Dorsey and Woody Herman bands.

Elgart spent only a short time with Spivak because it wasn't his type of music, he said.

"I got my brother, Les, in Charlie's band in mid-1942 because Charlie needed another trumpet player, but I didn't stay too long," Elgart said. "Charlie had a beautiful rubato sound on his trumpet but he couldn't swing at all."

Elgart stayed with Wald for over two years during the early 1940s. Wald, a fine clarinetist who died in 1973, was taken to task by many critics for imitating Artie Shaw rather than developing a musical style of his own.

"Yes, Jerry was like a clone of Artie," Elgart said. "He hired a lot of guys from the Shaw band. It was a good band with a lot of fine musicians, like tenor saxist Bobby Dukoff and guitarist Art Ryerson."

In 1944, Elgart played in the early manifestations of Herman's explosive First Herd, which featured such stellar musicians as Flip Phillips, tenor sax; Davey Tough, drums; Chubby Jackson, bass; Bill Harris, trombone; Pete Condoli, trumpet.

"Woody had such wonderful musicians and a great band, but some of the guys were terrible readers," Elgart said. "Woody started doing 'head arrangements' before he did any recording with that band. That's how the whole thing started."

In 1953, Elgart met Charles Albertine and recorded two of his experimental compositions, "Impressions of Outer Space" and "Music for Barefoot Ballerinas." Released on 10-inch vinyl records, these recordings became collector's items for fans of avant-garde jazz, but they were not commercially successful at the time. Elgart and Albertine put together a more traditional ensemble and began recording them using precise microphone placements, producing what came to be known as the "Elgart Sound." This proved to be very commercially successful, and Elgart enjoyed a run of successful albums and singles in the 1950s.

Albums recorded under the name of "Les and Larry Elgart Orchestra" include *Impressions of Outer Space* (Brunswick Records, 1953); *Prom Date* (Columbia Records, 1954); *Campus Hop* (Columbia, 1954); *Sophisticated Swing* (Columbia, 1953); *Just One More Dance* (Columbia, 1954); *The Band of the Year* (Columbia, 1954); *The Dancing Sound* (Columbia, 1954); *For Dancers Only* (Columbia, 1955); *The Elgart Touch* (Columbia, 1955); *The Most Happy Fella* (Columbia, 1956); *For Dancers Also* (Columbia, 1956); and *Les and Larry Elgart and Their Orchestra* (Columbia, 1958). Albums recorded by Larry Elgart himself include *Band With Strings* (Decca, 1954); *Larry Elgart and His Orchestra* (Decca, 1954); *Barefoot Ballerina* (Decca, 1955); *Larry Elgart and His Orchestra* (RCA Victor, 1959); *New Sounds at The Roosevelt* (RCA Victor, 1959); *Saratoga* (RCA Victor, 1960); *Easy Goin' Swing* (RCA, 1960); *Sophisticarted Sixties* (MGM Records, 1960); *The Shape of Sounds to Come* (MGM, 1961); *Visions* (MGM, 1961); *The City* (MGM, 1961); *Music in Motion!* (MGM, 1962); *More Music in Motion* (MGM, 1962); *The Larry Elgart Dance Band* (Project Records, 1979, as a reissue of *New Sounds at the Roosevelt*); *Flight of the Condor* (RCA Victor, 1981); *Hooked on Swing* (RCA / K-Tel International, 1982);

Hooked on Swing 2 (RCA Victor, 1983); *Larry Elgart and His Swing Orchestra* (RCA Victor, 1983); *Let My People Swing* (K-Tel Records, 1995, also a reissue of *New Sounds at the Roosevelt*); *Sensational Swing* (K-Tel, 1995, compilation); *Live at th Ambassador* (Quicksilver Records, 1998); *Latin Obsession* (Sony International, 2000); and *Bandstand Boogie* (2003). One commercially successful-selling album from the Larry Elgart canon was *New Sounds at the Roosevelt*, recorded on the RCA-Victor label. Tenor saxophonist Al Cohn contributed four originals on this fourteen-track album of ten modern-sounding standards. This album has since been reissued in 1995 under the title of *Let My People Swing*. Elgart and his band were booked for six weeks at the famed Roosevelt Hotel in New York City when the album was recorded in January and April of 1959.

"(Band booker) Willard Alexander sold the Roosevelt Hotel on the idea of changing its ballroom dance band routine," Elgart said. "Guy Lombardo had been the house band there for the past thirty-five years. Some people didn't like us because they wanted Lombardo's style of music and our band was exactly the opposite. People who dance to Lombardo's kind of music can't dance to the normal swing fashion. But we we had a successful run there."

In 1954, the Elgart Brothers left their permanent mark on music history in recording Albertine's "Bandstand Boogie" (January 29, 1954, on the Columbia label) for the legendary television show originally hosted by Bob Horn, and two years later, Dick Clark. Clark took the show national, to ABC-TV in 1956, and remained as host until 1987. Variations of the original surfaced as the show's theme in later years.

"'Bandstand Boogie' has become one of the most recognizeable theme songs around," Elgart said proudly.

But it wasn't until Elgart and His Manhattan Swing Orchestra recorded the *Hooked on Swing* album in 1982 that he received his biggest commercial success that revived a tremendous interest in his band.

"RCA had issued *Hooked on Classics* which was a huge success and everybody tried to do a follow up version to that record with swing," Elgart said. "At the time I was approached by the president of RCA Records to do the swing follow up. When our record came out you couldn't imagine how many other albums came out in that swing format. Ours was the only one to hit big."

Hooked on Swing was an instrumental medley of swing jazz hits including: "In the Mood," "Cherokee," "American Patrol," "Sing, Sing, Sing," "Don't Be That Way," "Little Brown Jug," "Opus No.1," "Zing Went the Strings of My Heart," and "String of Pearls" that became so popular it cracked the US *Billboard* Pop Singles chart (at No. 31) and Adult Contemporary chart (No. 20). This was the final hit for any artist in the year-long "medley craze," that lasted from 1981 to 1982. The LP album also hit No. 24 on the US charts.

Hooked on Swing 2 (released in 1988) and *The Best of Hooked on Swing* (released in January 1992) albums soon followed. The latter album includes an updated version of "Bandstand Boogie." *Hooked on Swing 2* debuted at No.89 on the album charts, and soon after Elgart was back to the jazz touring circuit. He continued to tour internationally and record into the 2000s.

Although Elgart won't admit it, many believe that his *Hooked on Swing* series may have been the seeds that were planted that ultimately gave birth to the current neo-swing craze.

"There are two crazes currently going on at the moment: rock/swing and Latin." he said. "The swing music that is out there isn't really swing but it's called swing and that part is good. It's like the recycling of other styles and when it comes around it comes around in a different way. It's really a combination of swing and rock."

Cashing in on the current popular Latin music craze, Sony Records recently rereleased Elgart's 1989 album, *Latin Obsession*.

"The album contains all authentic Latin tunes that are precisely played with wonderful percussionists," Elgart said.

Ever since *Hooked on Swing* was released, a greater number of young people have been attending Elgart's performances, he said.

In addition to playing for dances, Elgart and his orchestra also play a variety of concert dates throughout the year.

In 1995, Elgart and crew were chosen to perform the final concert at the closing of the famed Ambassador Auditorium in Pasadena, California. An album and video were made of that historic event entitled *Live From the Ambassador.*

As a solo artist, Elgart himself has made guest apperances with major symphony orchestras such as the Philly Pops, the Tulsa Pops with pianist Peter Nero, the West Virginia Pops with Maestra Rachel Worby, and the Boca Raton Pops with Crafton Black.

"I have three different kinds of books that I use," Elgart said. "One book is for playing for dances, the other is for sit-down concerts, and then other is for symphonic/pops dates where the orchestrations have been enlarged for a full symphonic orchestra."

Elgart said he has bands located in different parts of the country which makes it easier for him to travel. "The musicians that make up my different bands are all top-notch and they know exactly what is expected of them," he explained.

Elgart plans to take an all-star aggregation with him to perform at the 2000 Summer Olympic Games in Sydney, Australia, beginning in September, he said.

"We've played quite extensively in Australia over the years at the Victoria Arts Centre in Melbourne and at the Sydney Opera House," Elgart said. "Back in 1992, we performed for the Prime Minister's Olympic Ball which helped raise over one million dollars to send Australian athletes to the Barcelona Games. I was the only American artist invited to perform at the ball. We were invited to play for this Olympiad and we are honored."

With his 78th birthday approaching this year, Elgart doesn't have any plans of slowing down.

"This thing of leading a band is fun and enjoyable otherwise I wouldn't do it," he said.

Elgart keeps himself in great shape by walking four miles a day along the beach, lifting weights and doing back exercises.

"I don't use a sax strap and holding on to that also tends to be bad for your posture," he said.

When not fronting his band, Elgart looks forward to spending time with Lynn, his wife of thirty- seven years who also acts as his manager, and with his children and grandchildren.

Elgart said he is happy to have reached so many generations with his music.

"I guess it's been the length of time doing what I do that has been my contribution," he said.

** Coda - Here is an update on Larry Elgart since this article was published.

Larry Elgart and his Orchestra continued to perform throughout the early 2000s.

In October 2003, the Collectables label released the CD, *Bandstand Boogie,* a compilation of ten tunes previously recorded by Les and Larry Elgart from the 1950s.

Elgart, together with his wife, Lynn, had written a memoir of Elgart's life in music. Published by Archway Publishing in 2014, the book is titled *The Music Business and the Monkey Business.*

Larry Elgart died on August 29, 2017, in Sarasota, Florida. He was 95.

Besides his wife of 54 years, the former Lynn Walzer, Elgart is survived by two sons, Brock and Brad, four grandchildren, and four great-grandchildren. Elgart's first marriage to Grace Sims, ended in divorce.

Alto saxist Larry Elgart, 77, at the Jackson Rancheria Hotel and Casino in Jackson, CA, on January 13, 2000. – *Photo by Stephen Fratallone*

Larry Elgart, pictured above and below, fronting his band for a January 13, 2000, dance at the Jackson Rancheria Hotel and Casino in Jackson, CA. – *Photos by Stephen Fratallone*

Larry Elgart, 77, and his alto sax still swinging in 2000.
 — *Photo by Stephen Fratallone*

Swinging With A Basie-ite

Saxist, Leader and Arranger Frank Foster Shares Life With And After Count Basie

The following article on Frank Foster was originally published in the June 2000 issue of Jazz Connection Magazine.

When tenor saxophonist Frank Foster was fifteen years old, he had an ambition to play with the Count Basie band. Little did he realize that ten years later, his dream would come true, and he would eventually go on to lead Basie's band after the Count's death.

"I never thought I would be a sideman in Count Basie's band, but I really wanted to," said Foster last month in a telephone conversation from his home in Chesapeake, Virginia. "I grew up listening to the Count's music as I did Duke Ellington's and Jimmy Lunceford's."

Foster, a mainstay in the Count Basie orchestra throughout most of the 1950s through the early 1960s, helped to provide an exciting and distinctive sound with the group not only with his saxophone artistry, but with his arranging prowess as well. He also helped to create such memorable Basie standards as "April in Paris" and "Shiny Stockings."

Most music critics talked about the Basie band during this time as a "well-oiled machine," Foster said.

In 1950, Basie was leading an octet. But by mid-1951 he was reforming a big band, and with that band he discovered virtually new music. The earlier ensemble from the 1930s through the 1940s had been essentially a function of its soloists, and spontaneity was everything. In the 1950s, the soloists were a function of the ensemble, and precision and discipline were the basis of it all.

"Many critics said that the soloists in this band weren't as brilliant as the soloists in his 1930s and 1940s bands," Foster said. "I somewhat disagree with these critics because Basie had some great soloists during this period, guys like Joe Newman and Thad Jones on trumpets; Frank Wess on tenor sax; Marshall Royal on alto sax; Benny Powell and Al Grey on trombones; and Sonny Payne on drums. They may have been a little more derivative than earlier soloists, but that couldn't be helped."

Born on September 23, 1928, in Cincinnati, Ohio, Frank Benjamin Foster III grew up listening to all genres of music. His mother appreciated opera and would take her youngest son to all the major operas before he was ten years old, he said.

"I love classical music," he said.

Foster started listening to jazz at age eight when his fourteen-year-old brother played records made by the great Black jazz bands of the day: Basie, Ellington and Lunceford.

Taking up the clarinet at age eleven and then the alto saxophone at thirteen, Foster was enamored with the playing styles of alto saxophone giants Johnny Hodges, Benny Carter, Willie Smith and Earl Warren, he said.

"I really loved how Basie's lead alto saxist, Earl Warren played," Foster said.

By the time he was a senior in high school, Foster was leading his own twelve-piece band for which he did all the musical writing.

Around 1945, Foster became "under the influence" of bebop innovator and alto saxophonist Charlie Parker, he said.

"I was so much under his influence that I thought about switching to the tenor sax," he said.

He took up the tenor sax while attending the historically black Wilberforce University (now Central State University) in Ohio, because of the over-abundance of alto saxophonists at the school, Foster said.

Electing not to complete his senior year in college, Foster went to

Detroit in 1949 with trumpeter Snooky Young, who was then leading a ten-piece band.

While in Detroit, Foster's clarinet, tenor and alto saxophones were stolen and he ended up staying in the "Motor City" for two years. During that period, he was able to rub shoulders with such jazz notables as vibraphonist Milt Jackson, tenor saxist Wardell Gray, trumpeter Thad Jones and his younger brother, drummer Elvin Jones, he said.

With the Korean War raging in the Far East, Foster entered the Army in 1951 and was assigned to the Army band.

"Being in the Army band kept me involved in playing and writing music," Foster said.

While in Korea in February 1953, Foster got a hold of a *Down Beat Magazine* which contained a feature article about Count Basie and his orchestra. The article included inside photos of Eddie "Lockjaw" Davis and Paul Quinichette who were the tenor stars of that band.

"I thought to myself, 'I sure would love to be with that band!'" Foster said. "Little did I know that in five months time I would be!"

In June 1953, Foster was discharged from the Army. Returning to Detroit, he received word that Basie was looking for a saxophonist to replace Davis, who was leaving. Foster auditioned for Basie and in July he joined the band.

"It was somewhat like being in a dream," Foster said.

During the eleven years he spent with Basie (1953-1964), Foster helped to form the "new" Basie sound with firmly built structures that his arrangements provided. He also joined the pantheon of exciting saxophone soloists that has always been a Basie trademark.

The Basie band scored a big hit and critical acclaim on their 1955-56 Verve album, *April In Paris*. The title track from that album (and yes, that is the Count himself telling the band to take it "One more time!" and "One more once!" at the coda) has since become synonymous with Basie just as "One O'Clock Jump," "Jumpin' at the Woodside," "Tickle Toe," "Every Tub," "9:20 Special," and "Taxi War Dance" had fifteen to twenty years earlier.

The album's success was due to a large part because of Foster's arrangements. Along with "April in Paris," his composition of "Shiny Stockings" was one of the first classics of that new Basie style with its awe-inspiring brass ensemble with every nuance and every shake executed to perfection. Later, two sets of lyrics were written for the tune, one by Ella Fitzgerald and the other by Jon Hendricks.

Other striking Foster contributions to the Basie repertory have been "Down for the Count," "Blues Backstage," and "Blues in Hoss' Flat."

"For Count Basie to play an arrangement, it had to swing," Foster said. "It had to go down fairly easily. It didn't have to be easy music, but it did have to swing. You had to feel it. If you didn't feel it and if it didn't swing and if it was too busy, he wouldn't play it. He often used this expression with me: 'Foster, kid, don't put too many *Pregnant 19ths* in the arrangement.' A *Pregnant 19th,* by definition, is too many busy notes."

It was a lesson that Foster has appreciated from Basie and that he has taken with him throughout his musical career.

"It's letting simplicity play the biggest role in the arrangements that I write for the band," he said. "It's trying not to have too much 'busy-ness' going on."

Although there were many memorable performances played during his time with Basie, Foster did single out as special the Newport Jazz Festival gigs from the 1950s that featured guest soloists and Basie alumni Lester Young, Harry "Sweets" Edison and Roy Eldridge, and a command performance for Queen Elizabeth II of Great Britain and her royal family.

"I remember hearing Princess Margaret after the command performance telling Count Basie that he had a wonderful band," Foster said.

Since Foster was one of Basie's primary arrangers, he was in close proximity to his former boss to offer assessments about him as a bandleader, a musician, and as a person.

"As a leader, Basie was very easy to work for," Foster said. "All you had to do was to show up for work on time looking good, sober, and ready to perform."

Most people got the impression that Basie wasn't that great a pianist, but Foster disagrees.

"Basie was an accomplished pianist," he said. "He had more piano techniques than one might imagine. Although he had a simplistic style of playing, he was well-versed in the stride piano style. He knew what he wanted. He had musicians that were above him in knowledge of harmony and composition but he earned all our respect by the way he handled himself and the band.

"We (the members of the band) used to think that if someone who played a little more modern was at the keyboard, things would be better and we'd have a better time. We also noticed that when someone else sat down at the keyboard even though we'd admired their playing, it wasn't the same as having the 'Ol' Man' there. It was good, but it wasn't effective. We had people like Oscar Peterson, Erroll Garner and Nat Piece and none of them had the same impact playing with the orchestra as Basie had! We held Basie in eternal esteem and respect for that!"

As a person, Basie was quiet, laid back, and unassuming, Foster said.

"He was more easily approachable than might have been imagined," he said. "So many people were in awe of him that they didn't speak to him."

Amidst the constant traveling, Foster wasn't home enough to be with his first wife and two young children, so he left Basie to rectify that while musically branching out on his own.

"I needed to stay home more and to stretch out musically to get back into a modern jazz arena," Foster said. "I needed to get out of the 'Basie mold.' The Basie tradition was wonderful. I was a hard be-bopper and I wanted to get back into some more modern approaches to music."

During this period, Foster tried to establish a tradition of his own by becoming involved with recording and leading small groups as well as an eighteen-piece Big Band which became known in the early 1970s as "Frank Foster's Loud Minority." The band is active today.

"It's a modern band sound that is totally my concept," Foster said. "It touches on the Basie tradition but doesn't thrive on it. The element of swing is there all the time. It's more of a concert-type group than a dance band."

Although the band has never worked more than a dozen times per year and is not a traveling road band, it is a situation that Foster hopes to change, he said.

In addition to "Loud Miniority," Foster played with Elvin Jones from 1970 to 1972, and in 1972 and 1975, with the Thad Jones-Mel Lewis Big Band.

During the first half of the 1970s, Foster found himself emersed in the world of academia as an Artist-in-Residence at the New England Conservatiory of Music in Boston in 1971, and later that same year teaching for the New York City Public School System in District 5, Harlem, as part of a team of six professional musicians assigned to the Federal Government's Title I Program: Cultural Enrichment Through Music, Dance, and Song.

From 1972 to 1976, Foster was also a full-time Assistant Professor in the Black Studies Program at the State University of New York at Buffalo (SUNY).

The decade of the 1980s brought more changes to Foster's career as well as opportunities. In 1984, Count Basie died and the Basie Estate wanted the band to continue.

The band was first under the direction of tenor saxophonist Eric Dixon, a Basie alumnus. But the Basie Estate didn't care much for the idea of someone in the band directing and then sitting down to play. They wanted a leader who stood out in front. Trumpeter Thad Jones was then chosen because of his experience as co-leader of the contemporary Thad Jones-Mel Lewis Band.

Already stricken with cancer by the time he assumed the new directorship in February 1985, Jones resigned a year later after the traveling became too much for him.

Next in line for consideration for the musical directorship was Foster because he had bandleader experience and for his prolific Big Band arrangements both inside and outside the Basie band.

Foster agreed to front his former boss's band and stayed on to direct the Count Basie Orchestra for nine years, from 1986 to 1995.

As many of the original bandleaders passed away, their estates made provisions to keep their bands going, being often referred to as "ghost bands."

"When people refer to us as a 'ghost band,' I say, 'I don't see any ghosts up here,'" Foster quipped.

Being musical director of the Count Basie band had it's ups and downs, Foster said.

"The ups were I had excellent musicians and the band was tight," he said. "The down side was the people who didn't want to hear anything new. They just wanted to hear the old stuff. Being a creative artist, I have to continue creating new music. For someone to thwart that was very frustrating."

Under Foster's leadership, however, band personnel remained constant with very few turnovers.

"Most everyone in the band stayed," Foster said. "We'd have four chairs that would turn over on occasion - one of the tenor sax chairs, one each from the trombone and trumpet chairs, and the guitar chair."

Guitarist Freddie Green was the only original member of Basie's band who played under Foster's leadership, having started with the Count back in 1936. After Green's death in 1987, the band had a hard time finding someone who did what he did so well for over fifty years - playing rhythm on an unamplified guitar.

"No one really wanted to do what Freddie did," Foster said. "We went through a lot of guitarists."

After almost a decade at being the helm of the Basie band, Foster resigned for the same reason as he first resigned from Basie thirty-four years earlier - there was too much traveling involved, he said.

Trombonist Grover Mitchell is the current musical director of the Count Basie Orchestra.

Although he appreciated the opportunity to lead the Basie orchestra, the only bands Foster now wants to lead are his own, he said.

Besides "Loud Minority," Foster also heads up a ten-piece dance band called "Swing Plus" (a twelve-piece band), and a quintet, "Non-Electric Company" (a jazz quartet/quintet), that is strictly an acoustic jazz ensemble.

"Jazz is entirely improvisational and to a large degree, compositional,"

Foster said. "It's largely blues oriented and that's the feel that has to be imparted. It's also a form of music that I insist came out of the Black experience in this country. Jazz is democratic music because any race, nationality and sex can participate. I think it should always be with the acknowledgement that had it not been for the Black experience in America, we wouldn't have jazz as it is."

"Loud Minority" has recorded two albums: *Manhattan Fever* (1968) and *Shiny Stockings* (1977), both on the Denon label from Japan, and both of which have recently been made available in CD format in the U.S.

During the late 1970s and early 1980s, Foster also led a small group, "Living Color," which recorded an album for a Finnish record company called *Living Color: Twelve Shades of Black*.

A spin off from the "Living Color" group is "Swing Plus," which has not recorded as yet, Foster said. As a soloist and as a recording artist, Foster's music has grabbed more attention in Europe and Japan than in America.

In the early 1980s, Foster teamed up with fellow ex-Basie-ite saxophonist/flautist Frank Wess to record an album for Pablo Records entitled *Two Franks* and another album for the Concord Jazz label called *Frankly Speaking*.

Foster received two Grammy Awards: the first, for his Big Band arrangement of the Dianne Schuur composition "Deedles' Blues" ("Best Arrangement Accompanying a Vocal," 1987), and the second for his arrangement of guitarist/vocalist George Benson's composition, "Basie's Bag" ("Best Jazz Instrumental Performance, Big Band," 1990). His other Grammy nomination was for his Big Band arrangement of Charles Trenet's composition "Beyond the Sea."

In 1983, Dizzy Gillespie personally commissioned Foster to orchestrate one of the jazz icon's compositions, "Con Alma," for a scheduled performance and recording with The London Philharmonic Orchestra directed by Robert Farnon.

In 1987, Foster was awarded an honorary doctorate by Central State University in Wilberforce, Ohio. He also composed and orchestrated material for The Carnegie Hall Jazz Ensemble, The Detroit Civic Symphony Orchestra, The Ithaca College Jazz Ensemble, The Jazzmobile Corporation of New York City, the Lincoln Center Jazz Orchestra, The Malaysia Symphony Orchestra, The Metropole Orchestra of Hilverum, Netherlands, and the Thad-Jones-Mel Lewis Orchestra.

On June 24 of this year, the two Franks (Foster and Wess) will unite once again, backed by a sextet, at the Baltimore Jazz Society Festival in Baltimore, Maryland.

Last month, Foster performed with a local quartet during a four-day stay in Israel and has also toured this year in Canada, Australia, and along the East Coast in the U.S.

Foster and his second wife and manager, Cecilia, run their own music publication business called "Swing That Music." They have a son and daughter together along with two grandsons. Foster has two sons from his previous marriage as well as two grandsons.

"I distribute my own Big Band charts and arrangements," Foster said. "Most of these charts were performed and recorded by the Count Basie Orchestra. Of the fifty or so arrangements I sell, some are Basie, some are post-Basie. It's classic jazz for discerning listeners."

Most orders have been for college ensembles, although some charts have been purchased by private groups, Foster said.

Even at age 71, Foster still maintains a clear and vibrant artistic vision for himself.

"I want to be more active as a writer," he said. "As a player, I want to contribute to my own genre. I don't fancy myself as one of the foremost players of the scene today. I just want to be a stylist as a player. I'm an advanced post hard bop player. I want to carry the Big Band into the twenty-first century with a 'Fosterian' concept, that is, my own idea of what a Big Band should sound like in this day and age. That sound should be characterized by heavy activity with the brass ensemble. Eighty percent should swing and twenty percent could be a non-rhythmic concertized presentation. I want the swinging rhythm there with the brass shouting contemporary phrases and sophisticated harmonies, but not into the realm of the avant-garde."

Even though Foster has been and continues to be a tenor saxophone stylist, it is in the area of Big Band arranging where he feels he has made a lasting contribution, he said.

"I don't think I've contributed as a player in an innovative manner because I'm not an innovator," Foster said. "I have contributed to the Count Basie tradition of the 1950s and 1960s. I think I'm a damn good arranger and bandleader who hasn't yet gotten his big moment of glory. I'm still looking to work my own band to force my style on the world, whatever part of the world is ready for it! I've been doing this for over fifty years and I have not become a major force in the world of band leadership. I'm just angry enough to stick around until it happens!"

For information concerning "Swing That Music," write to: Swing That Music 1706 Woodgrove Street Chesapeake, VA 23320 (757) 436-0520 FAX (757) 312-8188 Toll Free Number: 1- 877-THE BAND

** Coda - Here is an update on Frank Foster since this article was published.

In 2002, the National Endowment for the Arts presented Frank Foster with its NEA Jazz Masters Award, the highest honor in jazz.

Foster was commissioned by The Harpers Ferry Historical Association of West Virginia to compose a jazz suite of ten to fifteen minutes' duration in connection with the Niagara Movement, relating to John Brown's famous raid on Harpers Ferry. The suite was performed by the Count Basie Orchestra at Harpers Ferry as part of the three-day Niagara Movement celebration in August 2006.

Jazz at Lincoln Center commissioned Foster to compose and arrange music for the Lincoln Center Jazz Orchestra, directed by Wynton Marsalis, for performances on March 13–15, 2008, with "A Man and a Woman" as the theme. Foster wrote the words, music, and orchestrations for "I Love You (Based on Your Availability)" and "Romance Without Substance is a Nuisance," both performed by vocalists Dennis Rowland and Marlena Shaw.

When the Count Basie Orchestra directed by Grover Mitchell was enlisted for Tony Bennett's 2008 album, *A Swingin' Christmas*, Foster was tapped to do the arranging duties.

On March 20, 2009, the Chicago Jazz Ensemble, directed by Jon Faddis, performed a three-part suite by Foster titled "Chi-Town is My Town and My Town's No Shy Town" at the Harris Theater in Chicago.

In 2009, Foster selected The Jazz Archive at Duke University to be the home for his numerous compositions, arrangements, and personal papers.

As a champion for humanitarian causes, Foster became a great supporter of The Jazz Foundation of America in their mission to save the homes and the lives of America's elderly jazz and blues musicians including musicians who survived Hurricane Katrina. After receiving help from the Jazz Foundation, he supported the cause by performing in their Annual Benefit Concert "A Great Night in Harlem" in 2008. He donated his gold-plated tenor sax to be auctioned by the Jazz Foundation of America, the proceeds of which went to support the foundation's non-profit programs, especially working gigs and educational programs for victims of hurricane Katrina in New Orleans and the Gulf Coast.

Frank Foster suffered a stroke in 2001 that impaired his left side to the extent that he could no could no longer play the saxophone. After continuing to lead the "Loud Minority" on limited engagements for much of the 2000s, he turned his leadership responsibilities for the band over to trumpeter Cecil Bridgewater, a prominent New York City jazz musician.

Until his death, Foster continued composing and arranging at his home in Chesapeake, Virginia, where he resided with his wife and personal manager of nearly forty-five years, Cecilia Foster. He died of kidney failure on July 26, 2011. He was 82.

Along with his wife, Foster is also survived by two children from their marriage, Frank Foster IV and Andrea Jardis Innis; two sons from his first marriage, Anthony and Donald; and six grandchildren.

Foster wrote his candid musical story in a 256-page book, *A Jazz Master: Frank Foster, An Autobiography*, published posthumously by PFDGS Media (2014). It was his final request to his wife to make certain that his book was published after his death. Foster's book can be purchased at www.Amazon.com

Frank Foster blowing his tenor sax just prior to his stroke in 2001.

Frank Foster performing in concert in the early 1990s.

Frank Foster blowing up a storm.

The front cover to Frank Foster's book, *A Jazz Master: Frank Foster, An Autobiography*, published posthumously in 2014 by PFDGS Media.

Flyin' Home (To Idaho)

Vibes Great Lionel Hampton Keeps The Music Going In His Life With Namesake Jazz Fest

The following article on Lionel Hampton was originally published in the February 2001 issue of Jazz Connection Magazine.

The way vibraphone great Lionel Hampton sees it, in order for good jazz to be good it has to have a good beat, good ideas, and it has to swing.

"It has to have heart, feeling and a lot of soul," said Hampton via telephone last month from his apartment in New York City. "That's the lesson that has been handed down in music. It's got to swing."

Now at age 92, and coupled with a number of strokes that has left his speech slurred, his hearing diminished and his stride a bit slower, Hampton continues to produce magical and vibrant jazz especially when the month of February rolls around. That's when he takes to the stage to host his Lionel Hampton Jazz Festival at the University of Idaho at Moscow, Idaho.

Now in it's 34th year, the four-day Fest (it's the first jazz festival ever named after a jazz musician and the first jazz festival ever named after an African-American) is a combination of entertainment and education. It boasts a roster of the world's most revered jazz masters performing in the University of Idaho's vast Kibbie Dome. This year's gala takes place February 21-24, 2001. Among the prestigious musicians performing will be Hank Jones, piano; Ray Brown and Christian McBride on bass; Herb

Ellis and Russell Malone, guitar; Benny Golson, Joe Lovano and Paquito D'Rivera, saxophone; Clark Terry, trumpet; Bill Watrous and Carl Fontana, trombone; Ben Riley, drums; and Nancy Wilson, Lou Rawls, and Freddy Cole, vocals.

The festival is also a showcase of performance competitions for students from elementary through college level. Each performance is judged by leading jazz educators who provide immediate feedback. The winners have the opportunity to perform in special winners' concerts.

In addition, jazz musicians share their expertise in more than thirty workshops. Each day is made complete by an evening concert led by Hampton and these all-star musicians. Because of the wide availability of musical education in schools, Hampton admitted that the caliber of musicianship is at a higher level today than at any time during the previous seven decades.

"It all comes from the heart," he said.

In addition, the Lionel Hampton Jazz Festival brings visiting jazz musicians to more than twenty elementary schools throughout the region. Each presentation consists of musical numbers, information about jazz, and demonstrations of jazz techniques. The program brings jazz to children who might otherwise not have a chance to participate in the festival.

"Lionel is like Louis Armstrong," said jazz trumpeter Freddie Hubbard, as quoted in a previously published article. Hubbard got his first horn when Hampton donated instruments to his drum and bugle corps in Indianapolis. "He's someone who brought music to the people."

And it's the music that keeps Hampton going. When sitting alone, he appears to be a tired, old man. But when the music plays, a metamorphosis occurs. The batteries are recharged and he becomes rejuvenated with the energy of a young man.

"Whenever I play, I'm looking for new things, for surprises," Hampton said.

One of the more exciting and honored surprises Hampton has experienced in his life was in 1987 when the University of Idaho School of Music was renamed to the Lionel Hampton School of Music. Like the festival that bears his name, this is the first school of music named after a jazz musician and the first school of music ever named after an African-American. The school was named to honor Hampton and his considerable contributions to jazz and American culture.

The school is well known for outstanding education in music theory, composition, history and performance of all genres.

"We have great teachers at the Lionel Hampton School of Music," Hampton proudly said. "The teachers insist students know their instrument, know harmony and scales, things like that. These help make a person a better musician."

Born on April 20, 1908 in Birmingham, Alabama, Hampton grew up in Kenosha, Wisconsin, and began his career as a drummer in Chicago.

His first teachers were the Dominican Sisters at the Holy Rosary Academy. By the time he was 20, he was living in Culver City, California, and working in clubs and recording studios.

During a 1930 session he met and recorded with Louis Armstrong, who encouraged him to change instruments that forever altered the course of jazz. During a session break, Armstrong pointed to a set of vibes at the back of the studio and asked Hampton if he knew how to play them.

Taking up the challenge, Hampton, who was well-schooled in his keyboard studies, picked up the mallets and said he'd give it a go. He played Armstrong's "Cornet Chop Suey."

Armstrong was so amazed that he wanted Hampton to play the vibes on the next tune they were to record. That tune was Eubie Blake's "Memories of You." It became a tremendous hit for Armstrong and the young Hampton and has remained a classic throughout the years.

Hampton was a respected name among the jazz community appearing on many recording dates with such immortal artists as Coleman Hawkins, Benny Carter, Barney Bigard and Jack Teagarden. He also was a member of the Les Hite band in the early 1930s, playing drums.

But it wasn't until 1936 when he was hired by clarinet-playing bandleader Benny Goodman that Hampton was brought to national prominence.

Goodman heard Hampton for the first time in person at the Paradise

Club in Los Angeles and hired him on the spot. Goodman had a trio within his Big Band which featured Goodman, Teddy Wilson on piano and Gene Krupa on drums. The trio quickly became a quartet, with the addition of Hampton on the vibes.

"Next thing you know, I was on stage jamming with these great musicians," Hampton recalled. "That's one session I'll never forget."

The Benny Goodman Quartet made immediate musical history, not only for the brilliant music they produced, but because they were the first racially integrated group of jazz musicians to perform publicly.

"It helped open new lines between blacks and whites," Hampton said. "It even helped pave the way, I think, for Jackie Robinson to break the color barrier in professional sports."

While with Goodman, Hampton participated in the first-ever jazz concert given at Carnegie Hall on January 16, 1938. He, along with vocalist Martha Tilton and trumpeter Chris Griffin, are the three surviving Goodman band members members from that historic concert.

Among the classics the Benny Goodman Quartet recorded were "Moonglow" (August 21, 1936); "Avalon" (July 30, 1937); "Stompin' at the Savoy (December 2, 1936); and "Vibraphone Blues" (August 26, 1936, with vocal by Hampton).

Hampton now stands alone as the only living member of that famed BG Quartet. Krupa was the first member to pass away in October 1973, with Goodman and Wilson both following in 1986.

After Krupa and Wilson left to form their own bands, Hampton stayed with Goodman as a featured performer with the Benny Goodman Sextet, which also included Charlie Christian on guitar; Fletcher Henderson and/or Johnny Guarnieri on piano; Artie Bernstein on bass; and Nick Fatool on drums. The Sextet performed at Goodman's second Carnegie Hall appearance on October 6, 1939, as part of John Hammond's "Spirituals to Swing Concert."

In 1937, Hampton organized for RCA-Victor some superb recording groups that included jazz stars such as Krupa, Harry James, Jonah Jones, Charlie Christian, Ziggy Elman, Nat "King" Cole.

One spectacular session, on September 11, 1939, Hampton put together the sax team of Benny Carter, Coleman Hawkins, Chu Berry and Ben Webster along with trumpeter Dizzy Gillespie, guitarist Charlie Christian, bassist Milt Hinton, and drummer Cozy Cole to cut four sides: "When Lights Are Low," "One Sweet Letter From You (vocal by Hampton)," "Hot Mallets," and "Early Session Hop."

Feeling the need to branch out on his own, Hampton left Goodman to form his own action-packed band in 1940. Throughout its career the band reflected its leader's personality - fun, moving, high-energy and always swinging.

The release of a succession of highly successful records under his own name soon followed including "On the Sunny Side of the Street" (on which he sang as well as played vibes, complimented by Johnny Hodges' stirring alto sax), "Central Avenue Breakdown" (May 10, 1940, with the Nat "King" Cole Trio, on which he played piano with two fingers, using them as if they were vibes mallets), "Jack the Bellboy" (May 10, 1940, playing drums with the Nat "King" Cole Trio).

Hampton flew to the top of the charts with his theme song, "Flying Home" (May 26, 1942, with its classic tenlor sax solo by a young Illinois Jacquet) and "Hamp's Boogie Woogie" in 1943.

Hampton employed a phenomenal array of sidemen, literally a *Who's Who* in jazz, who got their start with the vibes great. Among these were Illinois Jacquet, Dexter Gordon, Quincy Jones, Wes Montgomery, Clark Terry, Cat Anderson, Charles Mingus, Lucky Thompson, Ernie Royal, Joe Newman, Art Farmer, Benny Golson, Clifford Brown and Fat Navarro. Also, among his protégés were singers Dinah Washington (who was discovered and named by Hampton), Joe Williams, Betty Carter and Aretha Franklin.

In 1943, Hamps band sported Nat "King" Cole on jazz piano, and in that same year made some recordings with crooner Bing Crosby.

An accomplished composer, Hampton co-wrote "Flying Home," with

Benny Goodman, and the ballad, "Midnight Sun," with Sonny Burke and Johnny Mercer based on the chords of "How High the Moon."

He also composed two major symphonic works, *King David Suite* and *Blues Suite*, which have been performed often by leading philharmonic orchestra throughout the world.

Hampton also appeared as himself in a number of movies and documentaries including *Hollywood Hotel* (1937) as a member of the Benny Goodman Quartet; *A Song is Born* (1948); *The Benny Goodman Story* (1955); and *Benny Goodman: Adventures in the Kingdom of Swing* (1993).

In addition to his musical contributions, Hampton's philanthropic endeavors are equally vast, devoting much time and energy to public service projects outside the entertainment field. A staunch supporter of public housing, he developed the Lionel Hampton Houses in the early 1970s in uptown New York and shortly thereafter built the Gladys Hampton Houses, named after his late wife, who died in 1971. The Hampton's were married for 35 years and had no children.

Currently, Hampton is active in the planning stages of developing his "dream," as he calls it- the Lionel Hampton Institute For Music in Central Harlem - a university where "young black kids can learn to be doctors, lawyers, IBM technicians and, if they desire, musicians," he said.

In 1986, Hampton formed the Lionel Hampton Jazz Endowment Fund which seeks to help underprivileged people. The program was started after Hampton gave a sold-out concert at New York's Lincoln Center, collecting over $100,000 in receipts for the evening.

A few days later, he was invited to perform at the White House for then President Ronald Reagan. He asked the President what he should do with the money. President Reagan suggested to Hampton that he keep it to start an endowment.

"That's how it got started," Hampton said. "We even had the President's backing."

The Endowment Fund is designed to help those people who are financially in need, whether it be senior citizens needing food and clothing or an unwed mother seeking affordable housing, Hampton said. Needs are determined by Board members who review every case. If a case warrants Board approval, financial assistance is granted.

"Anytime you can help people with money, that's the highest good," Hampton said. "The Endowment Fund works on the same principle as going to the bank and getting a loan. It's something that will help people for life."

Hampton also makes time to serve as Honorary Chairman of the Jazz Foundation of America's Musicians' Emergency Fund, a newly-formed volunteer organization dedicated to aiding jazz musicians who have fallen on hard times.

In addition to humanitarian endeavors, Hampton is also a dedicated supporter of political causes. For years he has worked and contributed money on behalf of Republican presidential candidates. He is also a big backer of New York Mayor Rudolph Giuliani and played at the mayor's inaugural bash. He has been an honored guest at the White House many dozens of times and has performed there frequently. Hampton had been a regular guest of former President Bill Clinton, a jazz enthusiast.

Wishing to celebrate Hampton's 90th birthday is grand style, President Clinton invited the jazz giant and his New York Big Band for a special appearance in the East Room of the White House with an audience of one hundred fifty Washington friends and notables. The ceremony was also designed to celebrate Hampton's seven decades of monumental contributions to jazz music.

With the strains of "Hail to the Chief" echoing throughout the magnificent East Room, the President and First Lady, Hillary Rodham Clinton, entered the room. Mrs. Clinton stood to deliver a long and impassioned speech addressed to Hampton thanking him for his years of music beloved by the world and the White House's intent to broaden the education of jazz in schools throughout the U.S.

Hampton and the band swung into "Hamp's Boogie Woogie" and several other chandelier-shaking numbers, ending with his signature tune, "Flying Home."

Following "Flying Home," Hampton announced that "One of the greatest saxophone players in the world happens to be in our audience. May I ask him to rise?"

Then, Hamp implored, "Mr. President, could I ask you to come up on stage and play a number with my band?"

The East Room resounded with thunderous applause as President Clinton stood up and stepped on the stage and asked to borrow a saxophone from one of Hampton's sidemen, whispered to Hampton who then lifted his hands to conduct as the President began a lyrical rendition of "My Funny Valentine." The President's tone was sure, clear and moving.

Hampton has received innumerable prestigious awards over the years. Among those he is most proud are the title Official American Goodwill Ambassador, bestowed by presidents Dwight Eisenhower and Richard Nixon, the Papal Medal from Pope Paul VI, eighteen Honorary Doctorates from universities, the Gold Medal of Paris, France's highest cultural award, and a "star" on the Hollywood Walk of Fame.

In 1992, he received the highly-coveted Kennedy Center Honors Award, shared with Mstislav Rostropovich, Paul Taylor, Joanne Woodward, Paul Newman and Ginger Rogers.

In January 1997, he received The National Medal of the Arts at the White House from the Clintons.

Hampton's stateside and overseas tours often feature the exciting seventeen-piece Lionel Hampton New York Big Band, considered by many critics to be the best Big Band of its type in the world. How does this band measure up to some of the more stellar bands he's led from the 1940s?

"We have a great saxophone section and brass section," Hampton said. "It's up to you to judge."

Hampton also frequently appears as leader and soloist with his eight-piece group of renowned jazz musicians known as the Golden Men of Jazz, which includes Hank Jones, piano; Clark Terry and Harry "Sweets" Edison, trumpets; Al Grey, trombone; Buddy Tate and James Moody on saxophones; Milt Hinton, bass; and Grady Tate, drums.

Hampton's own long-time record label, Glad-Hamp Records, has released many dozens of recordings. Recent discs on the Telarc label include *Lionel Hampton and the Golden Men of Jazz - Live at the Blue Note* (1991) and *Lionel Hampton and the Golden Men of Jazz - Just Jazz - Live at the Blue Note* (1992).

On the MoJazz label, he recorded *For the Love of Music* in 1995. Appearing with Hampton on this album are Joshua Redman, Dianne Reeves, Chaka Khan, Tito Puente, and Stevie Wonder, among others. The album contains an eclectic mix of pop and straight ahead jazz in which Hampton dives into hip-hop grooves without compromising his improvisational standards.

"It's something different," Hampton said. "There's always something new in jazz. It helps keep me young."

The album is also a testament to Hampton's versatility and adaptability as an artist. While many artists from the Swing Era couldn't make the transition to the new jazz idiom of bop, Hampton adapted better than most and it kept his bands from going out of style. Years later in the early 1970s, he also dabbled with light rock.

"I've never feared changes in jazz," he said. "That's what jazz is about. I always keep my ears and my heart open. As long as I can feel the beat, it's good."

By keeping his ears and heart open, are some of the ways Hampton renews himself, he said.

"I look for different sounds," he said. "I just pick out the sounds that I think sound the best."

Besides maintaining his artistic integrity, Hampton remains extremely popular as an entertainer. That, he said, is the secret of keeping things in balance.

"I'm just a go-getter!" he said with a laugh. "There are a lot of good musicians, but they are not entertainers. Showmanship is important. Getting the audience involved is the key. My band was criticized as being a 'circus.' All that jive came from us. Now others are doing it."

In March 1995, Lionel Hampton suffered a mild stroke and was hospitalized for ten days. He practiced a diligent program of physical therapy and resumed his career in short order.

In January 1997, a vicious fire engulfed his apartment and destroyed everything he owned, including manuscripts, recordings, photographs, his piano and his vibes. Despite these set backs, Hampton was determined to keep the music going, he said.

His deep faith in God, his indomitable self-determination and his contagious optimism carried him through the rough times. "I have a good background," he said with a laugh.

It may be argued that such fortitude has more to do more with survival than with anything else. Survival has been very much on our minds recently. The losses of Tex Beneke and Tito Puente last May and more recently, Les Brown last month, are reminders that the ranks of Big Band Era leaders are thinning.

When asked if he considers himself a survivor as a bandleader, Hampton replied, "I don't want to go into that."

With a long and distinguished musical career, the "King of the Vibraphone" has pretty much seen it all.

So, with that in mind, does he feel there is anything new in jazz today?

"It seems to be going back to the days when I started," Hampton replied. "That's good."

Certainly Lionel Hampton is leaving his personal legacy in jazz, pointing to the jazz festival that bears his name, he said.

"If we can help pass on the music to kids, what better legacy is there than that?" he quipped. "And," he added humorously, "I hope they say about me that he's as good now as he was when he was 17."

There's no debating as to whether Hampton's fire and passion for the music still burns bright or whether he still swings hard. *It* does and *he* does.

"I just try to play like hell," he said.

** Coda - Here is an update on Lionel Hampton since this article was published.

Lionel Hampton died of heart failure at Mount Sinai Medical Center in New York on August 31, 2002. He was 94.

He is interred at Woodlawn Cemetery, the Bronx, New York City, immediately adjacent to both Miles Davis and Duke Ellington's graves. His funeral was held on September 7, 2002, and featured a performance by Wynton Marsalis and David Ostwald's Gully Low Jazz Band at Riverside Church in Manhattan. The procession began at the Cotton Club in Harlem.

Lionel Hampton, 79, with his Big Band performing at Pepperdine University, Malibu, California, on October 22, 1987.
– *Photo by Stephen Fratallone*

Lionel Hampton performing with an eight-piece band on the Tomorrowland Stage at Disneyland in May 1972. – *Photos by Stephen Fratallone*

An energetic Lionel Hampton, 77, with his vibes at Disneyland on August 11, 1985. – *Photo by Stephen Fratallone*

Lionel Hampton, 77, fronting his Big Band on the Plaza Garden Stage at Disneyland on August 11, 1985. – *Photos by Stephen Fratallone*

- Photo by Stephen Fratallone

The Pied Piper of Jazz

Famed Bandleader Woody Herman Honored By Tributes From Fans and Friends

The following article on Woody Herman was originally published in the 1999 issue of Jazz Connection Magazine. Material was republished from various articles written by the author from The Simi Valley (CA) Enterprise and The Fillmore (CA) Herald.

The name of Woody Herman means many things to many people but the common denominator of those who have known and worked with the celebrated bandleader can be summed up in one word: love.

"Everybody loves him," said crooner Tony Bennett. "He's the father of all great American musicians of our time."

Bennett, along with a host of many of Herman's friends and fans, paid tribute to the ailing jazz great at the Wadsworth Theatre in West Los Angeles on Friday, October 23, 1987. In addition to being a concert to honor "The Woodchopper," it was a benefit to help pay some of Herman's health bills.

Sponsored by radio station KKGO-FM, the concert was broadcast live. Although not present at the affair, it was reported that Herman was listening to that broadcast from his bed at Cedar Sinai Medical Center in Los Angeles.

The famed clarinetist and jazz innovator has been in failing health in recent months and has been hospitalized since October 1, suffering from congestive heart failure, emphysema and pnuemonia.

The idea for the tribute concert was the brain child of KKGO-FM station owner Saul Levine after he had heard about Herman's health issues and poor economic situation.

"Herman epitomizes the Big Band Era," Levine said. "As a jazz station, we've been playing his music for twenty-eight years."

The radio station has also initiated the Woody Herman Tribute Trust Fund, which according to Levine, has raised about $35,000.

"The money collected goes to offset Herman's medical expenses," said Linda Davis, Director of Marketing and Promotion at KKGO-FM. "All the net proceeds from the concert goes directly to the trust fund."

The trust fund was established to help musicians who face situations similar to that of Herman's.

The response was tremendous as organizers of the event raised $50,000 from ticket sales and special tribute posters alone to the near-sellout crowd – not to mention the labor of love given by the performers.

In addition to Bennett, other headliners who performed gratis were Rosemary Clooney, Dudley Moore, Doc Severinsen and *The Tonight Show* Orchestra, Mary Ann McCall, one of Herman's early band vocalists, Maxene Andrews, one-third of the famed Andrews Sisters singing trio, and comics John Byner and Pete Barbutti. Also appearing were a number of notable musicians who have "graduated" through the ranks of the Herman "Herd," including bassist Chubby Jackson, pianist Nat Pierce, arranger Ralph Burns, trumpeters Pete Candoli and Shorty Rogers, and saxophonist Dick Hafer.

Pierce and Rogers led the Herman alumni band on a number of tunes synonymous with the Herman library, including "Woodchopper's Ball," "Blue Flame," "Four Brothers," Early Autumn," and "The Good Earth."

"I've always admired Woody and I am very happy to do something for him," said comedian Dudley Moore, explaining his presence at the tributre concert. "I've followed him over the years and he has been a great source of inspiration."

Herman's inspiration was present in Moore's performance, as the British comic demonstrated his talents as an accomplished pianist.

"I performed on the same bill with Woody and Mel Tormé during the late 1960s in New York," said comedian John Byner. "Woody has a big heart and a big soul. He's a wonderful guy."

"People who know him will never have a bad word to say about him," said Nat Pierce, Herman's friend and colleague for thirty-six years. "None of us who ever played with him never felt we were actually working *for* him. It was more like we were working *with* him. He appreciated what we were doing and he let us know it. And the guys appreciated and respected him, so they worked all the harder."

"I think of how much he did for me and how very good he was to me," said vocalist Mary Ann McCall. "Woody is like a brother to me and we are very close. We always have been. His was the first band I ever sang with ("The Band That Played the Blues," during the mid-1930s) and he gave me a chance to sing the way I wanted to sing. That was just beautiful to me."

"Woody has always been like my daddy and whatever little reputation I've gained is through his efforts," commented Chubby Jackson, who was Herman's enthusiastic bassist with the First Herd from 1944 to 1946. "He let me do what I wanted to do. I never felt like I was working for the guy. That's the way the whole band felt. Woody's a natural friend."

"Somebody asked me in an interview recently what I thought about the fact that Woody Herman is destitute," said Tony Bennett. "I said, 'He's not destitute. Every musician in the world loves him. If you are talking bucks, that's one thing, but knowing that your peers adore you is a pretty good way to live.'"

Last month, the seventy-four-year-old Herman was threaten with eviction from his Hollywood Hills home for non-payment of rent. In 1985, landlord Willian Little purchased the jazz man's home in an Internal Revenue Service auction. After a court hearing, Herman was given permission to remain in the residence, at which time KKGO-FM agreed to pay Herman's back rent of about $4,600.

There's a bill now in Congress for Herman's financial relief from the IRS, which was introduced on September 15 (1987), by Rep. John Conyers Jr., D-Michigan.

"The IRS should make an exception to forget that tax problem," Bennett said.

Whether or not Congress is willing to forget Herman's debt remains to be seen, but the Wadsworth Theatre celebration proved that unlike old soldiers, old bandleaders are not forgotten.

"I'm overwhelmed by the support shown by the many fans and celebrities here tonight. It's beautiful," said the bandleader's daughter, Ingrid Herman-Reese.

"If Woody could be here tonight, I think he would be delighted that everybody is rooting for him," Moore said.

Woodrow Charles Thomas Herman was born on May 16, 1913, in Milwaukee, Wisconsin, the only child to Otto and Martha (Bartoszewicz). His father, a successful shoemaker and a lover of show business, was American-born German and his mother was born in Poland who immigrated to America as an infant with her family.

Through the coaching of his father, the young Herman began his show business career at age six as part of a touring kiddie revue. Three years later, he was a child prodigy clarinet player, singer, and tap dancer in adult vaudeville shows and was billed as "The Boy Wonder of the Clarinet."

Herman also took up playing the alto saxophone during this time as his jazz education expanded by listening to such "hot" players as C-Melody saxophonist Franke Trumbauer, Joe "King" Oliver's band featuring Louis Armstrong, and the Mound City Blue Blowers led by Red McKenzie. Featured players in this band included Coleman Hawkins, Jack Reagarden, Eddie Condon, Gene Krupa, Muggsy Spanier, Jimmy Dorsey, Pee Wee Russell, and Glenn Miller.

In his sophomore year at St. John's Cathedral High School, Herman joined the Joe Lichter band out of Chicago whose band was working at a Milwaukee ballroom. At age seventeen, Herman dropped out of school and went on the road with Tom Gerun's band from San Francisco. Another member of the sax section was Al Morris from Oakland, California, who later became a singer and called himself Tony Martin.

While the band was playing in San Francisco, the seventeen-year-old Herman met Charolette Neste, a stunning redhead, also seventeen, who was dancing in a musical revue. For six years they kept a romance going, much of it by telephone and letters; they were married, when they both were 23, on September 27, 1936, just weeks before he started his band. On September 3, 1941, their only child, Ingrid, was born.

After leaving Gerun, Herman had brief stints with the Harry Sosnick and Gus Arnheim outfits before joining Isham Jones in 1934, who is best known as a composer ("It Had to Be You," "I'll See You in My Dreams," "The One I Love Belongs to Somebody Else," "There Is No Greater Greater Love," "Swinging Down the Lane," and "On the Alamo") and leader of an excellent dance band.

When Jones decided to retire two years later because off ill health, Herman and several other key mermbers formed a cooperative orchestra in which all owned stock. Herman became leader because of his show-business personality. The new outfit was christened as "The Band That Plays the Blues," first appearing at Brooklyn Roseland Ballroom at Fulton and Flatbush avenues on the night of November 3, 1936, when President Franklin D. Roosevelt was elected to a second term.

From that point on, Heman began a jazz legacy that blossomed. The band's first pair of recordings on the Decca label came on November 6, 1936, with "Wintertime Dreams" and "Someone to Care for Me" (both vocals by Herman). Personnel in that band included Clarence Willard and Kermit Simmons, trumpets; Neal Reid, trombone; Joe Bishop, flugelhorn; Murray Williams and Don Watt, alto saxes; Saxie Mansfield and Bruce Wilkins, tenor saxes; Nick Hupfer, violin; Horace Diaz, piano; Chick Reeves, guitar; Walt Yoder, bass; and left-handed drummer Frank Carlson.

The band steadily progressed into popularity. Mary Martin sang with the band and waxed a number of tunes: "Who'll Buy My Violets" and "Listen to the Mockingbird" (December 22, 1938); and "The Maids of Cadiz" and "Il Bacio" (January 24, 1939). That same day The Band That Plays the Blues backed up the Andrews Sisters on their recording for Decca on "Begin the Beguine." Less than three months later, Herman would record what would be the biggest hit he ever had with "Woodchopper's Ball" (April 12, 1939).

In his autobiography, *The Woodchopper's Ball*, Herman recounts how his hit song got its name: "Walt Yoder come up with the title. It happened one day after he had gone to see the Sportsmen's Show at the Boston Garden. While wondering around there, he came upon a group of woodchopper's competing against the clock for prizes. That's all there was to it. And our most famous head arrangement got its name."

On the flip side of "Woodchopper's Ball" featured Mary Ann McCall on her first outing with the band, singing "Big-Wig in the Wigwam." McCall stayed with Herman through the end of 1939, before singing with Charlie Barnet's band. She returned to the Herman band in late 1945, and married Herman tenor man Al Cohn in 1949.

While the band retained a steady personnel, the addition of other key players added more punch to the band's sound. Joining the band during this period was Tommy Linehan, piano; Hy White, guitar; and Cappy Lewis and Steady Nelson, trumpets; and Jiggs Noble, Gordon Jenkins, Nick Harper, along with Joe Bishop sharing the arranging duties.

After "Woodchopper's Ball," the Herman band recorded other hit tunes with "Blues on Parade" (December 13, 1939); "Golden Wedding" (December 27, 1940); "Blue Flame" (February 13, 1941, the band's theme song); "Bishop's Blues" and "Woodsheddin' With Woody" (both on August 21, 1941); "Blues in the Night" (November 10, 1941, vocal by Herman); "Down Under" (July 24, 1942); and "Who Dat Up Der?" (November 17,1943, vocal by Herman), which became an overnight success.

In 1938, Herman organized a small six-piece jazz ensemble from his big band – a band-within-a- band - calling themselves "Woody Herman and His Woodchoppers." Personnel included Herman, clarinet and vocals; Joe Bishop, flugelhorn; Tommy Linehan, piano; Hy White, guitar; Walt Yoder, bass; and Frank Carlson, drums. The group waxed just a handful of tunes.

By 1940, Herman organized another small group called "Woody Herman and His Four Chips," comprised of Herman, Linehan, White, Yoder, and Carlson. This group documented four tunes during this period: "Chips' Boogie Woogie" and "Chips' Blues" (both on September 9, 1940); "Elise" (August 28, 1941); and "Yardbird Shuffle" (September 10, 1941).

On February 13, 1941, "Woody Herman and His Woodchoppers" were back in the Decca recording studios with "South" and "Fan It" (vocal by Herman). Herman and the rhythm section remained the same, but trumpeter Cappy Lewis and trombonist Neal Reid were added to the ensemble. Other recordings this group made include "Too Late" and "Ft. Worth Jail" (both on August 28, 1941, both vocals by Herman); "Three Little Sisters"(April 23, 1942, vocal by Herman); and the ever-popular "Deep in the Heart of Texas" (January 18, 1942, vocal by Bing Crosby).

With America entrenched in a world war and many musicians getting drafted and a musicians' union strike in full swing, Herman looked during this transitional period to reorganize his "Band That Plays the Blues" into something different, something more powerful and pulsating.

Beginning in 1944, Herman acquired some superb young musicians that kept the quality of music high: Flip Phillips on tenor sax; John LaPorta, alto sax; Chubby Jackson, bass; Ralph Burns, piano and arranger; Neal Hefti, Ray Wetzel, Pete and Conte Candoli, Sonny Berman, Carl "Bama" Warwick, trumpets; Bill Harris, trombone; Billy Bauer, guitar; Majorie Hyames and later Red Norvo on vibraphone; and Davey Tough, and later Don Lamond, drums. Frances Wayne was the band's girl singer, who later married Neal Hefti.

Herman's new band was given the moniker of "Woody Herman's Thundering Herd" by jazz critic George T. Simon. The name fit as the band "thundered" as one of the most exciting and inventive big bands with its exuberant and talented musicians playing modern, swinging scores, many written by arrangers Ralph Burns and Neal Hefti. Burns was Herman's piano player as well as a composer-arranger. Hefti was a trumpet player. Both were credited by Herman with being "as much responsible for our sound as anyone at that time."

Hit after hit soon followed on Columbia Records with "Apple Honey" (February 19, 1945); "Caldonia" (February 26, 1945); "Northwest Passage" and "Goosey Gander" (both on March 1, 1945); "The Good Earth" (August 10, 1945); "Bijou" (August 20, 1945); "Your Father's Moustache" (September 5, 1945); "Wildroot" (November 16, 1945), a Neal Hefti composition named for Herman's radio sponsor; and "Blowin' Up a Storm" (December 10, 1945).

While the band could swing, it could also play ballads with tenderness and warmth as on Frances Wayne's showcase tunes of "Happiness Is a Thing Called Joe" (1945) and "Gee, It's Good to Hold You" (September 5, 1945); and on "Laura" (February 19, 1945), with vocal by the boss.

The Herman Herd won numerous jazz polls and garnered a huge fan base. One such fan of Herman's music was classical composer Igor Stravinsky, who wrote a neo-classical piece especially for the band called *Ebony Concerto*. Stravinsky's composition debuted along with the Herman Herd at Carnegie Hall on March 26, 1946.

With most of the big bands giving up the financial struggle, Herman disbanded the "First Herd" in December 1946. He wanted to spend more time with his family in the home they recently purchased in the Hollywood Hills from actors Humphrey Bogart and Lauren Becall, and for Herman to help his wife, Charolette, overcome her issues with alcoholism and addiction to pills.

After about seven months into "retirement" and his wife established in her process of recovery, Herman organized another band. The so-called "Second Herd," formed in Los Angeles in the fall of 1947, lasting until late 1949.

The band was also known as "The Four Brothers Band," derived from the song "Four Brothers" (December 27, 1947) written by Jimmy Giuffre. The "Four Brothers" piece is based on the chord changes of "Jeepers Creepers," featuring a three-tenor and one-baritone saxophone section, a configuration that Herman has kept with every big band that followed. The original Four Brothers were Stan Getz, Zoot Sims, and Herbie Steward on tenors and Serge Chaloff on baritone.

In addition to the Four Brothers, the new outfit contained holdovers from the First Herd including Shorty Rogers on trumpet; Don Lamond on drums; and Walt Yoder, who was also a member in "The Band That Plays the Blues," returning on bass. A bandful of young, sharp players filled the rest of the lineup. The trumpet section also held Ernie Royal, Bernie Glow, Stan Fishelson, and Marky Markowitz. Earl Swope, Ollie Nelson, and Bob Smith anchored the trombone section; Gene Sargent played guitar; and Fred Otis was the pianist.

Notable hits with the Second Herd include "Keen and Peachy" (1947); "The Goof and I" (1947); the bop scat vocal, "Lemon Drop" (December 29-30, 1948, with Herman, bassist Chubby Jackson, and vibes player Terry Gibbs on the scat vocal); "Keeper of the Flame" (December 29-30, 1948); and the pensively reflective Ralph Burns arrangement of "Early Autumn" (December 29-30, 1948), a milestone recording that made Stan Getz a star.

By 1949, the Second Herd was named the "Best Band of 1949" by readers of the jazz magazine *Down Beat*. But that wasn't enough to keep the band financially going, so Herman once again disbanded to work for a while with a sextet.

In the early 1950s, Herman geared up to form another big band, this time called his "Third Herd." With more top sidemern playing for him – including Nat Pierce on piano, and Carl Fontana and Urbie Green on trombones – Herman successfully toured Europe and stay at the top of his field. Noteworthy recordings made by the Third Herd during this period include "Four Others" (September 11, 1953); "Mulligan Tawny" and "The Third Herd" (both on May 21, 1954).

Because of his father-like attitude and his constant time on the road traveling with his band, Herman was given the nickname of "Road Father."

The advent of the 1960s ushered in a financial nightmare for Herman by way of the IRS. It turned out that no taxes had been paid by his business manager for three years (1964-66); neither had there been any payroll tax returns filed for the band during that time. The entire burden fell on Herman. Ever since then, his life and career have been in the huge shadow of an ongoing battle with the IRS.

His indebtedness to the Internal Revue Service was a large burden that kept Herman on the road and working in an effort to keep up the interest payments. In 1985, Herman's house was seized by the government and auctioned off. He lived there, but only on a month-to-month basis worked out with the buyer.

Herman continued trucking with bands into the 1960s through the 1980s, adding elements of rock and jazz-fusion into his musical library. Gone were the ballrooms that once showcased bands. They were replaced by other venues such as theaters, college campuses for jazz education workshops, jazz festivals, and amusement parks such as Disneyland.

In the early 1970s a brand new audience found the sound of Woody Herman fresh and exciting with the noted bandleader garnering a pair of back-to-back Grammy awards for "Best Large Jazz Ensemble Album" with *Giant Steps* (Fantasy Records, released 1973) and *Thundering Herd* (Fantasy Records, released 1974). He received his first Grammy Award for the album, *Encore!* (Phillips Records, 1963) for "Best Instrumental Jazz Performance by a Large Group." Herman was also awarded the Grammy Lifetime Achievement Award in 1987.

Other noteworthy albums recorded by Herman and crew during this period include: *Heavy Exposure* (Cadet Records, 1969); *Brand New* (Fantasy Records, 1971); *The Raven Speaks* (Fantasy Records recorded August 28-30, 1972); *Woody Herman Presents a Concord Jam* (Concord Records, 1981); *My Buddy: Rosemary Clooney with Woody Herman and His Band* (Concord Jazz, 1983); and *50th Anniversary Tour* (Concord Jazz,

1986). This album was recorded live at The Great American Music Hall in San Francisco, CA, in March 1986.

Herman's final album that he recorded was *Woody's Gold Star* (Concord Records). Recorded live on March 3, 1987, at the Willows Theatre in Concord, California, the album can be considered Herman's last will and testament giving to jazz lovers the best in Big Band jazz.

By the 1980s, Herman had returned to straight-ahead jazz, dropping some of the newer rock and jazz-fusion approaches.

In 1981, Herman and the band established a base of operations in a hotel nightclub in New Orleans. He hoped to settle down in New Orleans as a way of relief from life on the road, but it wasn't meant to be. By late 1982, the New Orleans club folded.

A week later, Charlotte, the bandleader's wife of 46 years died in Los Angeles.

During the summer of 1986, Herman celebrated his 50th year as a bandleader giving special concerts at various venues across America. The celebration was highlighted on July 16 of that year with a sell-out performance at The Hollywood Bowl.

Appearing at that concert was Herman leading his Young Thundering Herd which included Roger Ingram, Ron Stout, Scott Wagstaff, Mark Lewis (the son of former "Band That Plays the Blues" trumpeter Cappy Lewis), and 21-year Herman band veteran Bill Byrne on trumpets; Paul McKee, Kim Kugler, and John Fedchock, trombones; Dave Rieckenburg, Jerry Pinter, and Frank Tiberi, who has been with Herman since 1969, on tenor saxes; and Mike Brignola, baritone sax; Joel Weiskopf, piano; Dave Carpenter, bass; and Joe Pulice, drums.

An All-Star Alumni Band including Pete Candoli, Bill Berry, Conte Candoli, Don Rader, and John Audino, trumpets; Dick "Slyde" Hyde, Buster Cooper, and Carl Fontana, trombones; Dick Hafer, Med Flory, Bob Cooper, Jack Nimitz, and Herman Riley, saxophones; Nat Pierce, piano; Monty Budwig, bass; and Chuck Flores, drums.

Special music was also performed by Herman veteran pianist Jimmy Rowles and his daughter, trumpeter Stacy Rowles.

Classical clarinetist Richard Stoltzman helped to recreate Stravinsky's *Ebony Concerto* with help from the Young Thundering Herd and Carol Robbins on harp and Rick Todd, French horn. Special guest appearances included Stan Getz, tenor sax, singer Rosemary Clooney who sang "My Buddy," and trumpeter Arturo Sandoval.

Other 50th Anniversary performances include Marsee Auditorium at El Camino College in Torrance, CA, on September 20, 1986; and Shades Nightclub in Thousand Oaks, CA on September 25.

I wrote the following Herman band review at the Shades Nightclub performance for the October 2, 1986, issue of *The Fillmore Herald*, where I had been working at the time as a staff reporter: *Woody Herman keeps on going. His friends affectionately call him "Father Time" because at age 73, the celebrated bandleader is one of the last giants of the Big Band Era that still keeps working year round.*

For Woody Herman fans such as myself, "The Woodchopper" and three-time Grammy Award Winner, symbolizes the very best that Big Band jazz has to offer.

This year marks the 50th year for Herman as a bandleader, scheduling three hundred concerts and performances in conjunction with his Golden Anniversary Tour. Early this summer Herman celebrated with a star-studded concert at the Hollywood Bowl that had the audience of 12,000 clammering for more. I know, because I was one out of that great throng wishing the night would have continued on forever.

On September 25, the Herman Herd thundered in to Shades Nightclub in Thousand Oaks and almost blew the roof off! Save for the Hollywood Bowl Concert, the Herd sounded better than ever. Surprisingly, Herman, who doesn't often yield to nostalgia, played tunes mostly with the swing-beat of the Big Band Era. Opening the set with a medley from the Duke Ellington canon, he had the crowd jumping with "It Don't Mean a Thing (If You Ain't Got That Swing)."

Performing some selections from his recently released album from Concord

Records, "Woody Herman and His Big Band 50*th* Anniversary Tour," the band displayed a reverent reading on a John Fedchock arrangement of John Coltrane's pensive "Central Park West." Ever the showman, Herman also demonstrated that being a septuagenarian isn't any excuse for drawbacks on vocal duties. Singing "I've Got the World on a String" and "Baby, I've Got News for You," he had the audience up for a standing ovation.

One of the more powerful numbers in the Herman library is a composition by Aaron Copeland entitled, "Fanfare for the Common Man." Of course, "Woodchopper's Ball" proved once again to be the crowd favorite.

What makes Woody Herman timeless is his uncanny sense of musicianship. He has the knack for picking outstanding arrangers and sidemen by providing for them a showcase for their talents. Many jazz greats have graduated through the Herman Herd and now second generation players are making their mark on the Herman legacy. Trumpeter Mark Lewis, son of trumpeter Cappy Lewis, who played in Herman's band during the 1930s and early 1940s, displayed great style and range as a featured soloist on "Blues For Red."

Reflecting as to how the anniversary tour has been going so far, Herman commented afterwards, "It's been excellent. We've had big crowds almost everywhere we've played."

When asked what has been his most enjoyable experience so far on the tour, Herman replied, "The number of people who have come out to hear us play."

The patrons who were fortunate enough to catch Herman's gig at Shades appeared to leave refreshed and renewed with a bit of reverence and awe for this "Musical Institution"of a man.

As Herman's theme song, "Blue Flame," was being played during the closing of the final set, my wish was once again for the night to continue on forever. I took comfort in the fact, however, that Woody Herman and his Young Thundering Herd will still keep on going!

During 1987, Herman and his Young Thundering Herd played more combination jazz clinics/benefit concerts at schools as they did at Pasadena City College (CA) on February 22.

By the fall of that year, Herman's health was in rapid decline. On October 1, Herman was too ill to perform a concert with his band at the Ventura High School Auditorium in Ventura, CA. As a special favor to Herman, bandleader Les Brown served as Guest Conductor for the event.

On Thursday, October 29, 1987, Herman died of congestive heart failure at Cedars-Sinai Medical Center in Los Angeles. He was 74. He is survived by his daughter, Ingrid Herman Reese, and two grandchildren.

More than 200 relatives, guests, friends and other music greats – including Les Brown, Ray Anthony, and Nat Pierce – gathered with Herman's family, for a traditional Roman Catholic funeral Mass on November 2 at St. Victor's Church in West Hollywood.

Herman is interred in a niche in the columbarium behind the Cathedral Mausolem at Hollywood Forever Cemetery.

** Coda - Here is an update on Woody Herman since this article was published.

Before Woody Herman died in 1987, he delegated most of his duties to Frank Tiberi, the leader of his reed section. After Herman's death, Tiberi became the leader of the Woody Herman Orchestra, which remains active to this day.

A documentary film titled *Woody Herman: Blue Flame- Portrait of a Jazz Legend* was released on DVD in late 2012 by the jazz documentary filmmaker Graham Carter, owner of Jazzed Media, to salute Herman and his centenary in May 2013.

Woody Herman, 59, leading his Young Thundering Herd at Disneyland on December 28, 1972. - *Photo by Stephen Fratallone*

Woody Herman, 73, at Shades Nightclub in Thousand Oaks, CA, on September 25, 1986. – *Photos by Stephen Fratallone*

Above: Woody Herman and the Herd at Shades Nightclub in Thousand Oaks, CA, on September 25, 1986. Saxophonist Frank Tiberi is pictured front row, far right. – *Photo by Stephen Fratallone*

Left: Woody Herman, 73, playing his soprano sax at his 50th Anniversary Concert at the Hollywood Bowl on July 16, 1986. – *Photo by Stephen Fratallone*

Herman leading his Young Thundering Herd at that same concert with special guest soloist Stan Getz, pictured in front.
– *Photo by Stephen Fratallone*

The Best Kept Secret In Jazz

Bandleader Elliot Lawrence Makes Mark In Big Band Jazz, Television, Movies, Theater

The following article on Elliot Lawrence was originally published in the January 2003 issue of Jazz Connection Magazine

Elliot Lawrence may very well have been the best kept secret in jazz. As a bandleader who started his journey toward musical prominence toward the latter part of World War II while many bandleaders were throwing in the towel, Lawrence's music is now just a memory. But his hard-to-find music is deserving of a second listen.

"When we started our first records for Columbia, we did very well," said a very youthful-sounding Lawrence, 77, via telephone from his apartment overlooking New York City's Central Park. "The big bands had their ups and downs like the stock market and when I came in it was toward the end of a high rise and gradually, the bands slipped away."

But Lawrence didn't slip away. Holding on with aggregations that boasted outstanding musicianship, he employed some of the most versatile jazz musicians in the business like Red Rodney, Gerry Mulligan, Alec Fila, Zoot Sims, Herbie Steward and outstanding arrangers like Johnny Mandel, Al Cohn, Ralph Burns, Nelson Riddle, Neal Hefti, Tiny Kahn, and Mulligan to write for him.

From 1955 to 1957 Lawrence recorded some of the most exciting big band jazz ever to be waxed for Fantasy Records stocking his personnel with some of music's finest soloists: trumpeters Nick Travis, Ernie Royal and Bernie Glow; trombonists Urbie Green and Eddie Bert; saxophonists Sims, Cohn, Hal McKusick, Eddie Wasserman, and Sam Marowitz; and drummer Don Lamond.

Fantasy Records has released some of Lawrence's sizzling big band jazz recordings from this period with *The Elliot Lawrence Band Plays Gerry Mulligan Arrangements*, showcasing Mulligan's compositions and arrangements, and *The Elliot Lawrence Big Band Swings Cohn And Kahn*, featuring generous amounts of the arrangers Cohn, Kahn,and Mandel.

"I think the best things we did artistically were for Fantasy," Lawrence said. "Those were really our best albums. Fantasy gave us the opportunity of recording what I really wanted to. That really worked."

And although the 1955-1957 Lawrence band was really one of the best bands anywhere, sadly, it was not well known.

"It really didn't get any of the recognition that we really thought we needed," Lawrence said.

While Lawrence made important contributions to jazz and the Big Band scene (recording steadily as a leader from 1946 to 1960), he mostly worked in the studios. After 1960 he stopped recording jazz altogether to compose, arrange and conduct for films, television and Broadway musicals.

"In the beginning, I loved the band business," Lawrence said. "It was a very exciting time. When I decided not to continue with the band business, one of the defining moments of my life was when Stan Kenton flew out from California to personally tell me that I can't give up the band. He told me that there is hardly anyone left that knows what the music business is about. But I had decided that I was going somewhere else and went into television and theater. I think I entered the music scene at the right time but I didn't make good career choices. It was great to have a band but I stayed with it too long as I might have done other things. I think I've been successful in my field and I'm happy."

Lawrence was born Elliot Lawrence Broza on Valentine's Day 1925 in

Philadelphia. His parents, Esther and Stan Lee Broza, were both connected with radio. His mother was a script writer and his father, a producer and director. Lawrence began playing piano at age two, long before he could read music. At age four, the young musical prodigy was touring local theaters with his father's *Children's Hour* show.

An attack of infantile paralysis threatened to end Lawrence's career shortly after it had begun. But he triumphed over the handicap and was back at the keyboard within a year.

Even though he was classically trained, Lawrence always had a soft spot in his heart for jazz, he said.

"I was always interested in jazz music," he said. "I started out very young and I by-passed the early jazz field."

In his teens, Lawrence studied with well-known conductor Leon Barzin. He was such an outstanding pupil that the Maestro asked him to consider making a career in classical music.

But Lawrence turned his attention toward a different direction. The teen prodigy began arranging and composing as soon as he started Berwyn High High School. In fact, he wrote the Berwyn High Alma Mater song. He also organized his own orchestra, "The Band Busters," and was featured on WCAU in Philadelphia. The band was so popular it was engaged for proms at nearby colleges.

As a student at the University of Pennsylvania, Lawrence conducted the football band and won a number of prizes and awards, including the Thornton Oakley Gold Medal for creative art, the highest award at the university.

After graduating from the University of Pennsylvania at the age of 19, Lawrence became the youngest executive in radio when he was appointed musical director of WCAU, leading one of the most impressive studio bands in the country.

In 1945, CBS started its *Listen to Lawrence* series. The program was so popular that within the first six months more than 100,000 fan letters were received. Noted critic George T. Simon wrote a rave review of the band in the March issue of *Metronome* which helped to peak national interest in the young and talented bandleader.

Some critics mistakenly were of the opinion that Lawrence patterned his band after that of pianist Claude Thornhill, although elements of Thornhill can be clearly heard in the young bandleaders music, Lawrence said.

"That idea came about because both Claude and I played piano," Lawrence said. "Neither of us were never great jazz players who played a lot of notes. As a result, a lot of our ballads sounded alike. I always had one French horn in my band. Later on, I had an oboe and a bassoon when other bands didn't."

In the early summer of 1945, Lawrence gave up his successful radio show in order to try the national big band scene. The Lawrence band made its first national broadcast on the Armed Forces Radio Service *One Night Stand* program from the Tune Town Ballroom in St. Louis on June 23. By early August, the band was broadcasting for AFRS *Basic Music Library* from New York.

In the band at that time was teen trumpeter Red Rodney, who already played with Dizzy Gillespie and who would later gain notoriety playing with Charlie Parker. He would become a stalwart of bebop jazz up until his death in 1994. In addition, there was 18-year-old tenor saxophonist Gerry Mulligan, a fellow Philadelphian who attended West Catholic High School. Mulligan was also gaining respectability as a fine composer and arranger. He would go on to be one of the giants of the baritone sax and one of the Founding Fathers of the West Coast "cool" jazz movement in the early 1950s.

"Gerry and I sort of grew up together," Lawrence said. "He left school and moved in with my family. Gerry had his problems through his life. He was also a character. He would sell the same arrangement to different bands. We all thought we were getting the original copy and he was selling them somewhere else at the same time! (laughs)"

After recording fourteen sides for Associated Transcriptions on February 13, 1946, both Rodney and Mulligan left Lawrence to join drummer Gene Krupa's band, who was playing more bop-oriented music.

"Red and Gerry's leaving the band hurt us," Lawrence lamented. "We were just getting things going and getting more air time when they left."

In April 1946, Lawrence and his band signed on with Columbia Records joining the roster already heavy with top-named outfits such as Gene Krupa, Benny Goodman, Harry James, Count Basie, Les Brown, Claude Thornhill, and the high-flying Woody Herman Herd.

"I always loved Woody's band," Lawrence said. "They came to Columbia just a short time before we did. I really thought the recordings Woody did with that band for Columbia at that time were just fantastic."

The Lawrence band waxed its first commercial recordings May 1 on the companys red label, with "Heart to Heart" (the band's theme song), "Strange Love" (vocal by Jack Hunter), "Remember Me?" and "In Apple Blossom Time," a Lawrence arrangement. The former three cuts were either rejected or unissued leaving "In Apple Blossom Time" to be released on the flip side of "Strange Love," another Lawrence arrangement, which was re-recorded eleven days later.

On that recording session of May 12, the band cut five tunes, all Lawrence arrangements, with "I Know" and "Once Upon a Moon" (vocals on both by Jack Hunter), "Who Do U Love, I Hope" (vocal by Rosalind Patton), and a swinging instrumental, "Five O'Clock Shadow," an original Lawrence composition.

"We were trying to be a dance band," Lawrence said of his band's sound. "The 'hot' or 'rhythm' tunes that we played were in the bebop style for a dance band. The band was on that kick very early. Gerry (Mulligan) wrote for me in that style right from the beginning."

Members of the band for those inaugural Columbia recordings included lead trumpeter Alec Fila, a veteran of the Benny Goodman orchestra, and a classically-trained oboist named Mitch Miller, who became the A&R man for Columbia in 1951, and who would have recording hits of his own in addition to hosting a popular television show in the early 1960s.

From June 22-29, 1946, the Lawrence band played at the Steel Pier in

Atlantic City, and opened at New York's famed Cafe Rouge in the Hotel Pennsylvania on July 1 without any previous "big name" booking, something no other band had been able to do. During his engagement there, Lawrence appeared on twenty radio shows and took his entire orchestra on NBC's *Chesterfield Supper Club*. He continued to tour colleges and ballrooms across America, and opened at Frank Daily's Meadowbrook in Cedar Grove, New Jersey, on September 3, staying two weeks.

From November 1946 to June 1948, trombonist Barney Liddell was with the Lawrence band. Liddell would later anchor Lawrence Welk's trombone section for many years and could be seen on the Champagne Music Maestro's weekly television shows.

Because of his young age and being an untested newcomer to Columbia, the recording executives, led by former bandleader Mitchell Ayers, had Lawrence record many of the less-than-fine quality of popular songs of the day. As a result, his commercial output didn't adequately reflect the band's actual working library of original scores.

"I made a lot of mistakes," Lawrence said. "What we were asked to record for one reason or another were big mistakes. The first band (from the radio station in Philadelphia) really didn't express what I wanted. By the time I had my second band, which was a great band, it didn't do a lot of recording and the band business was on the way down and we were on the way down. Once we got on Columbia, I wasn't smart enough to stand up what I thought should have been recorded. Unfortunately, I was wed by A&R people. I later admired the rock artists when they began to wade their own careers and to do what they wanted to do. The times back then aren't like the times today when artists pick material and really work for a long time on their recordings."

"You Broke the Only Heart That Loved You" (recorded July 24, 1946, with vocals by Rosalind Patton and Jack Hunter) was probably Lawrence's biggest hit on Columbia. However, Lawrence also composed and arranged some other excellent swing numbers for the label, including "Box

155" (recorded September 16, 1946), "Sugar Beat" (recorded February 3, 1947), and the bebop opus, "Elevation" (April 13, 1949), co-written with Mulligan, which was later named as "one of the top 50 jazz recordings of the twentieth century" by the Smithsonian Institution.

"Gerry and I wrote 'Elevation' early on," Lawrence recalled. "We had a tough time convincing Columbia to let us record it."

"Elevation" would be one of the last tunes recorded by Lawrence for Columbia before his departure from the recording company in October 1949. In the three-and-a-half-years that Lawrence was on the Columbia roster (barring the 1948 musicians' union strike), he waxed forty-five singles, excluding numerous V-Discs and transcriptions. (Hindsight Records compiled in an album some of those transcriptions that the Lawrence band did for Associated Transcription from 1946-1947 called, *The Uncollected Elliot Lawrence 1946*.)

Some Elliot Lawrence studio recordings and radio broadcasts can be purchase through the Song Search CD Store at www.songsearch.net or Metolius Music Company at www.metoliusmusic.com

The Lawrence Band performed for the hometown crowd in Philadelphia during Game 1 of the 1950 World Series, playing the bandleader's original song, "The Fightin' Phils." The song didn't do much to inspire the Phillies as the National League champs lost the World Series to the New York Yankees in four straight games.

During the early 1950s, Lawrence continued to lead a solid outfit broadcasting over radio and recording for Decca and King. (Decca released an LP album, *Prom Night*, comprised of a number of singles recorded from June 1950 to February 1951.) But the band was not without its problems.

"We had a really big drug problem," Lawrence said. "Out of the seventeen guys in the band, fifteen were on heroin at the time. It was a really wonderful band, but because of the drugs, I had to disband."

So, in early 1953 Lawrence broke up his band, reorganizing the following year.

As times became harder for big bands, Lawrence eventually abandoned his full-time band leading career, but occasionally re-formed the full-time group for special engagements and record dates. On such sessions his choice of musicians reflected his determination to look ahead.

While Lawrence wrote many arrangements for his own bands, he accommodated, but without wholly embracing, contemporary shifts in jazz. Into the 1950s, in addition to Mulligan, he also used arrangements by other young men who were testing the boundaries of big band music, notably Al Cohn, Tiny Kahn, and Johnny Mandel.

"A lot of the contemporary jazz sounds we had depended on who was with me," Lawrence said. "Johnny Mandel came in and wrote for the band. He's really a genius and he was a very influential person for the music of the time. Tiny Kahn was the drummer and also writing for us. Al Cohn was one of the tenor players and he was writing. We had a huge jazz talent."

Mandel, who would later achieve recognition for his Academy Award and Grammy Award-winning scores, joined Lawrence as a trombonist/arranger in early 1952 after doing an astonishing amount of work in the late 1940s arranging, writing, and/or performing with Alvino Rey, Artie Shaw, Jimmy Dorsey, Buddy Rich, Count Basie and the Henry Jerome orchestra.

Through the 1960s right up to the present, Mandel has continued to add to his vast body of work, including arrangements and/or production for Frank Sinatra, Michael Jackson, Quincy Jones, Miles Davis, Barbara Streisand, Anita O'Day, Mel Torme, Natalie Cole (seven arrangements on her 1991 Grammy-winning *Unforgettable* album), Shirley Horn, and Diana Krall, as well as his own solo work. He also scored the popular "Theme From M.A.S.H." as well as for TV's *Ben Casey* and *Cannon*, among others. In addition to his Academy Award (for the score to 1964's *The Sandpiper* which featured the song, "The Shadow of Your Smile"), and two Oscar nominations, he has won five Grammies and was nominated seven times, as well as garnering three Emmy nominations.

"Elliot is a wonderful guy and a beautiful guy to work for and with,"

Mandel said in a telephone conversation from his home in Malibu, California. "He just made everybody very comfortable to be there. That's why he could get the people he had like Al Cohn and Tiny Kahn. We loved playing for him because he let us do whatever we wanted. He loved us. What a joyful gig it was!"

Also working in Lawrence's band at the time were such stellar musicians as saxophonists Sam Marowitz, a Herman Herd alumnus, Hal McKusick, Al Cohn, and Al Steele; trombonist Ollie Wilson; and trumpeters Nick Travis and Al Porcino.

But the real backbone behind all the band's scores was Lawrence himself, Mandel said.

"Elliot was doing a lot of the arrangements," Mandel said. "Believe me, he wasn't starved for arrangers. He had Tiny Kahn, who was one of the best that I ever knew. As a drummer/arranger, he was the guy to have. And then there was Al Cohn. Ever since we were both 15, he was always a role model for me. The band was doing a lot of college proms and things like that. Elliot was chasing the college crowds then which was a good thing to do for a band like ours in order to keep that many people working at night."

Some of the scores that Mandel did for Lawrence which stand out as personal favorites of the super star arranger include "Any Time" and "Sing, Baby, Sing," two tunes he wrote in 1952 for the band's girl singer, Rosalind Patton, which were never recorded commercially; "Tape Worm" (recorded January 31, 1956), an upbeat instrumental; and "A Foggy Day" (recorded February 1, 1956), as a ballad tune.

As for Lawrence, some of his favorite Mandel tunes were the ones the band never recorded, he said.

"Johnny was influential in trying to lead me along the way he thought the band should go," Lawrence said with a laugh. "Al Porcino, who played trumpet in my band and who now leads his own jazz band in Germany, has put together what he considers the 100 greatest jazz arrangements. He's collected them from everybody and some of Johnny's works are on that list."

Mandel's arranging prowess helped Lawrence's band refine the Big Band jazz vocabulary during the Fantasy Record years of 1955-1957. Mandel's brilliant work was featured on such albums as *Elliot Lawrence Plays Tiny Kahn and Johnny Mandel Arrangements* (Fantasy 3-219); *The Elliot Lawrence Band Swinging at the Steel Pier* (Fantasy 3-236); *Elliot Lawrence Plays for Swinging Dancers* (Fantasy 3-246); and *Dream On... Dance On* (Fantasy 3-261).

"The band was great during this period," Mandel said. "It was just marvelous."

While Mandel never mentioned anything specific that he may of learned concerning arranging while working with Lawrence, (he did say, however, with tongue-in-cheek that he "stole from everybody!"), he does hold up Lawrence as a mentor, he said.

"Elliot was a mentor to all of us," Mandel said. "He used to walk around humming the things we wrote without us knowing he was doing it."

With his whisper-toned sound and harmonic genius, tenor saxophonist Al Cohn was a major contributor to the Lawrence musical library while being one of the most important post-Lester Young stylists of his generation.

Born in Brooklyn, New York, on November 24, 1925, Cohn started his career as a sideman between the years from 1944 to 1950, with Georgie Auld, Buddy Rich, Woody Herman and Artie Shaw. He was a later member of the "Four Brothers" band with Herman in the late 1940s (along with Zoot Sims, Herbie Steward and Serge Chaloff) and recorded his first sides as a leader for the Savoy label from 1950 to 1953. He later recorded on Prestige and Victor labels.

Some of his most prominent compositions include, "Ah Moore" and "The Goof and I." He also co-led a quintet with Sims, and recorded for the Xanadu label in the 1970s. In 1981, he scored a "comeback" with the Concord LP *Nonpareil* and worked with his guitarist son, Joe, as well as his wife, Mary Ann McCall, who sang with the Herman and Charlie Barnet bands. Cohn died on February 15, 1988, in Stroudsburg, Pennsylvania.

"Al Cohn was a genius," Lawrence said. "Not only did he write for my band, he was the Number One writer I used when I went into television. Al could write anything. When Johnny (Mandel) went to Hollywood, Al stayed in New York and we continued to work together. He is also one of the great underrated tenor players of all time."

In addition to arranging, Cohn was one of the steady batch of musicians that Lawrence used on his recordings throughout much of the 1950s, including the album, *Big Band Sound,* recorded on October 6, 1958, on the Sesac label.

During this period, Lawrence also recorded small group all-star jazz sessions for Air Force Reserve Transcriptions that featured such jazz notables as Roy Eldridge, Milt Hinton, Coleman Hawkins, Mundell Lowe, Teddy Wilson, Charlie Shavers, Lee Konitz, Woody Herman, Lawrence Brown, Chubby Jackson, Don Lamond, Hank D'Amico, Art Farmer, Georgie Auld, Kai Winding, Jimmy Cleveland, Tyree Glenn, Sam Most, Zoot Sims, Nick Travis and Urbie Green.

Other albums Lawrence recorded during the late 1950s include *Jazz Goes Broadway* (Vix, 1957); *Hi-Fi-ing Winds* (Vix, 1957); *Big Band Modern* (Jazztone,1958); *Winds on Velvet* (Surrey, 1958- 1959); and *Jump Steady* (Sesac,1960), his final album as a commercial bandleader.

As television became increasing popular by the mid-1950s, Lawrence found a new home for his musical talents, composing for a variety of TV shows including *The Red Buttons Show* from 1954- 1955 (he co-wrote the show's theme song, "The Buttons' Bounce," with Red Buttons, Jack Wolf, and Allan Walker), as well as for soap operas including *The Edge of Night* and *As the World Turns.*

In 1953, Lawrence and his band backed up Red Buttons on a pair of hit novelty songs for Columbia Records with "Strange Things Are Happening" (written by Lawrence and Allan Walker) and on the record's flip side, "The Ho Ho Song."

Through the formation of his own musical production company, Elliot Lawrence Productions, Lawrence contributed to the musical cues and background music heard on *The Edge Of Night*, which ran for twenty-eight years. The show's final telecast aired on December 28, 1984.

"*The Edge Of Night* was on for quite a few years before I joined on," Lawrence said. "I was also asked to write a new theme for that show. I did some new things on the show as well." Elliot Lawrence Productions also took over the music of another soap opera, *As the World Turns*, in the fall of 1981. After Lawrence went into semi-retirement in the late 1980s, *ATWT* and other Procter and Gamble soap operas were done by RTG Music. Composers associated with RTG Music included James Lawrence, Elliot's son.

"Doing the soap operas just fell in my lap," Lawrence said. "I did strictly for the money. It helped pay the bills. I had four children I had to put through school. I took all the soap operas I could get." So successful was Lawrence's hand in working on soap operas that at one time, there were five shows of which he was affiliated that were being aired every day, he said.

"I had a lot of help doing the soaps," Lawrence said. "Al Cohn wrote some things. My son, James, helped me a lot. He's very talented. He still works with me." In addition, Lawrence has worked on both *The Anne Bancroft* and *Night of a Hundred Stars* television shows, among others. His numerous film score credits include *Network* (1976), a black comedy, starring William Holden, Faye Dunaway, Peter Finch and Robert Duvall.

"There was a lot more music in that film before it was was edited," Lawrence said.

Lawrence also worked the 1971 Academy Award-winning film, *The French Connection*, starring Gene Hackman.

"Originally, the producers weren't happy with the music in the first seven minutes of the film, so they came to New York and I rewrote that portion of it even though my name isn't on the credits," Lawrence said.

Lawrence also serves as musical director for the Emmys as well as being a seven-time Emmy Award winner, earning the coveted trophy for "Outstanding Music Direction." Last September, Lawrence was nominated once again for an Emmy (his fourteenth nod) for his work as musical director for the Kennedy Center Honors. The winner in that

Emmy category went to Mark Watters, Musical Director for the Opening Ceremony in the 2002 Winter Olympics at Salt Lake City.

"I knew I wasn't going to win," Lawrence said matter of factly. "That show was really terrific." For the past quarter century, Lawrence has also worked as musical director for The Kennedy Center Honors in Washington, D.C., a television special which pays homage to artists for their contributions to the performing arts. This year's show was taped on December 2 and was aired over CBS on December 27. The gala was attended by President and Mrs. George W. Bush and Vice-President and Mrs. Richard Cheney. This year's honorees were Elizabeth Taylor, James Earl Jones, Chita Rivera, Paul Simon, and James Levine. Throughout the show, Lawrence could be seen briefly conducting the orchestra and smiling at the various celebrities who came on stage to perform and/or to make presentations.

Another place which Lawrence has had an impact was on Broadway, working as musical director/conductor for such popular musicals as *Bye Bye Birdie; How To Succeed in Business Without Really Trying; Golden Boy; Sugar; Here's to Love; Golden Rainbow; The Unsinkable Molly Brown;* and *The Apple Tree.*

"I started working in the theater through television," Lawrence said. "I went to Russia to conduct for *The Ed Sullivan Show* when Gower Champion said to me that I should be doing theater. He asked me to come to Broadway to conduct a new show he was producing which was *Bye Bye Birdie* (1960 starring Chita Rivera and Dick Van Dyke). That's how I got started in theater. From there I did *How to Succeed in Business Without Really Trying* (1961 starring Robert Morse and Rudy Vallee) and many others. I really love my theatrical conducting." In addition to conducting, Lawrence wrote music to Martin Charnin's words for the 1969 musical, *La Strada,* augmenting songs written by Lionel Bart.

"There were two songs of his that stayed in, but the rest were ours," Lawrence said. "We thought it was a pretty good show, but we closed the third night, I think." The last Broadway show Lawrence conducted was in the 1970s.

As a result of his connection with the theater, Lawrence was the logical choice to be the musical director for the Tony Awards, honoring the best in live theater production.

Last June was Lawrence's 37th year as musical director for the Tonys.

"I've done every one since the first year we went on national television," Lawrence said.

He's also a 1962 Tony Award winner in the now defunct category of "Best Conductor and Musical Director," for *How to Succeed in Business*. He was also nominated for a Tony for the first Broadway musical he conducted: *Bye Bye Birdie*.

"Doing the Tonys, Emmys, and the Kennedy Center Honors are things I'm proud of," Lawrence said.

Working as musical director/conductor for these various television specials along with his tenure in the theater, Lawrence has, in a sense, come full circle in his career, he mused.

"I trained as a serious classical musician," Lawrence said. "When I got to the University of Pennsylvania with my band, my musical teachers told me leading a band wasn't the thing to do. When I came back to TV and the theater, it's what I had trained to do as a conductor. The band business was wonderful but my health didn't take it so well. I had asthma. After eight years of touring, my health wasn't in great shape. That's when I made the switch into the early days of television." These days Lawrence still spends his time composing and arranging and doing musical directing for special projects such as last year's Fourth of July gala with the Washington Symphony, he said.

"I do whatever comes my way," he said.

Despite having a successful career as a bandleader along with his work in television, films and theater, Lawrence feels that his contributions to the history of American popular music are not as much as he would like, he said.

"When I started in the theater, the arrangements in the musical theater were done primarily by Robert Russell Bennett and Hans Spielack. The theater had a certain kind of arranging and sound. When I started in

Bye Bye Birdie, and from then on, I tried to change how music sounded in the theater. I feel responsible for a lot of the ways bands in the pit sound. They came into the twentieth century instead of being rooted in the nineteenth century as the way musicals were done before that. Any show I worked on I tried to make the music something really special. In TV, music tends to be put on the back burner. For television people, it's all in the picture. Money is spent on what you see, not so much on what you hear. That's what I have been struggling with, as have others. It's a fight every time you are on a program." Having been blessed with such immense artistic creativity, Lawrence digs deep into the "wells" of past musical experience for refreshment in order to forge ahead with new products.

"It's the things you build up over the years from the time you study to the time you listen to Ravel, Debussy, Ellington, and then Woody's band," Lawrence said. "You try to put it all together to make something really special. That's what American music is. One thing I feel strongly about is that Wynton Marsalis has given the impression that jazz and great American music is a black art only. That's not true. There's a great deal that comes from the black experience, but so many of the great writers were white. These writers influenced the bands so much. I feel insulted when people like (jazz trombonist and arranger) Billy Byers don't get their due because of Wynton's take on jazz. Music shouldn't have been divided by color, that's the trouble. It wasn't a deal where everybody worked together."

** Coda - Here is an update on Elliot Lawrence since this article was published.

At age 91, Lawrence is retired and living in New York City and only works on projects that interest him.

Elliot Lawrence in an early publicity photo from 1946.

Elliot Lawrence pictured recently during an interview.

The Elliot Lawrence Orchestra, circa, 1947. Seated to the right of Lawrence at the piano are band singers Rosalind Patton and Jack Hunter.

Maestro Elliot Lawrence from the mid-1950s.

Elliot Lawrence at the piano with three members of his orchestra in 1946: Tony Ryya, French horn; Bert Gassman, oboe; and Earl Shuster, bassoon.

Elliot Lawrence with drummer/arranger Tiny Kahn from 1952.

Is Everybody Happy?

Showman Ted Lewis Often Overlooked For His Contributions To Early Jazz

The following article on Ted Lewis was originally published in the August 2001 issue of Jazz Connection Magazine

To his family and friends in Circleville, Ohio, he was known as Theodore Leopold Friedman. But to his many adoring fans that spanned over seven decades, he was known as Ted Lewis, "The High-Hatted Tragedian of Song," "The Jazz King," and "The Medicine Man For Your Blues." With his trademark battered top hat, clarinet and twirling cane and renowned for his famous question, "Is everybody happy?" Lewis was an icon in vaudeville and led one of the most commercially-successful jazz bands throughout the 1920s and early 1930s.

As a bandleader, Lewis claimed he had the first of the big bands and employed an extraordinary array of talented musicians including such future jazz headliners as Benny Goodman, Jimmy Dorsey, Muggsy Spanier, Bunny Berigan, Jack Teagarden, Frank Teschemacher, Manny Klein, George Brunies and others. As the leader one of the best-selling jazz bands of the 1920s, Lewis was also Columbia Records' best-selling artist, recording such hits as "When My Baby Smiles at Me" (his theme), "Me and My Shadow," "Tiger Rag," "Dip Your Brush in the Sunshine," "St. Louis Blues," "On the Sunny Side of the Street," "The Blues My Naughty

Sweetie Gave to Me," "Some of These Days," and "Three O'Clock in the Morning."

As a jazz pioneer, most modern jazz histories overlook or down-play Lewis' role in the development of the idiom. When he is mentioned, he is often dismissed as being commercial or "corny." Lewis always considered himself more of a showman rather than a musician (although he was a better player than he got credit for being). In an interview published in 1970, Lewis himself admitted that many jazz aficionados think of him as his music as too corny.

This month marks the thirtieth anniversary of Lewis' passing. Lewis died quietly in his sleep on Wednesday, August 25, 1971, in his apartment on Central Park West in New York City. He was 81.

He was born on June 6, 1890, in Circleville, Ohio, one of four sons of Benjamin and Pauline Friedman. His parents owned Friedman's Bazaar, a large clothing emporium specializing in women's wear. His earliest employment consisted of "sweeping up" both inside and outside the Friedman store. In his spare time, he mowed lawns to earn money for a clarinet and upon its purchase, became a member of the Circleville Boys' Band.

His parents hoped he would go into business, but the younger Friedman, to the horror of his parents, was drawn to the life of a performer, influenced heavily by the circus.

Lewis' first professional singing job was in a Circleville movie house, earning four dollars a week and having to learn a new song each night.

The elder Friedman's enrolled their son in a Columbus, OH, business school but it did nothing to make him forget an entertainment career.

By age 16, Lewis had begun working in vaudeville, playing tent shows and other bottom-of-the-bill engagements, and gradually built a reputation for himself. His name change came about through an accident involving his partnership with a fellow named Lewis. An erroneous marquee billing as "Lewis and Lewis" seemed an omen, and he kept the new name imposed on him.

In 1915, Lewis married the former Adah Becker on the stage of a burlesque theater in Rochester, New York. Adah also acted as Lewis' secretary and business manager. They were married 56 years at the time of Lewis' death.

In 1916, while in New York, Lewis put together his first band, a five-piece ensemble called the Ted Lewis Nut Band. The following year he was playing in a band led by pianist Earl Fuller. It was in Fuller's group that Lewis rose to fame.

The success of the Original Dixieland Jazz Band in 1917 (they recorded the first ever jazz record to be released on the Victor label) opened the doors for other hot and novelty syncopated orchestras and Fuller's Famous Jazz Band was one of the most successful of the bunch. Lewis' wild stage antics and crazy clarinet sound stole the show. (Lewis played his clarinet "gas pipe" style, over blowing and creating a shrill tone that was very useful on novelty tunes but frowned on by most players in most settings.)

Lewis, as part of Fuller's band, was hired by Rector's Cafe in Manhattan, one of the largest entertainment venues of that period. It was during this time that Lewis added two final ingredients to his new persona - his distinctive battered top hat acquired in a dice game at Rector's in 1916 from a cab driver called "Mississippi" - and the catch-phrase, "Is everybody happy?" He began posing it to his audience at Rector's, and it stuck.

"After the opening number something told me to say, 'Is everybody happy?' and the house came down," Lewis said in a previously published interview.

In a short time, Lewis was appearing on stage at the Greenwich Village Follies, Ziegfeld Midnight Frolic, and Keith's Palace. He was the first show business celebrity who ever been a headliner at three Broadway night spots at the same time.

Such overwhelming popularity prompted Lewis to open his own cafe in 1918, the Bal Tabarian, an elegant club catering to the white-tie-and-tails set. Later, with partner Gil Boag, Lewis delved into another swank spot, The Montmarte, and then the last of his night club ventures, The Ted Lewis Club at 52nd Street and 7th Avenue.

In 1919, Lewis signed on with Columbia Records and recorded his first single "Wond'ring" and "Blues My Naughty Sweetie Gives to Me" (both on October 1). Two months later, Lewis introduced and made the first of four recordings of "When My Baby Smiles at Me" (December 9), which he co-wrote with Bill Munro and Andrew Sterling and which became his theme song. (The second recording of the tune was for Columbia on November 22, 1926; the third, for Decca on July 16, 1938; and the last for RKO-Unique Records in 1956).

By the mid-1920s, Lewis was one of Columbia's top selling artists and one of the world's top entertainers and bandleaders. His 1926 version of "Tiger Rag" (July 16) sold 5½ million copies!

Although Lewis took the role of singer himself on his recordings, he did have Ruth Etting cut sides with him, as did Thomas "Fats" Waller (on "Dallas Blues" and "Royal Garden Blues" both recorded on March 6, 1931) and Sophie Tucker who recorded "Some of These Days" (November 23, 1926), which became a million seller.

By the end of the 1920s, Lewis was so popular and distinctive a musical personality that Columbia devised a customized label design for him - a silhouette of the bandleader in his top hat that now embossed his records. In December of 1929, he signed a new contract with the label guaranteeing him $42,000 plus royalties on each record pressed, each year for two years. Even though Lewis was successful commercially, he was never reticent to bring in excellent musical talent. He recognized his own musical limitations, but never let the other musicians limit him. He paid his feature soloists well and did his best to keep them happy.

In 1928, Lewis added ex-New Orleans Rhythm Kings trombonist George Brunies to his band, and early the following year trumpet man Muggsy Spanier came aboard. Clarinetist/saxman Don Murray also added an exciting dimension to Lewis' band. His tragic death in June

1929, in a car accident was a blow to the band. Lewis soon recruited a young Chicago-based player, Frank Teschemacher, (who also died in an automobile accident in 1932), who was heavily influenced by the cornet playing of Bix Beiderbecke.

While he was willing to record with the band, Teschemacher begged off the group's tours. His replacement was Jimmy Dorsey, who was a widely idolized clarinetist. Dorsey not only energized the band, but proved one of the attractions on the band's 1930 tour of Europe. The band was at its peak and their 1930 sides, including "Aunt Hagar's Blues" (January 20) and "Sobbin' Blues, Parts 1 and 2" (April 24), were appealing and popular and they were attracting a lot of jazz listeners thanks to Dorsey and company.

After a brief and unexpected retirement, Lewis was back in business in 1931. The band was regrouped with a few changes. Dorsey had left and was replaced by a promising young clarinetist named Benny Goodman. Goodman's first recording with the Lewis band was "Dip Your Brush in the Sunshine" (April 13, 1931) which features exciting solos by the 21-year-old clarinetist and by Muggsy Spanier on trumpet.

Lewis' recordings during this period, while featuring superb playing, failed to sell the way his 1920s sides had. The Great Depression's economic upheaval spread to virtually every corner of America. Lewis' contract with Columbia ended in 1933, and he signed on with Decca Records.

He was never to enjoy anything like his old successes, despite remaining a popular personality with music that was attractive and lively even if it didn't swing. The Swing Era was beginning and many of his former sidemen such as Goodman and Dorsey were forming their own bands and Lewis' brand of Dixieland-based novelty numbers no longer commanded huge sales.

Among Lewis' nearly 100 hit recordings are the Top Ten hits: "Blues (My Naughty Sweetie Gives to Me) (No.5, 1920), "When My Baby Smiles at Me" (No.1, 1920), "I'll See You in C-U-B-A" (No. 4, 1920), "Fair One" (No.

9, 1921), "Margie" (No. 4, 1921), "All By Myself" (No. 1, 1921), "Second Hand Rose" (No. 2, 1921), "Everybody Step" (No. 3, 1922), "O! Katharina" (No.1, 1925), "Where'd You Get Those Eyes?" (No. 3, 1926), "I Love You (My Love Song)" (No. 3, 1929), "Lady Luck" (No. 3, 1929), "Yellow Dog Blues" (No. 4, 1930), "Just a Gigolo" (No. 1, 1931), "Somebody Loves You" (No. 2, 1931), "An Ev'ning in Caroline" (No. 2, 1931), "In a Shanty in Old Shanty Town" (No.1, 1932) and "Lazybones" (No. 1, 1933).

Lewis also did radio, including the *Valspar Paint Program* and the *Merritt Beer Program* and was featured on the *Coca Cola Spotlight Show* as late as 1945. Lewis never liked radio as he was a vaudeville-based performer with a visual as well as a musical act. From his point of view, the physical presence, the top hat, the bits of visual humor and dancing were as important as the music.

One of Lewis' most memorable bits was to the tune, "Me and My Shadow," introduced in 1925, in which he danced on stage with his spotlight-generated shadow. Eventually an African-American dancer was added to duet with Lewis as his "shadow" on stage. The first, and probably most famous of his "shadow," was Eddie Chester. Chester was followed by four other African-American "shadows," including long-time associate Charles "Snowball" Whittier, making Lewis one of the first prominent white entertainers to showcase African-American performers.

Oddly enough, Lewis never recorded "Me and My Shadow" until 1956 when it appeared as one of the tracks on the album *Me and My Shadow* (RKO-Unique Records). The album generated such popularity for Lewis' music that a follow-up album, *A Million Memories*, was recorded a year later.

Lewis continued to play the top clubs in America and Europe before World War II, earning top-dollar and top billing wherever he played, and made specialty appearances in films like *The Show of Shows* (1929), *Happiness Remedy* (1931), *Here Comes the Band* (1935), *Manhattan*

Merry-Go-Round (1937), *Hold That Ghost* (1941, starring Abbott and Costello along with The Andrews Sisters), the 1942 musical short, *Is Everybody Happy?* and *Follow the Boys* (1944) There were two films made about Lewis, both entitled *Is Everybody Happy?* The first was made in 1929 and is a fictionalized account of the Master Showman's life. In 1943, Columbia Pictures retold Lewis' life story with Larry Parks playing Lewis. (Parks also played Al Jolson in *The Al Jolson Story*).

As late as 1950, Lewis still recorded for Decca. Concert work was what interested him and he made occasional appearances on television, right up to the end of the 1960s at the country's biggest resorts and hotels. He played his last show, still wearing his top hat, at the Desert Inn in Las Vegas in 1967.

Besides sharing the stage with such show business greats as Sophie Tucker, Fannie Brice, George Jessel, Al Jolson, Eddie Cantor and Will Rogers, Lewis also gave command performances for seven United States Presidents, including Theodore Roosevelt, Woodrow Wilson, Herbert Hoover, Franklin Delano Roosevelt and for King George V of England.

On July 15, 1956, Lewis appeared as the mystery guest on television's *What's My Line?*

On June 5, 1977, the Ted Lewis Museum was dedicated in Circleville, Ohio, to honor its most famous son. Lewis' widow, Adah, was on hand for the dedication. She died on May 31, 1981. She is buried beside her famous husband in Forest Cemetery in Circleville.

The Ted Lewis Museum is housed in the only remaining edifice which stood on the original circle. The museum contains memorabilia items from over seven decades of Lewis' illustrious career such as honorary plaques, awards, photos, letters, contracts, scrapbooks, keys to cities, original orchestrations, early record collections and the movies he made, according to Polly Miller, Coordinator of the museum.

The museum archives also serve as a valuable resource for researchers of early twentieth century American music. Persons desiring research and study of Lewis' music are welcome by appointment as the museum is staffed entirely by volunteers.

"We are proud to keep Ted's quality of music, showmanship, and his outstanding supporting members, each spotlighted within his museum," Miller said. "We have had visitors from every State in the Union and fifteen foreign countries. Each year we give tours for hundreds of school children who come in groups. When funds permit, we present scholarships or monetary donations to benefit musical education in schools."

The Ted Lewis Theater within the museum provides a chance for visitors to see Lewis in performance by means of tapes from his movies and TV appearances. Even his battered top hat and clarinet are prominently displayed in a memorial case that is the spotlighted focal point of the museum.

The Ted Lewis Museum is open from 1 to 5 p.m. Fridays and Saturdays and is closed on holidays. Visitors and tours by special arrangement should write the museum at The Ted Lewis Museum, 133 West Main Street, Circleville, Ohio 43113 or telephone the museum at (740) 477-3630. The museum also operates a website at www.tedlewismuseum.org

So where does Ted Lewis fit on the continuum of jazz? Or does he? Did he even make a contribution to jazz, and if so, what should his contribution to jazz be remembered as?

This writer thinks Lewis does hold a prominent place in the continuum of jazz, at least during the early days of the musical form. Unfortunately, many early jazz pioneers, like the Original Dixieland Jazz Band, when they reached commercial success were often dismissed for their contributions. While it is true that some groups of jazz musicians were often prejudiced against and denied opportunities to record their work, musicians like Lewis and the ODJB, did bring jazz music into the mainstream and helped to popularized the genre.

While the Ken Burns documentary, *Jazz,* that was shown over PBS stations earlier this year, was a bold and monumental task at tracing the roots and influence jazz music has had on our culture, it's weakness lies (among other things) in the *omission* of such early jazz pioneers as Ted Lewis and others.

It appears that in Mr. Burns' documentary any jazz musician of non-color who has achieved any commercial success in the formation of jazz during the infantile years, is not worth mentioning. I also realize that if such a documentary were to include *all* contributors to jazz irregardless of race, the project would take much longer to air than the original 10-hour segment.

Celebrated jazz trumpeter Wynton Marsalis has been quoted as saying, "Jazz is democracy in music." If that statement is correct, which I believe it is, then we need to acknowledge *all* the Founding Fathers who have put their own individual stamp on so vast a musical art form, making it theirs. Certainly Ted Lewis is one such Founding Father.

It has been said that Lewis was a magician in the art of extracting drama from jazz. Throughout his career he maintained one method, one style of administering song and dance. His theory was that the only way to reach the public with music was to give it to them in a form which they could understand and thus enjoy.

Was that commercialism? Or artistic compromise? Or just demonstrating good musical taste?

While it may be argued that Lewis was more of a personality than a musician, one writer described him at one level like Al Jolson, but with a more genial and low-key personality. Unlike Jolson, Lewis had no voice to speak of, and yet people loved hearing him talk his way through lyrics, almost like a modern day rapper. He wasn't a great musician, but he hired great ones and let them do their work the way they liked. He also had a feel for the blues, as many of his vast recordings bear witness.

This writer also concludes that Ted Lewis' contribution was taking music and molding it to reflect the spectrum of human emotion, albeit, in a kind of *schmaltzy* way, that made it artistically creative, commercially successful, and above all, fun to listen. In short, his music made "everybody happy!"

* Special thanks to Bruce Eder, Dave Lewis, Polly Miller and Dennis Pereya for contributing to this article.

** Coda - Here is an update on Ted Lewis since this article was published.

In 2005, Dawn Williams wrote *Me and My Father's Shadow: A Daughter's Quest and Biography of Ted Lewis "The Jazz King"* (SunriseHouse Publishers). In the book she claims and substantiates to be the illegitimate child of Lewis, conceived during the heat of a passionate moment with a friend's wife.

While Lewis' paternity was known only by a select handful of close associates, it was kept hush-hush from the one person to whom it should have mattered to the most – the child he fathered and the child he never knew, a daughter, named Dawn Williams.

The Ted Lewis Orchestra was formed under the direction of Joseph Rubin to provide nostalgic entertainment in memory of the late jazz man/entertianer. Rubin, who is also the curator of the Ted Lewis Museum, impersonates Lewis in dress, mannerisms, and song on stage (complete with battered top hat), fronting a thirteen-piece band. Also part of this entertainment revue are The Reed Sisters along with Marvin J. Malone II, as Rubin's "shadow." Rubin also leads the five-piece Ted Lewis Jazz Band (clarinet, C-Melody sax, trumpet, trombone, piano and drums), the same size aggregation that Lewis started out with in 1917. A female vocalist is also part of the group. Ted Lewis' arrangements have been meticulously transcribed from original records and manuscript parts so listeners will hear this music just as it was played almost a century ago!

For information about the Ted Lewis Orchestra and Jazz Band, contact Rubin at: jrubin@tedlewisorchestra.com

Ted Lewis publicity photo from the early 1940s.

Ted Lewis and His Band in 1928.

Ted Lewis and His Orchestra in 1943.

Ted Lewis from 1941.

Wildly Imaginative

Arranger-Bandleader Billy May Leaves Legacy On Making A Tune Sound Great

The following article on Billy May was originally published in the July 2000 issue of Jazz Connection Magazine.

The way Billy May sees it, being an arranger requires a good imagination. And May himself has been described by Big Band critic George T. Simon as "wildly imaginative."

May, a huge man with a dry wit that was reflected in much of what he wrote, has been one of the most exciting arrangers to come out of the Big Band Era. One of the biggest hits and signature sounds of the Swing Era, the chipped saxophone riff on the classic "Cherokee," was arranged for Charlie Barnet's orchestra in 1939 by May. After playing trumpet and arranging for Barnet and Glenn Miller, May went into the recording studios to gain prominence as a much-in-demand arranger for Capitol Records backing up such singing stars as Frank Sinatra, Nat "King" Cole and Peggy Lee. For a brief period in the early 1950s, he was even a successful bandleader in his own right, often performing the hottest show in town.

"I guess some of the things I have done musically were very successful," said May, 83, via telephone from his home in San Juan Capistrano, California. "We got lucky."

May is free to consider the outcome of his work as having to do with luck, but many critics see it as coming from his keen "inspired imagination." Many would even go far as to say it's pure genius.

These critics see May's music as reflecting the combination of energy, enthusiasm, fun and creativity that is filled with exhilaration, excitement and ebullience.

"Obviously, you approach the material you are to arrange with a lot of factors in mind such as the composition itself, the targeted listeners, the artist who will be recording it, etc.," May said about how he receives the inspiration to do arrangements. "Sometimes suggestions are given by those who hire you. Doing something for Time/Life Records is different than doing something for Frank Sinatra. You have to consider all the factors."

Born November 10, 1916, in Pittsburgh, Pennsylvania, May started his musical training on the tuba at age fourteen, due to health reasons.

"I suffered from asthma as a boy and the doctor suggested that I play a horn to increase my lung capacity," May said. "I talked to the band teacher about it and he gave me a tuba."

May became interested in arranging because he had so much time to observe the other instruments when he played the tuba, he said.

"I was intrigued with arranging right from the beginning," May said. "The tuba had the bass part in the band and I began noticing that some arrangements had more interesting bass parts than others."

By the time he graduated from Schenley High School in 1935, the Big Band Era was just starting, and May had begun taking up playing the trombone and trumpet.

During the ensuing years, May worked with a variety of Pittsburgh bands, he said.

It was a chance meeting with bandleader Charlie Barnet during the band's stopover in Pittsburgh in the summer of 1938 that forever changed May's life.

"I had heard Charlie's band and I fell in love with it," May said. "I went to Charlie and asked if I could write an arrangement for him. He said sure and that his band was going to rehearse the following day. I stayed up all night and wrote a chart. I brought it to him and he liked it very much. He made a deal with me and then went out of town and didn't pay me. Shortly after that, Charlie went on another one of his marital adventures and broke up band."

Not to be discouraged, May kept on fine-tuning his arranging skills while continuing to play with local bands.

In early 1939, while tuning in on the radio, May heard a broadcast of Barnet's band from New York. Not to be denied, he wrote the saxophone playing bandleader a letter asking him for the money he owed him for the arrangement.

"Instead of sending money, Charlie called me and asked me to come to New York to work with him," May said. "I did arrangements and played trumpet in the band."

It didn't take long for May to come up with a hit arrangement for the Barnet band. He took an Indian-inspired tune that British bandleader Ray Noble had played in a suite and wove it to fit Barnet's hard, swinging style.

"Someone was fooling around with the plunger mutes on the trombones doing a 'wah-wah' sound," May recalled. "I got the idea of using the three trombones starting off the piece that way."

The result was a wild, romping version of "Cherokee," recorded on July 17, 1939, which became Barnet's biggest hit and the bandleader's theme song.

"It became the most popular record Charlie ever made," May said.

Other members of the Barnet band who were on the recording include Robert Burnet and John Owens, trumpets; Don Ruppersberg, Bill Robertson, and Ben Hall, trombones; Kurt Bloom, Gene Kinsey, James Lamare, and Don McCook, saxophones; Bill Miller, piano; Bus Etri, guitar: Phil Stephens, bass; and Cliff Leeman, drums.

In fact, "Cherokee" became one of the biggest hit tunes of the Swing Era - an anthem of sorts for the period - probably second only to Glenn

Miller's "In the Mood." The song also became a key inspiration for bebop players a few years later. Charlie Parker's "Ko- Ko" is based on the chord changes in "Cherokee."

With May and alto saxophonist/arranger Skippy Martin and trombonist/arranger Lyle "Spud" Murphy joining Barnet's band, things started to really cook. The band waxed a number of great sides for Bluebird including "The Count's Idea" and "The Duke's Idea" (tribute pieces for Count Basie and Duke Ellington, respectfully, both recorded on September 10, 1939); "The Right Idea" and "The Wrong Idea" (both on October 9, 1939); "Comanche War Dance" (January 3, 1940); "It's a Wonderful World" and "720 in the Books" (pair of vocals by Mary Ann McCall on February 7, 1940); "Leapin' at the Lincoln" (March 21, 1940); "Southern Fried" (September 17, 1940); and "Redskin Rhumba" (October 14,1940). Barnet used his own composition of "Redskin Rhumba," a follow-up to "Cherokee," as his closing theme.

May revealed a significant flair for satire on a composition titled "The Wrong Idea," composed with Charlie Barnet, that ridiculed the bland "Mickey Mouse" style of safe big-band music with specific musical mockery of bandleader Sammy Kaye, known for his "swing and sway" trademark.

Another gem that May arranged for the Barnet library were the quirky slow blues piece, "Pompton Turnpike" (July 19, 1940). May is heard on the muted trumpet passage in the call-and-response pattern opposite to Barnet's soprano saxophone.

Just as Barnet and his orchestra was riding the crest of popularity, disaster struck.

While playing at the Palomar Ballroom in Los Angeles in October 1939, a fire swept through the famed dance spot destroying the band's instruments and music.

"It was a very orderly fire," May recalled matter-of-factly. "The fire started after we left the bandstand at intermission. Once it got started, it had lots of fuel. The first casualties were the instruments and the music. I even lost my horn."

It was May who headed the undertaking of rewriting the entire Barnet book from scratch, with a little help from friends, he said.

"It wasn't so bad," May said. "We had a lot of guys to help us. Skippy Martin and myself had written most of the stuff for the band. Benny Carter and Jimmy Mundy came to help. Within two weeks we had the book in order to go out and start working."

That same year, May wrote a suite for the 1939 New York World's Fair called "Wings Over Manhattan," a piece that was inspired by Duke Ellington's musical influence. Barnet eventually recorded the tune on the Bluebird label in two parts on September 17, 1940.

May stayed with Barnet for almost a year-and-a half, from July 1939 to mid-October 1940.

The final recordings May did with Barnet occurred on October 14 with "I Hear a Rhapsody" and "Isola Bella" (both vocals by Bob Carroll); "Whatcha Know Joe?" (vocal by trumpeter Ford Leary and the vocal group, The Three Moaxes); "Buffy Boy," "Lumby," and "Redskin Rhumba."

"Charlie was a wonderful guy," May said. "He was born in a wealthy family and had money all his life. He was the original spoiled little rich kid but he was a good guy about it."

Right after he recorded those final cuts for Barnet, Glenn Miller hired May to play lead and jazz trumpet as well as to arrange for his band. Also joining the Miller band at the same time was Ray Anthony, who, with his warm low register sound was a very capable fourth trumpet man.

"Glenn was looking for a trumpet player and someone recommended me to him," May said. "I originally didn't want to go with Glenn because I liked Charlie's band better. Glenn also offered me $100 more than what I was making with Charlie and the money was too good to turn down."

Being with Miller was certainly a different experience than being with Barnet, May said.

"There's was more freedom in Charlie's band," May said. "It was more of a free-swinging band and you could do more of what you wanted.

There was definitely more improvisation. Glenn was pretty much a 'do-it-the-same-way-every-night' kind of a leader."

During his tenure with the trombone-playing bandleader, May shared arranging duties with Miller, Jerry Gray, and Bill Finegan.

One of the first recordings May did with Miller was his relaxed swinging arrangement of "Along the Santa Fe Trail" (vocal by Ray Eberle on November 8, 1940). Other Miller band personnel on that recording included Dale McMickle, Johnny Best, and Ray Anthony, trumpets; Jimmy Priddy, Paul Tanner, and Frank D'Annolfo, trombones; Willie Schwartz, Hal McIntyre, Ernie Caceres, Tex Beneke, and Al Klink, saxophones; Chummy MacGregor, piano; Jack Lathrop, guitar; Trigger Alpert, bass; Maurice Purtill, drums.

During this time, May helped to record many of the hits that have become Miller signature tunes such as "Anvil Chorus" (December 13-27, 1940); "Song of the Volga Boatmen" and "Sun Valley Jump" (both on January 17, 1941); "Perfidia" (vocal by Dorothy Claire and The Modernaires, February 19, 1941); "It's Always You" (vocal by Ray Eberle, February 20, 1941); "Chattanooga Choo Choo" (vocals by Tex Beneke, Paula Kelly and The Modernaires, May 7, 1941); "Adios" (June 25, 1941); "Elmer's Tune" (vocals by Ray Eberle and The Modernaires, August 11, 1941); A String of Pearls" (November 3, 1941); "Moonlight Cocktail" (vocals by Ray Eberle and The Modernaires, December 8, 1941); "Don't Sit Under the Apple Tree" (vocals by Tex Beneke, Marion Hutton and The Modernaires, February 18, 1942); "American Patrol" (April 2, 1942); "I've Got a Gal in Kalamazoo" (vocals by Tex Beneke, Marion Hutton and The Modernaires); "Serenade in Blue" (vocal by Ray Eberle and The Modernaires) and "At Last" (vocal by Ray Eberle) – the latter three tunes on May 20, 1942; "Caribbean Clipper" (July 14, 1942); and "Juke Box Saturday Night" (vocals by Tex Beneke, Marion Hutton and The Modernaires, July 15, 1942).

Another stand out chart that May did for the Miller band - and many would argue it to be a classic – was a slow, ballad-like arrangement of the Duke Ellington-Billy Strayhorn opus, "Take the 'A' Train."

During this time, the Miller band also made two movies: *Sun Valley Serenade* (1941) starring Sonja Henie, John Payne and Milton Berle; and *Orchestra Wives* (1942) starring George Montgomery, Anne Rutherford, Caesar Romero and Jackie Gleason.

May's composition of "Boom Shot," written with Miller (May's wife Arletta originally received credit as co-author in his place), was included in the soundtrack of the 20th Century Fox movie, *Orchestra Wives*.

"Working with Glenn was a good asset to my career," May said.

Besides leading the nation's Number One Band, Miller was also an astute business man. During his two-year stint with Miller, May learned a lot from the trombone-playing bandleader as to how to make money in the music business, he said.

When Miller alto saxophonist Hal McIntyre left the band to form his own outfit in October 1941, May composed and arranged some charts for the McIntyre band library. He wrote "Daisy Mae" and "Friday Afternoon," which were recorded by McIntyre on the Victor label on April 1, 1942.

After Miller broke up his band on September 27, 1942, after playing their last date at the Central Theatre in Passaic, New Jersey, to go into the service, May became a staff trumpet player for NBC on *The Chamber Society of Lower Basin Street* show before he moved to Los Angeles in the spring of 1943 to do free lance arranging.

May did work for Ozzie Nelson and played trumpet in Nelson's band on *The Red Skelton Show*. When Skelton went into the service in 1944, *The Ozzie and Harriet Show* replaced it. May became bandleader and arranger for Nelson's show during from 1944 until 1952 when it went on television.

May met Paul Weston, musical director of the new Capitol Records, and began ghost-arranging for him in 1944.

In August 1945, May recorded his first session as a Capitol Records orchestra leader backing up singer Ella Mae Morse on "Rip Van Winkle" and "Buzz Me."

In December of that year, May led a studio orchestra for Capitol that cut eight instrumentals of his own arrangements: "Body and Soul," "Honeysuckle Rose," "Sweet Lorraine," "Sunset and Vine Blues," "I Got Rhythm," "I May Be Wrong," "I Surrender, Dear" and "Just You, Just Me." Comprising that studio band were Paul Geil, Uan Rasey and Irv Shuken, trumpets; Les Jenkins and Bill Shaffer, trombones; Les Robinson and Heine Beau, alto saxophones; Hap Lawson and Harry Scuchman, tenor saxophones; Bob Poland, baritone saxophone; Buddy Cole, piano; Dave Barbour, guitar; Phil Stephens, bass; and Nick Fatool, drums.

During this period May also wrote arrangements for the bands of Les Brown and Alvino Rey.

When Capitol decided to put out a series of children's story-song records, May was given the musical responsibilities, producing over sixty such albums over the next ten years featuring Disney cartoon characters, Warner Brothers' Looney Tunes characters, and Bozo the Clown. On March 28, 1946, May teamed up with Pinto Golvig to wax the first of the Bozo the Clown series with *Bozo at the Circus*, a four-record set. Next, came *Bozo and His Rocket Ship* (March 24, 1947, two records); *Bozo Under the Sea* (October 1947, two records); and finally, *Bozo's Song* (December 1947).

Other children's records that May worked on for Capitol include a collaboration with cartoon character imitator Mel Blanc on "Bugs Bunny Meets Elmer Fudd, Pts. 1 & 2"; "Daffy Duck Flies South, Pts. 1 & 2" and "Porky Pig in Africa, Pts, 1 & 2" (all on April 23 and 25, 1947); "Bugs Bunny and the Tortoise" (December 1947); "Woody Woodpecker" (with the Sportsmen, June 1948); "Bugs Bunny Meets Hiawatha" and "Daffy Duck Meets Yosemite Sam" (both April 1950); "Tweety Pie" (May 1950); "I Tawt I Taw a Putty Tat" (July 1950); and "Bugs Bunny and the Pirate, Parts 1 & 2" (January 1954).

He also worked with James Baskett on a series of Brer Rabbitt recordings (September 1946); with Johnny Mercer, Luana Patten and Bobby Driscoll on "Mickey Mouse and the Beanstalk" (July 6-7, 1947); with Henry Blair on "Sparky and the Talking Train" (August 22, 1947) and

"Sparky's Magic Piano" (September 1947); and with Don Wilson on "Little Toot."

During his first few years at Capitol Records, May wrote for and led studio bands for a variety of artists including Clark Dennis, Margaret O'Brien, Jerry Lewis, Margaret Whiting, Baby Snooks, Peggy Lee, Kay Starr, Gisele MacKenzie, Nellie Lutcher, Ella Fitzgerald and Nat "King" Cole (most notably on Cole's version of "Walkin' My Baby Back Home," on September 4, 1951).

In addition, May also did work for Phil Harris and The King Sisters with "Stone Cold Dead in the Market," "The Coffee Song," "My Honey's Kiss," and "You, So It's You," for RCA Victor in February 1946.

It was the result of recording a dance album of Arthur Murray favorites in June 1951 that thrusted May into the world of band leading and a trademark sound.

"When I was doing those Murray sides, I was fooling around with the saxophone sound - the 'slurping saxophone' sound, as it's been called - and I thought that this would be a good time to experiment with Capitol's money," May said. "Capitol liked the sound so much that they forgot about the Arthur Murray records and put out a single. That snowballed into a big demand to see Billy May and his band all over the United States."

This "slurping saxophone" sound - voiced in thirds, something like a bluesy glissando - instantly became a much-sought-after "new sound."

"Individual saxophone players such as Johnny Hodges and Willie Smith were doing that (slurping sound) for a long time," May said. "I was thinking that I could get the saxophone section to do it. I was fooling around with the saxes and figured out which pitches worked best for the altos and tenors. I developed it and the guys I used in the band were happy to do it."

The band's theme song, "Lean Baby" (August 22, 1951), became a big hit. Other hits include "Fat Man Boogie" and "When My Sugar Walks Down the Street" (both on August 22, 1951); "All of Me" (June 25,1951); and "Charmaine" (December 12, 1951), which was charted for two weeks, peaking at No. 17.

On September 24, 1951, Capitol released these recordings by the May band. All were well received, and the band established itself placing 10th in *Down Beat* Magazine's "Best Band" category for 1951.

Many of the personnel on May's studio recordings included old band chums who were working in the studios after World War II: trumpeters Johnny Best, Uan Rasey, Conrad Gozzo and Manny Klein; trombonists Ed Kusby, Murray McEachern, Joe Howard and Si Zentner; saxophonists Les Robinson, Willie Schwartz, Ted Nash, Skeets Herfurt, Fred Fallensby, Don Raffell, and Chuck Gentry; pianist Buddy Cole; guitarist Barney Kessel; bassist Joe Mondragon; and drummer Alvin Stoller.

In order to capitalize on the public's interest, May took the band out on the road. On February 22, 1952, he opened at the Rainbow Gardens in Pomona, California. During that year, May's band was a top draw wherever they went and moved up to 5th Place in the *Down Beat* poll.

In mid-1953, Capitol released *Big Band Bash*, a 12-inch LP album of compilation recordings that May's band did between December 5, 1951 and January 23, 1953. The album showcases the best of the Billy May "sound" set to his swinging arrangements.

After almost two years of the constant traveling with his band, May threw in the towel.

"Soon after we launched the band, I found out I didn't miss the road," May said. "Even though the band did well wherever we played, we were playing the same joints I played with Barnet and Miller years earlier. I also didn't have the tolerance to do anniversary requests and shmooze with the audience. I really went out because my first marriage had its challenges in one way or another."

The band made its final appearance during an October 1953 engagement at the Hollywood Palladium.

Wanting out of the band business, May sold the band (reportedly for $35,000) to former Miller alumnus trumpeter Ray Anthony, he said. Anthony, who was already leading a band at the time and was a major recording artist for Capitol, bought the music and the rights to use May's name.

"I retained the right for records, television and movie work," May said.

May then headed back into the Capitol studios to continue to lead studio bands.

On April 17, 1954, in the wake of the popularity of the motion picture, *The Glenn Miller Story*, May cut a Glenn Miller tribute album played by Miller alumni for Gene Norman's 76 label. The album contains ten of Miller's most popular instrumentals. Joining May on the recording were Johnny Best, Zeke Zarchy and Clyde Hurley, trumpets; John Halliburton, Murray McEachern, Paul Tanner and Joe Yukl, trombones; Russ Cheever, Willie Schwartz, Eddie Miller, Babe Russin and Chuck Gentry, saxophones; Jack Russin, piano; Dick Fisher, guitar; Rollie Bundock, bass; and Jack Sperling, drums.

In October 1957, May teamed up for the first time with singer Frank Sinatra to record the album, *Come Fly With Me*. When Capitol released it in early 1958, the album shot to Number 1 on the *Billboard* pop chart.

"There was some good writing in there and it was a successful album," May said.

In May 1958, May cut an album of unusual interest. He dropped the use of reed instruments altogether for a "brass choir" sound on *Big Fat Brass*. It won for May a Grammy at the First Annual Grammy Awards for "Best Performance by an Orchestra." Personnel on that album include Johnny Best, Frank Beach, Pete Candoli, Conrad Gozzo, Manny Klein and Uan Rasey, trumpets; Ed Kusby, Tommy Pederson, Si Zenter, trombones; George Roberts, bass trombone; Vince de Rosa, Jack Cave, Jimmy Decker, Dick Perissi, Art Franz, French horns; Red Callender, tuba; Veryle Mills, harp; Paul Smith, piano; Al Hendrickson, guitar; Joe Mondragon and Ralph Penner, bass; Alvin Stoller, drums; Lou Singer and Ralph Hansell, percussion.

The chemistry between May and Sinatra was there on the *Come Fly With Me* album and the pair collaborated again on March 3, 1958, this time with songstress Keely Smith, on four tunes: "Nothing in Common" and "How Are You Fixed for Love?" (duet with Sinatra and Smith); and "The Same Old Song and Dance" and "Here Goes" (both vocals by Sinatra).

The next album project between May and Sinatra took place in December 1958, with *Come Dance with Me*. It also would be a smash hit album, staying on the charts for 141 consecutive weeks and earning for May his second Grammy Award in 1959 for "Best Arrangement." May also worked on Sinatra's follow up album, *Come Swing with Me* (1961). (May would be nominated for seven Grammys during his career.)

The May-Sinatra collaboration continued throughout the 1960s to 1979, on Capitol and on Sinatra's Reprise label. May arranged and conducted the first album, *The Past*, of Sinatra's *Trilogy* series in 1979.

Singers Bing Crosby and Rosemary Clooney cranked out two "traveling" duet albums with May: *That Travelin' Two-Beat* and *Fancy Meeting You Here* (both for RCA-Victor in 1958).

Albums with singers Keely Smith, *Cherokeely Swings* and *Politely* (December 1958), both on Capitol, and Anita O'Day, *Anita Swings Cole Porter with Billy May* (April 2 and 9, 1959) on Verve, soon followed.

May's work backing up singers was basically just a job to him, he said.

"It's like anything else, some of them were good and some of them were not so good," he said. "It was money."

But May did name-drop Patti Page, Peggy Lee, and Gerry Southern as some of his favorite female singers that he's worked with, while Sinatra, Vic Damone, and Perry Como rank as favorite male singers.

In April 1961, May and his Orchestra backed up Johnny Mercer and Bobby Darin on the swinging album, *Two of a Kind* (Atco Records).

May also worked in television and films. He composed the theme to the TV detective series, *Naked City*; *The Mod Squad*; *Emergency*; and his jazz style re-arrangement of Nikolai Rimsky-Korsakov's "Flight of the Bumblebee," which was the theme music for *The Green Hornet* (1966), which featured a trumpet performance by Al Hirt. May also composed the music for the "Batgirl Theme" song, which was used in the *Batman* (1966) television series when the Batgirl character was added to the cast in 1967.

He wrote the scores for the films including *Sergeants Three* and *Nightmare* (1956), in which he also played a bandleader in a dimly-lit nightclub; *Johnny Cool* and *Tony Rome* (with Frank Sinatra, November 1967). During this time May was also the musical director for satirist Stan Freberg's radio comedy series.

May first collaborated with Freberg in March 1952, on a Capitol Records' recording of "Abe Snake for President." Two years later, the pair teamed up again to record three more singles: "Sh-Boom," "Wide-Screen Mama Blues" and "Try" (all July 1954). May and Freberg would continue to record their off-beat brand of humor throughout the remainder of 1950s and '60s, including "Wun'erful, Wun'erful," a parody on bandleader Lawrence Welk (August 1957) and the 1961 comedy album, "*The History of the United States, Vol. I*," which earned a Grammy Award for Freberg.

May's arranging prowess was applauded by Big Band enthusiasts when he was asked in the early 1970s to arrange and lead authentic recreations for the Time/Life Records' series, *The Swing Era*. Bandleader Glen Gray had originally done some of these Swing Era recreations for Capitol Records five years earlier, May said.

In the meantime, F. M. Scott, an executive from Capitol, left and went to work for Time/Life. When Time/Life wanted to put out its own Swing Era material, Scott knew where Gray's masters were. Both record companies talked and a deal was cut, according to May.

"Time/Life started out using some of Gray's old masters but they needed more," May said. "They hired me to expand it. By the time we had the package completed (fourteen volumes, each containing thirty songs), the company had received an overwhelming response. I went to work for them for one album and I ended up working for them for three years!"

May's keen intellect and agility for musical scoring is legendary among studio musicians. He was once quoted as saying, "I write faster than anyone better and better than anyone faster."

An example of this occurred during a recording session with jazz pianist George Shearing on his *Burnished Brass* album, Shearing was playing the melody of a piece he wanted May to arrange. After one run-through, he started to repeat it and describe how he wanted it arranged. May interrupted him, saying, "Well, take it from after the bridge because I've got that much orchestrated already."

In 1996, May reunited with Stan Freberg to provide the music to his *The History Of The United States, Part II*, which earned a Grammy nomination. "It was really great," May said of the Freberg project.

In 1987, May was honored for his arranging talents during the Second Annual "Salute to the Songwriters" awards at the Dorothy Chandler Pavilion in Los Angeles. The event was headed by songstress Rosemary Clooney.

Now retired completely from the music business, May has since given up playing his trumpet and spends time with his wife, Doris, and four daughters, Cynthia May, Laureen Mitchell, Joannie Ransom, and Sandra Gregory. He also occupies the remainder of his free time with other things, such as his model train collection, he said.

When it comes to the music of today, May has little appreciation for it, he said.

"I don't like much of the current music," he said. "It's a generational thing."

May has also been a regular attendee at the Big Band Academy of America's annual reunions held the first weekend in March at the Sportsmen's Lodge in Studio City, California.

Although his vast contribution and legacy to American popular music has been immortalized on records, in films and on television, May is uncertain as to its significance, he said.

Yet, he candidly offers this bit advice for aspiring arrangers: "Don't do it!" he said jokingly. "If you really want to be an arranger, the best thing to do is to just keep your ears open."

** Coda - Here is an update on Billy May since this article was published.

On March 4, 2001, May was honored by the Big Band Academy of America as a recipient of its Golden Bandstand Award.

Billy May died on January 22, 2004, of heart failure at his home in San Juan Capistrano, California. He was 87.

Billy May from 1952.

Billy May, 85, with friend and colleague Van Alexander at the Big Band Academy of America's annual Reunion at the Sportsmen's Lodge in Studio City, CA, on March 4, 2001. – *Photo by Stephen Fratallone*

Billy May, 86, at the Big Band Academy of America's annual reunion on March 3, 2002, at th Sportsmern's Lodge in Studio City, California. - *Photo by Stephen Fratallone*

Billy May, 85, receiving the Golden Bandstand Award from Milt Bernhardt, President of the Big Band Academy of America on March 4, 2001. - *Photos by Stephen Fratallone*

My Buddy

Bandleader Buddy Moreno Remains A Musical And Broadcasting Icon In The St. Louis Area

The following article on Buddy Moreno was originally published in the October 2001 issue of Jazz Connection Magazine.

The way Buddy Moreno sees it, he's strictly a survivor from the Big Band era.

"That's exactly what I am, a survivor," said Moreno, 89, via telephone from his home in Florissant, Missouri, a suburb northwest of St. Louis. "I guess there's nothing wrong with that, is there?"

Moreno, a personable guitarist/singer who forged a name for himself with the Griff Williams, Dick Jurgens, and Harry James bands and who later went on to lead a dance band of his own during the late 1940s, still leads a band today for special occasions and also has had a lengthy career in radio.

"I think my band was quite good," Moreno said. "It was a good sounding commercial band."

Unfortunately for Moreno, he started his band near the end of the Big Band Era and while his music did have some popular appeal, it just didn't take off as a result of bad timing.

"Things happen and sometimes we just don't know why they happen," Moreno said.

In his book, *The Big Bands*, jazz writer Gorge T. Simon described Moreno as "a grinning, seemingly ever-joyous guitarist ... who on novelty and uptempoed [sic] tunes projected a pleasant personality and voice to match."

Born Carlos Jesus "Buddy" Moreno on July 14, 1912, in Los Angeles, California, as the only child to a Spanish father and an Irish mother. Moreno grew up in San Francisco. He began his career in high school as a singer forming a trio that copied the vocal arrangements of the renowned Rhythm Boys - Bing Crosby, Harry Barris, and Al Rinker.

"It was a fun thing as far as high school was concerned," Moreno said. "It was a way to charm the girls."

But the trio began to look at their craft with some seriousness and in 1929, they landed a job singing for the weekend crowd at the exclusive Olympic Club, Lakeside, in San Francisco for five dollars a night.

"One of the members of our trio was Walter King. His father, who led an orchestra at the time, helped get us the job," Moreno said.

After singing at various venues in and around the San Francisco area for a few years, Moreno joined the newly formed Griff Williams band in 1933 initially as the band's vocalist. The association would last for seven years.

Williams was a pianist who led his college band while attending Stanford University. In 1932, he joined the Anson Weeks Orchestra, who was very popular at the Mark Hopkins Hotel in San Francisco, staying only a few months before forming his own outfit. A society band, the Williams Orchestra had it's first booking at San Francisco's Edgewater Beach Hotel beginning in October 1933.

"Griff did a lot of 'debutant-type' parties around the San Francisco area," Moreno said. "He needed a lead singer and hired me for some of those jobs. We started out together. After he left Weeks to form his own band, he asked me to join him."

With a lot of idle time on the bandstand between vocals and when the opportunity of an open chair in the rhythm section becoming available, Moreno invested in some "insurance" in order to keep his job by learning to play the guitar, he said.

"Griff didn't want to use a banjo in the band anymore," Moreno. "He let Bob Logan, our banjo player, go. I asked Griff if I learned how to play the guitar would he put me in the band? He said yes. I took lessons and practiced like mad anywhere and anytime I could. After I mastered the instrument, I joined the band as a rhythm guitarist and vocalist."

Eventually, Williams also became a popular draw at the Mark Hopkins. By the late 1930s, Williams relocated to Chicago. During World War II, the band spent four years at the Stevens Hotel in Chicago, which at the time was known as the world's largest hotel. After the war he concentrated on working in Chicago and San Francisco. He disbanded in 1953 to work for a magazine publishing company in Chicago. He occasionally put together bands to work at society events. In 1956, Williams was given a local television show in Chicago. He died of a heart attack three years later.

"Griff was a fine player and had a very good, successful band," Moreno said of his former boss. "He looked like Fred Astaire. Because he was a Fred Astaire look-a-like, he would also dance around a bit in front of the bandstand. He was a very personable guy. All of the socialites loved him."

Some of the songs that Moreno recorded while with the Williams band that featured his vocal talents include "Oh, You Gorgeous Dancing Doll" and "Down by the O-H-I-O" (both recorded May, 1940); "That's For Me" and "Yum-Yum" (both recorded June, 1940), all on the Varsity Record label.

"Our first recordings were made in Chicago at a very obscure studio on Wabash Avenue," Moreno recalled. "They weren't too terribly good. At least I wasn't happy with them. They never really amounted to anything."

Wanting to "move up" musically from the strictly society sounds of the Williams ensemble, Moreno received three offers simultaneously from three of the top bands of the day - Eddy Duchin, Hal Kemp, and Dick Jurgens.

"Griff's band was playing at the Chase Hotel in St. Louis in December 1940 when I got the calls," Moreno said. "I didn't know which one I wanted to take."

After some thought, Moreno opted to go with Jurgens.

"I knew Dick from the West Coast and he had a college-type band that was young and exciting," Moreno said. "Plus, he was gun-ho. I was happy with my decision."

Ironically, while Moreno was finishing his stint with Williams, Kemp was killed in a tragic automobile accident in Madera, California, on December 19, and a little while later, Duchin's medical issues began to surface.

Taking guitarist Ronny Kepper's place in the Jurgens band, Moreno also shared the boy singer duties with Harry Cool, a tall, handsome, virile, curly-haired baritone whom Perry Como had recommended highly to Jurgens.

The Jurgens band was a very commercial, romantic-sounding outfit known for its full, lush ensemble sound and danceable melodies. From the late 1930s throughout the early 1940s, the Jurgens band was the toast of Chicago, drawing huge crowds during its stints at their home bases, the Aragon and Trianon ballrooms.

"I really don't know why Dick's band was so extremely popular with Chicagoans," Moreno said. "That's a question that is kind of hard to answer. The band was very solid, very commercial and played the way the people wanted to dance. The band itself was very personable. All the patrons knew each and every band member and called them by their first names."

When the band would go on tour to play at such places at Catalina Island off the Southern California coast or at New York's Strand Theater, other name bands would be hired to fill in for Jurgens at the Aragon and Trianon ballrooms. When Jurgens would return to Chicago, dancers would welcome him back like a conquering hero worthy of a Roman triumph.

"Dick was more of a front man and was very good at what he did," Moreno said. "The crowds in Chicago just adored him. He insisted on every one in the band having a neat appearance at all times."

During the two years that Moreno was with Jurgens, he made over twenty studio recordings on the Okeh (a Columbia affiliate) and the Columbia red label as the featured vocalist. Some of those sides include "San Antonio Rose" (November 26, 1940); "Pardon Me for Falling in Love" (February 17, 1941 - this was a Griff Williams composition that was never recorded by Williams); "I've Got a Bone to Pick with You"

(April 10, 1941); "Around and Around She Goes" (September 19, 1941); "Yankee Doodle Ain't Doodlin' Now" (February 20, 1942); "Happy in Love" (January 16, 1942); "Everything I've Got" and "I'm So-So-So in Love" (both recorded on June 22, 1942). But it was the band's biggest hit, "One Dozen Roses" (recorded March 4, 1942), which helped to give more recognition to Moreno's vocal talents.

"'One Dozen Roses' was a big one for Dick," Moreno said. "We would get requests to play it everywhere we went."

With America at war in 1942, many bands were breaking up as both sideman and bandleaders alike got "caught in the draft" or were enlisting to heed their country's call for military service. Jurgens was no exception.

Jurgens was called into the Marines and when he put his band members on notice, they all decided to stick it out until the very end.

"We really had such a tight band that all the fellows made a pact to stay together until Dick actually left to go in the service," Moreno said.

The band's last public performance was on Sunday evening January 17, 1943, at the Aragon Ballroom. The event was broadcasted over radio as part of the *Fitch Bandwagon* program. Thousands of loyal Dick Jurgens fans packed the North Side dance hall to say goodbye to the Windy City's favorite bandleader.

Many offers came in during the windup and the most interesting one for Moreno came from bandleader Ted Weems who wanted the displaced singer/guitarist to replace Perry Como, he said.

"Ted called me from New Orleans and said that his whole band was being inducted into the Merchant Marine and asked if I would like to be the boy singer for his new band," Moreno said. "Perry Como was singing with Weems at the time and was classified 4-F. Ted's manager was a friend of mine and he suggested that I go with the band. I hated turning it down but I also knew my service time was drawing near."

Moreno's decision proved to be prudent because shortly after the call from Weems, Moreno received a call from trumpeter Harry James, who led one of the hottest bands in the country.

"I told Harry about the pack the guys in the band made with each other," Moreno said. "I then said if after that time his offer was still good, I'd love to join his band." James' offer was indeed still good, so Moreno joined the popular trumpet player's band in March 1943 in California.

By that time, the recording ban between the record companies and the musicians' union was into its eighth month, denying bands and its singers the opportunity to wax commercial studio recordings. But that didn't disappoint Moreno, he said.

"Just the fact that I was singing with Harry was exciting enough for me," Moreno said. "It was a great experience and a challenge. We worked the Hollywood Palladium and the Paramount Theater and the Astor Roof of the Hotel Astor in New York - all the big places. We even did the *Chesterfield* radio shows."

By 1943, James was one of America's most successful bandleaders. He sported many top-notched musicians like Corky Corcoran on tenor sax; valve trombonist Juan Tizol, who had come over from Duke Ellington's band; and Willie Smith, Jimmie Lunceford's former alto saxophonist. James rounded out the American Dream on July 5 of that year by marrying Betty Grable, pinup girl of a million G. I.s.

"Harry was without a doubt the finest trumpet player I have ever known," Moreno said. "He's still tops. He was also a very fine leader."

Moreno was with the band for only a short time before Helen Forrest, James' celebrated girl singer who helped to record many hits for the trumpeter, left to go out as a single.

"Helen was the greatest," Moreno said. "As far as I'm concerned, she was the best of the Big Band singers."

Forrest was replaced briefly by another Helen - Helen Ward, who gained notoriety singing with Benny Goodman's orchestra in the mid-1930s.

After Ward's departure, Kitty Kallen, who had left Jimmy Dorsey, stepped in when the band returned to the Astor Roof on May 22.

"Kitty was fabulous, too," he said.

During his year-stay with James, a number of Moreno's vocals have been preserved thanks to radio remotes and V-Disc recordings. Some of these recordings include "Remember" (from a remote broadcast from the Hotel Astor on June 5, 1943); "Nice Work If You Can Get It" (broadcast from the Hollywood Palladium on November 25, 1943); "Always" (broadcast from the Hollywood Palladium in January 1944); and three V-Disc recordings dated November 17, 1943: "Oh, What a Beautiful Morning!"; "Better Give Me Lots of Lovin', Honey"; and "Mexico City."

Moreno appeared in the films *Two Girls and a Sailor* (1944, starring Van Johnson, June Allyson, and Gloria DeHaven) and *Bathing Beauty* (1944, starring Esther Williams and Red Skelton) along with the rest of the James band.

Prior to leaving James for military service in March 1944, Moreno helped his boss to make a decision by offering his opinion about a singer they both heard over the radio.

"I was riding in the car with Harry to the Hollywood Palladium one night and we were listening to the Eddie Oliver band out of Chicago over the radio," Moreno recalled. "Someone was singing named Buddy DiVito. Harry asked me what I thought. I said he sounded fine. Harry then called him to join the band."

DiVito may not have been the most famous of all of the boy singers who sang with James, but he worked for the celebrated trumpeter the longest, until 1948.

When Uncle Sam took out his option on Moreno, he was initially drafted as an infantryman into the Army and was trained in chemical warfare, Moreno said.

Once the Army learned of Moreno's background, he was then transferred to Special Services hooking up with Bill Finegan, former arranger for Glenn Miller and Tommy Dorsey, who was in charge of the military band at Camp Shanks, New York. Finegan would later go on to co-lead a band during the 1950s with fellow arranger, Eddie Sauter.

Upon his discharge from the Army in 1947, Moreno went out as a single for a while, he said. He worked a few dates in New York with a band led by Eddie Stone, the former violinist/novelty singer with Freddy Martin.

After some frustrating experiences, Moreno gave up on the idea of being a single, he said.

"I wasn't happy because I was never sure as to the amount of players I would get for a job," he said. "Sometimes I'd wind up with a trio of guys who couldn't read."

Then Music Corporation of America (MCA), Moreno's booking agency, urged the guitar-playing singer to put together a commercial band.

"I thought it was a good idea and I went out to find the guys I wanted," Moreno said.

The band, patterned after the Jurgens unit, debuted at the Casa Loma Ballroom in St. Louis in the fall of 1947.

"I always liked the Jurgens sound with the full ensemble," he said.

Moreno's new outfit incorporated a little from each of the three bands from which he played, he said.

"From Griff I developed a love of Cole Porter and George Gershwin tunes," Moreno said. "When I built my library of standards, I used those composers. I incorporated some of the show band gimmicks that Dick used. All the guys in the band acted in some skits. From Harry, I utilized big swing arrangements."

By 1947, many of the noted and more established bands of the day were throwing in the towel because venues to feature such groups were drying up. The idea of forming a new band during such "lean" days in the music business didn't seem to faze Moreno, he said.

"I didn't give that too much thought," he said. "I just enjoyed doing it. I enjoyed playing at the places we played. I had a bunch of good guys. We went on for as long as we could."

When Moreno went looking for a band vocalist, little did he know he would be getting a wife as well.

"MCA knew I was looking for a girl singer to compliment me," Moreno said. "I was looking for a blonde with good looks. They told me of a gal named Perri Mitchell who was singing with a band in Minneapolis.

We were playing in Chicago at the time and so MCA brought her down for an audition. I liked how she sang and I hired her."

Less than three years later, in 1950, the bandleader and the band singer were married.

Was it love at first sight?

"Not really," Moreno said. " thought Perri sang well and I had no intentions of marrying her at first. We sort of grew on each other."

On November 20, 1947, the Moreno band recorded some transcriptions in Chicago for Lang-worth Transcriptions, their first as a unit. The selections included "Carolyn" (an original composition by Moreno), "Just an Old Stone House," "They're Mine, They're Mine, They're Mine," "I Concentrate on You," "I Went Down to Virginia, Josephine," and "I-I Love" (a duet with Perri Mitchell).

With another recording ban due to take effect staring January 1, 1948, and studio space limited, it was nearly impossible for Moreno to get back in the studios to recording anything further before year's end. He didn't think the ban hurt him any, he said.

"It just didn't allow me to make any records for a year," he said.

During his days in the Williams band, Moreno became friends with Harold Kaplar, the owner of the Chase Hotel in St. Louis. Kaplar signed Moreno and his band for the entire summer at the Chase. When the Chase Hotel engagement ended, the band hit the road to play the Peabody Hotel in Memphis, the Ansley Hotel in Atlanta, and the Aragon and Trianon ballrooms in Chicago, among others.

When 1949 rolled around, Moreno and company were eager to get back into the studios to record. They continued to make transcriptions through Lang-worth such as "How It Lies, How It Lies, How It Lies," "Doo Dee Doo on an Old Kazoo," "My Bashful Nashville Girl from Tennessee," "I'll Remember April," and "Gee, I Wish You Were My Sweetheart" (all recorded March 23, 1949 in New York).

Moreno was also able to sign a record contract that year with RCA-Victor to wax such tunes as "Carolyn," "I-I Love" (vocal duet with Perri

Mitchell), "This Will Be the Best Years of Our Lives" (with back up by trumpeter Charlie Spivak), "Doo Dee Doo on an Old Kazoo," "Johnny, Get Your Girl," "How It Lies, How It Lies, How It Lies," "Honey Bun," "Thank You," "My Bashful Nashville Gal from Tennessee," "Open Door Polka" (vocal duet with Perri Mitchell) and "Drop Daid Little Darlin.'"

He later recorded for Circle Records.

Now married and with the band business getting slimmer and slimmer, Moreno was looking for more stability in life for he and his wife. This would be the beginning for him of a long love affair with radio. MCA helped him find work in radio as a disc jockey. He was teamed up at WHHM in Memphis with Ted Weems for a year. When the contract expired, Weems went back on the road with another band while Moreno went back to St. Louis.

Beginning June 30, 1958, Moreno had a local television program, *The Buddy Moreno Show*, on KOMX-TV in St. Louis. The show lasted for eighteen months and was broadcasted five days a week and was supported by a nine-piece band which Moreno fronted, he said.

"We had guest stars come on the show like Jack Teagarden or whoever happened to be in town," Moreno said. "It was a fun show."

After the show was cancelled due to economic restraints, Moreno organized a sweet band based at the Chase Hotel, a stint which lasted over ten years.

When that ballroom in the Chase Hotel closed, Moreno returned to radio and succeeded in joining KWK as an all-night DJ. After spending ten years at that radio station, he then became Program Director of WEW radio also of St. Louis, doing a four-hour daily record show. He helped steer that station into a Big Band nostalgia format, which proved successful.

In the 1960s, Moreno traveled with Bob Hope to entertain American military personnel around the world.

"That was such a rewarding experience in so many way," Moreno said. "The boys in uniform over there really appreciated what we were doing for them."

In addition to his involvement in radio, Moreno also served as the musical director for the Fox Theater and Municipal Opera orchestras in St. Louis.

For the past five years Moreno has hosted a live jazz-big band program on Saturday afternoons from 4-7 p.m. (Central Time) over WSIE-FM (88.7), a 50,000 watt, National Public Radio, 24-hour jazz station at Southern Illinois University-Edwardsville, which serves the St. Louis region.

"I'm still a disc jockey but I do interviews, too," Moreno said. "I also play some of the newer big band and swing stuff that's out there and good small group jazz. It's more than enough radio for me."

Do any callers to the station ever request hearing a tune played by the Buddy Moreno band?

"No," Moreno said with a laugh. "They just call to talk."

Moreno continues to lead a band for special dates a few times a year in and around the St. Louis area, he said. He still does the Chuck Norman Benefit at the Regal Riverfront Inn every year. He is scheduled to perform at the12th Annual Gateway Jazz Festival on Oct. 4 at the St. Louis Airport Hilton Hotel. (www.gatewayjazzfestival.com)

"My singing was alright," Moreno said of his style. "I didn't thrill anyone with it but I found my style. It's a happy version of people singing happy tunes."

The Moreno's have called Florissant, Missouri, located seventeen miles from St. Louis, home since 1957. They have two children, a daughter, Julie, 48, and a son, Rick, 44. In 1997, Perri Mitchell Moreno died.

Julie is a professional singer who has worked the Las Vegas and Tahoe show circuit, the Municipal Opera and various nightspots around the U.S. Her strong, bluesy vocals are reminiscent of those of singer Annie Lennox. She currently sings with the rock group, "Pavlov's Dog 2000," and sings with her father whenever his band scheduled to perform. Rick is a clinical psychologist in private practice who also heads the Missouri State Mental Hospital in St. Louis and plays drums on the side.

With over seventy years in the music business it doesn't seem that

Moreno is any where close to retiring.

"I've enjoyed what I've been doing on radio, on TV and with the band and as long as I can keep it up, I will," Moreno said. "I'm getting kind of rickety right about now. I had a couple of metal hips put in but I'm doing alright."

While Moreno's musical legacy is probably more readily felt within the St. Louis area than from without, he remains uncertain as to what that legacy might be, he said.

"Gosh, I don't know," he said. "I've gotten letters from people telling me I'm a musical icon and that I've given folks a lot of pleasure with my music. If I have given them pleasure with my music then what better legacy can I leave?"

** Coda – Here is an update on Buddy Moreno since this article was published.

Moreno died at Delmar Gardens North, an assisted-living facility in Florissant, Missouri, on Sunday, November 29, 2015, at the age of 103. In addition to his wife, Moreno was preceded in death by his son, Ricardo "Rick" Moreno.

His survivors include his daughter, Julie (Michael) Hamilton; his daughter-in-law, Chris Moreno; and two granddaughters, Kara and Amanda Moreno.

He is interred at the Jefferson Barracks National Cemetery in St. Louis.

Buddy Moreno wishing a fan "Best Chesterfield Wishes" from his sponsor, Chesterfield cigarettes.

Buddy Moreno having some fun with two of his band members on a Latin tune.

The Buddy Moreno Orchestra, circa 1947. Buddy Moreno is seated in the center with his female band singer and future wife, Perri Mitchell, seated to his right.

Buddy Moreno pictured a few years before his death with friend Dick Ulett.

Buddy Moreno during his time as radio host.

Remembering Tommy

Buddy Morrow Insures Tommy Dorsey's Music Is Alive and Well

The following article on Buddy Morrow was originally published in the June 2000 issue of Jazz Connection Magazine.

Buddy Morrow has had a lot of experience being a ghost.

The trombonist/bandleader was more than a ghost in the early 1950s when he led his orchestra to record such hits as "Night Train," "One Mint Julep," and "Hey, Mrs. Jones." When the Glenn Miller estate was looking for someone to lead its "ghost" band, they wanted Morrow.

Now, for the past 23 years (and still going!), Morrow has been the musical director of the Tommy Dorsey ("ghost") Orchestra insuring that the Dorsey sound is alive and well. And Morrow will be the first to tell you that Dorsey was very special.

"Tommy open a lot of doors for me," said Morrow, 81, last month via telephone from his home in Maitland, Florida. "I worked in Tommy's band from 1938-39. He helped give me a goal and a way of presentation as a musician and as a leader."

Dorsey, known as "The Sentimental Gentleman of Swing," led one of the best all-around dance bands during the 1930s and '40s. He was a very demanding musician who knew what he wanted and who also demanded a lot from the musicians who worked for him. To achieve the sound he wanted, he hired many talented composers and arrangers such as Matt

Dennis, Paul Weston, Sy Oliver and Axel Stordahl. He showcased singers who could project a variety of musical moods wonderfully: Jack Leonard, Jo Stafford, Connie Haines, The Pied Pipers, and Frank Sinatra, the biggest name singer of the era to have come through the Dorsey camp.

Over the years, many top-notch musicians filtered through the Dorsey ranks such as Bud Freeman, Heine Beau, Don Lodice, Buddy Rich, Skeets Herfurt, Max Kaminsky, Johnny Mince, Buddy DeFranco, Peewee Erwin, Ziggy Elman, Joe Bushkin, Charlie Shavers, Babe Russin, Bunny Berigan and of course, Buddy Morrow.

"Tommy loved talent and wanted to showcase it whenever he could," Morrow recalled. "He was also unpredictable. He could be a wonderful friend and a formidable enemy. If you take Jackie Gleason, Frank Sinatra, and Buddy Rich and put them all together, you'd have Tommy Dorsey. He was the nicest guy in the world yet he could be the toughest guy in the world. He could also be very generous when it was his idea."

It was Dorsey's generous words uttered to his young teenage trombonist that proved to be prophetic.

"Tommy once told me, 'Someday you are going to lead this band,'" Morrow said. "I was nineteen at the time. It took a little while, but, here I am!"

Born Muni Zudekoff (aka Moe Zudekoff) on February 8, 1919, in New Haven, Connecticut, to Sophie and David Zudekoff. He was the fifth of six siblings, all musicians, having received early musical training on the violin and cello. At age twelve he was given a trombone at school because they were short on trombonists that year.

"No one knew how well I was going to do on the horn," Morrow said. "After about six months, it was evident that the trombone and myself were going to do pretty well together."

By age 15 he was playing with the Yale Collegians, a group of college musicians.

Acting on the advice of a friend, he headed for New York City to pursue a career as a musician. In November 1936, he hooked up with clarinetist Artie Shaw who was forming a new band at the time consisting of a string quartet, two trumpets, one trombone, a tenor sax and rhythm section. It became known as "Art Shaw and His New Music."

"We had four future bandleaders in Artie's group," Morrow pointed out. "There was Lee Castle on trumpet, Tony Pastor on tenor sax, myself, and Glenn Miller's arranger, Jerry Gray, who played violin and accordion."

In December of that year, Shaw recorded "Sobbin' Blues" and "Cream Puff": (both on December 23) on which the teenage Morrow's trombone could be heard.

After six months of struggle, Shaw scrapped the string quartet and formed a more conventional swing band which featured bigger and more blasting brass sections.

"It was a wonderful band and very musical," Morrow said. "Artie was a brilliant leader. In my observation, he was like the Tchaikovsky of Jazz, playing with a much bigger sound with too many ideas. While Artie's main rival on the clarinet, Benny Goodman, was like the Picasso of Jazz, playing with very clear beautiful lines."

When Shaw disbanded his orchestra in February 1937 to reorganize, Morrow stayed in New York and applied for admission to the Julliard School of Music. Showing up for the initial audition without any music, Morrow basically winged it.

"I was trained as a youngster in classical music and so I played some examples from the classics that I knew," he said. "The committee wanted me to play something more complicated so I played a tough trumpet solo piece that I had studied. I played the heck out of it! Somewhere along the way, I had forgotten the remainder of the piece, so I improvised. Two weeks later, I got accepted with a full scholarship!"

By the time he was ready to enter Julliard, Morrow accepted an offer to join society pianist Eddie Duchin in May 1937. He stayed with the band about a year, replacing Frank Saracco as the sole trombonist.

In the summer of 1938, Morrow joined the Tommy Dorsey orchestra.

During his brief stay with Dorsey, Morrow helped to record a pair of huge Dorsey standards: "Boogie Woogie" (September 16, 1938) and

"Hawaiian War Chant" (November 29, 1938).

Other various personnel during Morrow's stint with the Dorsey band included Pee Wee Erwin, Lee Castle, Yank Lawson, Max Kaminsky, and Charlie Spivak, trumpets; Les Jenkins and Earle Hagen, trombones; Johnny Mince, clarinet/alto sax; Fred Stulce and Hymie Shertzer, alto saxes; Skeets Herfurt, Dean Kincaide, and Babe Russin, tenor saxes; Howard Smith, piano; Carmen Mastren, guitar; Gene Traxler, bass; and Maurice Purtill, drums. Vocalists were Jack Leonard and Edythe Wright.

Morrow would have been contented to stay longer with Dorsey but he rebelled when Dorsey hired a third trombonist, Elmer Smithers, and paid him $40 a week more than what Morrow was earning. When Morrow protested, Dorsey gave him a $10 raise as compensation. Instead, Morrow joined up with Paul Whiteman in early January 1939, replacing the legendary Jack Teagarden, who left to form his own outfit. With Whiteman, Morrow was earning $50 a week more than he had with Dorsey.

But there is one thing that Morrow appreciated from his time spent with Dorsey - something that money couldn't buy and which he has carried with him throughout his musical career - and that is, phrasing.

"Phrasing is a wonderful thing through the art of trombone playing," Morrow said. "There has to be a sense of fluidity, a sense of being able to contribute something musically. That's what I appreciated most from Tommy. Up until Tommy came along, the trombone had been appreciated, but unused in the manner in which Tommy used it. He was a great ballad player with excellent taste. He was a perfectionist with his musicians as he was with himself."

Whiteman, who had pioneered a symphonic approach to dance music and had gained the misnomer as "The King of Jazz" was "a great storyteller and he knew how to choose and showcase talent," Morrow said.

He performed with Whiteman's Concert Orchestra for their Decca/Brunswick recording of Gershwin's *Concerto in F*.

A stint with Bob Crosby soon followed, beginning in the summer of 1941 - this time with a name change from Muni Zudekoff to "Muni Morrow."

"The name change came as a result of a very convenient telephone book," Morrow related. "I opened the page and Wham! There I had it! I later went by the name of 'Buddy.'"

Morrow cut twenty-eight sides with the Crosby Orchestra including such notable recordings as "Vultee Special," "Russan Sailors' Dance," and "Zoot Suit" (vocal by Nappy Lamar - all three on January 20, 1942); "Sugar Foot Stomp" and "Jimtown Blues" (both on January 27, 1942); and "Chain Gang" (February 17, 1942).

Other personnel in the Crosby band at the time were Yank Lawson, Max Herman, and Lyman Vunk, trumpets; Floyd O'Brien and Elmer Smithers, trombones; Matty Matlock, clarinet; Arthur "Doc" Rando and Art Mendelsohn, alto saxes; Eddie Miller and Gil Rodin, tenor saxes; Jess Stacy, piano; Nappy Lamar, guitar; Bob Haggart, bass; Ray Bauduc, drums. Along with Crosby, Liz Tilton, and later Muriel Lane, supplied the vocal duties.

Morrow was not part of the Bob Cats, an eight-man Dixieland band, that was a signature part of the Crosby set up. Floyd O'Brien held that trombone position.

When America entered World War II, Morrow served in the Merchant Marine, then in the Navy for three years. He got his first experience leading a band as a Musician First Class while serving in the Navy on Staten Island from 1941 to 1944.

After the war, Morrow joined Jimmy Dorsey. On one occasion when Dorsey took ill, Morrow filled in as leader. He soon formed his own band.

RCA-Victor signed Morrow to record under his own name but by the early 1950s, the band wasn't enjoying the commercial success it had earlier.

Then one night in Detroit, the famed radio disc jockey, Ed McKenzie, known to his listeners as "Jack, the Bell Boy," suggested to Morrow that he record an exciting rhythm and blues number called "Night Train," composed by former Duke Ellington saxophonist, Jimmy Forrest. Forrest recorded the tune in November 1951 on the United Records label earning for himself a major rhythm and blues hit.

Morrow recorded it and the song became a national sensation selling over a million copies. The band had established itself as one of the big musical attractions on the road.

"I had no idea that 'Night Train' would become a standard when I recorded it,"Morrow said. "It was part of our last desperate attempt to create something that was marketable."

"Night Train" reached No. 27 on the charts, and No. 23 in the UK Singles Chart in March 1953.

Several different sets of lyrics were then written for the song. The earliest, written in 1952, are credited to Lewis P. Simpkins, the co-owner of United Records, and guitarist Oscar Washington.

Other hit recording followed for Morrow including "One Mint Julep," "I Don't Know," and "Hey, Mrs. Jones."

Among Morrow's albums are *Night Train; Big Band Guitar* (RCA-Victor, 1959); *New Blues Scene; Impact* (RCA-Victor, 1959, about American television themes); *Double Impact* (RCA-Victor, 1959, more American television themes); *Campus After Dark;* and several albums in tribute to both Tommy and Jimmy Dorsey.

Morrow returned to the studios for awhile and appeared on the Sid Caesar and Perry Como shows. He conducted for the Jimmy Rodgers television show and was on staff at NBC for years as a featured player on the *Tonight Show.*

He was also a frequent performer leading his Big Band at Disneyland, when the renowned theme park featured its Big Band Showcase during the summers.

From September 17, 1974 to March 30, 1975, Morrow was tapped to direct the World Famous Glenn Miller Orchestra, succeeding Peanuts Hucko in that capacity. Morrow was the fourth leader of the GMO since its inception in 1956.

Then in 1977, he took over at the helm of the seventeen-piece Tommy Dorsey Orchestra when its trombonist/leader Murray McEachern died.

Since Dorsey's death in November 1956, other leaders who preceded Morrow in this assignment were saxophonist Sam Donahue and trombonist Warren Covington.

Morrow's artistic vision made him the right choice for the job.

"I've always looked to playing my best and looking at what was going on around me," Morrow said. "My motto has always been, 'Anything you can do, I can do better.' I practiced until I could do it better. I'd make sure that I'd always wanted to add a little something more to the cake. Every time one picks up a horn, there's a certain amount of artistic endeavor there."

Morrow will admit that his music would have its place in nostalgia if it weren't for him leading the Tommy Dorsey band.

"Oh sure," he said. "My band ended up being a rhythm and blues band before we started misnaming it with rock and roll."

Morrow takes his job as leader of the Tommy Dorsey Orchestra very seriously. For him, it's like being on a mission.

"The mission is to play the Tommy Dorsey arrangements as they were supposed to be played and with the perfection that Tommy insisted upon," Morrow said. "We do that with complete regard for what I consider his way of doing things."

Yet the band does not play Dorsey standards as if it were a live 78 RPM record. They sometimes take an old arrangement and "tweak" it a little to give it a contemporary edge, Morrow said.

"You have to go with the times," he said.

While every tune in the band's library it not strictly a Dorsey tune, the band does play other selections that fit the *parameters* of the Dorsey sound, Morrow said.

"We are permitted by the Dorsey estate to play non-Dorsey tunes but we use them sparingly," Morrow said. "To use them all the time I might as well drop the Dorsey name and go as Buddy Morrow and his Orchestra. We have a certain percentage that we adhere to pretty well."

Sometimes band members want to disregard their mission and branch out to play other material. When that happens, Morrow has to step in to police the action, he said.

"As bandleader, I'm somewhat of a dictator and that's the way the band has to be," Morrow said. "The band has to reflect what is demanded. I do what I think is right. You have to look at your audience and decide what brings out the best in all. It's a lesson in plain common sense, which is very uncommon. I know we have a job to do and it's my effort to see that we have audience satisfaction."

It is Morrow's hope that listeners will walk away from a Tommy Dorsey Orchestra performance whistling some of the tunes, he said.

"More than anything, I want listeners to walk away with a big smile knowing that they had a good time and knowing we did what we were supposed to do," Morrow said.

Although turnovers in the band are a constant problem, the average age of the band members is about twenty-five, Morrow said.

"We get good musicians any way we can find them," he said. "It's tough to find guys who can double out of Tommy's book."

Depending on the condition and place, attendance by more young people at a Tommy Dorsey Orchestra performance has increased over the years, Morrow said.

While spending about forty-two weeks a year on the road, Morrow and company perform seventy percent of there gigs in concert settings, he said.

"It's a concert of dance music," he said. "It was dance music at the time, and it's now become a type of presentation that is a little different than five or six guys on stage electrifying an audience."

Last month, the band spent nine days performing aboard a Rotterdam Cruise line from New York to Lisbon, Portugal. The band itinerary also includes four or five cruises a year down the Mississippi River, Morrow said.

The Tommy Dorsey Orchestra also maintains a web site which also includes the bands performance schedule. The web site address is: www.tommydorseyorchestra.com.

Morrow has also been asked to reproduce a lot of the Dorsey material to be recorded on CD. Although still in the planning stage, final approval for the project would have to come from the Tommy Dorsey estate, he said.

"We will be coming out with a new product of old tunes," Morrow said.

Having spent over two decades of leading the Tommy Dorsey band with its sometimes grueling travel schedule, Morrow brings mental freshness to his role as musical director by approaching every performance as though it was his first, he said.

"We have to do that in order to have the strength and the emotional stamina to do what is needed for the Tommy Dorsey band," Morrow said. "Tommy had very high standards for his music. It's up to us to be part and partial to those particular standards."

For Morrow, every Tommy Dorsey tune has a certain gem-like quality to them and he is particularly attracted to the ballad selections that are in the band's library.

"I loved the ballads and how they they were constructed and how they featured Tommy," Morrow said. "I'll never forget a recording that Tommy made with Jack Leonard doing the vocal on 'All the Things You Are.' It's a beautiful piece. It set a certain standard for trombone playing. It's one of my favorite arrangements."

However, Morrow's favorites are what the public enjoys the most, he said.

"In that respect, the altruism stops at the cashier's table," he said.

With over sixty-five years in the music business and with no signs of slowing down, Morrow said he would still do it all over again.

"I'd be more flamboyant about it, though," he said. "I would know that we were in a very special period and we were playing a very special kind of music that would last a long time and would have its place. The audiences are at its biggest at the day the music is developing. The music we have here in our band is quality. Even though it's old and wrinkled, it still has value!"

It's Morrow's quality of musical artistry and taste that he offers as his legacy to music, he said.

"My legacy is being one of the top trombone players in the world and still being at an age to tell you how it's done," he said. "It's also hopefully exhibiting good taste and a respect for *all* music that's done with good taste of what was wanted by the composer or arranger. To this day, the arrangers don't have the credit that they deserve. They are instrumental in making a band sound great."

** Coda – Here is an update on Buddy Morrow since this article was published.

In 2009, Morrow was awarded the International Trombone Association's Lifetime Achievement Award, an award that is given to a person who has significantly changed trombone playing around the world.

Morrow led the Tommy Dorsey Orchestra from 1977 through September 24, 2010, when he appeared with the band for the final time. Morrow died in the morning on September 27, 2010, at his home in Maitland, Fla. He was 91.

Morrow is survived by his third wife, Carol Morrow; their daughter Sara, of Los Angeles; a son, Peter, of Hillsdale, New Jersey, from his first marriage, to Lucille Ross; a daughter, Catherine, of Marietta, Georgia, from his second marriage, to Clare Eggleston; and three grandchildren.

Terry Myers succeed Morrow as the director of the Tommy Dorsey Orchestra.

Buddy Morrow as a fledging bandleader during the late 1940s.

Buddy Morrow, 82, as director of the Tommy Dorsey Orchestra, playing at Feather Falls Casino in Oroville, California, August 7, 2001. – *Photos by Stephen Fratallone*

Buddy Morrow, 81, directing the Tommy Dorsey Orchestra for a dance on June 8, 2000, at the Jackson Rancheria Hotel and Casino in Jackson, CA. – *Photo by Stephen Fratallone*

Buddy Morrow at 81, at Jackson, CA.
– *Photo by Stephen Fratallone*

When His "Singing Guitar" Talks, People Listen

Famed Bandleader Alvino Rey Helped Introduce Electric Steel Guitar To Music World

The following article on Alvino Rey was originally published in the May 2000 issue of Jazz Connection Magazine.

When bandleader Alvino Rey first started picking on the guitar as a young man, he never thought that his instrument of choice would be as popular as it is today.

"I honestly had no idea," Rey said via telephone from his home in Sandy, Utah. "Ever since rock 'n roll came on the scene, it seems like now every kid wants to play the electric guitar."

Rock 'n roll may have popularized the guitar, but it was musicians like Rey, who led a family-oriented commercial dance band during the late 1930s and '40s which featured his "Singing Guitar" and the female quartet, The King Sisters, that helped introduce the electric guitar to the music business as a solo instrument.

"It (the electric steel guitar) was something new at the time, so I guess I could be called an innovator of sorts," said Rey, now 88. "Originally, it was a Hawaiian steel guitar and over the years I added pedals to it in order to make the chord changes."

This was during the time when plectrists such as Rey as well as Les

Paul and the late Charlie Christian were considered by many to be the top guitarists during the Swing Era.

Rey was born Alvin McBurney of Scotch-Irish ancestry on July 1, 1908, in Oakland, California. Some sources list the year of his birth as 1911. While growing up in Cleveland, Ohio, Rey first took up playing the banjo for several years before switching over to guitar.

"I then heard a few wonderful guitar players and that's when I got interested in the guitar," he said.

One of those wonderful guitarists that Rey heard was Eddie Lang. Along with jazz violinist Joe Venuti, Rey became enamored with both men's artistries, he said.

As a teen, Rey even put together a little jazz combo similar in style to that of Lang and Venuti.

It wasn't until a trip made to New York City when the young eighteen-year-old budding guitarist met his idol for the first time and as a result, got a "pre-owned" damaged guitar out of the encounter.

"Lang was the first person I went to see when I got to New York," Rey recalled. "I went up to his hotel. He was very nice. He had two guitars in his room. He was going to send one back to the manufacturer because it had a crack in it. I asked him if I could have the guitar. He gave it to me."

It was while working as a solo act that Rey adopted his new stage name.

"The entertainment people thought that McBurney wasn't a good name," Rey said. "It's different now. All the funny names or unusual names come in as big as anything. My Spanish teacher called me *Alvino* for Alvin. That's how it started out. I made the name legal in 1946 when I got out of the Navy."

Rey soon found a spot in Phil Spitalny's orchestra in 1927. This was before Spitalny surrounded himself with a bevy of female musicians for his *Hour of Charm* radio series in the late 1930s.

Soon after the stock market crashed in 1929, Spitalny's band broke up and Rey returned to his native San Francisco and worked for three years as a staff musician at NBC radio.

It was while working on radio that Rey introduced the electric steel guitar.

Rey love to tinker. At age fifteen, Rey invented an electrical amplifier for the guitar, but failed to have it patented. He did patent a number of improvements years later. But it was while tinkering with Hawaiian or "lap" steel guitars, he added pedals to the instrument to get shifts in the tuning. That eventually led the Gibson Guitar Company to conduct research-and-development work that evolved into the pedal steel guitar that is widely used in country music.

The unusual instrument also caught the attention of bandleader Horace Heidt. Heidt was a smart businessman who led a successful show band during the 1920s through the 1950s. He was astute enough to recognize fine talent and had the savvy to know what would draw public interest to his shows.

"When I wasn't working with the radio orchestra, I did a solo act playing the Spanish guitar and the electric steel guitar at the Orpheum Theatre in San Francisco," Rey recalled. "No one had ever heard of the electric steel guitar and people made a big fuss over it. After seeing how the instrument was accepted by listeners, Horace then asked me to join his band."

That was in 1933. During his five-year stay with Heidt, Rey, along with pianist Frankie Carle, alto saxophonist and arranger Frank DeVol, trombonist Ernie Passoja, and the vocal foursome of the King Sisters - Alyce, Luise, Donna and Yvonne - helped to establish Heidt as a dance band rather than just a stage band.

Heidt was always looking for talent that was new and different to present to his public and he insisted that his musicians be full of musical tricks and gimmicks. Rey, for instance, created all sorts of novelty effects with his electric guitar, he said.

Heidt was a hard-nosed bandleader who could be difficult to deal with, especially with members of his band. He is also credited for nurturing, at least on the surface, a "family feeling" among his band - and he never let anyone forget his paternal role in that family.

"Horace was strict but he was very personable with the public," Rey said. "He had his symptoms with the band. He'd like some musicians and there were some he didn't like. I always got along fine with him."

On June 16, 1937, Heidt and His Brigadiers began recording for Brunswick after a nearly eight-year absence from the recording studios. Rey and the King Sisters helped Heidt wax four sides on that session with "Hot Lips" (vocal by The King Sisters), "Gone With the Wind" (vocal by Larry Cotton), "The Bells of St. Mary's" and "The Farmer's Daughter, Marianne" (both vocals by Bob McCoy and The Glee Club).

During that thirteen-month period to July 8, 1938, Rey helped Heidt record eight-three tunes for Brunswick.

In May 1937, Rey married Luise King. In 1938, when Heidt's Musical Knights band (as it was now called) landed a spot at the Baltimore Hotel in New York, Heidt was bitter and irritated that the sponsor signed them up because they were impressed by Alyce King's vocals. He took the first opportunity to fire her - when she dropped her microphone and it hit an audience member. The other Sisters immediately resigned, followed by Rey, and then saxophonist Frank DeVol.

Rey went on to form his own band, utilizing the King Sisters as his prime attraction. They settled in Los Angeles, California. The Kings came from Utah and making their home in Los Angeles was a lot closer to their native "Beehive State" than New York.

Radio station KHJ asked Rey to form a studio band. Assured of work, Rey sent for Frank DeVol to create a new library for the band and asked friend and saxophonist Arthur "Skeets" Herfurt to leave Tommy Dorsey in order to assume the lead alto chair.

Rey's new band quickly gained popularity with West Coast audiences as a result of transcribed radio shows.

"We started out as more of a swing band and played more jazz," Rey said. "We played a lot of pieces what the musicians liked."

Rey and his band only stayed on the West Coast for about a year before being booked in New York's Biltmore Hotel and at the Rustic Cabin across the Hudson River in Englewood, New Jersey.

"We took only two of the L.A. musicians with us to New York because they had musicians' union cards for New York," Rey said. "We then formed a new band made up mostly of East Coast musicians."

Rey's East Coast debut at The Biltmore Hotel didn't fare well as hotel management insisted that the band play soft, quiet background music for its customers instead of its big swing arrangements. As a result, the band was fired. But the Rustic Cabin engagement a week later, proved to be a completely different experience. College kids came out in droves to hear the band and they loved what they heard. The band broadcasted nightly over WOR radio and gained a huge following.

It was during this time that Rey developed his "singing guitar" trademark.

"The name sort of fit us," Rey said. "The talking guitar bit was more of a style, too. We tried to build all our music around the guitar. As you would hear the band on the air, you'd also hear the guitar. Then we'd get carried away with jazz and forget about the guitar. The band was made up of such fine musicians that sometimes we'd get a little too far out and loud for the customers."

Starting in 1939, for the band's opening theme, Rey employed a weird but successful effect that sounded like electronic voices. Rey used a carbon throat microphone to modulate his electric guitar sound. The mike, developed for military pilots, was worn by Rey's wife Luise, who stood behind a curtain and sang along with the guitar lines. The novel combination was called "Singing Guitar," and later became known as the Sonovox. Along with early Vocoders (initially called Voders), which were initially developed to scramble messages between the Pentagon and field commanders during World War II, the Sonovox innovation was one of the first known talk box experiments.

"We had some microphones that were the opposite of throat microphones," Rey described. "It was like a loud speaker unit fastened to your throat. The guitar would play musically into it and the voice, usually done by my wife, Luise, would mouth the words and it would come out with an eerie effect almost like that of an alien."

In 1940, Rey signed on with RCA-Victor to make records with its affiliate and less-expensive label, Bluebird. The band's first recording session took place in New York on November 18 with "St. Louis Blues," "Tiger Rag," and "Row, Row, Row Your Boat" (all three vocals by The Four King Sisters), and "Rose Room," an instrumental.

In the band at the time were Frank Strasek, Paul Fredericks and Danny Vannelli, trumpets; Jerry Rosa and Wallace "Blue" Barron, trombones; Kermit Levinsky and Bill Sine, alto saxophones: Skeets Herfurt and Jerry Sanfino, tenor saxophones; Milt Raskin, piano; Dick Morgan, guitar; Gene Traxler, bass; and Bunny Shawker, drums.

From November 18, 1940 thru July 24, 1942, Rey and company recorded seventy commercial sides for Bluebird and Victor, including the band's closing theme song, "Nighty Night," sung with a sultry vocal by Yvonne King on February 3, 1941.

Joining the band in early 1941 was pianist Edwin LeMar Cole, better known as Buddy Cole. He would later marry Yvonne King.

On November 21, 1941, the band recorded its playful version of "Deep in the Heart of Texas." The piece became a huge hit for Rey, due to the energetic novelty singing styles of sax man Skeets Herfurt and trombonist Bill Schallen. The record's "B" side, "I Said No!" a provocative-sounding vocal by Yvonne King, also recorded that same day, also became a chart-topper. In fact, during February 1942, both songs were listed on *Billboard's* Top Ten Chart, along with the bands of Glenn Miller, Woody Herman, Sammy Kaye, Jimmie Lunceford, Harry James and singer Kate Smith.

Other popular recordings comprising the Rey canon during this time include the flag-waving "Tiger Rag;" "The William Tell Overture, Parts 1 & 2" and "Where You Are" (vocal by Alyce King, both on Feb. 3, 1941); "In the Hall of the Mountain King" (June 10, 1941); "The Skunk Song" (vocal by Dick Morgan, October 24, 1941); "Little Hawk" (January 27,

1942), the surreal "Picnic in Purgatory" (vocal by Charles Brosen, March 12, 1942); and a care free version of "Strip Polka" (vocal by The King Sisters and Chorus, July 24, 1942).

In 1942, Rey was selected top guitarist by readers through *Metronome Magazine's* readers' poll. On January 16 of that year, Rey became a Metronome All-Star, joining fellow poll winners clarinetist Benny Goodman, trumpeter Cootie Williams, trombonist J.C. Higgenbotham, alto saxophonist Benny Carter, tenor saxophonist Charlie Barnet, pianist Count Basie, bassist John Kirby, and drummer Gene Krupa, to cut a rousing recording of "I Got Rhythm."

"It was quite an honor being named to the Metronome All-Stars," Rey said. "It was a thrill being able to cut a record with those giants of jazz."

Earlier that same year, a young Kai Winding became a member of Rey's trombone section.

Rey, his orchestra, and the King Sisters also appeared in several movies including *Larceny With Music* (1943 - starring Allan Jones and Kitty Carlisle); *Jam Session* (1944 - starring Ann Miller and Jess Barker also with Louis Armstrong, Charlie Barnet, Glen Gray, Teddy Powell, and Jan Garber and their orchestras, and The Pied Pipers) and *The All-American Band,* an RKO film made in response to fan voting, Rey said.

In late 1942, Rey formed what he called "the best band I ever had; it was my favorite."

Unfortunately, musicians' union president James Caesar Petrillo called a musician's strike against the record companies that began on August 1 and Rey's "best band" never got to record. In addition to sporting many fine jazz musicians, the band also employed the stellar arranging talents of Neal Hefti, Ray Conniff, Johnny Mandel, and Billy May.

"It was large band," Rey said. "We sort of outdid Stan Kenton. We had the best musicians in the country and the band really swung well. We had six saxes, ten brass with four bass trumpets, and seven vocalists, including Andy Russell."

In addition to singing, Russell also played drums. Other noted Big Band era drummers who passed through the Rey band during this period were Don Lamond, Irv Cottler, Nick Fatool, Davey Tough and Mel Lewis.

Although no commercial studio recordings were made with this 1942-43 band, numerous radio transcriptions from the Hollywood Palladium and the College Inn do exist. Rey is spending a great deal of time these days preparing them for sale on CDs, he said.

"Because of the record ban at that time, we weren't allowed to sell these radio transcriptions," Rey said. "I'm surprised as to how many of these air checks I have. Some of them are wonderful! In those days we were broadcasting using one microphone. There are very few turn tables that can play these 16-inch records and there is one at nearby Brigham Young University. We are transcribing everything on to CD and we are trying to polish them up to get the "pops" out of everything. It's a big challenge for me but I'm enjoying it."

In 1943, Rey took a war-plant job with Vega Aircraft in Los Angeles where he inspected radio parts for the B-29 Flying Fortresses. Working the night shift, he still tried to keep his band going during the day with weekly radio broadcasts and irregular personal appearances.

"In 1943 everyone was getting drafted," Rey said. "I still played mostly on weekends. Most of the guys did this kind of thing in order to get out of the draft."

Time caught up with Rey and the following year he was inducted into the Navy, utilizing his specialty in the field of electronics as a part-time instructor at radar school.

"I knew more about electronics than I did about music," Rey said. "For the war effort, I thought I'd be more valuable to be in something that was important like electronics."

After the war, Rey settled in Los Angeles and formed another band while signing on with Capitol Records. During his time at Capitol, he produced a 1946 cover hit of Slim Gaillard's "Cement Mixer (Puddy Puddy)," which became a hit and jazz-oriented pieces such as "High Octane," "Steel Guitar Rag" and "Cumana," a fast mambo-fused tune composed by jazz pianist Barclay Allen, Harold Spina, and guitarist Roc Hillman. Rey also recognized the singing talents of Blossom Dearie, then a member of his "Blue Reys" vocal group.

With the Big Bands quickly fading out, Rey's orchestra didn't stay together for much longer. Rey returned to do studio work only to lead a band occasionally for special television performances and for casuals around the country, he said.

Rey was also a featured member of Carl Cotner's small musical group, "The Melody Ranch Hard-Way Six," on Gene Autry's *Melody Ranch* radio shows in the early 1950s.

The King Family, whom Rey married into, was large and musical. After their presumed retirement, an unusual extended-family charity performance in the mid-1960s at Brigham Young University led to renewed interest in their careers.

When the three dozen members of the King Family appeared on ABC's *Hollywood Palace* variety show, they drew more than 50,000 fan letters of appreciation. ABC brought them back into the spotlight as stars of *The King Family*, a wholesome hour-long program that involved as many as sixty relatives.

"We had tremendous exposure with the TV show," Rey said. "I think it helped revitalized our careers. It certainly kept my name in the limelight."

The King Family television show lasted off and on for about five years, beginning in 1965, Rey said.

"It was a family-oriented show," Rey said. "We tried to play good music on it. We had a very good band and wonderful arrangers such as Lennie Niehaus, Ralph Carmichael, Dick Grove and Perry Botkin, Jr. The show caught on for a few years and then began to drop off. We don't know exactly why. Maybe people got tired of seeing the same thing over and over again."

Members of the King Family included Karleton Driggs (brother of the King Sisters), his wife, Hazel, and their three children, Bill Driggs III, Don Driggs and Raymond Driggs; Bill Driggs, Jr. (brother of the King Sisters) and his wife, Phyliss, and their three children, Stephen, Debra and Jonathan; Maxine King and her husband, LaVern Thomas, and their two children, Carolyn and Tom; Luise King (wife of Alvino Rey) and their three children, Robert, Liza and Jon; Alyce King and her husband, actor Robert Clarke, and their son, Cameron. Alyce was previously married to the late Sydney de Azevedo and has two sons by that marriage, Lex and Ric; Donna King and her husband, Jim Conkling, and their five children, Candy Wilson (who is married to Robert Wilson), Jamie, Christopher, Xandra, and Laurette Conkling; Yvonne King, by a previous marriage to the late Buddy Cole, has two daughters, Tina and Cathy Cole. She was married at the time of the show to bandleader Del Courtney; and Marilyn King and her two children, Susannah and Adam Lloyd. She was married at the time of the show to Kent Larsen, now deceased.

Although Rey has been a giant in the jazz and pop music fields, his first love is playing classical guitar. It's his favorite form of music, he admitted.

"My right hand never worked well to play a lot of classical stuff," Rey lamented. "I had some mechanical trouble with my right hand. I don't have any problems playing with the pick. As much as I love classical music, I never tried to aspire to be a classical guitarist."

But that never discouraged Rey from absorbing as much classical guitar as he could. He even learned from the best: the late, great Andres Segovia.

"I spent many years with Segovia both in Spain and at his seminars here in America," Rey said. "It was a big thrill in my life to study with him. I learned a lot of expression from him. Segovia was a determined player. He never did anything but play the guitar. He'd even lay there in bed not even dressed and practice guitar!"

Rey's whole life has been absorbed in music. His enthusiastic interest in music still remains to this day. He continually sharpens his guitar skills by practicing all the time and by performing solos and concerts with symphony orchestras throughout the country, he said.

"I've always been excited about jazz and I love jazz music very much," he said. "Unfortunately, there was never much money in jazz so that's why I went into more commercial things."

With having played so many important engagements over the years since his band was formed, Rey lists playing for Ronald Reagan's gubernatorial and presidential inaugural balls as his most memorable performances.

In 1979, Rey and his family moved from Southern California to relocate in Sandy, Utah, a suburb of Salt Lake City.

In the 1980s, Rey and his band made a tour of college campuses with the King Sisters and former Claude Thornhill star vocalist Fran Warren.

Rey and the King Sisters no longer perform together as a group but they do see each other frequently at family gatherings, he said.

Rey still records with small groups and his latest release, *Keep on Smiling,* an album of most requested tunes, was recorded on his Alysa Record label three years ago. His current project, *Song of the Islands,* an album of Hawaiian music played on his Hawaiian steel guitar, has not yet been released, he said.

"I'm just waiting to get the album cover made for it," he said.

Many of Rey's CDs may be purchased through Alysa Records at P.O. Box 901321, Sandy, Utah 84090.

Rey has three grown children - a daughter, Liza Rey Butler (born May 13, 1947), who is an international harpist and with whom Rey performs on occasion; and two sons, Robert (born May 3, 1946) and Jon (born February 4, 1952), who are musical but are not in the music business; and six grandchildren and a great-grandson, he said. Rey's two grandsons, Win and Will Butler, are members of the Canadian indie rock group, Arcade Fire.

In 1997, after 60 years of marriage, Luise King Rey died at age 83. She gave her final performance before 15,000 people at a Utah centennial celebration the previous year. In 1996, sister Alyce King Clarke died. Today, four King Sisters remain: Maxine, Donna, Yvonne and Marilyn.

In 1983, Luise King Rey wrote *Those Swinging Years* (Olympus Publishing), a book about Rey's band and the King Sisters' rise to fame.

While Rey continues to make wonderful music, he admits that he is ignorant of what young people listen to these days, he said.

"I don't know that much about it," he said. "I don't why some of the pop music that's out there is so successful. The music seems to fit the kids today as to what they want. The kids I know today are good classical players and there are also a few good jazz players among the bunch."

Playing good music has always been a trademark of Alvino Rey. Having led one of the most successful, popular, and many would even say fun bands during Big Band Era, Rey believes that having given his public years of good musical entertainment would be his contribution to the history of American popular music.

"We always thought we were playing good music," he said. "We wanted a good band and we all agreed that this kind of music is what we liked. I think we were right."

** Coda – Here is an update on Alvino Rey since this article was published.

Rey remained an amateur radio operator for years, holding his call handle as W6UK.

In 2001, Rey released his *Song of the Islands* CD.

On March 3, 2002, Rey, along with the King Sisters were the recipients of the Golden Bandstand Award from the Big Band Academy of America. The 94-year-old Rey attended the affair at the Sportsmen's Lodge in Studio City, CA, and performed "Cumana" on guitar in amazing and thrilling fashion, along with technical precision and imagaination.

In 2004, after breaking his hip and suffering complications including pneumonia and congestive heart failure, Rey died on February 24, 2004, at a rehabilitation center in Draper, Utah, hear his home in Sandy. He was 95. He is interred at Cypress Lawn Memorial Park in Colma, California.

Alyce King Clarke died on August 23, 1996. She was 81.

Donna King Conkling died on June 16, 2007. She was 88.

Yvonne King Burch died on December 13, 2009, at age 89.

Marilyn King Thomas died on August 7, 2013. She was 82. She was the last of the King Sisters.

Alvino Rey, seated at his Gibson Electraharp electric steel guitar, surrounded by the King Sisters: (l-r) Yvonne, Donna, Luise, and Alyce, from a Gibson Guitar ad from early 1942.

Alvino Rey, 94, with his guitar at the Big Band Academy of America's annual reunion on March 3, 2002, at the Sportsmen's Lodge in Studio City, CA. – *Photo by Stephen Fratallone*

At age 94, Alvino Rey wows the audience at the BBAA with his flaw- less version of "Cumana" on the guitar. – *Photos by Stephen Fratallone*

Remembering Artie Shaw

Jazz Giant/Bandleader Artie Shaw Dies at Age 94

The following article on Artie Shaw was originally published in the January 2005 issue of Jazz Connection Magazine - with contributions from Associated Press news sources.

Artie Shaw, the jazz clarinetist and big-band leader who successfully challenged Benny Goodman's reign as the King of Swing with his recordings of "Begin the Beguine," "Oh! Lady Be Good," and "Star Dust" in the late 1930s, died on Thursday, December 30, 2004, at his home in Newbury Park, California. He was 94. He apparently died of natural causes, his lawyer, Eddie Ezor, told The Associated Press.

Artie Shaw's virtuosity on his instrument, his group's highly original arrangements and his explosively romantic showmanship made him one of the most danced-to bandleaders of swing and one of the most listened-to artists of jazz. He quit performing in 1954, but the many re-releases of his discs, a ghost band, and his informed but often sardonic comments on music and many other subjects kept him in the public ear.

Although his musical career closely paralleled that of Benny Goodman, his archrival, who died in 1986, the two men had little in common in their approaches to music.

"The distance between me and Benny was that I was trying to play a musical thing, and Benny was trying to swing," Shaw said several years ago. "Benny had great fingers; I'd never deny that. But listen to our two versions of 'Star Dust.' I was playing; he was swinging."

Shaw impressed and amazed clarinetists of all schools. Barney Bigard, the New Orleans clarinetist who was Duke Ellington's soloist for fourteen years, said he considered Shaw the greatest clarinetist ever. Phil Woods, a saxophonist of the bebop era, took Charlie Parker as his inspiration on saxophone, but he modeled his clarinet playing on Shaw's. John Carter, a leading post-bop clarinetist, said he took up the instrument because of Shaw.

And in 1983, when Franklin Cohen, the principal clarinetist of the Cleveland Orchestra, was to be featured playing Shaw's "Concerto for Clarinet," he listened to Shaw's recording of the work and said he found his playing unbelievable.

"Shaw is the greatest player I ever heard," he said. "It's hard to play the way he plays. It's not an overblown orchestral style. He makes so many incredible shadings."

Shaw was born Arthur Jacob Arshawsky in May 23, 1910, in New York City. He grew up in New Haven, Connecticut, where he was stung by anti-Semitic insults.

He was playing professionally at age fourteen and touring at sixteen. The youngster settled in Cleveland for a time, working with Cleveland's top band leader, Austin Wylie. Shaw did the arranging and rehearsing for Wylie's band. He joined Irving Aaronson's band at nineteen, moving to Hollywood. Shaw's influences ranged from Louis Armstrong to Debussy, Bartók and Stravinsky. Shaw settled in New York and, at the age of twenty-one, quickly became the best lead alto sax and clarinet player in the Big Apple, with many performances on the radio and visits to the recording studios. He backed up jazz singer Billie Holiday on some of her earliest recordings.

He was asked to play a concert at the Imperial Theater in New York in May 1936. It was called a swing concert, and it included well-known swing bands like the Casa Loma Orchestra and the bands of Tommy Dorsey and Bob Crosby. Although Shaw was not yet known to much of the public, he was asked to put together a small group to play while the band onstage was changed.

"Just for kicks, I thought I'd write a piece for clarinet and string quartet, plus a small rhythm section," Shaw recalled. "Nobody had ever done that, sort of a jazz chamber-music thing."

His "Interlude in B-Flat" brought down the house. The audience refused to stop applauding, but Shaw had nothing else to play because this was the only thing he had written for the group. Finally, they played it again. On the basis of this success, he was urged to form a band. It was a twelve-piece ensemble consisting of Shaw himself on clarinet, one trumpet, one trombone, one tenor sax, two violins, one viola, one cello, and a standard rhythm section of piano, guitar, bass, and drums. Peg LaCentra was the band's female vocalist.

The new "Artie Shaw and His Orchestra" recorded their first four sides on the Brunswick label on June 11, 1936, with "The Japanese Sandman," "A Pretty Girl is Like a Melody," "I Used to Be Above Love" and "No Regrets," with vocals on the latter two numbers by Wes Vaughn, the band's guitarist.

Personnel on that recording included Willie Kelly, trumpet; Mark Bennett, trombone; Tony Zimmers, tenor sax; Julie Schechter and Lou Klayman, violins; Sam Persoff, viola; Jimmy Oderich, cello; Fulton McGrath, piano; Wes Vaughn, guitar; Hank Wayland, bass; and Sammy Weiss, drums.

Members of that early band included four future bandleaders: tenor saxophonist/vocalist Tony Pastor; trumpeter Lee Castaldo (Castle), who would go on to lead the Jimmy Dorsey Orchestra after Dorsey's death in 1957; trombonist Moe Zudecoff (aka Buddy Morrow), who led his own band in the 1950s and has been the musical director of the Tommy Dorsey Orchestra for the past 25 years; and violinist/arranger Jerry Gray, whose arrangements were later to be an important part of Glenn Miller's musical library in both his civilian and military outfits.

The band had a unique sound but wasn't a commercial success. The string quartet approach was discarded and in early 1937, Shaw reorganized his band in a conventional Big Band format with standard instrumentation promising it would be "the loudest band in the whole damn world." The band, called "Art Shaw and His New Music," was developing its sound and in addition to Pastor and Gray who stayed on from the first band, boasted fine sidemen such as trumpeter Johnny Best; trombonist George Arus; lead alto saxophonist Les Robinson; and drummer George Wettling.

In 1938, Shaw became a star with his recording of Gray's arrangement of the Cole Porter tune, "Begin the Beguine" (recorded July 24), which Shaw joking referred to as "a nice little tune from one of Cole Porter's very few flop shows."

Band members making this definitive recording were Chuck Peterson, Johnny Best, Claude Bowen, trumpets; George Arus, Ted Vesley, and Harry Rogers, trombones; Les Robinson and Hank Freeman, alto saxes; Tony Pastor and Ronnie Perry, tenor saxes; Les Burness, piano; Al Avola, guitar; Sid Weiss, bass; and Cliff Leeman, drums.

Other hits soon followed including "Indian Love Call," "Back Bay Shuffle," "Any Old Time" (all three tunes were recored on July 24 with Billie Holiday featured on the vocal on the latter tune, the only commercial recording she waxed with the Shaw orchestra); Shaw's mournful theme song, "Nightmare" and "Non-Stop Flight" (both on Septenber 27); and "Softly As in a Morning Sunrise" (November 17).

With regards to Holiday, Shaw is credited with being the first white bandleader to employ a black female singer as a full-time member of his band. Situations for Holiday became ugly when the band toured the South, and soon after she left the band. It was during this period that Helen Forrest joined on as the band's vocalist making her recording debut on September 27, 1938, with "You're a Sweet Little Headache" and "I Have Eyes." She cut some impressive sides during this time with "Thanks For Everything" (November 17, 1938); "Deep Purple" (March 12, 1939); "Day In, Day Out" (August 27, 1939); and "All the Things You Are (October 26, 1939).

Throughout 1939, the Shaw band was gaining popularity and winning many swing band polls. Band personnel was beefed up with the addition of tenor saxophonist Georgie Auld, trombonist Les Jenkins, and drummer Buddy Rich, who helped swing the band on more "flag-waving" hits such as "The Donkey Serenade" (January 23, 1939); "Rose Room" (January 31, 1939); "One Night Stand" (March 17, 1939); "Traffic Jam" (June 12, 1939); "Serenade to a Savage" (June 22, 1939); and "Oh! Lady Be Good" (August 27, 1939).

The band appeared in its first movie, *Dancing Co-Ed* (1939), starring Lana Turner, Ann Rutherford, and Richard Carlson and was the feature band for a year on the *Old Gold* cigarette radio program (from November 20, 1938 to November 14, 1939) with comedian/humorist Robert Benchley acting as emcee.

Unable emotionally to cope with the pressures of stardom, Shaw left the bandstand while playing at the Café Rouge at the Hotel Pennsylvania in New York City and took a protracted holiday to Mexico in November 1939, handing the reigns over to Tony Pastor. The band stayed together for about three months until the men took jobs with other big name bands.

"I wanted to resign from the planet, not just music," Shaw said later. "It stopped being fun with success. Money got in the way. Everybody got greedy, including me. Fear set in. I got miserable when I became a commodity."

He disappeared to what was then a little-known village in Mexico - Acapulco - where he was ignored for three months until he rescued a woman from drowning and reporters found out who he was.

While in Mexico, Shaw became musically invigorated. By January 1940, he returned to the United States with the idea of forming a sixty-five-piece orchestra. That size orchestra never materialized, but owing RCA-Victor six more recordings on his contract, Shaw recorded with thirty-two studio musicians including woodwinds, French horns, and a full string section along with the normal dance band instrumentation and produced another smash hit, "Frenesi" (March 3, 1940), a tune he had heard a group playing on a wharf in Acapulco.

A touring band with a string section was organized, collecting more hits, including "Temptation" (September 7, 1940); "Star Dust" (October 7, 1940); "Concerto for Clarinet, Parts 1 and 2" (December 17, 1940); "Moonglow" and Dancing in the Dark" (both on January 23, 1941). Shaw's new band included such virtuosos as trumpeter Billy Butterfield; trombonists Jack Jenny and Ray Conniff; tenor saxophonist Jerry Jerome; electric guitarist Al Hendrickson; and drummer Nick Fatool. Robinson remained as Shaw's lead alto saxophonist.

In 1940, Shaw co-starred with Fred Astaire, Burgess Meredith and Paulette Goddard in the "B" flick, *Second Chorus*.

Shaw was signed to be the house bandleader for the *Burns and Allen Show* for twenty-six weeks emanating from Hollywood, beginning in July 1940.

During this period, Shaw formed his six-piece combo, the Gramercy Five (named after a New York telephone exchange), which included Shaw on clarinet; Butterfield, trumpet; Johnny Guarnieri, harpsichord; Hendrickson, guitar; Jud DeNaut, bass; and Fatool, drums.

This "first" Gramercy Five group cut eight exciting sides during its short-lived existence: "Special Delivery Stomp," "Summit Ridge Drive" (named for the street Shaw lived on in Hollywood), "Keepin' Myself For You" and "Cross Your Heart "(all four tunes recorded on September 3, 1940); and "Dr. Livingstone, I Presume?" "When the Quail Come Back to San Quentin," "My Blue Heaven" and "Smoke Gets in Your Eyes" (the latter four all on December 5, 1940).

While this current band of Shaw's drew critical acclaim, Shaw himself grew restless. Shortly after the start of 1941, he disbanded. In the fall of that year he organized another group with alumni from his other bands: saxophonists Auld and Robinson; trumpeters Lee Castle and Max Kaminsky; trombonists Jack Jenny and Ray Conniff; pianist Johnny Guarnieri; and a host of other brilliant musicians such as drummer Dave Tough, and black trumpeter/vocalist Oran "Hot Lips" Page, whose vocals on "Take Your Shoes Off, Baby" (October 30, 1941) and "St. James Infirmary, Parts 1 and 2" (November 12, 1941), were high spots of Shaw's recordings this period.

Upon America's entry in World War II as a result of the Japanese attack on Pearl Harbor, Hawaii, Shaw put his band on notice and enlisted in the Navy. Later that month, he flew to California and married Elizabeth Kern, the daughter of Jerome Kern, his fourth marriage.

In January 1942, Shaw waxed eight tunes before reporting to the Navy. Recording three vocals with the Shaw band during these last recording sessions was Fredda Gibson, who later became known as Georgia Gibbs, who forged a stellar solo career as a pop vocalist during the next decade. She was featured on "Somebody Nobody Loves," "Not Mine," and "Absent-Minded Moon."

After an initial period of anonymity in the service, Shaw became a chief petty officer and was ordered to form a band. When he heard the band members he had been given, he went AWOL ("tacitly," he said) in order to see the Secretary of the Navy, James V. Forrestal.

"I want to get into the war!" Shaw told him. "And if I have to run a band, I want it to be good."

Shaw left the meeting with permission to enlist a band to be taken to the Pacific. He recruited some of the best musicians he had worked with in civilian life, including trumpeters Johnny Best, Max Kaminsky, Frank Beach, and Conrad Gozzo; saxophonist Sam Donahue; drummer Dave Tough; and Claude Thornhill on piano also doing some arrangements.

As a morale-boosting outfit, Shaw's Navy band toured Pacific combat zones and played for troops in the jungles, airplane hangars, and on decks of ships. Shaw was medically discharged two years later in 1944 due to exhaustion.

Upon his return to civilian life and after regaining his health, Shaw's troubled marriage to Betty Kern ended in divorce and he organized another band in the fall of 1944 - a seventeen-piecer without strings which featured stars like Roy Eldridge on trumpet; Ray Conniff on trombone (also on arrangement duties); Dodo Marmarosa on piano; and Barney Kessel on guitar.

This 1944-45 band cut some exciting sides for RCA-Victor including "'S Wonderful" (arranged by Conniff) and "Bedford Drive" (both on September 1, 1945); "Lucky Number" (June 14, 1945); "The Maid With the Flaccid Air"(July 19, 1945); and "Dancing on the Ceiling" (July 24, 1945).

A second reincarnation of The Gramercy Five was formed with Eldridge, Marmarosa, Kessel, bassist Morris Rayman, and drummer Lou Fromm. The group cut six sides including "The Grabtown Grapple," "The Sad Sack" and "Scuttlebutt" (all three on January 9, 1945) and "The Gentle Grifter," "Mysterioso" and "Hop, Skip and Jump" (all three on July 31, 1945).

From the fall of 1945 to 1947, Shaw switched record companies and signed with a new label called Musicraft Records, producing some of the best big band tracks of his career. Recording once again with strings and a host of excellent studio musicians, Shaw waxed a pair of big jump tunes: "The Hornet" and "The Glider" (both on September 1945); an outstanding vocal version of "My Heart Belongs to Daddy" (June 13, 1946) sung by Kitty Kallen, who had left the Harry James band for a solo career; and some brilliant singing by a young Mel Torme and his Mel-Tones on two Cole Porter tunes: "What Is This Thing Called Love?" (June 19, 1946) and "Get Out of Town" (June 25, 1946), among others.

Shaw organized several other big bands, including a very good but short-lived 1949 bop-oriented jazz band, another reincarnation of his Gramercy Five, and a symphony orchestra which appeared at Carnegie Hall.

In 1951, Shaw again quit the music business, this time moving to Duchess County, New York, where he bought a 240-acre dairy farm and wrote his first book, an autobiography, *The Trouble With Cinderella: An Outline of Identity* (1952).

In 1946, Shaw was present at a meeting of the Independent Citizens' Committee of the Arts, Sciences and Professions. Olivia de Havilland and Ronald Reagan, part of a core group of actors and artists who were trying to sway the organization away from Communism, presented an anti-Communist declaration which, if signed, was set to run in newspapers. There was bedlam as many rose to champion the communist cause, and Artie Shaw began praising the Democratic standards of the Soviet constitution.

In 1953, Shaw was forced to testify before the House Un-American Activities Committee for his leftist activities. The committee was investigating a peace activist organization, the World Peace Council, which it considered a Communist front.

In 1954, Shaw made his last public apperance as an instrumentalist when he put together a new Gramercy Five made up of such superb modern musicians as pianist Hank Jones; guitarist Tal Farlow; and bassist Tommy Potter. The group's music has been documented on two CDs by MusicMaster called *Artie Shaw: The Last Recordings, Rare and Unreleased* and *Artie Shaw: More Last Recordings, The Final Sessions.*

Shaw packed his clarinet away once and for all in 1954. The following year, he left the United States and built a spectacular house on the brow of a mountain on the coast of Northeast Spain, where he lived for five years.

On his return to America in 1960, he settled in Lakeville, Connecticut, a small town in the northwestern part of the state, where he continued his writing. In 1965, he finished a second book consisting of three novellas, entitled *I Love You, I Hate, Drop Dead: Variations on a Theme.*

In 1973, Shaw moved back to California again, this time settling in Newbury Park, a part of Thousand Oaks in Ventura County, about 40 miles west of Los Angeles.

In 1983, he formed The Artie Shaw Orchestra to play his old arrangements and some newer music. It was directed by Dick Johnson, a saxophonist and clarinetist, and Shaw appeared with it occasionally as a non-playing conductor.

"I did all you can do with a clarinet," he said in a 1994 interview. "Any more would have been less."

In 1989, Shaw's third fictional work was published, *The Best of Intentions and Other Stories.* For the past decade he had begun writing a three-volume novel about a troubled young musician, Albie Snow. The tome is entitled *The Education of Albie Snow*. The work remains unpublished.

The mercurial Shaw struggled with both an attraction and an aversion to fame. He hated publicity. Nevertheless, he was a notorious ladies' man, and among his eight wives were glamour figures Lana Turner (wife No. 3, 1940); Betty Kern (No. 4, 1941, producing a son, Steven Kern); Ava Gardner (No. 5, 1945), Kathleen Winsor (No.6, 1946), who wrote the best selling historical novel, *Forever Amber*; Doris Dowling (No.7, producing a son, Jonathan Shaw); and Evelyn Keyes (No. 8, 1957). His first two wives were Jane Cairns (1932–33) and Margaret Allen (1934–37). All his marriages ended in divorce.

Throughout his life, Shaw became a cattle farmer, a producer and distributor of films, a successful competitor in shooting high-powered target rifles (he was ranked fourth in the United States in 1962), an expert fly fisherman, and a lecturer on the college circuit offering a choice of four subjects: "The Artist in a Material Society," "The Swingers of the Big Band Era," "Psychotherapy and the Creative Artist" and "Consecutive Monogamy and Ideal Divorce," in which he presented himself as "the ex- husband of love goddesses and an authority on divorce." His source material for this last lecture came from his experience with eight wives.

"People ask what those women saw in me," Shaw said in an interview with *The New York Times*. "Let's face it, I wasn't a bad-looking stud. But that's not it. It's the music; it's standing up there under the lights. A lot of women just flip; looks have nothing to do with it. You call Mick Jagger good- looking?"

On May 24, 1987, Shaw was presented a Doctor of Humane Letters from California Lutheran University in Thousand Oaks, near his home in Newbury Park. He also gave a fifteen-minute commencement address that day to 225 undergraduates and 145 graduate students entitled "Three Chords For Beauty and One to Pay the Rent."

Shaw achieved enormous success, then walked away from it over and over again, always returning for another round. In the early 1980s, Shaw produced a critically acclaimed documentary, *Artie Shaw: Time Is All You've Got*. He received many awards and honors, among them a Lifetime Achievement Award from the National Academy of Recording Arts and Sciences (Shaw's recordings of "Begin the Beguine," "Star Dust," "Frenesi," and "Any Old Time" are in the Grammy Hall of Fame), and a pair of Grammy nods in 2003 for "Best Historical Album" and for writing the linear notes to the Bluebird Records five-CD set, *Artie Shaw: Self Portrait*.

Since 2004, the Selmer clarinet Shaw played on his classic 1938 recording of "Begin the Beguine" has been preserved in the National Museum of American History, a gift made when Shaw was honored with the James Smithson Bicentennial Medal for his lifetime achievement and contributions to American culture and music. Shaw's clarinet rests alongside such other jazz treasures as Dizzy Gillespie's angled trumpet, Ella Fitzgerald's red dress, and Charlie Christian's electric guitar.

John Hasse, the museum's American music curator, called Shaw "one of the giants of jazz, a singular man of extraordinary intellect and a legendary and great American."

Personal Encounters With Artie Shaw
by Stephen Fratallone/*Jazz Connection Magazine*

My first encounters with Artie Shaw begin in November 1979 while I was a student at California Lutheran University in Thousand Oaks, California. I happened to browse through the November 18 issue of the *Thousand Oaks News-Chronicle* when I saw article written about Shaw. To my delighted surprise, I read that Shaw lived in nearby Newbury Park.

Acting on a hunch, I looked in the telephone directory to see if he would be listed there. Sure enough, I saw printed on the page, "A. Shaw,

2127 W. Palos Court, Newbury Park." I took out my city directory and looked up where Palos Court was located. I hopped in my car and drove out to his house, more curious than anything as to what kind of home this musical giant lived in.

When I came to address I was impressed by the beauty of Shaw's home. It was a typical modern- looking California style home with a large drive-in courtyard. Timidly, I walked up to the front door. I noticed a note was posted for the UPS delivery person to bring all packages to the back door. As I was reading the note a familiar face startled me from the kitchen window off to the side.

"May I help you?" said the voice. It was Shaw himself! I recognized him from the pictures that were published in the newspaper. He was a half-bald gentleman with a mustache. Scared, I quickly mumbled an answer to the effect, "I'm sorry. I have the wrong house."

I immediately left feeling frustrated that I didn't stay to say that I was a fan of his. Thinking it over later, it probably would have made no difference if I had. I heard that Shaw did not seek fan adulation and his notorious gruff attitude would no doubt have made me feel cheap for doing so.

My next encounter with Shaw was six years later via telephone. I was working as a staff writer/photographer for a monthly feature magazine in Ventura County. Wanting to write about a celebrity that lived in Ventura County, I telephoned Shaw to request an interview. He was polite but very resolute in our brief conversation together. I must have approached Shaw in the wrong way or something, as he declined my request for an interview telling me that he was "a private citizen and didn't wish to talk about his past musical experiences." Um... OK.

On May 24, 1987, I attended the 24th annual graduation ceremony at my Alma Mater to hear Shaw deliver the commencement address and receive an honorary doctorate degree. Decked in a black robe while sporting a full beard with his right hand in a sling (resulting in a fractured wrist a few weeks before and as a result, he was unable to shave), Shaw gave the best commencement I had ever heard! The fifteen-minute speech, "Three Chords For Beauty and One to Pay the Rent," was witty and practical and not saturated with flowery clichés as so many graduation speeches are.

A few weeks later, the music professor at Cal Lutheran asked me if I would like to meet the new "Dr." Shaw as he was slated to give a lecture on campus to a group of senior citizens attending a week-long Elderhostle class. I jumped at the chance! I was introduced to him prior to the class. The first thing I noticed about this musical giant was how short he was! I was also surprised at his attire that day. He was wearing jeans, a work shirt, tennis shoes and a baseball cap. He still was sporting the beard as his wrist hadn't completely healed to where he could use it. He was very friendly and pleasant.

I asked if he would like to see the photos I had taken of him at the graduation a few weeks earlier. He said he liked the photos very much and one photo in particular, a close up of him speaking behind the podium, tickled his fancy. I gave it to him and he was very pleased. (I later sent him an enlargement of that same photo to autograph for me, which he did.) Inside the classroom, Shaw immediately told the group of about fifty seniors of his disinterest in discussing his years as a bandleader. He did, however, share his view about himself, music in general, and his opinions about the then current political climate.

"I pride myself as a semi-schizophrenic," he told the seniors. "I'm trying to understand the universe. There is no sense in the real world. I try to inject a bit of rationality in this wide-range of irrationality. So what am I doing? Criticizing the hell out of everything!"

Shaw went on to say that he has always considered himself an artist while the public has labeled him as an entertainer. That's the problem which caused him to give up the clarinet in 1954.

"I'm not conditioned to be an entertainer," he admitted. "An entertainer pleases others while an artist only has to please himself. The problem with that is artists are misunderstood by all. I'm not interested in the clarinet but in music. Shaw went on to discuss the problem of labelling.

"We speak our emotions into music. An artist should write for himself and not for an audience. If the audience likes it, great. If not, they can keep away. My situation is the same. Let them concentrate on my music and not on me. I like the music. I love it and live it, in fact. But for me, the business part of music just plain stinks."

Someone from the audience then asked Shaw about his impressions of "Rock 'N Roll." After a few moments about labelling certain music and what that means, Shaw said.

"Rock 'N Roll is the music of today. We live in hysteria and this music mirrors that just as 'swing' did during the Depression Era. We live in a chaotic, destructive and hostile world. Rock 'N Roll is hostile music."

Shaw did admit that he likes some things, of course, however, he said he doesn't like what the public is fed by the media.

"Sure I'm angry," he said. "It's hard to be at peace when things are not portrayed as they are. Look at the Iran-Contra hearings. It's enough to make you sick! That's why I left the United States years ago (to live in Spain from 1955-1960). I no longer live here. Physically I do, but not the rest of me."

In 1999, I had purchased some Artie Shaw CDs at a local music store. I sent the CD covers to Shaw requesting his autograph. He obliged. One of the CD covers I had sent to him was not returned. A few days later, I received a letter from Shaw's personal secretary stating that the reason why this particular CD cover wasn't returned was it was a pirated CD. The letter asked me to send that CD to Shaw and that he would reimburse me for the cost of the CD and postage. I did so.

In the meantime, I had written Shaw a letter requesting a fifteen-minute telephone interview to discuss the topic of music in general. I wanted to incorporate Shaw's interview with an interview I was hoping to do with Dick Johnson, the current musical director of the Artie Shaw Orchestra, as the ASO was slated to perform at the Jackson Rancheria in Jackson, CA. The article was designed to herald the coming of the ASO to the area. I never received a response back from Shaw.

Three months went by and I still had not been reimbursed by Shaw for the pirated CD I sent to him. I wrote back to Shaw's secretary about it and also put in another request for an interview. A week later I received a money order for the amount in question and a letter of apology for the delay but no response either way for an interview.

I kept thinking to myself, "What do I need to do get an interview with this guy?"

In 2003, Shaw was nominated for a Grammy Award for the linear notes he had written to a 5-CD boxed set of his music called *Artie Shaw: Self-Portrait*. I once again wrote to Shaw requesting a brief telephone interview to discuss the nomination, and the CD project itself. I never heard back from him.

Despite his flaws in interpersonal relationships, the world has lost a true musical artist and innovator in Artie Shaw. Thanks for the great music, Artie!

Resquiat in Pace!

Artie Shaw, "The King of the Clarinet," at the height of his career in 1939.

Artie Shaw and His Orchestra in a scene from the 1940 film, *Second Chorus*.

Artie Shaw from 1940.

Artie Shaw, 77, being introduced to the audience by Dr. Daniel Geeting of the Music Department at California Lutheran University, Thousand Oaks, on May 24, 1987.

Dr. Artie Shaw, 77, giving the commencement address at California Lutheran University, Thousand Oaks, on May 24, 1987. Shaw was presented with an honorary doctorate degree by CLU.
– *Photos by Stephen Fratallone*

Still "King Of The Stardust Ballroom"

Bandleader Orrin Tucker Renowned for Playing Music That Catered to Ballroom Dancers

The following article on Orrin Tucker was originally published in the May 2000 issue of Jazz Connection Magazine

Orrin Tucker dreamt of a career in medicine but when he became fascinated with a picture of a saxophone in a Sear Roebuck catalog, his interests shifted to music. It proved to be good Rx, as Tucker went on to lead one of the most popular hotel/ballroom orchestras during the Big Band era.

"I don't have any regrets choosing music over medicine," said the eighty-nine-year-old bandleader in a telephone conversation from his home in South Pasadena, California. "It's proven to be a good choice for me."

His 1939 hit recording of "Oh, Johnny, Oh, Johnny, Oh!" catapulted Tucker to prominence, leading one of the hottest bands in the land.

Born Robert Orrin Tucker on February 17, 1911, in St. Louis, Missouri, Tucker grew up in Wheaton, Illinois. The genesis of his musical career literally came out of the pages of that Sears Roebuck catalog where he saw a picture of a saxophone.

"The picture of that shiny saxophone fascinated me," Tucker said. "There were so many more buttons on it than on a trumpet and a violin was kind of forbidding. I thought I'd like to try the saxophone."

Tucker's yearning for a saxophone was also heightened after seeing Fred Waring and His Pennsylvanians perform during their yearly pilgrimage to Chicago, he said.

Saving his money, the teenage Tucker eventually bought an alto saxophone through the Sears Roebuck department store catalog. Having difficulty finding a saxophone teacher in the Wheaton area, Tucker became self-taught on the instrument, utilizing written instructional books to figure out fingering techniques.

"I really had to help myself in order to get started," he said. He later switched to playing the tenor saxophone.

While in high school, Tucker formed a dance band with his sights set on attending college and then medical school.

"I was just looking to be a general practitioner, a family doctor," Tucker said.

Many of those dances that Tucker played for were in Chicago and juggling dance hall schedules with train schedules sometimes didn't always work out for the budding bandleader.

"I would try to take the latest train possible back to Wheaton, but there were times when the dances would be over late and I'd end up sitting at the train depot all night in order to catch the 6 a.m. train back home," Tucker said.

Some individuals were not so understanding of Tucker's enterprises, least of all his high school principal.

"I remember getting off the early morning train carrying my instruments sloshing through the snow-covered streets," Tucker recalled. "I passed in front of the principal's home. He saw me as he came out the door to get his bottle of milk. Later that morning, he addressed the class saying, 'That Orrin Tucker will never amount to anything. He's always coming home during the early morning hours. He'll focus all his attention on playing for dances but doesn't pay any attention to his studies!'"

Some of the dance halls Tucker played at had dubious reputations and were run by gangsters. Chicago during Prohibition was a mecca for underworld racketeering.

"I worked for a few of those people," Tucker said matter-of-factly. "One of those people was Bugsy Siegel, the guy who owned all the original hotels in Las Vegas."

After graduating from Wheaton High School in 1929, Tucker learned that Northwestern University's School of Speech offered one one-year scholarship per year to an Illinois resident interested in studying theater arts. He made application for the scholarship and won it, figuring once enrolled, he could then take pre-med courses. After completing his freshman year, he transferred to North Central College in Naperville, Illinois, which was closer to Wheaton.

To help meet college expenses, Tucker formed a band to play at the Spanish Tea Room in Naperville. The band drew patrons from as far away as Chicago.

A local agent, noting his success, booked Tucker and his band into a three-week engagement at a New Orleans hotel during Mardi Gras. The band faired well which inspired Tucker to then focus all his energies to full time bandleading.

"That did it for me," Tucker said. "Staying in music was what I wanted to do. From then on, there was no turning back."

Tucker himself was a pleasant enough singer and his outfit was doing well enough since it was formed in 1933, but when he hired Bonnie Baker in February 1938 as his girl singer, the band's popularity increased.

"We were in Kansas City at the time and I received a telephone call from Louis Armstrong telling me about this singer named Evelyn Nelson he'd just seen at the Claridge Hotel in St. Louis," Tucker said. "He told me that she sings with a cute voice and that if I wrote cute songs for here, I could make her a star and in so doing help the band."

Acting on Armstrong's tip, Tucker went to check out the five-foot charmer from Orange, Texas. He was pleased with what he heard.

"It wasn't easy, but I talked her into joining the band," Tucker said. "I also talked her into changing her name. I'm very much in favor of a person's name to begin with consonants. I thought 'Bonnie Baker' was a strong name with confidence. It turned out to be true."

In 1938, Tucker signed on with Vocalion Records, a subsidiary of Columbia Records. The band made their recording debut on April 25, 1938, by waxing six sides, two of which feaured Baker's vocals: "Havin' Myself a Time" and "Especially For You." The remaining cuts featured Tucker on the vocals with "Cathedral in the Pines," "Ride, Tenderfoot, Ride," "I'll Dream Tonight," and "I Need Lovin'."

Band personnel on this session included Morton Wells, trumpet; Dick Robinson, trombone; Doc Morrison, Joe Srassburger, Norbert Stammer, alto and tenor saxes; Roy Cohan and Will Flanders, violins; Everett Ralston, piano; George Sontag, second piano and cello; Lorry Lee, guitar; Arnold Jensen, bass; and Phil Patton, drums.

Tucker started featuring material that showcased Baker's girl-like voice on such pieces as "Especially For You" and "Wouldja Mind?"

The next Vocalion recording session for the Tucker band came a year later on April 2, 1939, waxing a half-dozen tunes. Band personnel remained the same from a year earlier, but included the addition of Gil Mershon and Sam Sims comprising the vocal group, "The Bodyguards," (to "protect" Baker); and George Liberace on violin. He was the elder brother and business partner of famed U.S. entertainer/pianist Liberace.

The band's big break came when they were asked to record on Columbia's red label, which was recently purchsed by the Columbia Broadcasting System (CBS).

"We were playing at the Cocoanut Grove in Los Angeles in 1939 when Bill Paley, the President of CBS, called me wanting me to do the first recording session for his new company," Tucker said. "He said that Benny Goodman, who had just signed with Columbia, was set to do the second session. He suggested that we pick songs to record that were popular at our dances."

The recording date set for Tucker was August 20, 1939. It would become a turning point in his life.

One of the songs to come out of that recording session was an old World War I tune by Abe Olman and Ed Rose called "Oh, Johnny, Oh, Johnny, Oh!" Baker sang the vocal while adding her own coy enunciations of such provocative words as "Oh!" and "Uh-uh" along with a few extra sighs.

All of a sudden Tucker had himself a hit record and one of the hottest bands in the country.

"I didn't especially want to record it because it was too simple of a novelty song," Tucker recalled. "I didn't think it would be big. We had some other tunes that were strong ballads that I thought would be better sellers. 'Oh, Johnny' became a big national hit. It helped put Columbia Records in business."

"Oh, Johnny, Oh, Johnny, Oh!" reached No. 2 on the *Billboard* pop chart, remaining on the chart for fourteen weeks, and selling 1.5 million copies. The song was awarded a gold disc by the Recording Industry Association of America (RIAA).

In 1941, the Tucker aggregation starred in the film, *You're the One*, a Paramount motion picture movie written especially for the band, which co-starred Albert Dekker, Jerry Colonna, and Edward Everett Horton. Colonna recorded with Tucker for Columbia one of the songs from the film's soundtrack, "The Yogi Who Lost His Will Power," on November 11, 1940.

Tucker recorded almost eighty sides for Columbia and Vocalion from April 25, 1938 to March 31, 1942, including "Drifting and Dreaming" (the band's theme song on December 5, 1939); "How Many Times?" (August 20, 1939, vocal by Tucker); "Not Yet" (March 18, 1940, vocal by Baker); "Where Do I Go From You?" (March 18, 1940, vocal by Tucker); "Absence Makes the Heart Grow Fonder" (January 29, 1941, vocal by Baker); and "Calling All Hearts" (February 7, 1941, vocal by Tucker).

"Our usual policy would be Bonnie would sing a song on one side of a record and I'd sing a song on the other side," Tucker said.

The canon of Tucker's commercially recorded studio works occurred during this period. It was during this time that Tucker christened his girl singer with the prefix of "Wee."

"I introduced Bonnie over the radio saying, 'And now the shy voice of *Wee Bonnie Baker…*'" Tucker said. "People picked up on that and the name stuck."

Baker stayed with the band until 1942 when Tucker disbanded. She went on to have a solo singing career with the USO during World War II, and appearing regularly on the radio show, *Your Hit Parade*. She sang with other bands, made recordings, entertained in nightclubs and voiced the cartoon chracter "Chilly Willy" in the 1950s.

She gave up performing after suffering a heart attack in 1965. In 1976, she was a switchboard operator at a Fort Lauderdale, Florida medical center. She died in Fort Lauderdale on August 11, 1990, at the age of 73.

Shortly after America entered World War II, Tucker applied for active duty in the Navy. He left the orchestra on June 7, 1942 and by July 15, 1942, he was inducted for active duty, commissioned as a lieutenant. He was stationed for four years at Pearl Harbor, Hawaii, as a pilot instructor..

Because of his popularity as a bandleader before the war, he also was appointed Entertainment Officer at the base.

"I had double duty the whole damned time!" he said.

However, Tucker's notoriety as a musician kept him in good standing with his subordinates, thus creating a fine rapport between officers and enlisted personnel.

"At my first assignment, I was one of six white officers at an installation with 3,600 African American sailors," Tucker said. "The whole camp felt as if they knew me and the sailors would stop in my quarters to make friends."

Throughout the duration of the war, Tucker noticed that the servicemen were listening to loud, brassy jazz and swing bands. When he returned to civilian life in 1945, he elected to change his musical style. His post-war band included seven brass, five saxes and even two French horns. The musical arrangements were heavy and thick.

Tucker's new band started out at the Waldorf-Astoria Hotel in New York, then went on to the Empire Room in Chicago, and then made its way to Los Angeles to the Cocoanut Grove. Patrons received Tucker's new sound with mixed reviews. Hotel managers wanted the string section back and the brass section reduced to form a much lighter, sweeter sound.

"We were mostly a hotel band playing in dining rooms and this new sound that we were trying out was just too loud for that sort of thing," Tucker said. "Besides, the hotel managers threatened to cancel any return bookings if we didn't go back to the old sound, which I did."

The music that Tucker was noted for playing was labeled "Mickey Mouse" by swing fans, a term that never offended him, Tucker said.

"Every band that played hotel music was labeled a 'Mickey Mouse' band," he said.

Tucker knew his music and his public and was at his best playing for middle-aged dancers. When most of the Big Bands were fading away, he was still around, playing his music at some of the smarter spots, such as the Strand Theater in New York City; the Trianon Ballroom and the Stevens Hotel in Chicago; the Peabody Hotel in Memphis; the Casino Gardens in Ocean Park, California; and the Hotel Mark Hopkins in San Francisco.

During this time he made only a handful of commercial recordings. Other notable female vocalists who sang with Tucker were Scottee Marsh and Helen Lee.

Tucker and his band appeared in a made-for-television production of *Queen of the Stardust Ballroom,* which aired February 13, 1975 and cast Maureen Stapleton as a widow and Charles Durning as a postman who rediscover their youth while ballroom dancing. The televison received great reviews which gave Tucker the idea to buy an abandoned skating rink at 5612 Sunset Boulevard in Hollywood at the Hollywood Freeway and convert it into a dance show place, which he named "The Stardust Ballroom." His own band became its star attraction at the new venue until 1982, when he closed its doors due to economic factors.

Throughout the 1970s and 1980s, Tucker played annually at Disneyland, Las Vegas, and was a popular main stay at Myron's Ballroom in downtown Los Angeles.

"There aren't any ballrooms around," he said sadly. "If people do dance, they don't touch each other. They stand on the floor waving their arms up over their heads."

Tucker also noted that younger people are not attracted to his music.

"No, they wouldn't know me from a bale of hay," he quipped.

Tucker considers himself "semi-retired" and leads a band for special occasions, mostly in the greater Los Angeles area. In October, however, he and a fourteen-piece band will play aboard the *Queen Elizabeth* for a cruise from London, England, to Miami, Florida, he said.

"I haven't played my saxophone in about six months so I better get it out and get my chops up!" he said.

Tucker married Jill Powell, a model, in 1944, and the couple divorced in 1952. Since 1975, he's been married to Aline Cameron Tucker.

Tucker was recently hospitalized for six months as a result of spinal surgery. If that wasn't bad enough, in 1997, Tucker lost his collection of records and memorabilia in a fire.

Tucker feels that his contribution to the history of American popular music has been leading a very good and entertaining stage band, he said.

"I always tried to have a good theatrical show," he said. "My trademark for many years was having the band do some things with lights during a blacked out room."

To this day, Tucker remains philosophical about the path he chose in life.

"All through my life I am a person who wanted to be in a position to help people," he said. "I believe that the source of happiness is helping others."

Tucker believes he has done just that though his music, and rightly so.

Tucker maintains a website at: www.orrintucker.com Much of

Tucker's more "recent" music can be purchased through Bermuda House on their website at: www.bermudahouse.com

** Coda – Here is an update on Orrin Tucker since this article was published.

In 2003, Tucker was interviewed about his passion for music and his long career as a bandleader by the National Association of Music Merchants (NAMM) Oral History Program.

Tucker had been confined to a nursing home the last few years of his life. He died peacefully on Saturday, April 9, 2011. He was 100 years old.

He leaves his wife, Aline Cameron Tucker; a daughter, Nora Compere; and a grandson, Eric Compere.

Orrin Tucker and his star vocalist, "Wee" Bonnie Baker in 1940.

Orrin Tucker in a 1950s publicity photo.

Orrin Tucker, 90, at the Big Band Acaemy of America's annual reunion on March 4, 2001, at the Sportsmen Lodge in Studio City, California . – *Photo by Stephen Fratallone*

The "Ghost Bands"

A ghost band is, in the case of Big Band jazz, a band that performs under the original name of a deceased leader, typically performing the repertoire of the original bands. Ghost bands fall into three categories: (1) authorized, (2) unauthorized, and (3) unspecified.

Authorized ghost bands fall into two sub-categories: (a) authorized under the will of the decedent and (b) authorized by agreement with the heirs, successors, and assigns to the rights of the name.

Unauthorized ghost bands are those that exist in the face of opposition, or those that prevail in a legal challenge. Unspecified ghost bands subsist with no preference or will given. In this case, more than one band might subsist, and even remain unopposed if money is not an issue.

The phrase, "ghost band," sometimes is viewed as an underhanded way of saying that the ensemble is not the "real McCoy." Not being the "real McCoy" does not automatically mean "inferior." Some people hold to the opinion that ghost bands are unnecessary. If someone wants to hear what a particular band sounds like, all they have to do is listen to that band's original recordings. True enough. However, seeing and hearing the music played live right before one's eyes and ears as it was meant to be played brings into perspective a different dimention to the music that dusty old recordings can never achieve.

The author has included the following articles on seven leaders of such ghost bands – Michael Berkowitz and the New Gene Krupa Orchestra,

Les Brown Jr. and His Band of Renown, Chris Calloway and Cab Calloway's Legacy of Swing, Dick Johnson and the Artie Shaw Orchestra, Larry O'Brien and the Glenn Miller Orchestra, Don Pentleton and the Hal McIntyre Orchestra, and Bill Tole and the Jimmy Dorsey Orchestra - with the idea that what these bands are doing has some value not only from an entertainment perspective, but also from a legacy perspective of musical Americana. They come close, or as close as possible in this day and age – being far removed over the years from the "first generation" Big Band they represent - to being the "real McCoy." From a branding perspective, some repertory big bands, such as the Glenn Miller Orchestra, which has remained active for seventy-one years after its leader's death, embrace the phrase "ghost band" as a statement of commitment to the preservation of the original sound.

Those Drummin' Men

Drummer Michael Berkowitz Keeps Gene Krupa's Music Alive As Leader Of The New Krupa Band

The following article on Michael Berkowitz and the New Gene Krupa Orchestra was originally published in the November 2003 issue of Jazz Connection Magazine

Michael Berkowitz and Gene Krupa

Michael Berkowitz is drum crazy and he has Gene Krupa to thank for it. It was seeing his drumming idol perform for the first time and meeting him afterwards at a jazz club in Indianapolis in 1964 that inspired the then thirteen-year-old Berkowitz to forge a professional career in music. Since that magical moment, Berkowitz has gone on to become a much-in-demand traps artist performing and touring with a variety of giants in the entertainment industry as well as being a steady fixture in the New York City music scene. Now, thirty years after Krupa's death, Berkowitz is the leader of the newly-organized and licensed New Gene Krupa Orchestra, which keeps the music of the late drumming bandleader/icon alive.

"Gene was really the first drummer who brought the drums out from behind the band," said Berkowitz, 52, via telephone from his home in New York City. "He created a lot of excitement being the first and perhaps the only super star drummer in terms of having movie star good looks, charisma and musical talent. It's quite a legacy and sometimes it's overwhelming to think about it in those terms."

Krupa, the gum-chewing, hair-waving drummer known for his grimaces and torrid style of playing, would often be drenched in his own sweat after playing one exciting set after another. His own charisma, flare and innovative "drumnastics" gained him popular appeal.

"Everyone talk about the Gene Krupa charisma," Berkowitz said. "Gene had that magnetic ability that people just loved. It was great stuff. Even if he didn't have the greatest speed or a certain time as compared to Buddy Rich or Louis Bellson, Gene could do the simplest things and the crowd would just go crazy. Like Buddy once said, 'I'm playing all the drums and Gene gets all the applause.'"

While Krupa had many hit recordings during his thirteen years as a bandleader – "Wire Brush Stomp," "Drummin' Man," "Drum Boogie," "Let Me Off Uptown," "Leave Us Leap," "Boogie Blues," and "Lover," among others - the tune most closely associated with the drumming great is "Sing, Sing, Sing," a Louis Prima composition that the drummer recorded in 1937 as a member of Benny Goodman's orchestra. His tom-tom solo throughout the piece, considered a classic, is probably the most recognized drum solo in jazz history. And that famous solo has also recently found its way on television commercials.

"People hear 'Sing, Sing, Sing' everyday behind the cookie commercial," Berkowitz said. "Even though Gene recorded the song while he was a member of Benny Goodman's band, it's still Gene Krupa."

Despite his successes at the jukebox, many people are still unaware of the music that Krupa left behind, according to Berkowitz. And it's for that very reason that Berkowitz feels the need to "reintroduce" Krupa's music.

"It's important for me to push that music out there," Berkowitz said. "It's not just a bunch of drum solos. As Gene once said, 'You have to take a break every once-in-a-while. Even the *Super Chief* slows down.'" And like any good drummer in a big band situation knows, the traps man has to set the table for the band.

"A good drummer has to have good time, but the time has to pulsate and it's got to swing, as Gene used to say," Berkowitz said. "The drummer doesn't want to throw curves to the band. You want everyone to feel comfortable while giving support to everybody. You don't overplay and you don't underplay. You give things the right energy. You don't lay back too much and you keep things moving forward. And in this kind of band – Gene's band - you have to give it that excitement."

Eugene Bertram Krupa was born on January 15, 1909, in "Little Poland," the Polish immigrant district on Chicago's tough Far South Side. Both his parents, Bartley and Ann Krupa, were Polish immigrants. They were devoted Roman Catholics and raised a family of nine children, two girls and seven boys, of whom Gene was the youngest. The senior Krupa died when Gene was very young and his mother worked as a milliner to support the family.

Krupa's parents were very religious and had they're youngest son groomed for the priesthood. He spent his grammar school days at various parochial schools and upon graduation went to St. Joseph's College, a preparatory seminary in Rensselear, Indiana, for a brief year. Krupa's musical ambitions were too strong and he gave up the idea of becoming a priest.

Krupa played sax in grade school but took up drums by age eleven because they were the cheapest instrument in a music store where he worked. In 1921, while still in grammar school, Krupa joined his first band "The Frivolians." He obtained the drumming seat as a fluke when the regular drummer was sick. The band played during summers in Madison, Wisconsin.

Upon entering high school in 1923, Krupa became buddies with the "Austin High Gang:" cornetist Jimmy McPartland, bassist Jimmy Lannigan, tenor saxophonist Bud Freeman, clarinetist Frank Teschemacher, and drummer Davey Tough. In 1925, Krupa began his percussion studies with Roy Knapp. After joining the local union, he began showing up at clubs to play after-hours sessions with Mezz Mezzrow, Tommy Dorsey, Bix Beiderbecke and Benny Goodman. His own influences ranged from Tubby Hall and Zutty Singleton to Baby Dodds and, later on, Chick Webb.

Krupa was an innovator in many respects. In his recording debut on December 8, 1927 with the McKenzie-Condon Chicagoans (the band consisted of McPartland, Teschemacher, Freeman, Lannigan, Joe Sullivan, piano; and Eddie Condon, banjo), he was the first drummer to record a bass drum in the studio. The two titles, "China Boy" and "Sugar," became groundbreakers.

Krupa is also widely regarded as the first real drum soloist, who interacted with other players and took the instrument beyond its role as mere timekeeper. He also contributed to drum set innovations, helping the Slingerland Drum Company to invent tunable tom-toms (replacing tacked-on drum heads).

In the late summer of 1928, Krupa moved to New York, where he played in numerous orchestras and studio and pit bands and was later recruited by Red Nichols. Krupa, along with Goodman and Glenn Miller, performed in the pit band of two George Gershwin plays: *Strike Up the Band* and *Girl Crazy*.

In June 1933, Krupa married Ethel Maguire, the telephone operator at the Dixie Hotel, where he was staying while working on *Girl Crazy*. They divorced in 1942 and remarried in 1946, until her death in 1955.

Krupa played on some legendary "jazz" recordings with Bix Beiderbecke, Adrian Rollini and Joe Venuti. He also continued to work in commercial outfits like those of Iving Anderson, Mal Hallet, Buddy Rogers and Russ Columbo until 1934 when record producer John Hammond recruited Krupa for Benny Goodman's orchestra.

The Goodman group featured Krupa prominently in the full orchestra and with the groundbreaking Goodman Trio (with Teddy Wilson on piano) and Quartet (with the addition of Lionel Hampton on vibraphone). The Trio is possibly the first working small group which featured black and white musicians. Krupa's tenure with "The King of Swing" would see the Goodman band reach dizzy heights of popularity as the most successful band of the swing era, culminating in the legendary concert at Carnegie Hall on January 16, 1938.

The band was the first jazz act to play New York's Carnegie Hall. Krupa's performance on "Sing, Sing, Sing" at the concert has been hailed a classic. After the Carnegie Hall performance, tension began to surface between Krupa and Goodman. Audiences were demanding that Krupa be featured in every number and Goodman didn't want to lose the spotlight to a sideman.

Krupa left Goodman after a blow-up at the Earle Theatre in Philadelphia on March 3, 1938, and a month-and-a-half later he formed his own orchestra. His band was an instant success upon it's opening at the Marine Ballroom on the Steel Pier in Atlantic City on April 16 for a youthful and enthusiastic audience of 4,000 fans.

During the band's first few years, Krupa's new outfit included vocalist Irene Daye and such noted sidemen as tenor saxophonists Vido Musso and Sam Donahue; trombonist/singer Leo Watson; and trumpeters Shorty Sherock and Corky Cornelius, among others. Early popular favorites by the band included "Wire Brush Stomp" (recorded June 2, 1938); "Apurksody" (December 12, 1938), the band's theme song as the title spells the name Krupa backwards, plus the last four letters of rhapsody); "Drummin' Man" (November 2, 1939 with vocal by Irene Daye); "Blue Rhythm Fantasy" (January 2, 1940) which occupied two sides of the 78 rpm record; "Boog It" (February 12, 1940 with vocal by Daye); and "Drum Boogie" (January 17, 1941 with vocal by Daye). The latter tune would be Daye's final recording with the Krupa band as she left to marry Corky Cornelius, who joined the Casa Loma Orchestra. (A few years later after her husband, Cornelius, had died, Daye would sing for Charlie Spivak's band and would eventually become Mrs. Charlie Spivak.)

A whole new Krupa era began with the addition of singer Anita O'Day and trumpeter Roy Eldridge to the band in early 1941. The pair inspired the band, made it more colorful, and brought it to mew musical heights. With O'Day and Eldridge, the Krupa band made its greatest recordings and enjoyed its greatest popularity.

O'Day, an outstanding song stylist who came across as a hip musician, cut several sides that were chart toppers including "Georgia on My Mind" (March 12, 1941); "Just a Little Bit South of North Carolina" and "Slow Down" (both on March 19, 1941); "Green Eyes" (May 8, 1941); "Stop! The Red Lights On" (August 18, 1941); "The Walls Keep Talking" (vocal duet with Roy Eldridge on August 20, 1941); "Bolero at the Savoy" (November 25, 1941); "Thanks For the Boogie Ride" (vocal duet with Eldridge November 25, 1941); "Pass the Bounce" (vocal duet with Eldridge December 29, 1941); "That's What You Think" (February 26, 1942); "Barrelhouse Bessie From Basin Street" (April 2, 1941); and "Massachusetts" and "Murder, He Says" (both on July 13, 1942).

O'Day briefly rejoined the Krupa band in mid-1945 (leaving in early 1946) and helped to score more hits for the band with "Opus No. 1" (a Sy Oliver arrangement) and "Boogie Blues" (both on August 21, 1945), and "Chickery Chick" (September 26, 1945).

Eldridge's sensational and brilliant trumpeting stood out on such recordings as "After You've Gone" (June 5, 1941), and "Rockin' Chair" (July 2, 1941).

Together, O'Day and Eldridge recorded the band's all-time hit, "Let Me Off Up Town" (May 8, 1941).

Eventually O'Day left the band in the autumn of 1942 to marry golfer Carl Hoff, and subsequently worked briefly with Woody Herman and the Stan Kenton bands early in 1944. Crooner Johnny Desmond took care of the vocal department for a while to be replaced by Ray Eberle, who after leaving Glenn Miller, sang with the band for a short period.

In the summer of 1943, Krupa was arrested in San Francisco on questionable charges of possession of marijuana and contributing to the delinquency of a minor. Krupa was sent to San Quentin Prison and sentenced to 90 days, of which 84 were served. He was later cleared of the latter charges. During this time, Roy Eldridge led Krupa's band and eventually had to break up the group.

The following year Krupa briefly joined Tommy Dorsey's band. Despite his condemnation by the media concerning his drug charge, he was voted "Best Drummer" in the *Down Beat* Readers' Poll.

In re-forming his orchestra during the summer of 1944, Krupa made an effort to explore the new modernist trends rooted in the bebop jazz movement. Taken by the sound of the string section during his stint with Dorsey, Krupa used a string section for about eight months calling his outfit, "The Band That Swings with Strings."

Between 1945 and 1949 his band featured such arrangers as George Williams, Neal Hefti, Eddie Finkel, and baritone saxophonist Gerry Mulligan, who brought the band the instrumental score "Disc Jockey Jump" (January 22,1947). Krupa's musical line-up during this period featured a number of contemporary jazzmen, including explosive tenor saxophonist Charlie Ventura; clarinetist Buddy DeFranco; trombonists Frank Rosolino, Moe Schneider, and Warren Covington; trumpeters Red Rodney, Al Porcino, and Dan Fagerquist; and pianist Teddy Napoleon.

Other hit recordings during this period include "Leave Us Leap"

(January 22, 1945); "Lover" (September 26, 1945); and "Gene's Boogie" (February 5, 1947 with vocal by Carolyn Grey).

Following the Goodman pattern, trio performances formed a regular part of the band's performances. The Gene Krupa Jazz Trio, with Charlie Ventura on tenor sax, Teddy Napoleon, and later George Walters on piano, recorded classics of its own with "Dark Eyes" and "Body and Soul" (both on March 8, 1945); and "Stompin' at the Savoy" (June 1, 1945).

Krupa managed to keep the full band together until December of 1950, when most big bands had already fallen apart. His music hit the charts once again when he recorded with a small traditional jazz group for RCA-Victor called "Gene Krupa's Chicago Jazz Band," that included Wild Bill Davison, cornet; Cutty Cutshall, trombone; Peanuts Hucko, clarinet; Gene Schroeder, piano; Ray Biondi, guitar; Al Hall, bass; with Bobby Soots doing the vocals on "Bonaparte's Retreat" and "My Scandinavian Baby" (both on April 6, 1950). "Boneparte's Retreat" made *Billboard's* Top 20 Chart. During the week of September 1, 1950, the song, having been on the charts for only three weeks, was ranked at Number 20. The previous week it was ranked at Number 16. During that first week in September, Kay Starr's version was ranked at Number 6, having already been on the charts for thirteen weeks. Krupa's band was one of two bands making the Top 20 during this period. The other was Guy Lombardo with his "Third Man Theme," making the 17th spot.

Krupa kept a smaller version of the big band together through 1951. He disbanded that group in 1951 to tour with Jazz at the Philharmonic. In 1954, he and drummer Cozy Cole founded a percussion school in New York. Krupa spent the last twenty years of his life teaching while also studying timpani and classical percussion, various ethnic drumming concepts and occasionally leading small groups and recording with a big band as a session leader, including 1962's *Burning Beat* with Buddy Rich on the Verve label.

In 1959, Krupa married Patty Bowler and later divorced in 1968. They adopted two children, Mary Grace and Gene Michael, also known as "Bee Gee." Also in that year, actor Sal Mineo portrayed the legendary drummer in the Hollywood flop, *The Gene Krupa Story*. Krupa supplied the soundtrack drumming as well as a cameo appearance in the movie.

Other feature films Krupa appeared in include *The Big Broadcast of 1937* and *Hollywood Hotel* (1937 - both as a member of Benny Goodman's band); *Some Like It Hot* (1938); *Ball Of Fire* (1941, starring Gary Cooper and Barbara Stanwyck); *Syncopation* (1942); *George White's Scandals* (1945); *Beat the Band* (1947); *Boy! What a Girl* (1947); *Smart Politics* (1948); *Glamour Girl* (1948); *Make Believe Ballroom* (1949); *The Glenn Miller Story* (1953); *The Benny Goodman Story* (1955); and *Jazz Ball* (1956).

Movie shorts or "Soundies" that featured his band include *America's Ace Drummer Man* (1941); *Thanks for the Boogie Ride* and *Let Me Off Uptown* (both 1942); *Book Revue* and *Follow That Music* (both 1946); *Drummer Man* (1947); *Thrills of Music* (1948); and *Deep Purple* (1949).

Krupa also authored his own book titled *The Gene Krupa Drum Method* (1938) and began an annual Teen Drum Contest in 1939. The contest attracted thousands of contestants each year and saw drum legend Louie Bellson as the first year's winner.

After suffering a heart attack in 1960, Krupa became limited to sporadic performances. During 1972 and 1973 he played several reunion concerts with Benny Goodman's band - one of which resulted in the 1972 live album *Jazz at the New School*. In that same year Krupa joined Goodman, Hampton, and Wilson in a reunion of the Benny Goodman Quartet on the *Timex Jazz* television special.

In 1972, Krupa was elected by the readers into the *Down Beat* Hall of Fame.

In April 1973, Krupa's home in Yonkers, New York, where he had lived for the past twenty years, was destroyed by fire.

Krupa's final public performance was with a reunion of the old Benny Goodman Quartet at Saratoga Springs, New York, on August 18, 1973.

He died on October 16, 1973, of a heart attack at age 64. He had also been plagued by leukemia and emphysema. He was laid to rest at the Holy Cross Cemetery in Calumet City, Illinois.

Berkowitz began performing as a drummer at the age of eleven in his hometown of Indianapolis, Indiana. Largely self-taught, he learned from listening to big band recordings from his parents' collection and by watching jazz giants performing on television.

"During the 1950s and '60s, musicians were on TV much more than they are today," Berkowitz said.

The first time Berkowitz ever heard the name of Gene Krupa was as a youngster while watching an episode of the TV sit-com, *Dennis the Menace* (1959-1963), starring Jay North. In that particular episode, Dennis was going down the street beating a bass drum and Mr. Wilson told him, "Dennis, stop! You are no Gene Krupa." The inquisitive young Berkowitz then asked his mother who Gene Krupa was, and she told her son he was the famous drummer.

"From then on I began listening to Gene Krupa recordings and saw him play on various TV shows," Berkowitz recalled. "There was something about him and his playing that I liked."

A few years later, Krupa and members of his quartet came to Indianapolis to perform at that city's famed Embers Club. Berkowitz's parents took their young teenage son to the nightspot to see the legendary drum master. It was an event that made a lasting impression on the fledgling drummer.

"I was just amazed at the music I was hearing and seeing the charisma Gene had," Berkowitz recalled. "To go and see Gene Krupa play live with Charlie Ventura on tenor sax, John Bunch on piano, and Nobby Totah on bass, was absolutely wonderful!"

To put the icing on the cake, Berkowitz's parents took their son backstage after the performance to meet his drumming idol.

"It was an amazing moment when I actually got to meet Gene," Berkowitz said. "Gene was very nice, kind and gentle even though I asked some very stupid questions. (laughs) We had some pictures taken. I'm seated in a chair and Gene is over me. I'm in my green suit and green tie and basically looking scared out of my mind! After that, Gene would send me pictures of himself from time to time when he was on the road."

Six years later, Berkowitz would find himself back at The Embers

Club, this time as the house drummer/band contractor for the nightspot.

After studying music at Indiana University, Berkowitz began touring with Johnny Mathis, Andy Williams, and Henry Mancini. Mancini persuaded him to move to Los Angeles, where he became one of the city's busiest studio musicians, working with stars such as Liza Minnelli, Gloria Estefan, Linda Ronstadt, Ringo Starr, Helen Reddy, Seals and Crofts, The Association, Billy Joel, Steve Lawrence, Michael Feinstein, Elton John, Michael Crawford, Sting, Elton John, Bette Midler, Roberta Flack, Maureen McGovern, and Sarah Brightman, among others.

Berkowitz has worked closely for years with composer Johnny Green (of "Body and Soul" fame) and conductor of the MGM Orchestra, and with arranger/bandleader Nelson Riddle for fourteen years. It was Green who called Berkowitz a "Drummer-Conductor Extraordinaire."

The time Berkowitz spent rubbing shoulders with these two giants of music has allowed him to incorporate much of their gifts, knowledge and expertise into his own professional career, he said.

"Johnny was a great conductor and enthusiast," Berkowitz said. "I try to maintain that enthusiasm that he had at all times. He was just a whirlwind of positive vibes. Nelson was a perfectionist. He was like 'Eyeore,' always having a cloud over his head. I just had so much respect for him and continue to have such respect for him that I hope some of that professionalism and whatever it was that made Nelson so special, I get to carry it on."

Berkowitz has also led numerous orchestras including the Boston Pops, The London Symphony, The Cincinnati Pops, The Pittsburgh Symphony, The North Carolina Symphony, The Atlanta Symphony, The National Symphony; and is featured on recordings with Steve Lawrence, Placido Domingo, Linda Eder and countless original cast albums, movies, "jingles" and television performances.

In addition, the talented drummer has performed on many television programs including *The Academy Awards*; *The Tonight Show*; *The Tony Awards*; *The Today Show*; *A Capitol Fourth*; *Great Performances*; *Live From Lincoln Center*; and *Concerts at the White House*.

After moving to New York in 1980, Berkowitz was immediately in demand on Broadway, working shows such as *Evita*; *Pacific Overtures*; *The Tap Dance Kid*; *Do Re Mi*; and Jerome Robbins' *Broadway*.

Berkowitz's current projects include a new Jerry Herman musical, *Miss Spectacular*; *A Tribute to Sinatra* with the Cincinnati Pops for Telarc; a benefit performance of *West Side Story* for Katie Couric's Foundation (starring Robert DeNiro, Kevin Kline, Bette Midler, Chita Rivera, Rita Moreno, Josh Groban, Beyonce Knowles, the cast of *The Sopranos*; and and former New York Mayor Rudy Giuliani); and a special concert version of Jerry Herman's *Mack and Mabel*.

Berkowitz continues to work with *Broadway on Broadway*, a free concert in New York's Times Square featuring numbers from each season's Broadway Musicals, now in its 11th year and continuing to draw over 50,000 people. During the holiday season, he will be at Madison Square Garden from November 28 through December 28 for his tenth year in the pit for *A Christmas Carol*. As a leader of his own big band, Berkowitz has also led tribute bands to Gene Krupa, Harry James, Buddy Rich, Nelson Riddle, Artie Shaw, and Billy May. His band played at the world-famous Birdland for three sold-out nights in June.

Yet there is a difference leading an *authorized* band such as the New Gene Krupa Orchestra as opposed to putting together various tribute groups, according to Berkowitz.

"The first thing that makes a difference is the license," Berkowitz said. "It helps when booking a band. People want to know is this the *real* band? That gives it a sense of legitimacy that the tribute band does not. It's upholding a tradition, a standard. The level of what I expect of the musicians is 110 percent. You just want it to be the best possible product you can put on the stage. That's what it's all about."

But getting the Krupa estate to give Berkowitz its blessings to officially front the band that bears the legendary drummer's name was a four-year challenge, Berkowitz said.

The first person to hold the license was Ben Anthony who is now deceased. Then, Jack Platt, a childhood friend of Krupa's, held the license until his death in 1998. After Platt's passing, the Krupa estate wasn't ready to license the band to any one just yet, according to Berkowitz.

However, through persistent persuasion, Berkowitz obtained the licensing agreement from the Krupa estate on June 1 of this year, he said.

"We are just getting started," he said. "So far, I'm having a great deal of luck marketing the band through the Internet."

While the band may just be getting started, Berkowitz was hard at work behind the scenes long before the first band rehearsal was ever scheduled. He has devoted a lot of time and energy in putting together the Krupa library before he was officially given the license, he said.

"A lot of the music was lost in a fire in Gene's home in Yonkers and I spent a good amount of time reconstructing the book prior to having the band," Berkowitz said. "I've also recovered the book Ben Anthony had which contained a lot of stuff which I didn't have, tunes like "Wire Brush Stomp," "Massachusetts," and some obscure pieces."

Adding to the library are some recent arrangements that Quincy Jones and Billy Byers reworked of all the Krupa hits, Berkowitz said.

"The pieces have a modern sound to them," he said.

Personal favorites from the Krupa library for Berkowitz include "Gene's Boogie," "Massachusetts," and "Rockin' Chair," he said.

Although the fifteen-piece New Gene Krupa Orchestra is not a full-time road band, Berkowitz would like it to be, he said.

"It's a difficult thing," he said. "If Gene couldn't do it in 1951, and given the current state of the music business, it's more difficult now. I'd like to be working as much as possible. I think we'll do very well. We're playing at community concerts, community art centers and colleges. I don't envision us, at least in the near future, anywhere near like the Glenn Miller Orchestra, constantly being on the road."

For now, as a way of being more cost-efficient, when the New Gene Krupa Orchestra makes appearances, whether for stage shows or for dances, Berkowitz utilizes musicians from specific geographic areas across the country, he said.

"I have musicians on the East Coast, West Coast, and in the Midwest," he said. "I bring Lynn Roberts to sing at all our performances. She's fabulous. Lynn sang with Harry James, Benny Goodman, Tommy Dorsey and Dubby Spivak."

As of press time, the nearest venue to Northern California that the New Gene Krupa Orchestra is slated to perform at is at John Ascuaga's Nuggett Hotel in Sparks, Nevada, on February 25, 2004.

For a complete update on performances by the New Gene Krupa Orchestra, log on to Berkowitz's official website at: www.berkmusic.com

When circumstances permit, Berkowitz hopes that Anita O'Day would also sing with the band for special concerts. O'Day, who just turned 84 last month, recently moved to New York City from her residence in Hollywood, CA. Still in fantastic voice, she continues to perform and is scheduled to perform at The Fez on Lafayette in New York City on November 2 and November 9 as part of her birthday celebration. (See www.anitaoday.com)

"We would love to have Anita make an appearance with us when she's available," Berkowitz said. "She's basically only willing to do 'Let Me Off Uptown' and 'Boogie Blues.'" Since moving to New York, the likelihood of her doing some things with us are good."

While some of Krupa's music may be sixty-five years old, it still manages to attract a young audience wherever the band plays, Berkowitz said.

"What's great is that these young people show up and they know the music," he said. "Unfortunately, they dance the Lindy to everything. (laughs)"

Some critics have scoffed at the idea of a Gene Krupa "ghost" band being organized arguing that the real impact Krupa left in jazz was not with his big band, but rather, in his small group work. Berkowitz disagrees.

"That's not really a fair statement," he said. "I think Gene's impact was with his big band. The trio and quartet things were done later on. While we do "Dark Eyes," "Stompin' at the Savoy," and "Caravan" in a quartet format within the big band, to me, the big band is the reason why I wanted to do this. People can say what they want."

As the New Gene Krupa Orchestra gears up for bookings for a new concert season, Berkowitz is optimistic that the band will catch on. His goal is that when people are looking for a quality big band to play a date, the NGKO will be one of their top choices for consideration, he said.

"I'd like us to be a band that is thought of as the *alternative*," Berkowitz said. "The Glenn Miller Orchestra is the Rolls Royce of bands that are currently out there. If you can't get the GMO, I want the band to be the next band to be thought of. That's my goal. It's a lofty one but that's what I'm really trying to achieve here. If we aren't your first choice, we sure want to be your second choice based on professionalism, great music, great approach, and doing everything what we say we'll do. It's business."

And a possible recording project for the band is also on the horizon, according to Berkowitz.

"The only problem I'm having is what to record," Berkowitz said. "I'm not sure whether to re- record with the new band some of the things Gene did or to take other arrangements and lend the Krupa touch to them. I'm not sure which way to go."

No matter what direction Berkowitz may go when it comes to any recordings, his compass is firmly set on "forward" when it comes to making people more aware of the colorful Gene Krupa legacy, his music, and the new big band that bears his name.

"Gene left a legacy to big band jazz by bringing the drums out to the forefront and making the drummer the high-priced guy," Berkowitz said. "His energy, his spectacular charisma, and his style of playing are also legacies he left behind. The band itself was such a big success especially with Roy Eldridge and Anita O'Day. I don't know why people aren't more aware of that than they seem to be. But, we are going to do everything we can to make people aware of it now."

** Coda – Here is an update on Michael Berkowitz and the New Gene Krupa Orchestra since this article was published.

Berkowitz remains musically active in a variety of different ways. For the past ten years he has been the Principal Pops Conductor of the Santa Rosa Symphony in Santa Rosa, California.

Berkowitz and the Gene Krupa Orchestra recorded the CD, *Thinking of Gene*. The project was recorded live from Washington, D. C.

The band continues to perform throughout the country whenever it can.

Michael Berkowitz, above, and Gene Krupa, on their respective sets.

Maestro Michael Berkowitz.

Gene Krupa, the first super-star of the drums.

Michael Berkowitz remains a first-call drummer on various musical projects and as a conductor.

Les Brown Jr. and Les Brown
- *Photos by Stephen Fratallone/Jazz Connection*

Moving Full Speed Ahead

Les Brown Jr. Keeps His Dad's Band Of Renown Afloat And Charted On Course

The following article on Les Brown Jr. was originally published in the June 2001 issue of Jazz Connection Magazine

For sixty-four years, the music of Les Brown and His Band of Renown have been synonymous with quality music. The band's consistency in style, clean playing, and wonderful arrangements that got people moving out on the dance floor were the trademarks of the venerable bandleader right up until his passing on January 4 of this year at age 88.

With the Maestro's passing, Brown's son, Les Jr., has now taken over at the helm of the "Good Ship Band of Renown," keeping it afloat and charted on course.

"Dad kept the quality of music high and that will stay with us," Les Brown Jr. said after the Band of Renown played another stellar performance at the Jackson Racheria Hotel and Casino in Jackson, California, on June 14. "People are sorry that Dad isn't around and have expressed their sorrow. However, they love the fact the tradition is going on and that the band won't stop."

The senior Brown, who started leading a band in 1936, was awarded the distinction four years ago by the *Guiness Book of World Records* as the leader of the longest lasting musical organization in the history of Amnerican popular music. During this time Brown and his orchestra chalked up such popular hits as "Leap Frog" (the band's theme song), "Joltin' Joe DiMaggio," "Bizet Has His Day," "Mexican Hat Dance," "My Dreams Are Getting Better All the Time," and his two top hits, "Sentimental Journey," which he co-wrote in 1944 with Ben Homer and Bud Green, and which helped to launch Doris Day, Brown's girl singer at the time to fame, and Irving Berlin's "I've Got My Love to Keep Me Warm," recorded the following year and released in 1948.

In that year, Brown joined forces with Bob Hope as the comedian's musical director for his radio shows and later for television. He also accompanied Hope on eighteen Christmas tours to entertain U. S. troops.

Brown was also musical director for numerous TV specials as well as for *The Steve Allen Show* in the 1950s and for *The Dean Martin Show* from 1965 to 1974.

But don't call the Band of Renown a "ghost band" just yet, according to Brown Jr.

"People don't feel our band is a 'ghost band' like some others," Brown Jr. said. "There is still a Brown in front of the band."

In addition to Brown Jr., who is an alumnus of his father's band since age fifteen, the band is also home to a pair of long-time members – singer and former trombonist Clyde "Stumpy" Brown and singer and former baritone saxophonist Henry "Butch" Stone. Stumpy Brown is Brown Jr's. uncle who has been with the organization since July 1943. Now at age 76, Stumpy Brown is the band's manager and featured jump tune vocalist.

Stone, 88, and now legally blind, is the featured novelty tune singer. Although not blood-related, he is considered family nevertheless, having been a mainstay with the Band of Renown since 1941, scoring a hit with his signature tune, "A Good Man is Hard to Find."

Brown's band has always been a "family affair." Even middle brother Warren Brown was part of the trombone section from 1939 to 1942, and again briefly in 1946. He went on to become vice- president of music publication for Universal Studios. Now retired at age 85, he resides in Carlsbad, California.

The task of grooming his son for leadership of his band was something that Brown had envisioned for a long time, Brown Jr. said.

"Over the last three years, ever since Dad remarried, I began leading the band more and more," Brown Jr. said. "He wanted to do more traveling on his own and I took over at that point." (Brown was married for three years to Evelyn Joyce Wells. Brown's first wife of sixty-two years, Georgia Claire DeWolfe, died in 1996.)

With the passing of the baton, Brown also gave his son freedom to lead the band his own way, Brown Jr. said.

"Dad was great about it," he said. "When I say my own way, I mean he'd let me have my own way in counting off tempos. He'd come up to me afterwards and say that the show went well but that such- and-such tune was too fast or too slow, stuff like that. I said to him what he used to say to me for years, 'Get your own band!' We'd joke with each other that way."

While the senior Brown played the clarinet and alto saxophone, he gave up playing those instruments in public years ago in order to concentrate on conducting his band. Although he had a certain charm and charisma on the bandstand few could match, he wasn't the greatest speaker when utilizing a microphone, Brown Jr. said.

"A lot of people didn't know exactly what Dad was saying," he said. "I'm trained as an actor and as an MC. That's more what I do. I guide the band and I get the audience to listen. Dad prepared the band but I'm a better front man. And now I prepare the band the way he used to do it."

Much of Brown Jr.'s "education" about leading a band came as a result of just watching his father in action, he said.

"When I was twenty-five, I thought I knew it all because I'd been in the band for ten years first as a drummer, then as a singer," Brown Jr. said. "I thought to myself, 'Why couldn't my dad understand everything I know?' By the time he passed away, I realized that he knew it all and I didn't know much of anything about it. For the past three years I watched everything he did. I learned so much over those years that I didn't realize what I already knew, but I didn't let it sink in until I let go of all of the baloney. I learned everything about band leading from Dad – how to conduct the show, how to control the dynamics to what the job of the bandleader really is. The bandleader is the liaison between the audience and the band. The band has to trust me to set the tempo and to know what the audience wants to hear and how they want to hear it. So, I just watched. Dad didn't have to tell me. When he'd let me go out and lead the band he'd stay and watch and tell me what I was doing right and what I needed to work on."

While children of famous musical parents may want to explore other musical territories, Brown Jr.'s gravitation toward the music that made his father a household name stood him in good graces as he assumed his leadership role.

"Over the past five years I suggested to Dad to go back and play what worked best for him from the 1940s and 1950s when the band was at its peak," Brown Jr. said. "Rather than play a little rock or a little of this, I told him he should play what he knows. He was a swing band and one of the best. He listened and turned the library lover to me. I went through to find some of the old arrangements and put them back in the band book. When we'd play a tune, he'd say, 'That's a great arrangement. I had forgotten about it.' After fifty or sixty years, I can see how he would have forgotten them."

The Band of Renown has recorded a CD of classic Les Brown songs called *Session 55: The New Les Brown CD* (Jake/Doc Hollywood Records). Recorded in March 2000, this twenty-one track disc features updated and feshly recorded versions of standard's from the band's library as well as Brown signature tunes of "Leap Frog" and "Bizet Has His Day." The album showcases works by such stellar arrangers as Van Alexander, Frank Comstock, Bob Higgins, Ben Homer, Joe Garland, and by Brown himself. Singer Lou Rawls joins in as special guest on "I Only Have Eyes For You" and "They Can't Take That Away From Me." It's the last album

Brown conducted on and personally supervised. The CD is slated for release on July 17, according to Brown Jr.

For CD and musical arrangement purchases as well as current information about the Band of Renown, a website is maintained at: www.bandsofrenown.com.

Despite Brown's passing, the enthusiasm from audiences for the Band of Renown's music over the past six months has not waned, Brown Jr. said.

"I host a four-hour radio show on Sunday evenings called *The Music of Your Life*," Brown Jr. said. "The outcome and power of that show is now apparent to me when we do a job. People come to hear the band as a result of hearing the radio show and hearing the music. It's starting to catch on. People are coming to see what we are like now."

Even the enthusiasm of the audience at the Jackson Rancheria had not diminished since the Band of Renown made its second appearance there last July. Brown himself was schedule to front the band, but at the last moment deferred those duties to his son. The audience was told that Brown contracted a virus in his thoat that left him speechless. They were told it was nothing serious but it was just enough of a malady to keep him from doing his MC duties. Six months later Brown was dead, succumbing to lung cancer.

Not only has Brown's passing been the biggest change to the Band of Renown's make up, but Brown Jr. has initiated three other major changes as well, he said.

The first change has to do with his uncle, Stumpy Brown. For the past fifty-eight years, Stumpy Brown had been the anchor in the Band of Renown's trombone section as well as the band's jump tune vocalist. During the past two decades, he had also worked as the band's manager and booker. Since January of this year, he no longer plays trombone in the band.

"The burden of playing, singing, managing, and booking was getting to be hard on my uncle, so now I utilize him as a featured vocalist," Brown Jr. said. "It relieves him of the burden of having to play trombone every night because it becomes more and more physically difficult as he gets older." The second change has to do with featuring more vocals overall throughout a show.

"It's been my experience that people respond to vocals more today than they did during the Big Band Era when vocalists were considered like sidemen in a band," Brown Jr. said.

The final change has to do with the fruit of the band's labor – conducting band rehearsals immediately after playing an engagement.

"Since we've been putting a lot of the old arrangements back in the book, we have been rehearsing after we we play our job, making sure the notes are right and everything is there," Brown Jr. said.

In the weeks ahead, the Band of Renown have engagements in Newport Beach, California, and at the Stardust Hotel in Las Vegas, according to Brown Jr.

While the Brown Family has left a musical dynasty – beginning with R. W. Brown, Brown Jr's grandfather, who was a baker and played soprano saxophone and led the Tower City, Pennsylvania town band, earning him the sobriquet, "The March Prince," because of his fondness for John Phillip Sousa marches – it is uncertain at this point whether the next generation of Brown's will take over the baton to lead the Band of Renown.

"My daughter is an executive in the music business and isn't a musician, per se," Brown Jr. said. "I have a twenty-three-year-old son who has expressed an interest in singing. He's a little shy about it, but I'll try to get him over that. I'll definitely encourage him to think about the band."

But for the moment, Brown Jr. is carrying on the family tradition, a legacy rich in musical quality, longevity, service, fortitude and grace.

"Dad's legacy I think has to do with his great music and being the longest lasting bandleader in history," Brown Jr. said. "The other thing, of course, is the fact that millions of servicemen saw the band over eighteen Christmas tours. That's probably the greatest impact. He was part of that. I think we'll stick around to play his music for some time."

** Coda – Here is an update on Les Brown Jr. and the Band of Renown since this article was published.

Since 2004, Les Brown Jr. and his Band of Renown moved from Los Angeles to Branson, Missouri, an Ozark town in the southwest part of the state known as a family vacation destination. The move has allowed the band to work more readily.

The band's website is at: www.bandofrenown.com

Les Brown Jr. fronting his Band of Renown on July 13, 2000, for a dance at the Jackson Rancheria Hotel and Casino in Jackson, CA.
– *Photo by Stephen Fratallone*

Les Brown Jr. hamming it up with Butch Stone on one of Stone's novelty tunes on June 14, 2001, at the Jackson Rancheria Hotel and Casino in Jackson, CA. – *Photo by Stephen Fratallone*

Les Brown Jr. in 2000 and 2001.
- *Photos by Stephen Fratallone*

Les Brown Jr. doing what he loves doing best: conducting and fronting his Band of Renown for a dance while at the Jackson Rancheria Hotel and Casino in Jackson, CA, on July 13, 2000. – *Photos by Stephen Fratallone*

Les Brown Jr., above, on June 14, 2001, at a dance at the Jackson Rancheria Hotel and Casino in Jackson, CA; and below, he enthusiastically conducts his Band of Renown while his uncle, Stumpy Brown, 77, sings a jump tune for the Jackson crowd at the same dance.
– *Photos by Stephen Fratallone*

Hi-De-Ho, Neighbor!

Chris Calloway Pays Tribute To Her Father, Cab Calloway, And His Legacy Of Swing

Cab Calloway and Chris Calloway

The following article on Chris Calloway and Cab Calloway's Legacy of Swing was originally published in the January 2001 issue of Jazz Connection Magazine

Chris Calloway is on a royal mission. The singer/actress is heir to an American musical dynasty who is helping to keep alive the music of her late father, jazz icon, Cab Calloway, the "King of Hi-De-Ho."

"I'm the next generation of this legacy," Calloway said via telephone from her home in Santa Fe, New Mexico. "I grew up, came through and have been trained in this legacy, in this style, in this epic. I do represent a great American musical family. It's here for me to help perpetuate that and to use the media to get it to the forefront."

Although the world knew him as "The Hi-De-Ho Man" from his hit song, "Minnie the Moocher," vocalist and flamboyant bandleader Cabell "Cab" Calloway was an incubator of jazz talent and a timeless example of the Swing Era's appeal. He once forgot the words to this song and sang, "Hi-De-Ho" in its place, the phrase which eventually became his trademark.

For the last eighteen years of Cab Calloway's career, Chris Calloway had toured with her father. However, she didn't come to recognize or appreciate the impact of her father's music until he passed away in 1994.

"It was actually about five years ago when I began to realize what I had in terms of heritage and legacy," she said. "I worked with Daddy and did all the stuff that I had to do to be in his shows, but on the side I had my own band furiously trying to come out with Al Jarreau tracks. When the retro-swing craze took hold, I began to do some research on it. Now my dad's music is still fabulous. It's still valuable. Now I've taken it and made it my own."

The jazz icon's music has been virtually unheard from since his death because of litigation surrounding the alleged misappropriation of rights by the late bandleader's manager, Chris Calloway said.

"Dad's manager set him up to sign his rights away," Chris Calloway said. "It took us five years to fight these people but we got our rights back! That's the reason why no one has been hearing anything about Cab Calloway. Now we are footloose and free, so here we come!"

Chris Calloway will be starting the new year off with a bang as she takes the "Cab Calloway's Legacy of Swing" show on a fifty-five-city mation-wide tour beginning January 7, 2001. The second stop of the tour will be at California State University, Chico's Laxson Auditorium on January 8.

The show, adapted from its debut at the 1999 JVC Jazz Festival, incudes original Calloway arrangements, some of which have not been heard in fifty years. Fronting the thirteen-piece Hi-De-Ho Orchrestra will be Chris Calloway singing some of her father's signature tunes including "Minnie the Moocher," "Jumpin' Jive," "Boog It," and "Are You All Reet?" she said.

"The show is very similar to the Cotton Club-type experience," she said. "We'll be doing big band arrangements some of which are instrumental arrangements of original Cab Calloway charts. It's quite a treat for the band, myself, and certainly for the audience."

Also on the bill will be tap dancer Chester Whitmore, a protégé of famed tap dancer Fayard Nicholas, the elder Nicholas of the celebrated Nicholas Brothers dance team, and a group of Lindy Hoppers and other swing dancers.

"It's going to be a great show in the tradition of a revue," Chris Calloway said.

It was in front of these kinds of revues that Cab Calloway's star shined the brightest. A tall, handsome man with a million-dollar smile and a happy, friendly air, Calloway would launch the band into action. Then, with elbows flying, would furiously dance out from under his hat. He would encourage soloists with great roaring shouts. And he would get a stranglehold on a microphone and sing. He was so impetuous at what he was doing that he once danced off the bandstand and broke his ankle.

A consummate entertainer who could not arrange anything or play an instrument, except for occasional attempts on the drums, Calloway once told an interviewer, "A band must consist of good musicians, must have top-flight arrangements, must be well-rehearsed and completely led. But that isn't enough. People can't be held and entertained in a complete sense by sound alone. There must be something for the eyes to see."

Cabell Calloway was born on December 25, 1907, in Rochester, New

York. His father was a lawyer, his mother a teacher. Soon after his birth, the family moved to Baltimore, where he was reared. His older sister, Blanche, who was a singer and became famous in her own right as the first female Big Band leader of an all-male band, got him his first show-business job in 1927 singing in *Plantation Days*, a touring show in which she was featured.

When the tour ended in Chicago, Calloway entered law school at Crane College in the "Windy City." At the same time, he was playing basketball well enough to get an offer from the Harlen Globetrotters, but turned it down to pursue music.

He was moonlighting as a nightclub singer at the Sunset Café, where he met Louis Armstrong. Calloway eventually became the featured vocalist with the Alabamians, considered at the time to contain some of the best musicians of the period. In 1928, Calloway took over leadership of the orchestra and after a successful run, found himself in New York City.

By 1930, Calloway and his orchestra replaced Duke Ellington's orchestra at the Cotton Club in Harlem. The trademark Calloway image, which combined an almost catlike grace on the bandstand with a singing style that could be slyly insinuating one moment and wildly exuberant the next, came into full bloom one night in 1931 when he was leading his band in a radio broadcast from the Cotton Club.

Calloway had recently written "Minnie the Moocher," a new radio theme song for his band. The song combined a melody that was very close to the band's previous theme, "St. James Infirmary," with lyrics patterned on those of two other popular songs of the day, "Willie, the Weeper" an "Minnie, the Mermaid." As he started to sing the song, Calloway suddenly realized he could not remember the lyrics.

"I couldn't leave a blank there as I might have done if we weren't on the air," he wrote in his autobiography, *Of Minnie the Moocher and Me* (Crowell Publishing, 1976). "I had to fill the space, so I started to scat-sing the first that came into my mind."

What Calloway scatted was, *"Hi-de-hi-de-hi-de-ho. Ho-de-ho-de-ho-de-hee. Oodle-odlye-odlyee-oodlee-doo."*

"The crowd went crazy," Calloway recalled in his book. "I asked the band to follow me. I sang, *'Ho-de-hi-de-hi-de-ho.'* And the band responded, I sang, *'Dwaa-de-dwaa-de-dwaa-de-doo.'* I asked the audience to join in. They hollered back and nearly brought the roof down."

Many critics are of the opinion that Calloway's band from 1939 to 1942, was perhaps his finest. That band had a rich, clean ensemble slound, a persuative swing and great spirit about it, and brilliant soloists that included tenor saxophonist Chu Berry; trumpetrs John Burks "Dizzy" Gillespie, Jonah Jones, and Adolphus "Doc" Cheatham; bassist Milt Hinton; trombonist Tyree Glenn; and drummer Cozy Cole. Hinton, believed to have been the last surviving member of that great band, died on December 19, 2000. He was 90.

The Calloway band continued to play and record until 1948 when, as the Big Band Era faded, Calloway gave up the Big Band and performed with small groups.

In 1928, Calloway married Wenonah "Betty" Conacher and subsequently had four daughters: Camay, Chris, Eulalia, and Cabella. The marriage lasted until 1949.

In 1953, Calloway married Zulme "Nuffie" MacNeal. The marriage lasted until Calloway's death in 1994.

In 1952, Calloway played the role of the drug-peddling "Sportin' Life" in *Porgy and Bess*, a role that composer George Gerscwin had modeled on Calloway's colorful performing style. He toured in the show overseas and in the United States with great success for 3½ years.

In 1967, Calloway was back on Broadway in an all-African Amnerican version of *Hello, Dolly!* with Pearl Bailey. Calloway also appeared in many movies, starting with *The Big Broadcast of 1932*; *The Singing Kid* with Al Jolson in 1936; *Manhattan Merry-Go-Round* (1937); *Stormy Weather* with Lena Horne in 1943; *Hi De Ho* (1947); *St. Louis Blues* (1958); *A*

Man Called Adam (1966); *The Blues Brothers* (1980), which garnered renewed interest in Calloway; and *The Cotton Club* (1984). In the 1990s, Calloway's timeless appeal got him a cameo in a 1930s-themed Janet Jackson music video, *Alright*, that introduced a new generation to his crowd-pleasing genius.

Among the songs that Calloway made famous were "Reefer Man" (June 9, 1932); "Kicking the Gong Around" (December 18, 1933); "The Jumpin' Jive" (July 17, 1939); "Pickin' the Cabbage" and "Boog It" (both on March 8, 1940); "A Chicken Ain't Nothin' But a Bird" (October 14, 1940); "Are You Reet?" and "Ebony Silhouette" (both on January 16, 1941); and his biggest hit and signature tune, "Minnie the Moocher" (March 3, 1931, December 18, 1933, and again on February 2, 1942).

A lexicographer as well as a composer, Calloway compiled the *Hepster's Dictionary* (1938), a glossary of jive expressions, which was updated several time.

Some examples of jive talk found in Calloway's dictionary include *Armstrongs* (N), musical notes in the upper register, high trumpet notes; *Blap* (N), something very good, e.g., "That's a blap."; *Dillinger* (N), a killer-diller, something too hot to handle; *IGG* (V), to ignore someone, e.g., "Don't igg me."; *Main Queen* (N), favorite girl friend; *Slide Your Jib* (V), to talk freely; *Trickeration* (N), struttin' your stuff, muggin' lightly and politely; and *Yeah, Man*, an exclamation of assent.

On November 18, 1994, Calloway died in a nursing nhome in Hosekessin, Delaware, from complications he suffered from a stroke the previous June. He was 86. His body was cremated and his ashes were given to his family. Upon the death of his wife Zulme "Nuffie" Calloway on October 13, 2008, his ashes were interred next to her in the Rosewood Mausoleum at Ferncliff Cemetery in Hartsdale, New York.

A middle school in Wllington, Delaware, has been named after the jazz legend: The Cab Calloway School of the Arts. As the only middle school of its kind in the state, the school focuses on using the arts to supplement academics in order to strengthen intellectual, physical, social, and emotional growth of the whole student. Academic courses are offered in Language Arts, Math, Science, and Social Studies, supplemented by courses in the arts, including dance, drama, visual arts, vocal, instrumental music and communication arts.

Although the school currently does not offer any courses which specifically focuses on Calloway's music, Chris Calloway thought the addition of such a class into the schools curriculum was a cute idea, she said.

"I can see having a class in Scat 101 or something like that," she said with a laugh.

Despite the legendary status Calloway achieved, it wasn't always easy for his children growing up in his shadow. Chris Calloway explains:

"As a child, I was not prepared to deal with some of the things I had to deal with because my dad was a famous person. When we went out to dinner on occasion, it was drummed into us kids that we really really had to be on our best behavior. Our behavior was a reflection on our dad. That's a pretty heavy thing thing to dump on a kid! In that respect, it was a drag. My mother really let us know when we were living in White Plains, New York, that we were the first black family living in the neighborhood. She was very social-conscious. Our behavior and the way we carried ourselves had to show that we were 'model' children. That was a drag."

But seeing how much joy her father gave people left an impression on Chris Calloway, she said.

"It was always a thrill to see my dad interact with people and to see the joy on their faces," she said. "Evidentially, he impacted people's lives in such a way that they remember the exact moment when they saw him." (This writer can attest to that. I had the privilege of seeing Calloway perform during the summer of 1980 on the Tomorrowland Stage at Disneyland with former Big Band diva, Helen Forrest. Calloway was dressed in a white tuxedo with tails and at age 72, he pranced and strutted around the stage like an energetic 20-year-old.)

It wasn't until Chris Calloway was about ten years old that she first realized her father's celebrity status, she said.

"My dad was doing *Porgy and Bess* one summer at a theater-in-the-round in Massachusetts," Chris Calloway recalled. "The family went with him and we stayed at a cottage while he was doing the show. My sister and I would go nightly to work with him. He would make his appearance on stage and the place would just go crazy! There would be this electrical shock that would run through the theater. I thought to myself, 'Wow! This guy is really something else.' I was sitting there night after night seeing this person who created this magic every single night. It came to me that he was something special. He would be sitting in the wings at any venue looking like an old man. But when he was introduced to the audience, he would shoot up like something had gotten in side of him to produce this ball of energy. I think it had a great deal to do with how these kind of entertainers were brought up. Going through racial situations and the Depression, they really had to push. Performing on stage was not a casual thing. It was really life or death. That seemed to sustain my dad forever."

Most children consider the music their parents listen to as "square." Chris Calloway felt the same way about her father's music while growing up. It didn't become an issue for her until she was in college during the 1960s, she said.

"The hippie thing, Jimi Hendrix, The Beatles, and the protestors against the Vietnam War was the demarcation of our generation," Chris Calloway said. "Dad would say, 'I can't understand what the hell they're saying!' H-E-L-L-O! I suppose the jive talk that he helped to popularize in his music *was* understandable? He would be critical of the 1960s fashions. Did anybody ever wonder where those zoot suits he wore from the 1940s came from?"

Although Calloway wrote a dictionary on jive talk and spoke the vernacular as part of his public persona, it wasn't practiced extensively at home, Chris Calloway recalled.

"Jive talk was very subtly and very naturally used at home," she said. "It crept into conversations very lossely. Dad may have said something like, 'That was a *cool* thing,' or 'Don't *jive* around!' There were certain words and linguistic moments where it was used in that way."

While he was at home, Calloway laid his public persona to rest and was rather a quiet person, occasionally entertaining musician and show business friends, Chris Calloway said.

"When Daddy was home, he was down right dull!" she said. "He was very low key. He wasn't a big social guy. While he did have some entertainment friends visit on occasion, our home wasn't a party house. I remember we had Pearl Bailey, Lena Horne, Harry Belafonte, Louis Armstrong, and even Willie Mays come to the house. Since my dad's birthday was on Christmas Day, that always got to be a fun thing. It was tradition for as long as I can remember that Dizzy Gillespie would call my dad up on the phone and play 'Happy Birthday' for him on his trumpet."

There is a story that has been circulating for years stating that Calloway fired Gillespie from his band in 1941 after Gillespie allegedly threw "spitballs" at him during an engagement in Hartford, Connecticut. The two supposedly got into a fight and Gillespie stabbed Calloway in the leg with a small knife during the brawl.

"If Daddy were here, he'd hitting the ceiling!" Chrsi Calloway said. "He'd say, 'That's a bunch of crap! No one threw any spitballs at any one!' That story has almost reached mythological proportions."

Yet Calloway was not without his quirks and foibles. While being a privately spiritual person, the jazz legend was also a very superstitious person, often practicing certain ritualistic behaviors associated with people in show business.

"If you spilled salt, you had to throw it over your shoulder," Chris Calloway said. "No hats were to be place on the bed or shoes on the table. He would spit on the hem of your skirt before you went out on stage – old show biz rituals like that. Spiritually, my dad was very private. His religion, if you will, was the moment on stage interacting with the audience. That was his prayer. That was his church. He certainly believed in God. Coming out of the early twentieth century in to a black midle-class family, God and Jesus weren't something they tapped their tambourines to. His spiritual side was intimate and very quiet. He didn't talk much about it. He was more comfortable in front of 5,000 people than one- on-one."

Calloway's popular appeal with an audience stemmed from the belief that this was paramount for an entertainer to give oneself totally for the satisfaction of the audience.

"It was life or death," Chris Calloway said. "There wasn't anything casual about it. In my training with him, the mantra was, 'You owe everything to the audience. If they weren't there, there wouldn't be any reason for you to be there.' This came out of the modern trend of the time during the 1960s when performers would come out on stage in jeans and T-shirts or they would turn their backs on the audience or they would be grody with an audience. That was sacrilege to him! That was the ultimate violation of the ethic of an entertainer. In his peculiar psychology, that was his religion which made it all the more potent. He just gave his entire life to the audience."

When it came to his band's unique sound, it was Calloway's charismatic spirit which played a big influence, according to his daughter.

"I'm just coming to find out that the band is really going to sound like the energy and the spirit of its leader," she said. "The spirit and jolt that my dad gave those musicians was directly his. Musically, he relied heavily on the reeds. There are wonderful reed arrangements where the saxes are flowing in and out, a Chu Berry or Eddie Barfield kind of thing. The brass was biting with Dizzy and Jonah Jones. I think the band was underrated because of his persona. He wasn't Count Basie or Duke Ellington, who were playing musicians. What Cab played was 'body' persona, front man. He played front man just as hard as Ellington played piano or made arrangements."

Bitten by the "Show Biz Bug" ever since she first appeared on stage with her father in *Porgy and Bess*, Chris Calloway has always wanted to entertain. And being the daughter of a famous father didn't always guarantee instant success. She had to pay her dues. Her solo career had its humble beginnings at New York's Improvisation Club on West 44th Street, where such entertainers such as Liza Minnelli, Richard Pryor, and Rodney Dangerfield came in to try out material. Chris Calloway worked up a routine as a singing hat check girl.

"I was a theater major at Boston University and I went to New York to get some experience," Chris Calloway recalled. "Dad was not pleased with me for doing this. As a matter of fact, he was so mad, he threw a television set at me! I got this job as a hat check girl there. I would come threshing out of this closet twice an evening to start trying my stuff. It was a great time. When people found out who I was and when my dad came down one time, it was a really big thing. It was where I got my roots."

After seeing what his daughter could do in front of an audience, Calloway helped his daughter out by getting her engagements in the Catskill Mountains-circuit and at some cabaret clubs around New York City, she said.

"I picked up a manager and that was the beginning for me," she said.

During the mid-1960s, Chris Calloway worked about five jobs as a Go-Go girl with vibraphone great Lionel Hampton and his band.

"I was basically the little Go-Go girl that got members of the audience up to go-go dance with them while Lionel played the drums," she said.

At age 21, Chris Calloway made her television debut on *The Ed Sullivan Show* on March 19, 1967, with her dad, which began the musical partnership between father and daughter. Her Broadway career began that same year with the acclaimed all-black production of *Hello, Dolly!* starring Pearl Bailey and her father, followed by a significant nine-month tour of the musical review, *Eubie*.

But after two years of performing together, Chris Calloway was at the time a widow with a nine-month-old son to raise. She decided that she had had enough and moved to Los Angeles. It was in the "City of Angeles" that a dream came true for her.

"I had my own talk radio and music shows," she said. "I just moved to L.A. and I was listening to a talk show on the radio one day and the announcer on the show stated the program didn't have a permanent host. I called the radio station and told them that I'm their hostess for the show. I got interviewed for the job and was hired. I had a community service show called *Women's World*, dealing with women's issues and interests. It turned out to be a dream come true. I then hosted my own music show and that dream became a fabulous reality for me!"

After a few years working in radio, Chris Calloway rejoined her father during the last eighteen years of his life performing together with his Hi-De-Ho Orchestra touring the United States, Europe, South America, Japan, and Australia.

In her professional association with her father, Chris Calloway has gleaned a wide range of things that she uses today in her career, things such as dealing with club owners, being on the road and what to do after the show. But probably the two most important things have to do with the audience and the orchestra, she said.

"The first thing I've gleaned is to have ultimate respect for the audience," Chris Calloway said. "I'm blessed and what I believe has happened to me is a 50-50 thing. I came into this life with some God-given talent. The other half I gleaned from my working association with my dad. That has to do with watching him give his life to the audience. The second thing is watching how he handled the band. He wouldn't show his band the 'road map' of a tune. I thought to myself, how evil! One of two things would happen. The band would either kick it in the ass or you could see exactly where the weakness in the band was. I did not understand that until months ago when I was confronted with a band who couldn't play my stuff. There are things which I've come to understand as to why he handled himself the way he did. They all work. I've taken them and made them my own."

In putting together "Cab Calloway's Legacy of Swing" show, Chris Calloway received some encouragement and inspiration from some established swing groups in the San Francisco area, namely Lavay Smith and her Red Hot Skillet Lickers and The Ambassadors of Swing led by "Vice Grip."

"I called Lavay and asked her who does her charts and she referred me to Vice who is a total Cab Calloway fan," Chris Calloway said. "Vice invited me to sit in with his group and I've performed on several jobs with them. They got me moving to put this Hi-De-Ho Orchestra together."

Young people have also begun to take a renewed interest in Cab Calloway's music, referred to by many as "old swing," she said.

"These kids love it!" she said. "'Old swing' was my thing. I could never figure out how these retro-swing bands like Big Bad Voodoo Daddy or Squirrel Nut Zippers are considered swing. To me it's like rockabilly or sometning. It isn't swing. I'm in awe of Brian Setzer because he's on the cutting edge with what he does. He really does adhere to the Big Band sound. But he has taken it to a very contemporary moment and it works."

In helping to kick off the 2001 tour, Chris Calloway recorded and produced a new CD last year, *Celebration of a Legacy*, in which she sings some of her father's compositions with the Big Bsnd as well with a trio. In addition to reprises of "Minnie the Moocher" and "The Jumpin' Jive," the release also contains other Calloway charts of "Everybody Eats When They Come to My House," "Boog It," "The Jungle King," "Kickin' the Gong Around," "A Foo a Little Bally Hoo," "Calloway Boogie," and "Growlin' Dan." Timeless standards of "Stormy Weather," "I've Got the World on a String," "Blues in the Night," and "The Man That Got Away" complete the CD.

On a previous CD, *Live At Espiritu*, Chris Calloway is backed by her trio.

Future projects for the "Legacy of Swing" show include a tour of Europe after the national tour is completed, Chris Calloway said.

While the show is billed as "Cab Calloway's Legacy of Swing," it is Calloway's legacy as a dynamic entertainer that will always be remembered, Chris Calloway said.

"The bottom line is, it's all about the joy of Dad's music," she said. "The fact is when people feel the presence of his music and of his spirit and of his contribution, they leave feeling better than when they came. It's about a one hundred-percent commitment to them as an audience. That's what I do as well."

** Coda – Here is an update on Chris Calloway and Cab Calloway's Legacy of Swing since this article was published.

Chris Calloway died on August 7, 2008, after surviving breast cancer for eighteen years. She was 63.

A profile of Calloway, *Cab Calloway: Sketches*, aired on the PBS program *American Masters* in February 2012.

The Cab Calloway Orchestra is directed by Calloway's grandson, C. "CB" Calloway Brooks. He is the son of Camay Calloway Murphy.

An exuberant 72-year-old Cab Calloway leading the audience in a chorus of "Minnie the Moocher," from a scene in the 1980s comedy flick, *The Blues Brothers*.

Cab Calloway in a publicity photo, circa 1940.

The Hi-De-Ho Man, Cab Calloway, wearing a zoot suit from the 1940s.

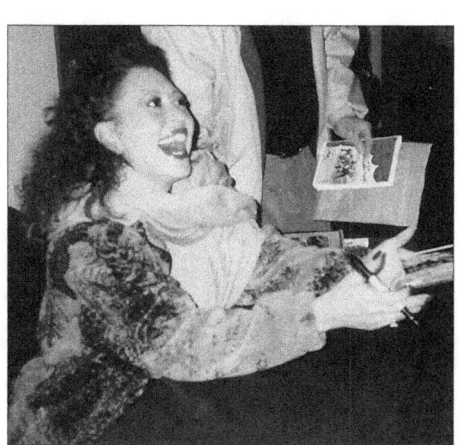

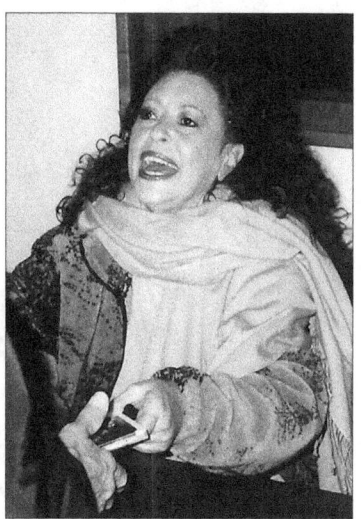

Chris Calloway greeting fans after her "Cab Calloway's Legacy of Swing" show at California State University, Chico, on January 8, 2001.
– *Photos by Stephen Fratallone*

A Cinderella Story

Dick Johnson's Dream Comes True As Director Of Artie Shaw's Orchestra

Dick Johnson and Artie Shaw

The following article on Dick Johnson and the Artie Shaw Orchestra was originally published in the March 2005 issue of Jazz Connection Magazine

The way clarinetist Dick Johnson sees it, his musical career as director of the Artie Shaw Orchestra for the past twenty-two years has been a Cinderella Story. Having paid his dues as a musician during World War II and working as a sideman in the bands of Charlie Spivak, Neil Hefti, Buddy Morrow, and Buddy Rich, Johnson was given the ultimate compliment by Shaw himself in 1983 asking him to lead a new Artie Shaw Orchestra. It was a dream come true for the veteran clarinetist.

"I idolized Artie since I was fourteen and it happened that he liked my playing and I got his band," said Johnson, 79, via telephone from his home in Brockton, Massachusetts. "That sort of threw me into a 'what-am-I-gonna-do-now?' mode. It has been a Cinderella Story for me. I've been doing it (leading the Shaw band) for quite a while and I'm having the time of my life."

During the heyday of the Big Band Era, clarinet virtuoso Artie Shaw led one of the most popular bands of all time, becoming one of music's biggest stars. His classic versions of Hoagy Carmichael's "Stardust" and Cole Porter's "Begin the Beguine" took the country by storm, placing him in competition with rival clarinetist Benny Goodman for the title of "King of Swing." Shaw was known as the "King of the Clarinet." A brilliant and adventurous talent with a restless soul, he sold millions of records and was hailed by both fans and his peers as one of the greatest swing musicians ever.

While Shaw's "new" band was one of many "ghost bands" (so named because the bands of deceased bandleaders were being led by others) to appear on the big band circuit during the 1980's, it is unique because the name-bearing bandleader (in this case Shaw himself) was still alive at its inception.

"Artie's band is unusual in that way because we did have Artie with us since the band's beginning right up until the time he died," Johnson said. "Having him around to support the band as a resource, a critic, a cheerleader, and as a friend was tremendous. No other band could say that about itself."

Shaw died on December 30, 2004, at age 94.

Northern California aficionados of Shaw's music can have the opportunity of hearing the new Artie Shaw Orchestra under the direction of Dick Johnson when they come to the Paradise Performing Arts Center in Paradise, California, on Friday, April 1, 2005 at 7:30 p.m. The band's appearance will be held in conjunction as a fund raiser for the PPAC. A portable wooden dance floor will be set up at the foot of the stage for those who wish to dance.

"We'll be playing most of Artie's hits," Johnson said, "Things like 'Dancing in the Dark,' 'Back Bay Shuffle,' 'Softly As in a Morning Sunrise,' 'Rose Room,' 'What Is This Thing Call Love?,' 'Stardust' and of course, 'Begin the Beguine.' In fact, 'Stardust' goes over bigger than 'Begin the Beguine.'"

Also look for a few selections from Shaw's small group, the Gramercy Five, Johnson said.

Shaw was born Arthur Jacob Arshawsky in May 23, 1910, in New York City. He grew up in New Haven, Connecticut, where he was stung by anti-Semitic insults.

He was playing professionally at age fourteen and touring at sixteen. The youngster settled in Cleveland for a time, working with Cleveland's top band leader, Austin Wylie. Shaw did the arranging and rehearsing for Wylie's band. He joined Irving Aaronson's band at nineteen, moving to Hollywood. Shaw's influences ranged from Louis Armstrong to Debussy, Bartók and Stravinsky. Shaw settled in New York and, at the age of twenty-one, quickly became the best lead alto sax and clarinet player in the Big Apple, with many performances on the radio and visits to the recording studios. He backed up jazz singer Billie Holiday on some of her earliest recordings.

Shaw's big break came when he asked to lead a small group for a swing concert at New York's Imperial Theater on May 24, 1936. Performing "Interlude in B-Flat," he provided an unorthodox band comprising a string quartet, a rhythm section minus piano, and his clarinet. The audience response was overwhelming and the buzz garnered Shaw both a record contract and his own orchestra, which he debuted the following month with a trumpet, trombone and tenor sax front line, a four-piece standard rhythm section, and a string quartet.

Members of that early band included four future bandleaders: tenor saxophonist/vocalist Tony Pastor; trumpeter Lee Castaldo (Castle), who would go on to lead the Jimmy Dorsey Orchestra after Dorsey's death in 1957; trombonist Moe Zudecoff (Buddy Morrow), who led his own band in the 1950s and has been the musical director of the Tommy Dorsey Orchestra for the past twenty-five years; and violinist/arranger Jerry Gray, whose arrangements were later to be an important part of Glenn Miller's musical library in both his civilian and military outfits.

The band had a unique sound but wasn't a commercial success. The string quartet approach was discarded and in early 1937, Shaw reorganized his band in a conventional big band format. The band, called "Art Shaw and His New Music," was developing its sound. In addition to Pastor and Gray who stayed on from the first band, this aggregation boasted fine sidemen such as trumpeter Johnny Best; trombonist George Arus; lead alto saxophonist Les Robinson; and drummer George Wettling.

In 1938, Shaw became a star with his recording of Gray's arrangement of the Cole Porter tune, "Begin the Beguine" (recorded July 24). Other hits soon followed including "Indian Love Call," "Back Bay Shuffle," "Any Old Time" (all on July 24 with Billie Holiday featured on the vocal on the latter tune); Shaws mournful theme song, "Nightmare," and "Non-Stop Flight" (both on September 27); and Softly As in a Morning Sunrise (November 17).

It was during this period that Helen Forrest joined on as the band's vocalist, cutting some impressive sides as "Thanks For Everything" (November 17, 1938); "Deep Purple" (March 12, 1939); "Day In, Day Out" (August 27, 1939); and "All the Things You Are" (October 26, 1939).

Throughout 1939, the Shaw band was gaining popularity and winning many swing band polls. Band personnel was beefed up with the addition of tenor saxophonist Georgie Auld, trombonist Les Jenkins, and drummer Buddy Rich, who helped swing the band on more "flag-waving" hits such as "The Donkey Serenade" (January 23, 1939); "Rose Room"

(January 31, 1939); "One Night Stand" (March 17, 1939); "Traffic Jam" (June 12, 1939); "Serenade to a Savage" (June 22, 1939); and "Oh! Lady Be Good" (August 27, 1939).

The band appeared in its first movie, *Dancing Co-Ed*, starring Lana Turner and Ann Rutherford, and was the feature band on the *Old Gold* radio program with Robert Benchley.

Unable emotionally to cope with the pressures of stardom, Shaw took a protracted holiday to Mexico in November 1939, handing the reigns over to Tony Pastor. The band stayed together for about three months until the men took jobs with other big name bands.

While in Mexico, Shaw became musically invigorated. By January 1940, he returned to the United States with the idea of forming a sixty-five-piece orchestra. That size orchestra never materialized, but on March 3, 1940, Shaw recorded with thirty-two musicians and produced another hit, "Frenesi." A touring band with a string section collected more hits, including "Temptation" (September 7, 1940); "Stardust" (October 7, 1940); "Concerto For Clarinet, Parts 1 and 2" (December 17, 1940); "Moonglow" and "Dancing in the Dark" (both January 23, 1941).

Shaw's new band included such virtuosos as trumpeter Billy Butterfield; trombonists Jack Jenny and Ray Conniff; tenor saxophonist Jerry Jerome; electric guitarist Al Hendrickson; and drummer Nick Fatool. Robinson remained as Shaw's lead alto saxophonist.

In 1940, Shaw co-starred with Fred Astaire, Burgess Meredith and Paulette Goddard in the "B" flick, *Second Chorus*.

In later highlights, Shaw formed his six-piece combo, the Gramercy Five (named after a New York telephone exchange), which included Shaw on clarinet, Butterfield, trumpet; Johnny Guarnieri, harpsichord; Hendrickson, guitar; Jud DeNaut, bass; and Fatool, drums. This "first" Gramercy Five group cut eight exciting sides during its short-lived existence: "Special Delivery Stomp," "Summit Ridge Drive" (named for the street Shaw live on in Hollywood), "Keepin' Myself For You" and "Cross Your Heart" (all on September 3, 1940); and "Dr. Livingstone,

I Presume?," "When the Quail Come Back to San Quentin," "My Blue Heaven" and "Smoke Gets in Your Eyes" (all on December 5, 1940).

While this current band of Shaw's drew critical acclaim, Shaw himself grew restless. Shortly after the start of 1941, he disbanded. In the fall of that year he organized another group with alumni from his other bands: saxophonists Auld and Robinson; trumpeters Castle and Max Kaminsky; trombonists Jenny and Conniff, pianist Guarnieri; and a host of other brilliant musicians such as drummer Dave Tough and trumpeter/vocalist Oran "Hot Lips" Page, whose vocals on "Take Your Shoes Off, Baby" (October 30, 1941) and "St. James Infirmary, Parts 1 and 2" (November 12, 1941), were high spots of Shaw's recordings during this period.

Soon after America's entry into World War II, Shaw enlisted in the Navy. He was given permission to lead a Navy band that included many outstanding musicians, some alumni of Shaw's civilian groups, including trumpeters Best, Conrad Gozzo, Kaminsky and Frank Beach; saxophonist Sam Donahue; drummer Tough; and Claude Thornhill on piano also doing some arrangements.

As a morale-boosting outfit, Shaw's Navy band toured Pacific combat zones and played for troops in the jungles, airplane hangars, and on decks of ships. Shaw was medically discharged two years later in 1944 due to exhaustion. Upon his return to civilian life and after regaining his health, Shaw organized another band in the fall of 1944 - a seventeen-piecer without strings which featured stars like Roy Eldridge on trumpet; Ray Conniff on trombone (and arrangement duties); Dodo Marmarosa on piano; and Barney Kessel on guitar.

This 1944-45 band cut some exciting sides for RCA-Victor including " 'S Wonderful" (arranged by Conniff) and "Bedford Drive" (both on September 1, 1945); "Lucky Number" (June 14, 1945); "The Maid With the Flaccid Air" (July 19, 1945); and "Dancing On the Ceiling" (July 24, 1945).

A second reincarnation of The Gramercy Five was formed with Eldridge, Marmarosa, Kessel, bassist Morris Rayman, and drummer Lou Fromm. The group cut six sides including "The Grabtown Grapple," "The

Sad Sack" and "Scuttlebutt" (all on January 9, 1945) and "The Gentle Grifter," "Mysterioso" and "Hop, Skip and Jump" (all on July 31, 1945).

From the fall of 1945 to 1947, Shaw switched record companies and signed with a new label called Musicraft Records, producing some of the best big band tracks of his career. Recording with strings, Shaw waxed two big jump tunes: "The Hornet" and "The Glider" (both September 1945); an outstanding vocal version of "My Heart Belongs to Daddy" (June 13, 1946) sung by Kitty Kallen; and some brilliant singing by a young Mel Torme and his Mel-Tones on two Cole Porter tunes: "What Is This Thing Called Love?" (June 19, 1946) and "Get Out of Town" (June 25, 1946), among others.

Before retiring from music in 1954, Shaw organized several other big bands, including a very good but short-lived 1949 bop-oriented jazz band, another reincarnation of his Gramercy Five, and a symphony orchestra, appeared at Carnegie Hall, and wrote his autobiography, *The Trouble With Cinderella: An Outline of Identity* (1952). He's also written two fictional works: *I Love You, I Hate, Drop Dead: Variations on a Theme* (1965) and *The Best of Intentions and Other Stories* (1989).

The mercurial Shaw struggled with both an attraction and an aversion to fame. He hated publicity. Nevertheless, he was a notorious ladies' man, and among his eight wives were glamour figures Lana Turner (wife No. 3, 1940), Ava Gardner (No. 5, 1945), Doris Dowling (No.7) and Evelyn Keyes (No. 8, 1957). Shaw was also married to Betty Kern (No. 4, 1942), daughter of composer Jerome Kern (producing a son, Steven), and Kathleen Winsor (No. 6, 1946), who wrote the best selling historical novel, *Forever Amber*. Shaw also had another son, Jonathon.

Shaw achieved enormous success, then walked away from it over and over again, always returning for another round. In the early 1980s, Shaw produced a critically acclaimed documentary, *Artie Shaw: Time Is All You've Got*. He received many awards and honors, among them a Lifetime Achievement Award from the National Academy of Recording Arts and Sciences (Shaw's recordings of "Begin the Beguine," "Stardust," "Frenesi," and "Any Old Time" are in the Grammy Hall of Fame), and a Grammy nod in 2003 for writing the linear notes to the Bluebird Records five-CD set, *Artie Shaw: Self Portrait*.

Since 2004, the Selmer clarinet Shaw played on his classic 1938 recording of "Begin the Beguine" has been preserved in the National Museum of American History, a gift made when Shaw was honored with the James Smithson Bicentennial Medal for his lifetime achievement and contributions to American culture and music. Prior to his death, Shaw was revising the novel which he'd worked on for three decades, the story of a jazz musician named Albie Snow.

A native Bostonian born on December 1, 1925, Johnson began his musical odyssey at age five studying the piano with his mother who was a piano teacher with a Master's degree from the New England Conservatory of Music. The relationship between Johnson and the piano didn't last long.

"I just hated the piano," Johnson confessed.

At age seven, he switched to the clarinet, and later to the alto saxophone.

Johnson became interested in jazz at age fifteen in 1941, and loved all the swing bands of the period. As a young clarinetist, he was especially attracted to the two master clarinet-playing bandleaders of the day: Shaw and Benny Goodman.

"I idolized both men," Johnson said. "The comparisons between Benny and Artie have gone on for years. There really is no comparison. They are apples and oranges. Artie played his way, so did Benny. As jazz players, Benny and Artie were head and shoulders above everyone."

But Johnson's ear (and heart) leaned more toward Shaw's lyrical style of playing after hearing the "King of the Clarinet's" knock out recording of "Concerto For Clarinet, Parts 1 and 2" (recorded December 17, 1940).

"I leaned more toward Artie's playing because he lunged ahead of everybody," Johnson said. "He was always trying to do something new. His playing was new. Many of the jazz greats have told me that Artie was the one they listened to. They got some of their licks from him."

Despite the numerous and different-sounding bands Shaw had, Johnson appreciated each and every one, he said.

"I love them all!" he said enthusiastically. "The first band got everyone, including me, forging ahead. Artie's second band with the strings recorded some of his biggest hits. I'd have to say that Artie's string bands really got to me. The Musicraft recordings he did with Mel Torme and the Mel-Tones, to me, those are perfection. The arrangements were beautiful. Artie's solos are beautiful. The Musicraft recordings were Artie's favorites, too. That band was unbelievable! Artie just kept lunging forward. It was the way music was going. Whereas, Benny (Goodman) still played unbelievable, but he stayed in the same groove, to some degree."

With the world at war, eighteen-year-old Johnson entered the Navy in 1944. He didn't begin to study music seriously until aboard ship. During his tenure in the Navy, he practiced the clarinet and alto sax as much as four hours a day.

"There were great musicians on the ship," Johnson said.

After his discharge in 1946, Johnson returned to his native Boston and studied clarinet for eighteen months with Norman Carrel of the Boston Symphony. He also gigged around the New England area until 1952 when he joined trumpeter Charlie Spivak's band.

In 1955, Johnson went with trombonist Buddy Morrow for a three-year stint. It was during his time with Morrow's band that Johnson was able to cut his first jazz albums under his own name: *Music For Swinging Moderns* (1956 - Mercury Records); *Most Likely* (1957 - Riverside Records) with pianist Dave McKenna, bassist Wilbur Ware, and drummer Philly Joe Jones, who recorded a number of albums with tenor saxophonist John Coltrane; and a live performance album at the 1958 Newport Jazz Festival for producer George Wein.

In 1958, Johnson returned to the Boston area and hooked up with Herb Pomeroy's band, a territorial outfit, and taught part-time at the Berklee School of Music. Johnson also did short stints playing alto sax with Benny Goodman from 1959 to 1960. (Johnson was later praised by Goodman in a New York City article.) In the early 1960s, Johnson teamed up with childhood friend and trumpeter Lou Colombo to perform and record. Johnson and Colombo have recently released a new CD together called *Artie's Choice! And The Naturals*, featuring guitarist Gray Sargent. Johnson continued to record in the 1970s with Colombo and McKenna as well as Tony DeFazio, Sonny Cain and Lou Santos. He also formed his own small band, "Swing Shift," and was signed to a recording contract with Concord Records.

In 1980, Johnson recorded with Woody Herman at the Concord Jazz Festival in Concord, California. The swinging performance was released on the Concord Jazz label as *Woody Herman Presents a Concord Jam*. Playing alto sax on that date, Johnson is also joined by tenor saxophonist Scott Hamilton, pianist McKenna, vibraphonist Cal Tjader, cornetist Warren Vache, guitarist Cal Collins, and drummer Jack Hanna.

That same year, Johnson received a very complimentary note from Shaw concerning his clarinet playing. That missive would be the start of a friendship between Johnson and the legendary clarinet-playing bandleader that would last for almost twenty-five years.

"My manager, Bill Curtis, met Artie in 1944 in Kingman, Arizona, after Artie returned to the States from his tour of duty in the Pacific," Johnson said. "Bill said to me that he would try to get a hold of Artie to see if he would write a blurb on my next album. Bill made contact with Artie and Artie agreed to listen to my album. A few weeks later, Artie sent a letter to Bill expressing his pleasure with my playing."

Shaw not only praised Johnson's playing, he elevated it to legendary stature. In that letter to Curtis dated December 18, 1980, Shaw wrote: *"You wanted to hear what I think of Dick Johnson's playing. Okay. As of this time, he's the best I've ever heard. Bar none. And you can quote me on that, anywhere, anytime!"*

"When I read that letter, I almost passed out!" Johnson quipped. "Here was my idol saying I was the best. I never expected he would ever say that about anyone, let alone me."

In 1983, Shaw was ready to have his "new" aggregation go on the road, tapping the 57-year-old Johnson to front it, while giving him complete artistic control, Johnson said.

"I had all of Artie's arrangements from his recordings so I was very familiar with his music before he even asked me to lead his band," Johnson said. "I had them all down. I was even able to play "Stardust," which is probably one of the hardest things for a clarinetist to play."

During the first few months of the band's genesis, Shaw himself would appear with the band in concert as conductor and story-teller. Even though Johnson was confident in his own musical abilities to play Shaw's music and to lead his band, he admittedly was initially nervous knowing that his idol and mentor was around, he said.

"I remember when we first started out, Artie was rehearsing the band daily for about a week at the Hilton Hotel in Boston and I got off my playing a few times," Johnson said. "Artie knew I was scared. Afterwards, he put his arm around my shoulder and said that I played some great stuff and that he loved the way I play alto sax. It was his way of easing me." Shaw's comforting gesture toward his new musical director worked, but there were times when Shaw's presence also brought a bit of "grounding" concerning Johnson's artistic bravado.

"The main thing is Artie liked the way I played, yet he could cut me down when needed, but he always did it in a nice way," Johnson said. One such "cutting" incident occurred when the orchestra was playing on a cruise ship from the United States to Spain. Shaw accompanied the band and rehearsed it a few times during the sojourn across the Atlantic Ocean. The first night the band played, Shaw was sitting in the audience, and Johnson, wanting to impress his boss, began showing off a bit as to what he could do musically on the clarinet.

"Afterwards, I went over to Artie's table and he told me that I played great," Johnson recalled. "But Artie also said to that the reason why I was showing off my chops was because he was in the audience. He assured me that he knew I had the chops. He was smiling when he said those things. It wasn't a bad put down, but my heart sunk a little bit. He said, 'When you need to do something like that, fine. But don't keep it going too long. Get the 'meat' out of a tune and get more lyrical.' The next night I got as lyrical as you could get! (laughing) Artie told me later that I had the idea and that I was now playing music. Artie was always my teacher but he did it in a nice way. He was always great with the band and he never raised his voice to me other than talking about someone else. He told me, 'The way you play, you should be out there with your own jazz group.'"

In spite of the well-meaning advice that Shaw passed on to Johnson, the two musicians got along very well together, and would often appreciate the playful humor each one had to offer.

"There were some things I played exactly like Artie did because that's what the people wanted to hear," Johnson said. "Artie told me to do what I wanted so that I wouldn't have to be *him* all the time. We were playing at the Blue Note in New York City in 1984. We played 'Rose Room.' Artie had a certain lick in the piece that I liked to play. Artie happened to beat the time off really fast. When it came to that part in the song where that certain lick was, Artie started grinning at me. I don't know how I did it, but I managed to play that lick. Artie apologized to me later saying he wasn't really thinking about the tempo because he figured I would do my own thing. That same night we played 'Concerto For Clarinet.' The last note goes up to a high C. When I went to whack out that high C, it came out a triple F. Artie started laughing. He said to me, 'Let me see your clarinet.' I then corrected myself saying, 'Sorry, folks.' And then I hit the C."

Shaw's jocularity was also demonstrated toward other musicians. When much ado was made of the rivalry between Shaw and Goodman, both clarinet giants took the competition in good graces and with a sense of humor, Johnson said.

"Whenever the situation would arise, Artie always had little 'zings' to say to Benny," Johnson said. "They were playful comments. Artie had nothing bad to say."

Shaw was a perfectionist and the music in his band library reflected the musical excellence he always strived for. With a band library that's "huge," and with fifty of those tunes from the library played regularly, the Shaw charts provide some challenge to band personnel, according to Johnson.

"For a good musician, some are, and some that are not hard," Johnson said. "Any guy coming in has his work cut out for him. If he's a good musician, he starts to relax."

While many big bands these days utilize regional players to fill its ranks when performing in certain geographic areas of the United States, the fifteen-piece Artie Shaw Orchestra with its four trumpets, five saxophones, three trombones, piano, bass and drums, is a road band. They perform together and they travel together.

"On the whole, our band is a relatively young band with the bulk of its musicians ranging in age from their late 20s to the 40s," Johnson said. "We have some who went to Berklee, a lot come from New York. Two of our saxophonists and our manager are in their seventies."

For years, the Shaw Orchestra utilized guitarist Joe Cohn, son of tenor sax giant and arranger Al Cohn and his wife, band singer Mary Ann McCall. However, when Cohn left, Shaw never used another guitarist.

"Joe was that good," Johnson said.

However, if and when the time comes for the Shaw Orchestra to record, Johnson says he plans on using his son-in-law, Gray Sargent, to fill the guitar void. Sargent currently performs with crooner Tony Bennett as a member of the songster's dynamic rhythm quartet.

Early on, the new Shaw band was averaging thirty-five weeks on the road. That's a good amount of time, by anyone's standards. But for the past few years, the band has cut its playing time to about twenty weeks a year. That sits very well with Johnson, he said.

"It's good for me because I have other things going on," he said.

With the amount of traveling and playing many of the same tunes over and over again, it becomes difficult at times to interpret such pieces in fresh ways.

"I change the tunes so I keep the guys in the band and myself interested," Johnson said. "Some bands go out and play the exact thing every night. That would drive me nuts. There is plenty of stuff in our book that we love to play."

In addition to playing all Shaw signature tunes, the band also steps "outside the box" on occasion and plays charts associated with other bandleaders such as Goodman, Count Basie, Duke Ellington, and the Dorsey's - Tommy and Jimmy both.

"These guys were the biggies and we play their themes and one of their big hit tunes," Johnson said. "It takes a short time to do in our presentation and the audience loves it."

Over the years, Shaw was quite proud of his new orchestra and of its musical director, according to Johnson.

"Anytime we needed new mics or stands, Artie paid for it himself," Johnson said. "He was very fair. He got ten percent of the band's gross and he paid me very, very well. It's always been more than I've ever made with any band. If the band wasn't making it, Artie would have stopped the band within the first couple of years."

With Shaw's death, ownership of the band was not passed on to his two sons, but rather to Shaw's long-time friend and attorney, Eddie Ezor, Johnson said.

"Eddie approached Artie on this before he died and Artie told Eddie that the band goes on just the same," Johnson said. "Artie and Eddie never signed a contract. They've known each other for years, and it was sealed with a handshake."

Prior to Shaw's passing, the band's focus was just performing the timeless music of Artie Shaw. Since his passing, it has become a mission to keep the clarinet giant's music alive. While seniors remain receptive to the music, a newer generation of listeners are not, Johnson intimated.

"I think it got to that point of being a mission," Johnson said. "We all thought it was going to be bigger than it was, but it really wasn't. The people who come to hear us are getting older. We've been booked at high schools but our audience is mostly seniors. Our music goes over like wildfire, but there are very few young people interested in it." As the band forges on, so does Johnson. But for how long? As seniors get older and pass on, audience support for Shaw's music performed live may also fade quicker than anticipated. As Johnson himself advances in age, and with no immediate clarinet-playing successor in mind, how will the Shaw legacy survive?

"I don't know of any younger guys coming up," Johnson said. "I'm sure there are plenty who can play the hell out of the clarinet, but nobody has been mentioned. There are guys out there who can play, but you just don't hear of them because nobody hires them to make a mess of records. I'm sure if something were to happen to me there would be somebody out there who can do it."

With the clarinet as a dying instrument in jazz groups and big bands, only a handful of noted players on the scene today are keeping the instrument in the musical forefront. Elder statesman Buddy DeFranco is one. DeFranco remains active performing and recording with his own group as well as heading a musical festival named after him at the University of Montana. It was DeFranco who took Johnson's place during the band's tour to Brazil a few years ago when Johnson was too ill to make the trek. Ken Peplowski, Eddie Daniels and contemporary jazzman Don Byron are other clarinet notables. Would they be interested in Johnson's job? Probably not.

While Johnson's virtuosity as a clarinetist is peerless, his contribution toward the instrument it will most likely be judged within the context of his musical association with Shaw.

"It's a thrill to play for seniors and for the musicians who are big on Artie Shaw," Johnson said. "It's about pleasing them and pleasing myself from an era that we went through. People would come back stage crying or we'd get standing ovations for things done well. People often times will come up to me and say that I play way better than Artie. I tell them, 'Wait a minute. Stop right there. When Artie did this, he did it over sixty-fiuve years ago and I don't play better than he. Nobody will ever play better than he did. He was one of a kind."

To celebrate his musical uniqueness, Shaw was invited to attend the 32nd Annual International Association of Jazz Educator's International Conference on January 7 in Long Beach, California, as a guest panelist and to be the recipient of the National Endowment Masters Award presented on behalf of President George W. Bush and Mrs. Bush. Shaw never received the honor. He died a week prior to the conference. Johnson attended the IAJE conference to accept the award for Shaw.

The following is the text of Johnson's speech. In his remarks, Johnson stated that Shaw should be more readily recognized for his contribution in the history of jazz as being the link between swing and bebop.

First off, I know that Artie Shaw would thank you implicitly for the National Endowment Masters Award and no one could be any prouder than me for being chosen to accept it for him. I am deeply honored and will never forget these moments.

I wrote the following article a few months ago to send to the various jazz tabloids. I called it "Artie Shaw: A Major Link in B-Flat and Thanks For The Legacy." I would like to take a moment and read it to you now.

Artie Shaw was arguably the greatest clarinetist ever. Granted, he was much heralded for his playing, for his bands and for his recordings. However, he was never seriously referred to as one of the major link tying the Swing Era to the BeBop Era.

Early proof of this is his 1938 band with its thousands of radio remotes from New York City, Chicago, Los Angeles, etc. Artie's playing was very obviously years ahead of his peers. One might call me opinionated, and I am!

There happens to be many stalwarts of jazz that think as I do. So I guess you might call them opinionated, as well. The following is a partial list of jazz giants that I am referring to. I have also made it a point to have had personal conversations about this with most of them: Cannonball Adderly, Ray Charles, Al Cohn, Rolf Kuhn, Buddy DeFranco, Paquito D'Rivera, Dizzy Gillespie, Art Pepper, Charlie Parker, Lee Konitz, Buddy Rich, Zoot Sims, Herbie Steward, Mel Torme, Phil Woods, and Lester Young.

In 1940, when Artie added strings, he was put down by Tommy Dorsey, Benny Goodman and Glenn Miller. But when the strings proved "acceptable," Dorsey had strings for Frank Sinatra. Harry James had them for Helen Forrest, Glenn Miller had them in the Army-Air Force Band. Even Gene

Krupa had them for a short time. Artie's biggest-selling records had strings: 'Stardust,' 'Moonglow,' 'Dancing in the Dark,' 'St. ames Infirmary,' 'Concerto For Clarinet.' Every one of those tunes had unsurpassable clarinet solos.

Speaking of 'Stardust'... I get many requests for a copy of Artie's chorus to which, I comply. If one can play it, bully for him! When the string band ended, Artie went back to using seven brass, five saxes and four rhythm and another great band evolved.

When World War II came along and Artie enlisted in the Navy, he brought the band out to the hectic Pacific Islands war zones. In his Navy band at the time were Conrad Gozzo, Dale Pierce, Max Kaminsky, and Frank Beach, trumpets; Sam Donahue, tenor sax; Tak Takvorian and Dick LeFave, trombone; and Davey Tough, drums.

After two years, Artie was medically discharged from the Navy and came back to the States and put another great band together featuring Roy Eldridge on trumpet. Artie made some beautiful jazz records then such as "S Wonderful,' 'The Glider,' 'The Hornet,' 'Let's Walk,' and 'Little Jazz,' featuring Roy Eldridge.

Artie's bands just kept growing musically and harmonically. Artie's last big band was the 1949- 1950 bebop band. With this band, Artie recorded a blues tune called 'Invendo' by Johnny Mandel. He made two takes of the bright blues piece in concert. He took four choruses on each take. Try to find those recordings and you will hear the best bebop jazz clarinet playing of all time! Musicians flipped over this band but the masses were screaming for 'Begin the Beguine.' Artie then threw in the towel and his big band career.

Artie then went to play with an updated Gramercy Five with guitarist Tal Farlow and pianist Hank Jones, plus vibes, bass and drums until 1954. He also did some studio standards with a large orchestra. Mel Torme and his Mel-Tones were featured on some of Artie's Musicraft recordings. Great records!

Artie then delved into some very difficult classical records and stopped playing altogether. Everyone said, 'How could you, Artie?' Artie had his reasons.

The following is a list is my version of the great trail blazers of jazz *who had just a little more to say than most up to the time of John Coltrane: Louis Armstrong, Art Tatum, Coleman Hawkins, Artie Shaw, Lester Young, Nat 'King' Cole, Charlie Christian, Roy Eldridge, Buddy Rich, Don Byas, Charlie Parker, Dizzy Gillespie, Bud Powell, Fats Navarro, Sonny Stitt, Sonny Rollins, Miles Davis, James Moody, Bill Evans, Jimmy Knepper, Scott LaFaro and John Coltrane.*

Ray Charles once wrote in an article that 'along with Art Tatum, Nat 'King' Cole, and Charles Brown, Artie Shaw was one of my favorite soloists. On any given night, Artie Shaw was the greatest clarinet player in the world.' Jazz history should have named Artie as the link between Swing and BeBop. There is a galaxy of recorded jazz clarinet by Artie. Seek them out and you'll never hear clarinet playing like that again! Artie made sure of that!

Thank you so very much for listening, folks! And thank you, Artie Shaw, for the boundless legacy of jazz clarinet. I hope you are accepting this honor where ever you are. So long, Artie!

Two days later, Johnson, accompanied by his wife, Rose, and manager, Bill Curtis, attended Shaw's closed-casket funeral at Chapel of the Oaks in Westlake Village, California, a short distance away from Shaw's home in Newbury Park. The funeral was by invitation only. Guests included piano great Marion McPartland and comedian Red Buttons who told of their personal stories about the late clarinet legend.

At the conclusion of the eulogies, Johnson played one full chorus of solo clarinet on "I'll Be Seeing You," segueing into three full choruses of traditional blues, before segueing back to the last half of "I'll Be Seeing You," according to Johnson.

"I'm sure Artie would have been pleased with his private tribute," Johnson said. "I know I felt on top of the world to have been chosen to do these finishing touches in celebration of Artie's life."

Shaw is interred at Valley Oaks Memorial Park in Westlake Village.

Like all musical legends who have passed on, the topic concerning their legacy will always be the subject of vigorous discussion. And Artie

Shaw's legacy is no exception. From Johnson's point of view, Shaw's lasting musical legacy is that of what he spoke of at the IAJE conference: the link from the Swing Era into the BeBop Era.

"When Artie played jazz on things like 'The Glider' or 'The Hornet,' he was playing with musicians who were starting to play with Charlie Parker, Dizzy Gillespie and those guys," Johnson said. "If you listen to Artie, he was already doing it (early bop ideas). It was just his way of playing. For me, he was arguably the greatest jazz clarinetist of all time. I say arguably because guys like Benny Goodman were, in their own way, just as good. For my cup of tea, Artie was the best. He put the jazz clarinet way ahead of its time for guys like Buddy DeFranco, Eddie Daniels, Ken Peplowski and Abe Most. All these guys are all/were great players. Artie was a trailer blazer of jazz."

** Coda – Here is an update on Dick Johnson and the Artie Shaw Orchestra since this article was published.

In 2006, Johnson and band recorded the CD, *Star Dust & Beyond: A Tribute to Artie Shaw*.

Dick Johnson died on January 10, 2010, in Boston, Massachusetts after a short illness. He was 84.

He is survived by Rose, his wife of 59 years; a daughter, Pamela Johnson Sargent; and a son, Gary Johnson.

Clarinetist Matt Koza has assumed the directorship of the Artie Shaw Orchestra. The band's website is: www.artieshaworchestra.com

Artie Shaw, right, passes the baton, or in this case, the clarinet, on to Dick Johnson in 1983 as Johnson was personally tapped by Shaw to direct the Artie Shaw Orchestra.

Dick Johnson soloing on his clarinet in 2002.

The Artie Shaw Orchestra under the direction of Dick Johnson.

Dick Johnson, left, fronting the Artie Shaw Orchestra in 2002.

Dick Johnson

For The Love of Glenn

Trombonist Larry O'Brien Keeps
The Glenn Miller Orchestra In A Moonlight Serenade

Larry O'Brien and Glenn Miller

The following article on Larry O'Brien and the Glenn Miller Orchestra was originally published in the March 2002 issue of Jazz Connection Magazine

When one thinks of bands from the Big Band Era, the orchestra of Glenn Miller usually tops the list. From 1939 to 1942, Miller led the Number One band in the country. The mention of his band evokes the most memories, it seems, of how wonderfully romantic that period all was. During the bands four years on the national music scene, they reclorded seventy Top Ten hits, many of which have become standards such as "In the Mood," "Chattanooga Choo Choo," "A String of Pearls," "Don't Sit Under the Apple Tree," and "American Patrol." His music is the one people most want to hear over and over again.

Now, nearly six decades after Miller's death, the orchestra that bears his name is still playing the great music he once helped to create. Under the direction of Larry O'Brien, the sixteen-piece Glenn Miller Orchestra is keeping the music of the late bandleader alive.

"Keeping the music alive is one way of looking at it, but keeping the band going with its musical integrity is really the greater issue," said O'Brien, 68, via telephone on Valentine's Day from the Marriot Grand Hotrl in Point Clear, Alabama, where the band was staying. "I want the band to be such that if Glenn were to come down from the clouds tomorrow and listen to the band, he'd say, 'Good job.'"

And would Miller approve?

"I think he would," O'Brien said. "I try to make it fun for the guys in the band and fun for the audience while maintaining the musical integrity. I've always felt that playing music well is its own reward."

Playing music well reaps for the band its most important reward, that is, the appreciation of its adoring fans, O'Brien said.

"I like to think of our band as a *finesse* band," he said. "We don't play just to get up there and bow the walls down on every number. We use a lot of dynamics. "That's the biggest comment we get from people. They say, 'What a pleasure to hear the band. You guys are playing *music*!' That's one of the things I insist upon is that we play everything correctly and musically."

Miller himself was known to be a stickler for maintaining standards of musical correctness with his band. While some orchestra leaders fronted free-swinging outfits and encouraged more musical freedom from among its musicians, Miller approached his job from a business man's point of view. He was more of the let's-do-it-the-same-way-every-night kind of leader. It was that type of philosophy coupled with the talented writers and arrangers he was associated with that made his music so appealing and commercially successful.

"The arrangements Glenn had in his book were good but fairly simple," O'Brien said. "They weren't trying to blaze new frontiers. They were just trying to give the people something to dance to and enjoy, something that was wholesome that had a lot of romance in it and love. There wasn't any hate in the music like you get in some of today's music. The reason why Glenn's music is so popuar today is that the band has maintained very high standards over the years. When people come to hear the Glenn Miller Orchestra, they know they're going to hear "A String of Pearls," "Little Brown Jug," "In the Mood," things like that."

Northern California fans of Miller's music can have the opportunity to dance and romance once again to all the great Miller classics when the Glenn Miller Orchestra plays for a free dance on Friday, March 15 at Feather Falls Casino in Oroville at 8 p.m., and for an evening dance the following night on the *USS Hornet* Museum in Alameda.

"Our listeners can expect to hear what I call 'The Golden Oldies,' ('In the Mood,' 'A String of Pearls,' etc.), O'Brien said. "I try to surround them with other attractive pieces that people will enjoy and some of which are more up to date. We try to space things out so that the program moves smoothly. I never get too far away from Glenn Miller. I also try to introduce tunes by Glenn that are not well known."

Alton Glenn Miller was born on March 1, 1904, in Clarinda, Iowa. He received his musical start while living in North Platte, Nebraska, by playing the mandolin and then trading it later for an old battered trombone.

In 1923, Miller entered the University of Colorado, although he spent more time traveling to auditions and playing where and whenever he could. After flunking three of his five courses one semester, Miller dropped out of college to concentrate on his career as a professional musician.

He toured with several orchestras and ended up in Los Angeles where he landed a spot in drummer Ben Pollack's group. In addition to playing his trombone, Miller also got a chance to write some arrangements for the band. Arriving in New York City, he soon sent for and married his collage sweetheart, Helen Berger, in 1928, and for the next three years earned his living as a free lance trombonist and arranger.

Miller played and recorded with Tommy and Jimmy Dorsey (who, on several of their records, featured crooner Bing Crosby), Gene Krupa, Eddie Condon, and Coleman Hawkins. During this period, Miller cut eighteen sides for Benny Goodman, and also worked for radio and studio conductors Victor Young, Carl Fenton, and Jacques Renard.

In 1934, Miller became the musical director of the Dorsey Brothers Orchestra. Personnel in that band included Charlie Spivak, trumpet; Roc Hillman, guitar; Skeets Herfurt, saxophone; Ray McKinley, drums; and Bob Crosby and Kay Weber, vocals.

When Tommy Dorsey abruptly left to form his own outfit in 1935, Miller then joined the Ray Noble Orchestra, which included Charlie Spivak, Pee Wee Erwin, trumpets; Bud Freeman, tenor sax; Johnny Mince, clarinet; and George Van Eps, guitar, among others.

In April 1935, Miller recorded for the first time under his own name. Using six horns, a rhythm section and a string quartet, he recorded "Moonlight on the Ganges" and "A Blues Serenade" for Columbia Records. Selling only a few hundred copies of the recordings, he continued his position in the Noble orchestra.

In 1937, Miller stepped out to form his own band. He recorded a few sides for Decca and Brunswick and did a couple of week-long stints in New Orleans and Dallas, and many one-nighters, but the band never caught on. Broke and depressed, he disbanded his orchestra. Having no idea what he was going to do next, he returned to New York City.

It is said that Miller could never remember precisely the moment he decided to emphasize his new reed section sound. But it was during this disheartening interim that he realized the unique sound – produced by the clarinet holding the melodic line while the tenor sax plays the same note, supported harmonically by thee other saxophones – just might be the individualistic and easily recognizable style that would set his band a part from all the rest. "A band ought to have a sound all of its own," Miller said. "It ought to have personality."

Miller formed his second orchestra in March 1938, which would later include Tex Beneke and Al Klink, tenor saxes; Hal McIntyre, alto sax; Willie Schwartz, clarinet; Ernie Caceres, alto and baritone saxes; Johnny Best, Ray Anthony, Billy May, Clyde Hurley, Bobby Hackett, trumpets; Paul Tanner, trombone; Chummy MacGregor, piano; Trigger Alpert, bass; Moe Purtill, drums; Ray Eberle, Marion Hutton, and Paula Kelly, vocals; and the vocal group, The Modernaires.

The band soon began breaking attendance records all up and down the East Coast. In 1939, the Miller Orchestra was invited by ASCAP to perform at Cranegie Hall with three of the greatest bands ever – Paul Whiteman, Fred Waring, and Benny Goodman – and created more of a stir than any of them.

There were record-breaking recordings as well, including "Tuxedo Junction" (recorded on February 5, 1940), which sold 115,000 copies in the first week of its release and went on to become a million-seller; "In the Mood" (recorded on August 1, 1939) and "Pennsylvania 6-5000" (April 28, 1940), all appearing on the inexpensively-priced RCA-Victor Bluebird label.

In early 1940, *Down Beat* Magazine announced that Miller had topped all other bands in its "Sweet Band Poll," capping off this seemingly sudden rise to the top. There was also Miller's *Moonlight Serenade* radio series for Chesterfield cigarettes which aired three times a week over CBS.

In 1941, the Miller band went off to Hollywood to work on its first movie, *Sun Valley Serenade*, which introduced the eventual million-selling song, "Chattanooga Choo Choo" (May 7, 1941), which featured Tex Beneke and Paula Kelly and the Modernaires.

The following year the band filmed *Orchestra Wives*.

The war was starting to take its toll on many of the Big Bands as musicians and the rest of the country's young men began receiving draft notices. On September 27, 1942, Miller's civilian band gave its last performance at the Central Theater in Passaic, New Jersey, before its leader left for military service.

On October 7, 1942, Miller reported for induction into the Army and was immediately assigned to the Army Specialist Corps. His commission to the rank of captain came after many months of convincing the military higher-ups that he could modernize the Army band and ultimately improve the morale of the men. Upon completion of his training, he was transferred into the Army Air Corps, where he ultimately organized the Army Air Force Band. Miller's goal of entertaining the fighting troops took another year to materialize, but in late 1943, he and the band were shipped out to England.

In less than one year, the Army Air Force under Miller's command engaged in over 800 performances. Of these, 500 were broadcasts heard by millions. There were more than 300 personal appearances including concerts and dances, with a gross attendance of over 600,000.

In the fall of 1944, the band was scheduled to be sent on a six-week tour of Europe and would be stationed in Paris during that time. Miller, now promoted to the rank of major, decided to go on ahead in order to make the proper arrangements for the band's arrival. On a cold, foggy December 15th, Miller board a transport plane to Paris with two other officers, never to be seen again. His disappearance over the English Channel remains a mystery to this day.

The Miller band became in reality, the first in a long string of "ghost bands" (so named because its original leader had passed away), making the circuit these days for Big Band enthusiasts. After Miller's death, Tex Beneke, Miller's discovery and pet sideman, first fronted the band in the musical style that made his former boss famous. It was called "The Glenn Miller Orchestra with Tex Beneke." Eventually, a riff between the Miller estate and Beneke occurred and Beneke went out on his own name, without any officially sanctioned Miller connections.

After *The Glenn Miller Story*, starring James Stewart and June Allyson, was released in 1954, there was renewed public interest in Miller's music. In 1956, the official Glenn Miller Orchestra was revived when Helen Miller and David McKay, the attorney in charge of the Miller estate, selected drummer Ray McKinley, a long-time friend and associate, to reorganize and lead the new group.

McKinley directed the Miller band for ten years before passing the baton to jazz clarinetist Buddy DeFranco, who stayed at the helm until January 1974. He was succeeded by Peanuts Hucko, star clarinetist in the Miller AAF Band, who fronted the band for nine months. Then trombonist Buddy Morrow got the nod and stayed until March 1975. After that, leadership was given to Jimmy Henderson, a lesser-known West Coast trombonist, who stayed until 1981. He was followed by O'Brien who stayed for two years before he was called away by other commitments. From 1983 to 1988, saxophonist Dick Gerhart assumed leadership before passing the baton back to O'Brien, who has been with the GMO ever since.

"I'v been here the longest," O'Brien said. "I've got that going for me. I believe the band reflects the personality of its leader. I think that was the case in previous leaders."

Larry O'Brien was born on July 15, 1933, in Jamaica, New York. His musical training began at John Adams High School in Jamaica, with trombone lessons by the band director. He also studied privately with trombonist Ed Kolyer who played in Broadway shows. O'Brien's idol on the trombone was Tommy Dorsey.

At age fifteen, O'Brien played first trombone with the New York City All-City High School Symphony Orchestra and at age sixteen, with the New York Philharmonic Orchestra Trombone Scholarship.

From 1952 to 1955, O'Brien did a three-year stint in the service attending the Naval School of Music in Washington, D. C., and was assigned to the 328th Army Band. After his discharge, he went to New York University earning a Bachelor of Science degree in education with his major in music.

It was while attending college that O'Brien joined the Sammy Kaye Orchestra, which was then performing at the Roosevelt Grill in New York City. He also toured and recorded with Kaye and was the featured soloist on the *Sammy Kaye Show* on television.

Kaye, who died in 1987, and was known for his "Mickey Mouse-style" of music, has been described as a demanding bandleader who knew precisely what type of sound he wanted. He drilled his orchestra intensely to get that sound. He got what he wanted, but it is said that band members detested his extreme dictatorial attitude.

"Sammy was a task master at times," O'Brien said. "Playing in Sammy Kaye's band was the equivalent of going to boot camp. He had very strict rules and everybody followed them. What we did was to play three hours straight when we did a dance. We took a half-hour break and played the last half-hour. He took all the ten-minute breaks at one time, which was legal. It was kind of a strange way to run a job. You had to make sure your kidneys were well-vented before you got on the bandstand. He didn't allow any drinking on or off the bandstand during a job."

Taking his cue from Kaye, O'Brien too, doesn't allow drinking of any kind, non-alcoholic or otherwise, on the bandstand. It has to do more with image than anything else, he said.

"I don't even allow bottled water on the bandstand," O'Brien said. "To us its water, but to the audience it's vodka. The only exception I'll make to that if we are playing outside under a burling, hot sun, then sometimes I'll allow it. You don't want to present any bad images. Musicians in our band today are trying to rub off the stigma that was attached to them from the bands of the 1940s and '50s were they did drink excessively and they did drugs and a lot of things that are socially unacceptable today. Today's musicians aren't like that at all. They are wholesome young men. I'm not saying they are angels, but they take care of business. We don't have an alcohol problem with our band."

O'Brien then did stints with the orchestras of Buddy Morrow, Ralph Materie, Ray Eberle, Billy May, Les Elgart, Boyd Raeburn, Art Mooney, and Lee Castle. In 1962, O'Brien was the featured soloist/lead trombonist with the Tommy Dorsey Orchestra when it was directed by Sam Donahue.

"I've gone through the Big Band mill, you might say," O'Brien said. "I did work mostly with East Coast bands. I haven't had that much to do with West Coast bands like Harry James, Les Brown, and Stan Kenton."

O'Brien spent several years as musical director for Frank Sinatra Jr. They toured worldwide for almost three years and appeared numerous times on *The Merv Griffin Show*, *The Tonight Show*, and *The Mike Douglas Show*. His association with Sinatra Jr. continued in various formats for sixteen years, touring Italy and performing in Las Vegas regularly with trumpeter and Stan Kenton alumnus Buddy Childers.

In 1979, O'Brien settled in Las Vegas playing with the Al Ramsey Orchestra at Caesar's Palace, backing up such stars as Frank Sinatra, Tom Jones, Sergio Franchi, Wayne Newton, Roy Clark, and others. He also toured with Pia Zadora and performed on her album, *Pia Today*, which featured the Sammy Nestico Orchestra. He's recorded two albums with the Russ Gary Big Band Express: *Have Horns Will Travel* and *A Time to Remember*.

O'Brien's association with the Glenn Miler Orchestra goes back to the early 1960s when he worked as a sideman in the band under Ray McKinley's leadership. Having that experience playing with the band is what makes his leadership somewhat unique.

"I don't think I bring anything different to this job than what these other gentlemen did," O'Brien said modestly. "They all certainly had their turn at bat with the band and did very well, especially Ray McKinley. His stamp is the one in which the band carries today. I may have more inside experience having been a sideman with the band. Barring the experiences that Ray and Peanuts Hucko personally had with Glenn, I don't think anybody else could say that."

During his short time as a sideman with the GMO, O'Brien learned a number of things from McKinley that he now incorporates in his leadership position. One such lesson has to do with setting tempo.

"I remember the first time Ray counted off 'American Patrol' with him playing the drums," O'Brien recalled. "I thought we'd never get through it, that it would take two days to play. By the time we had reached bar thirteen, I was stomping my foot right through the floor! That old man could play 4/4 swing time and just swing the whole band. I learned right then it's not the tempo you kick off, it's what you do with it when you got it."

By sitting in the brass section night after night, O'Brien admitted that he couldn't truly appreciate the full luster each arrangement had in the Miller book. It was only when he first fronted the band that he realized the music's impact, he said.

"The greatest revelation to me was the first btime I stood in front of the band and could hear all the parts," O'Brien said. "Before that as a sideman, I was struggling to maintain what the former section leader had laid down and I really wasn't listening to the whole sound. Now, while in front of the band, I could hear the arrangements and how lovely they were and how much time and thought had gone into them and why people like to still hear them today."

If listeners are expecting the band to play Miller standards as if it were a live 78 RPM record, they will be disappointed. Such older arrangements will be "tweaked" a little to give it a contemporary edge.

"We do this a lot with our vocalists," O'Brien said. "My philosophy is to use our vocalists as featured artists rather than as boy and girl singers. In the original Miller band Ray Eberle only sang ballads. Tex Benke sang the up-tempo tunes. Marion Hutton sang novelty numbers. A lot of those tunes don't make much sense today. If we played them, some people would enjoy them, I guess, but they would wonder what "Five O'Clock Whistle" was all about. Our male vocalist, Nick Hilscher, is a very fine vocalist and will sing some up-tempo songs, particularly a lot of the Frank

Sinatra stuff. He even looks and sounds a lot like Frank. When you hear him do a Sinatra tune, you'll say, 'Yeah, that's what young Frank must have sounded like.' Our female vocalist, Julia Rich, is another fine singer who will sing a nice ballad every set as well as an up-tempo song."

Three musicians from the band also join the feature vocalists on selected songs to form the vocal group, "The Moonlight Serenaders."

"These singers can do it all," O'Brien said. "We not only do 'Chattanooga Choo Choo' and 'Kalamazoo' but 'Jukebox Saturday Night,' 'People Like You and Me,' 'That Old Black Magic,' and 'Shoo-Shoo, Baby.' We do a different opener every night and we do different songs for the vocalists. I even mix up my feature songs. The audience knows they are going to hear the stuff they really want to hear but the other stuff is going to be a little surprise to them and hopefully, a pleasant surprise."

While every tune in the Glenn Miller Orchestra's library is not strictly a Miller tune, the band does play other selections that fit the perimeters of the Miller sound, O'Brien said.

"Music didn't die in 1944, Glenn died," O'Brien said. "I think we would be doing a disservice to our listeners and to Glenn's music by not continuing with it. We're very careful about that. We don't do anything that's too far out or what people can't enjoy. It's all good music but a lot of the arrangements are very up to date."

The band carries with them two libraries; one for concerts, one for dances, totaling 300 charts, O'Brien said.

"When we do a dance, like tonight, we have a lot of liberty what we can pursue," he said. "We play Latin music and walzes. We don't play dance music for concerts and we don't play concert music for dances. At a concert you'll hear "Rhapsody in Blue" or "Anvil Chorus," things like that. At dances you'll hear "Johnson Rag" or "Frenesi," things that are not so exciting that you'd want to put them in a concert."

The Glenn Miller Orchestra is the busiest band in the world, working 48 weeks a year since 1956, according to O'Brien.

"If we could stand it, they'd book us 52 weeks a year," O'Brien said with a laugh. "Luckily, we take a vacation once in a while."

The band does an annual tour of Japan from mid-November through mid-December.

Although turnovers in the band are a constant challenge, the average age of band members is around twenty-five, O'Brien said.

"It's about the same when Glenn led his band," O'Brien said. "All of those guys who were in the band who are old and dead now were young once. I feel that if I can keep a musician for a year, I'm doing pretty good. My dream is to have the same band for a year. I haven't realized that dream yet, but I've come close a few times. Something always happens; emergencies, family problems, etc. Glenn had the same problems. If you look at his discography, you'll see that there were a lot of changes in the band back then, too."

In addition to O'Brien, the band does have some stability thanks to a handful of tenured players who act as anchors such as lead trombonist George Reinert who has been with the band for eleven years; alto saxophonist/clarinetist Kevin Sheehan, a six-year veteran; and singer Julia Rich, who is a twelve- year veteran.

"I cherish these people because I know my trombone section is going to be in good hands with George leading it," O'Brien said. "I know the vocal group will be good with Julia in charge of it. The sax section is solid because of Kevin's influence."

While some of the younger musicians in the band are at first put off by the music they get paid to play, they seem to gradually hook into it and appreciate it, according to O'Brien.

"The music that we play is a different concept from anything that they have ever done," he said. "It's different phrasing. After a while they can see the validity of it and they can see how the music of today came from that. There's definitely a direct line there. They can connect with their Big Band roots, if you will."

Although it would appear that older people tend to "connect" more with the music of Glenn Miller than would younger people, O'Brien doesn't see it that way, he said.

"We've always attracted younger people," he said. "I don't think there's any more or any less. If you talk about the retro-swing craze, you have to talk about that besides us. The popularity of this band never waned."

For the band's tour schedule, log on to the band's website at: www.glennmillerorchestra.com

Although performing the same pieces night after night can become mundane at times, O'Brien brings freshness to his position by accepting the challenge of trying to win over his audience through good music and perhaps even a little reverie.

"Every audience we play for is a challenge to get them over to our side and to have them enjoy themselves and to get them to forget their troubles for a couple of hours," O'Brien said. "If they are old enough to relive some of those great old memories, great. If they aren't that old, maybe we can give people insights as to what it was to be young back then and to have it be so special."

The O'Brien-led GMO has recorded two CDs, *Moonlight Serenade* and *Here We Go Again*, both from 1992, including three Christmas albums: *In the Christmas Mood*, *In the Christmas Mood II* and *In the Nutcracker Mood*.

These CDs as well as videos and other merchandise from Glenn Miller Productions, Inc., can be purchased on line from the GMO website at: www.glennmillerorchestra.com

In the meantime, the band will continue its hectic touring schedule throughout the United States and Canada. They are slated to perform again this year, as they have done in years past, at the annual Glenn Miller Festival in Miller's birth town of Clarinda, Iowa. The festival is held in early June 9.

As always, O'Brien will be celebrating Glenn Miller's legacy in American popular music, a legacy that was saturated with love of country, duty, and sacrifice.

"I think Glenn showed us personal sacrifice," O'Brien said. "He gave up a very successful career by joing the Army. He didn't have to go into the service. He was exempt because of his age and because he was married with children. He wanted to do his part. I can appreciate that. My father was the same way. The day after Pearl Harbor was attacked he went down to join the Navy. He was exempt as well so he worked in a defense plant. Glenn did what he though what his job would be; to organize a band for morale. He was hugely successful at it. Unfortunately, he paid for it with his life. How selfless can you get? He didn't have to go in the service. He was making tons of money and riding the crest of his popularity. Even with a war going on he probably would have racked it in. Instead, he chose to serve his country, which is an exemplary thing for somebody to do." With over eighteen years (and counting!) accrued at the helm of the "Good Ship Glenn Miller," O'Brien shows no signs of retiring.

"I still have fire in my belly," he said. "I still enjoy it. I still enjoy the band very much. I still enjoy traveling. I still think I bring somethning to the music. As long as I'm alive, I want to be involved in music."

** Coda – Here is an update on Larry O'Brien and the Glenn Miller Orchestra since this article was published.

Larry O'Brien married Judy Malling on September 14, 2003, in South Bend, Indiana.

O'Brien appeared as a guest artist on crooner Nick Hilscher's 2003 debut CD, *Nick Hilscher Sings with the Glenn Miller Orchestra*, and on the 2003 release of the Cornerstone Jazz Trio's debut CD, *One For the Road!* The Cornerstone Jazz Trio was comprised of members of the GMO rhythm section: Andy Nevala, piano; Shawn Marko, bass; and Greg Parnell, drums.

O'Brien directed the GMO on the album, *On the Air*, recorded live from a XM Radio Broadcast. The CD was released in March 2004.

After almost 25 years as the Director of the Glenn Miller Orchestra, Larry O'Brien retired in December 2010. He and his wife, Judy, live in Hawaii.

Trombonist Gary Tole succeeded O'Brien as the leader of the GMO in January 2011, lasting at that position until December of that year.

Since January 2012, singer Nick Hilscher, former featured vocalist with the Glenn Miller and the Tommy Dorsey orchestras, currently leads the GMO.

Glenn Miller and His Orchestra at the Café Rouge in the Hotel Pennsylvania in New York City, circa 1940. At the microphone is singer Marion Hutton.

Larry O'Brien directing the Glenn Miller Orchestra for a dance at Feather Falls Casino in Oroville, CA, on March 15, 2002.
– *Photo by Stephen Fratallone*

Larry O'Brien with the Glenn Miller Orchestra on March 15, 2002, in Oroville, CA. – *Photo by Stephen Fratallone*

Larry O'Brien and the Glenn Miller Orchestra at the
Glenn Miller Festival in Clarinda, Iowa.

Larry O'Brien conducting the Glenn Miller Orchestra at Feather Falls Casino in Oroville, CA, on March 15, 2000.
- *Photo by Stephen Fratallone*

The Band America Loves

Drummer Don Pentleton Resurrects The Hip-Sounding Hal McIntyre Orchestra

Don Pentleton

Hal McIntyre

The following article on Don Pentleton and the Hal McIntyre Orchestra was originally published in the June-July 2004 issue of Jazz Connection Magazine

When recalling name bands from the Big Band Era, images of Benny Goodman, Glenn Miller, Artie Shaw, Harry James, Tommy and

Jimmy Dorsey, Woody Herman, Count Basie, Duke Ellington, Guy Lombardo and Sammy Kaye instantly come to mind. One such top band that emerged in the early 1940's that achieved commercial success but somehow never quite made it to the upper echelons as did the aforementioned groups, was led by alto saxophonist and Miller alumnus, Hal McIntyre.

After spending four years with Miller, McIntyre formed his own band (with Miller's blessing and financial support) in late 1941. Billed as "The Band That America Loves," McIntyre's outfit played at all the top spots, recorded a number of chart-topping tunes including "Daisy May," "The Commando Serenade," "Bayou Shuffle," an instrumental cover of "Sentimental Journey," and "Glow Worm" (with The Mills Brothers), was a favorite of G.I.'s overseas, and was one of the few big bands that kept working throughout the declining years of the 1950's.

"The McIntyre name is a pretty viable name," said Don Pentleton, director of the newly reorganized Hal McIntyre Orchestra, via telephone from his home in Boston. "It was, in its day, probably in the top ten or fifteen bands of the time."

Pentleton, a veteran big band drummer who has also performed with the Glenn Miller Orchestra, Hal McIntyre Orchestra, Guy Lombardo Orchestra, Skitch Henderson, Ella Fitzgerald and comedians Phyllis Diller, Pat Cooper, Frankie Fontaine, and George Jessel, has resurrected the Hal McIntyre Orchestra from virtual obscurity.

"Hal was 'The All-American Boy,'" recalled Paul Tanner, 86, in a telephone conversation from his home in Carlsbad, California. "He was a real gentleman."

Tanner and McIntyre were band mates in the famed Miller orchestra. Tanner holds the distinction of being the only surviving member of that great Miller civilian band since it was reorganized in 1938 to have participated in every RCA Bluebird recording, radio program, live performance and motion picture appearance.

"Hal was a people person and his audiences just loved him," Pentleton added. "You'd be surprised that I've received hundreds and hundreds of e-mails from people who wrote they are delighted to hear that Hal's band is coming back. Many people have stated that they remember meeting Hal and dancing to his band at such-and-such venue. They said what a charming and wonderful guy he really was."

Pentleton had developed a close relationship with the McIntyre family during his stint as the McIntyre band's drummer during 1970s and 1980s when the alto saxophone-playing bandleader's son, Hal Jr., led it. When Hal Jr., also an alto saxophonist, passed away in 1999, Pentelton seemed the logical and perfect choice to keep the music of Hal McIntyre going. He subsequently inherited the name rights and the band's book from the family. About a year ago, he got a burr under his saddle "to do something with the band," he said.

And Pentleton's motivation to do something with the band was "more of a personal thing rather than a public thing," he said.

"I bring the passion of wanting this thing to succeed," Pentleton said. "I have the experience of having played in the band and knowing and playing this music. I have an association with the family. I know how passionate they want this to succeed."

Harold W. "Hal" McIntyre was born on November 29, 1924, in Cromwell, Connecticut. By his late teens he was already the veteran of a series of groups and formed his own eight-piece band in 1935. He later landed his big break when offered a temporary gig playing alto sax with Benny Goodman. The Goodman stint lasted just ten days, but it brought McIntyre to the attention of Miller.

After working in the bands of Ben Pollack, Smith Ballew, The Dorsey Brothers, and Ray Noble, and after scuffling as a free-lance musician/arranger for radio and record dates, Miller formed his own band in January 1937. He assembled a band that included trumpeter Charlie Spivak, tenor saxophonist Jerry Jerome, bassist Rolly Bundock, pianist Chummy MacGregor, and McIntyre playing lead alto sax.

In March of that year, Miller landed a record date on Decca Records waxing six semi-Dixieland sides dominated by vocals. The records did not sell.

The band's second recording session occurred on June 9 for Brunswick. The four tracks recorded at that session, including Miller's arrangement of "I Got Rhythm," revealed the early stages of Miller's early style, like the biting, slightly piercing sound of the brass section, and Miller's distinctive reed sound of two clarinets and two tenors, each pair in thirds an octave apart. On "I Got Rhythm," McIntyre shares solo duties with Jerry Jerome, tenor sax; Tweet Peterson, trumpet; and Eak Kenyon, drums.

Throughout 1937, the Miller band did poor business and struggled for acceptance. In spite of two more recording sessions in November and December for Brunswick, bookings were sporadic. With morale in the band low, Miller decided to disband on January 2, 1938, after playing an engagement at the Ritz Ballroom in Bridgeport, Connecticut.

Vowing not to give up, Miller reorganized a new band two months later. Four players from his old band joined the new outfit, forming the nucleus of what was to be Miller's great civilian band which lasted until September 1942: first trumpeter Bob Price; bassist Rolly Bundock; and Miller's two close friends, pianist Chummy MacGregor and McIntyre on lead alto.

"Hal and Chummy were Glenn's two good friends in the band," Tanner said. "The rest of us in the band were all friendly, but those two were in Glenn's 'inner circle.'"

But friendship alone didn't cloud Miller's quest to hire outstanding musicians for his new band.

"Glenn thought Hal was a very good player and wanted him in his new band," Tanner said of McIntyre's return stint with the trombone-playing bandleader. "Hal played great lead alto sax in the band and occasionally played clarinet and improvised. He also played lead clarinet a little before Glenn settled on Willie Schwartz."

Rounding out Miller's new outfit were trumpeters Bob Peck and Johnny Austin; trombonists Paul Tanner and Al Mastren; lead clarinetist Willie Schwartz; alto saxophonist Bill Stegmeyer; tenor saxophonists

Gordon "Tex" Beneke and Stanley Aronson; and drummer Bob Spangler; male vocalist Ray Eberle; and in September of that year, Marion Hutton, who became the band's female vocalist.

Later additions to the Miller band during the ensuing four years included trumpeters Johnny Best, Clyde Hurley, Dale McMickle, Leigh Knowles, Zeke Zarchy, Billy May, Ray Anthony, and Bobby Hackett (who also doubled on guitar); trombonists Jimmy Priddy, Tommy Mack, and Frank D'Annolfo; saxophonists Al Klink, Ernie Caceres, Irving "Babe" Russin, and Skippy Martin; guitarist Jack Lathrop; bassist Herman "Trigger" Alpert and Edward "Doc" Goldberg; drummer Maurice Purtill; female vocalists Dorothy Claire and Paula Kelly; and the vocal group, The Modernaires (Chuck Goldstein, Bill Conway, Hal Dickenson, and Ralph Brewster); and arrangers Bill Finegan, Eddie Durham, and Jerry Gray.

During the Miller band's brief four years on the national scene, they recorded seventy Top Ten Hits, becoming the most popular band in the land. McIntyre had a hand in helping to record the majority of the Miller classics that have since become standards in Big Band music such as "Moonlight Serenade," "Little Brown Jug," "Sunrise Serenade," "In the Mood," "Johnson Rag," "Tuxedo Junction," "Danny Boy," "Pennsylvania 6-5000," "A Nightingale Sang in Berkeley Square," "Anvil Chorus," "Song of the Volga Boatmen," "Sun Valley Jump," "Perfidia," "Chattanooga Choo Choo," "I Know Why," "Adios," and "Elmer's Tune."

In fact, McIntyre was responsible in helping Miller to record "Tuxedo Junction" (February 5, 1940). The tune was written by bandleader/trumpeter Erskine Hawkins and two of his saxophonist's, Julian Dash and William Johnson. Hawkins recorded the tune on July 18, 1939 and his version was in the Top Ten of the *Hit Parade* by December of that year. The Miller band heard the piece for the first time on December 24, 1939, at the Savoy Ballroom when the Hawkins band played opposite them. Miller's musicians liked the tune and McIntyre picked up a lead sheet from one of the composers and gave it to Jerry Gray to write out an arrangement. The Miller men added their own ideas to the arrangement and the result was far different than Hawkins' version. It became a million-selling instrumental for Miller.

McIntyre also went to Hollywood in early 1941 with the Miller band to work on the motion picture, *Sun Valley Serenade*, starring John Payne, Sonya Henie, Milton Berle and Lynn Bari. It was the first of two films that featured Miller's orchestra.

At Miller's urging, McIntyre left his close friend to front his own band on October 6, 1941.

"Mac's" new band debuted shortly after at the Glen Island Casino in New Rochelle, New York. But it was until January 19, 1942, that the McIntyre band went into the recording studios to cut its first commercial sides for RCA-Victor. During that session, the band waxed four tunes: "Fooled," "Tangerine," and "I'll Never Forget" (all three with vocals by Carl Denny), and "Mandy is Two" (vocal by Penny Parker), which was rejected and never issued.

Band personnel for that session included trumpeters Paul McCoy, Horace "Steady" Nelson, Bill Rubenstein, Clarence Willard; trombonists Vic Hamann, Howard Gibeling, Don Ruppersberg; saxophonists Larry Kinsey, Dave Matthews, John Dee, Bob Poland; pianist Danny Hurd; guitarist Jack Lathrop; drummer Ralph Tilken; and bassist Eddie Safranski, who later went on to greater notoriety with Stan Kenton.

McIntyre also featured various vocalists on pretty ballad tunes. In addition to Parker and Denny, vocalists filtering through the band included Frances Gaynor, Jerry Stuart, Gloria Van, Ruth Gaylor, Helen Ward, Benny Goodman's former vocalist, Al Nobel, and Frankie Lester.

Despite the years he spent with Miller, it would seem logical that McIntyre would incorporate the "Miller sound" to his. But it wasn't the case. In fact, Mac's band sounded more like that of Duke Ellington in its influence, according to Pentleton.

"Hal's chief arranger was saxophonist Dave Matthews," Pentleton said. "He wrote, almost note-for-note, some of Duke's stuff."

Matthews, an outstanding tenor saxophone soloist in his own right who played with Harry James when the trumpet star organized his band three years earlier, and who later scored the hit song, "Shoo- Shoo Baby," for Ella Mae Morse in 1943 and who wrote many Ellingtonian arrangements for Woody Herman, loved the music of the celebrated composer, pianist and bandleader. Matthews was once quoted as saying that his only reason for using Ellington's music "was for the musical pleasure it gave me on hearing it played in arrangements - nothing more."

Also contributing to the McIntyre band's colorful sound were arrangements written by pianist Danny Hurd, trombonist Howard Gibeling and by McIntyre's friend and ex-Miller band mate, Billy May. Some of the more popular tunes that May helped pen (co-written with McIntyre) for the band included two swing charts: "Friday Afternoon" and "Daisy May" (other variations have it listed as Daisy Mae), both recorded for RCA-Victor on April 1, 1942.

It's interesting to note that on the original 78 RPM records of these two songs, the composers listed are Hal McIntyre and "Arletta" May. May, who died earlier this year at age 87, was legendary for his sense of humor. It's been reported that "Daisy" was May's favorite nickname for his first wife. Since he helped composed the piece, no doubt in her honor, he used her first name on the compositional credits. Coupled with the fact that both recordings were waxed on April Fool's Day, it could have been May's subtle way of expressing an inside joke.

With the United States already at war and a musicians' union strike set to begin August 1, 1942, the McIntyre band cut twenty-nine sides (two tracks were rejected) from January to July of that year.

Other big tunes that Mac recorded during this seven-month period include "The Commando Serenade" (February 2, 1942); "Play No. 49" (June 2,1942), both composed by McIntyre and Matthews and both pieces arranged by Matthews; "South Bayou Shuffle" (February 13, 1942); and "This is the Army, Mr. Jones" (July 22, 1942, with vocal by Jerry Stuart).

What most critics agree on is that the arrangements in the McIntyre band book were very contemporary in its sound.

"Hal's band was one of the 'hipper' bands of the 1940s," Pentleton said. "Hal liked the sound of his band."

While the McIntyre band was a very musical one, George T. Simon, the late big band music critic, felt that if the band had been built more around Mac's horn and less around the arrangements, the McIntyre band might have been much more successful.

McIntyre played with a lush tone, somewhat Johnny Hodges-like in nature. Yet in spite of being a masterful musician, he appeared to be much of an underrated alto saxophonist, being overshadowed by such alto giants of the time as Hodges, Benny Carter, and Willie Smith.

"Hal was very underrated," Pentleton said. "He didn't feature himself too much. He was more of an ensemble guy."

"I don't consider Hal being 'under' anybody," Tanner said. "If he had to compare himself to Johnny Hodges, that's a problem. Hal was a good sax player. Besides being a fine soloist, he was a good lead alto player in the saxophone section. When he was with Glenn, he didn't have much of a chance to solo. When Glenn featured saxophonists, he usually featured the section."

The band went on to headline venues including New York City's Commodore Hotel and Paramount Theater, Frank Dailey's Meadowbrook Club in New Jersey, The Hollywood Palladium, Chicago's Sherman Hotel, and other numerous ballrooms and hotels across the country. Mac's band even played at President Franklin Roosevelt's Birthday Ball at the Statler Hotel in Washington, D. C., on January 30, 1945.

During the war years, Mac and company regularly played overseas for U. S. troops. By doing so, he ran the risk of diminishing his career by not recording regularly and by not being more in the public eye at home. But that didn't matter to him because he wanted to make a contribution doing his part for the war effort, which the G.I.'s appreciated, according to Simon in his book, *The Big Bands*.

In fact, when McIntyre returned from such excursions, he was able to pick up where he left off. He and his band were featured in three motion pictures including *Sing Me a Song of Texas* (1945), starring Noah Berry, Rosemary Lane, Tom Tyler, and Connie Matthews; and *Eadie Was a Lady* (1945), starring dancer Ann Miller, who died earlier in this year.

In 1945, McIntyre scored a hit with an instrumental version of "Sentimental Journey," written by Bud Green, Les Brown and Ben Homer. The definitive version of that tune was recorded by Les Brown and his Orchestra with his girl singer, Doris Day, on the vocal. Brown's version charted at Number 1. Another competing version of the song was done by the vocal group, The Merry Macs (charted at Number 4).

"Hal had the first instrumental cover of 'Sentimental Journey,'" Pentleton said. "It helped put his kids through college."

Another chart-topper for McIntyre that year was "I'm Making Believe" (vocal by Ruth Gaynor, which reached the Number 14 position).

When the big bands began fading from the scene, McIntyre continued leading his orchestra well into the 1950s.

"Hal kept the band working right up until he died," Pentleton said. "It's my theory that had he lived, Hal would have taken his band on into the 1960s along with Woody Herman, Count Basie, and Stan Kenton. These were about the only big bands that really survived, and the McIntyre band was a survivor."

On April 7, 1952, his band provided the exciting back up for The Mills Brothers on "Glow Worm," which became one of the biggest hits for the legendary singing group. The melody had been outfitted with brand-new lyrics by Johnny Mercer and a rocking arrangement by Sy Oliver. It may be argued that "Glow Worm" was probably McIntyre's most popular tune as well, albeit incognito, because of the radio play it continues to receive over fifty years later. Many radio stations around the country that play a nostalgic music format invariably play The Mills Brothers/Hal McIntyre version of this recording. Listeners associate the tune with The Mills Brothers. However, how many listeners also associate the song with Hal McIntyre? Probably few in number.

Toward the latter part of the 1950s, McIntyre was experiencing some domestic problems in his life. He moved to California and he was separated from his wife and children. Some observed, as did Simon, that "his innate warmth and big grin were still present, but his inner spirit had begun to wane."

Tanner had even sensed a "quiet reserve" about his former band mate a few years earlier after crossing paths with him while on the road as a member of Tex Beneke's orchestra. Tanner played with the saxophone-playing bandleader from 1946 to 1951.

"Hal liked to socialize with the audience. In fact, he socialized with everyone," Tanner recalled. "When we came across Hal on the road, he didn't seem like he was 'one of the boys.' He was kind of outside the circle of the guys. I felt that he wasn't the usual glib, outstanding person as he was before. I often wondered if he felt awkward or felt badly about it. That was the only time I had contact with Hal after he left Glenn's band. His life took a different turn."

Before the McIntyre band's ranks finally splintered, tragedy struck. McIntyre died in a house fire at his home in Los Angeles on May 5, 1959, apparently caused by a carelessly discarded cigarette.

"Hal took the combination of the sweet Sammy Kaye-type band and mixed it together with a very hip Duke Ellington-type band and found middle ground," Pentleton said about McIntyre's musical legacy.

"His music was very danceable and even today, when we take the band out, the dancers love it. Musically, it's not over their heads. That's what people like and that's what made Hal a famous guy."

A number of original Hal McIntyre recordings have been released recently on CD and can be purchased over the Internet on Amazon.com at www.amazon.com Album selections include *The Issued Recordings of Hal McIntyre: 1941-1947* (Jazz Band Records 2001); *Hal McIntyre and*

His Orchestra 1942; *Hal McIntyre and His Orchestra 1944-1945*; and *'S Wonderful* (Collectors' Choice Music 2003).

The biggest challenge that Don Pentleton faced in putting together this new Hal McIntyre Orchestra was trying to plug the right people in the right places, he said. And those challenges were primarily aimed at the saxophone section, he said.

"I've overcome getting a lead alto player that played as well as Hal McIntyre did, and I've done it," Pentelton said enthusiastically. "His name is Dave Chapman. He's the perfect guy to play the Hal McIntyre lead alto book."

In addition, Pentleton also searched for a five-member sax section that would sound like the McIntyre sax section, said. "Luckily, I've overcome that as well," he said. "The band's book was written by a saxophone player for a predominately saxophone players' book."

In seeking out potential personnel for the band, Pentleton looked not to the music colleges of New England, but to more established veteran musicians in the area who know and are familiar with both the big band and McIntyre concepts, Pentelton said.

"I've got some people here in Boston that know how to play that concept of music," he said. "I didn't want to take a bunch of college kids out of the New England Conservatory of Music or Berklee College of Music and put the music in front of them and then say, 'OK, you can read the notes but you don't have the concept because you didn't grow up in those years and you don't have the background and the where-with-all to know how to play these notes properly with the proper feel.'"

Although the McIntyre band has yet to become a full-time road band, (although Pentleton is working with bookers to make it one) it boasts a traveling party of seventeen, including its band manager and the band's girl vocalist, Alanna Manning, who has been the Hal McIntyre vocalist during Hal McIntyre Jr.'s tenure.

A small tour is in the working stages for this summer, according to Pentleton.

"We are working with a booker in Redondo Beach, California, who was a big Hal McIntyre fan," Pentleton said. "He'll plug us for some dates in Southern California."

Pentleton credits numerous Big Band specialty media, in both print and radio, and especially Charles DeStanfo, who runs the front offices of the Glenn Miller Orchestra, in helping to get the word out about the Hal McIntyre Orchestra.

"I'm thankful that people are interested in this band," Pentleton said. "The band has had some down time, so it's not easy to do this. There are many people in our corner doing all they can in helping to support us."

Plans also have been solidified for the band to record a new CD this fall, according to Pentleton.

"I'm getting all the tunes together," Pentleton said. "I'm also getting the ASCAP (American Society of Composers, Authors and Publishers) authorization, which you have to dig way, way back to get the rights to find out if certain songs have gone by the entitlement years or if I have to pay a royalty."

Although the impending CD doesn't have a title as yet, its contents will be a musical mixed bag of old and new, according to Pentleton.

"We are going to bring back a lot of the original music that's rewritten so it sounds like a 2000s big band instead of a 1940s big band," Pentleton said. "However, I've intermingled a lot of the original Hal McIntyre charts from the 1940s because the band was very hip for its time. That music still sounds good today."

But so far, during the band's brief exposure to the public, it has been received enthusiastic support from both young people and seniors alike, Pentleton said.

"When we play a venue, we get a pretty good mix of older and younger people," Pentleton said. "In fact, we did a few college dates here in New England and the kids turned out en mass. A number of these colleges have ballroom dance clubs and that type of dancing has caught on with the college students. Young people's interest in swing music has tapered off a bit from five years ago, but it's being carried on now on a smaller scale."

And when young persons who come out to hear the Hal McIntyre band perform and have questions as to who he was and what the band is all about, Pentleton is ready to tell them all about it.

"We have handouts at the door about the band's history and I encourage them to check out the band's website," he said.

Pentleton is also trying to get across a musical statement to his younger listeners about the Hal McIntyre Orchestra both past and present. It's a musical statement about the brilliance of "The Band America Loves."

"I'm trying to give the younger people a little insight as to what that music and what that particular band had to offer," he said. "The Hal McIntyre Orchestra was very unique amongst big bands for its hip sound. It caught everybody. The voicings in the sax section were very hip. He always got very great high-note lead players. The band was very, very good. I'm trying to give that back."

To learn more about the Hal McIntyre Orchestra, past and present, log on to www.halmcintyre.com

** Coda – Here is an update on Don Pentleton and the Hal McIntyre Orchestra since this article was published.

The Hal McIntyre Orchestra under the direction of Don Pentleton continues to perform.

Hal McIntyre in 1941

Hal McIntyre as a fledgling bandleader in 1942.

Ruth Gaylor, left, and Hal McIntyre, right, in a scene from the Columbia Pictures feature film, *Eadie Was a Lady* (1945).

The Hal McIntyre Orchestra in 1942 playing for a War Bond Rally/Dance.

Don Pentleton, center in dark sports coat, fronting the Hal McIntyre Orchestra under his direction.

Don Pentleton on drums, keeping time for the Hal McIntyre Orchestra in 2004.

The Band America Loves

Don Pentleton engaging the audience as the director of the Hal McIntyre Orchestra.

Oodles Of Noodles

Trombonist Bill Tole Assumes
New Leadership of The Jimmy Dorsey Orchestra

Bill Tole   Jimmy Dorsey

The following article on Bill Tole and the Jimmy Dorsey Orchestra was originally published in the January 2002 issue of Jazz Connection Magazine

For trombonist Bill Tole, he sees his mission as the new leader of the Jimmy Dorsey Orchestra as that of keeping the music of the late bandleader alive.

"There still is a lot of interest in Big Band music of the name bands, like Jimmy Dorsey's," said Tole via telephone from his hotel room in Oroville, California, where the Jimmy Dorsey band was set to play a New Year's Eve dance for seniors on December 30, 2001, at Feather Falls Casino. "We just want to keep the music going."

The fourteen-piece Jimmy Dorsey Orchestra is one of many "ghost bands" (so tagged because it's original leader has passed away) making the circuit these days for Big Band enthusiasts.

"I think all the Big Bands now are ghost bands," Tole said. "About the only active bandleader that's left is (trumpeter) Ray Anthony."

Tole was a natural choice to assume the leadership of the Jimmy Dorsey band as he has been involved with the music of Jimmy and Tommy Dorsey for years. He first grew up listening to the recordings both bandleaders had made and after graduating from college, he joined the Tommy Dorsey Orchestra when Warren Covington was the band's musical director. He later joined the Air Force dance band, "The Airmen of Note," occupying the first trombone chair and was also assistant leader during his four-year tenure with that ensemble. After establishing himself as a much-in-demand studio musician and as a successful leader of his own swinging outfit in the Los Angeles area, Tole was asked to play the role of Tommy Dorsey in the 1977 film, *New York, New York*, starring Liza Minelli and Robert DeNiro.

Jimmy Dorsey was born on February 29, 1904, in Shenandoah, Pennsylvania, the son of a coal miner turned music educator, and was the older brother of Tommy by a-year-and-a-half. Dorsey started off playing the trumpet but switched to the alto saxophone in 1915, and then learned to double on the clarinet. During the 1920s, Dorsey relocated to New York City doing freelance radio and recording work. He was a member of cornetist Red Nichols' Five Pennies jazz band and joined Ted Lewis in 1930, with whom he toured Europe.

Jimmy Dorsey was considered one of the finest clarinet and alto saxophone players of his day and was always playing solos that amazed his fellow musicians as well as his audiences. He and brother Tommy formed the twelve-piece Dorsey Brothers Orchestra in 1934. Band personnel at the time included Glenn Miller, Charlie Spivak, Ray McKinley, Roc Hillman, Skeets Herfurt, and Bob Crosby and Kay Weber sharing vocal chores.

Since assuming the leadership of the band in 1935 after his brother and co-leader, Tommy, walked off the bandstand due to an argument over the tempo of a tune, The Dorsey Brothers Orchestra became the Jimmy Dorsey Orchestra, and included musicians such as Bobby Byrne, Ray McKinley, Freddy Slack, Tutti Camarata, Donald Matteson, Roc Hillman, and Skeets Herfurt along with vocalists Bob Eberly and Kay Weber.

Jimmy's band scored many hits such as "Parade of the Milk Bottles Caps" (recorded July 7, 1936); "John Silver" and "Dusk in Upper Sandusky" (both on April 29, 1938); "Hold Tight" (with The Andrews Sisters on November 21, 1938); and his theme song, "Contrasts" (April 30, 1940), which was a variation of his earlier composition of "Oodles of Noodles." (July 14, 1932).

Dorsey's two band singers, Bob Eberly and Helen O'Connell, also contributed heavily to the pantheon of hits both individually and collectively. Eberly's hits include "They Can't Take That Away From Me" (March 17, 1937); "Our Love Is Here to Stay" (January 25, 1938); "Deep Purple" (February 10, 1939); "Stairway to the Stars" (June 16, 1939); "The Breeze and I" (April 18, 1940); "I Understand" (December 9, 1940); and "Maria Elena" (March 19, 1941).

O'Connell's solo chart-toppers include "All of Me" (March 3,1939); "Six Lessons From Madame La Zonga" (April 9, 1940); and "Arthur Murray Taught Me Dancing in a Hurry" (December 10, 1941).

But it was the Eberly-O'Connell duets which would help to make the Jimmy Dorsey band one of the biggest draws in box-office history up to then with such classics as "Brazil" (July 14, 1942); "Yours" (February 3, 1941); "Amapola" (February 3, 1941); "Green Eyes" (March 19, 1941); and "Tangerine" (December 10, 1941). These songs have since become standards in Big Band music.

A good part of Dorsey's success over the years was attributable to other singers and sidemen who worked for him including Kitty Kallen, Bob Carroll, Ray McKinley, Freddie Slack, Bobby Byrne, Roc Hillman, Tutti Camarata, Charlie Teagarden, Herbie Haymer, Lee Castle, Bobby Dukoff, and Ralph Muzillo, among others.

In 1943, Dorsey's band had reached its peak. The band made a number of movies including *I Dood It* (1943) and *Lost in a Harem* (1944) with Abbott and Costello. In 1947, Jimmy and Tommy Dorsey starred in their biographical film called *The Fabulous Dorseys*. In the early 1950s, J. D. led a number of Dixieland revivals, resulting in well-received recordings.

Jimmy Dorsey had eleven number one hits with his orchestra in the 1930s and the 1940s: "Is It True What They Say About Dixie?" "Change Partners," "The Breeze and I" "Amapola," "My Sister and I," "Maria Elena," "Green Eyes," "Blue Champagne," "Tangerine," "Besame Mucho" (Kitty Kallen on the vocal), and "Pennies from Heaven" with Bing Crosby.

In 1935, he had two more number ones as part of the Dorsey Brothers Orchestra: "Lullaby of Broadway" and "Chasing Shadows." His biggest hit was "Amapola," which was Number One for ten weeks in 1941 on the *Billboard* pop singles chart.

Jimmy and Tommy Dorsey reunited on March 15, 1945, to record a V-Disc at Liederkranz Hall in New York City. Released in June, 1945, V-Disc 451 featured "More Than You Know" backed with "Brotherly Jump." The songs featured the combined orchestras of Jimmy and Tommy Dorsey.

In 1953, Jimmy and Tommy Dorsey united eighteen years after Tommy had walked off the Glen Island Casino bandstand. The band was basically Tommy's, but both of them led it. The brothers continued to work together until Tommy death in November 1956.

Early the following year, Jimmy Dorsey recorded an old ballad called "So Rare," with something of a rock 'n roll beat to it, that featured his alto sax. It would be his last hit, a million-seller. It reached No. 2 position, and was on the record charts for twenty-six weeks. He was given a gold record for the song two days before his death from lung cancer on June 12, 1957.

In 1996, the U.S. Postal Service issued a Jimmy Dorsey and Tommy Dorsey commemorative postage stamp (32-cents).

"In a way, Jimmy was the lesser known of the two Dorsey brothers," Tole said. "By the same token, Jimmy was a better jazz player than Tommy on their respective instruments. Tommy was a great trombonist and ballad player. Tommy started the ballad trombone playing. He created a style that everyone has followed ever since. At that time there was really just Tommy Dorsey and Jack Jenny who did all the pretty ballads and had the chops to do it. Jimmy was probably more of a player, a sideman. He was a fantastic technician either as a ballad player or as a jazz player."

The Jimmy Dorsey Orchestra continued for the next thirty-three years under the leadership of trumpeter Lee Castle, an alumnus of the Jimmy Dorsey band. Jim Miller joined the orchestra as a trombonist and became assistant leader in 1980. In November 1989, Miller became the band's leader after Castle's death.

In March 1992, Miller became the owner of the Jimmy Dorsey Orchestra. In 1998, Miller and company recorded a CD of Big Band standards called *On Tour Swingin' Today*. Not only is Tole on that album, but he also helped assemble the musicians for the recording, he said. By late 2001, Miller retired from leading the band due to health issues and passed the baton to Tole.

"I've been subbing as leader of this band for the past several years so it was a natural progression," Tole said. "As the leader and not the owner, I can safely say I can have the fun without the headaches."

Born and raised in Pittsburgh, Pennsylvania, Tole comes from a musical family. His father was a high school band director for many years and is currently still active as a professional trombone and piano player. His mother also plays the piano and for many years performed with master chorales in the western Pennsylvania area. They have both been a tremendous influence on Tole developing an appreciation and love for the art. He is the oldest of four children. His sister, Nancy Knorr, is the featured vocalist with the Jimmy Dorsey Orchestra and is the lead singer and leader of the famous "Pied Pipers," the vocal group which helped to create so many hits for Tommy Dorsey in the early 1940s. His brother, Gary, is a busy studio musician and leader of his own band in the Los Angeles area.

"There was always music going on in our house," Tole said. "I grew up with Big Band music."

Wishing to pursue a career as a musician, Tole attended Duquesne University School of Music. Following his stint in the Dorsey band and in the military service, he quickly became a much sought after musician. Tole moved to New York City in the mid 1960s and played for many of the top Broadway shows, worked club dates and was busy doing recordings in the studios.

However, a change in the studio scene relocated Tole to Los Angeles in 1967 where he continued his professional career. He has performed with many of the great stars in the music business. Some of the Big Band leaders he has played with include Ray Anthony, Tex Beneke, Louis Bellson, Les Brown, Bob Crosby, Harry James, Quincy Jones, Nelson Riddle and Si Zentner. The great singing stars include Frank Sinatra, Tom Jones, Ella Fitzgerald, Pearl Bailey, Tony Martin and many more.

"I started my own band in 1970 because I had a bunch of Big Band arrangements and a lot of the musicians I worked with wanted to get together to play some charts all the way through instead of just thirty seconds for a film clip," Tole said. "From there things began to roll."

Tole is very much in demand as a soloist, teacher and clinician in the United States for United Musical Instruments and he has also performed in Great Britain, Australia and Japan as a clinician and lecturer.

As the leader of his own orchestra, Tole has recorded a number of CDs including *Music From New York, New York* (Calliope Records); *On the Move* and *Big Band Memories*; and *The Modernaires Now* (Alpha-Omega

Records) with the Modernaries and special guest Tex Beneke. Recorded in 1996, it was Beneke's last recording before passing away in May 2000.

Tole's current release is an album with the Pied Pipers called *Dream*. Tole also maintains a web site that contains information about CD purchases and touring schedules for the Jimmy Dorsey Orchestra, his own band and for the Pied Pipers at www.billtoleorchestra.com

But Tole adamantly admits that Jimmy Dorsey's music is special, he said.

"The style of Jimmy's band followed along the lines of the Benny Goodman and Woody Herman swing bands," Tole said. "Jimmy had tremendous facilities and great chops on the clarinet and alto sax. He could hit high notes that weren't even on the horn! Perhaps with the successes of clarinet greats like Benny Goodman and Artie Shaw, the audience finally woke up and realized that Jimmy can play, too! For a while there Jimmy and Tommy were both top bands that were battling each other with just a slightly different style."

Under Tole's leadership, the focal point of the Jimmy Dorsey Orchestra is not only to play the big hits like "So Rare," "June Night," "Johnson Rag," "J. D.'s Boogie Woogie," "Green Eyes" and "Tangerine," but to also highlight numbers from the Dorsey Brother's band (both 1934-1935 and 1953- 1956) as well as some of Tole's own material, he said.

"We bring these two eras - a twenty-year span - into the forefront," Tole said. "I'm not trying to change the style of the band but rather add a percentage of some of things that I've done in the last twenty years and some of the things that I've done with Les Brown and Nelson Riddle to the book."

Of course, Tole cannot resist devoting a section of an evening's program paying tribute to the man who made Jimmy Dorsey a bandleader, that is, his brother, Tommy. Tole loves to bring out the big T. D. charts such as "I'm Getting Sentimental Over You" (T. D.'s theme song), "Marie" "On the Sunny Side of the Street," "Song of India," and "Opus One." It's not everyday that an audience can see and hear "Tommy Dorsey" (referriung to Tole's portrayal of the bandleader in the movie) play his golden trombone with such fluidity!

Besides providing additional support in the trombone section, an important part of Tole's function in the band is to play counter-melody movements between himself and the alto saxophonist which was a prevalent sound during the Dorsey Brother's recordings from the 1950s and some from the mid-1930s, he said.

"In addition to fronting the band, that's where I fit in," Tole said.

And Tole leaves all the original Jimmy Dorsey solo spots (either on clarinet or alto sax) to his lead alto saxophonist, he said.

"A lot of people ask how come the leader of the Jimmy Dorsey Orchestra isn't a sax player," Tole aid. "I don't have an honest answer to that question. But we just try to be honest to Jimmy's music as we can."

Providing the "Helen O'Connell touch" is Nancy Knorr, the J. D. band's featured vocalist since 1992. Also a native of Pittsburgh, Pennsylvania, Knorr is a classically trained violinist. At the age of 12, she was performing with the Pittsburgh Youth Symphony Orchestra. She attended West Virginia University School of Music and continued her education at St. Louis University. She was a member of the St. Louis Philharmonic Orchestra and many chamber groups. As a singer, Knorr has performed with Warren Covington and his Orchestra, the Tommy Dorsey Orchestra and Tex Beneke and his Orchestra. She has performed with symphony and pops orchestras and has shared the stage with Toni Tennille, Jack Jones, Hal Linden, Doc Severinsen and Les Brown. She was also a featured performer on a PBS special, *Those Fabulous Forties*. She is also the leader of "The Pied Pipers" vocal group.

"We always feature Nancy doing a Helen O'Connell set singing her biggest hits like "All of Me," "Amapola," "Green Eyes" and "Tangerine," Tole said. "When it comes to doing the big duet hits that Helen did with Bob Eberly, Nancy sings those songs in one tempo. The audience seems to respond favorably to it."

O'Connell was Jimmy Dorsey's girl singer 1939 to 1943, afterwards embarking on a solo career. In the late 1950s, she was co-host of the *Today Show* with Dave Garoway. For nine years, she was Bob Barker's sidekick on the Miss Universe Pageant, and appeared in the "nostalgia" revue, *4 Girls 4*, during the late 1970s alongside Rosemary Clooney, Margaret Whiting and Rose Marie.

O'Connell died of cancer in September 1993, at age 73. She was married at the time to noted studio arranger, composer and orchestra leader Frank DeVol.

"I worked with Helen at the Huntington Hartford Theater on Vine Street in Los Angeles when she did *4 Girls 4* and she was singing the hits of the Jimmy Dorsey band in one tempo," Tole recalled. "Shortly before she passed away, Helen did a tour with Jim Miller and the J. D. band and she sang all her hits that same way. After she passed away, her husband, Frank, gave my sister, Nancy, all her charts. We're actually playing the original charts that Helen had done on the adaptation."

While *some* comparison can be made toward leadership of the J. D. band between Bill Tole and his sister, Nancy Knorr, to that of the Dorsey Brothers, Tole doesn't see it that way, he said.

"I suppose some parallels can be drawn, but Nancy and I better not have an argument as to who is going to walk off the stage!" Tole said jokingly.

Although performing the same pieces night after night can become mundane at times, Tole brings freshness to his position as a leader by having the attitude that everything he does as a musician is a form of emoting at the moment and to doing it well, he said.

"I just keep trying to get it right!" he said with a laugh. "Anytime I play, the situation is just a little different. My mood may be different. One night the mouthpiece on my trombone may feel a little different on my lip. Or maybe my lip is sore after working a hard job with someone else. Every time I play, it's a challenge. I try to perform a piece to the best of my ability at that moment. Everything comes from right now instead of what is going to be or what was."

On the surface the music of Jimmy Dorsey may be more appealing to older persons, but attendance by younger people at J. D. orchestra engagements has been increasing, Tole said.

"I think it's a combination of the jazz programs started in high schools and colleges that brings the listeners to our shows and the dance craze with the swing movement that started a few years ago that brings the dancers," Tole said.

And these kids seem to be "connecting" with the music.

"The young people seem to be 'connecting' with the swing numbers," Tole said. "They do the West Coast Swing to 'June Night' because it has a shuffle drive to it. I throw a few things of mine that go along with what they want to do."

While the "generation gap" between seniors and young people seem to narrow at dances, common ground is not always easy to find.

"The only criticisms I've heard from the young people have to do with tempo," Tole said. "They are listening and dancing to songs that were recorded at faster tempos that older people today danced to when they were younger. Now, the older people need the tempos to be bit slower."

Although it has been a slow year for all the bands, things are beginning to looking better for the J.D. band during 2002. They are averaging ten to fifteen engagements a month, Tole said.

"Right now the majority of our work are concerts and dances with the bulk being concerts," Tole said.

While Tole offered no concrete goals for the Jimmy Dorsey band in the year 2002, some special projects are being considered, he said.

"We are talking about putting a tour together of the Jimmy Dorsey band and the Pied Pipers to go to Australia and New Zealand," Tole said. "I have been going there with my band every year for the past ten years. I'm also working on putting a tour together of the J. D. band with a Big Band era singer like Beryl Davis."

Even though Tole wears three hats - two as a bandleader and the other as a studio musician - his first love will always be toward playing Big Band music.

"It seems that I always had bands," he said. "I led a band in high school and then started a jazz band while in college. Besides studio work, basically all I've ever done was Big Bands."

** Coda – Here is an update on Bill Tole and the Jimmy Dorsey Orchestra since this article was published.

The Jimmy Dorsey Orchestra under the direction of Bill Tole continues to perform and tour. The band's website address is: www.jimmydorseyorchestra.com

Jimmy Dorsey in a publicity photo with his alto saxophone, circa 1936.

Jimmy Dorsey and his Orchestra in 1938. Pictured with Dorsey (standing) are guitarist Roc Hillman, second from bottom to Dorsey's right; trumpeter Tutti Camarta, above Dorsey's left ear; trombonist Bobby Byrne, top right; singer Bob Eberly, second from bottom on left; drummer Ray McKinley, third from top left; and pianist Freddie Slack, behind McKinley.

Jimmy Dorsey in 1955.

Bill Tole fronting the Jimmy Dorsey Orchestra for a senior's New Year's Eve dance on December 30, 2001, at Feather Falls Casino in Oroville, California. – *Photo by Stephen Fratallone*

Bill Tole soloing on his trombone as the director of the Jimmy Dorsey Orchestra on December 30, 2001, at Feather Falls Casino in Oroville, California. – *Photo by Stephen Fratallone*

Author Photos with the Bandleaders

With Van Alexander, 93, on September 21, 2008.

With Tex Beneke, 73, on March 7, 1987.

With Les Brown, 87, on December 2, 1999.

With Bobby Byrne, 83, on March 2, 2003.

With Benny Carter, 79, on October 25, 1986.

With Del Courtney, 90, on January 17, 2001.

With Bob Crosby, 72, on July 1, 1985.

With Larry Elgart, 77, on January 13, 2000.

With Lionel Hampton, 77, on August 11, 1985.

With Woody Herman, 73, September 1986.

Author's Photos with the Bandleaders | 479

With Billy May, 86, on March 2, 2002.

With Buddy Morrow, 82, August 7, 2001.

With Alvino Rey, 94, on March 3, 2002.

With Orrin Tucker, 90, on March 4, 2001

With Les Brown Jr. on March 7, 2004.

With Chris Calloway on January 7, 2001.

www.ingramcontent.com/pod-product-compliance
Lightning Source LLC
Chambersburg PA
CBHW060313230426
43663CB00009B/1689